ABW Management

Modern China Series

ABW Management

Theory and Practice by Wang Hai

Zhang Xiuyu

North American Business Press

ABW Management

ISBN: 9781948915120

NORTH
AMERICAN BUSINESS
P R E S S

North American Business Press
Atlanta, Georgia
Miami, Florida
New York, New York,
Toronto, Canada

FIRST PRINTING, 2019

About Modern China Series

China, as one of the oldest civilized regions in the world, has emerged as something of a "new world" because it is working to embrace its own essence and heritage and link them to viable economic strategies. In the last 25 years, China has made tremendous strides by doing so. The country and her people have every right to take pride in these accomplishments. With these successes under their belt, many Chinese leaders and intellectuals anticipate continuing growth. China's plans and strategies, furthermore, are often based upon this premise.

There is tremendous interest in the US on the Chinese economy and business environment. China has emerged as a global super power, and scholars and businessmen in the US are keenly interested in learning how this is going to continue to affect them and how they can do business with China. In response to growing interest from international and Asian scholars, North American Business Press is pleased to announce our Modern China Series (MCS) books, which is first of such series in the US and has garnered tremendous interest both in the US and around the world. With our first book reaching stores in September 2011, this initiative is aimed at developing relationships between NABP and Chinese scholars who desire to promote their academic and applied business writings to the rest of the world.

We have had overwhelming demand for the Modern China Series from both authors who would like to publish in the series and people who would like to read the books. Currently, there are ten books published in the series and, additionally, we have a couple of dozen books that we are considering for the series. The books have been viewed by tens of thousands of people from the U.S. and the rest of the world.

We have published books relating to several areas revolving around the Chinese business environment. We have a few that focus on the best practices in marketing in China; a couple relating to "best practices" in doing business in China; and a few on the outlook of the Chinese economy. The market for the Modern China Series is huge. There are tens of thousands of scholars that are keenly interested in the continued growth of the Chinese economy and the implications that will have on the business world. Even more significant are the millions of businessmen that are interested in the impact that China will continue to have on the global economy. It is difficult to pin down the exact demand for the series, but it Is very large.

We have big plans for growing the Moderns China Series. This has the potential to one of the most significant economic/business series ever produced. We are very selective with the books that we will add to the collection, but we encourage any scholars who think they have unique and interesting perspectives on China to submit their books to us. From the readers perspective, we are committed to producing high quality books on a regular basis so that readers should expect a steady stream of insightful books to be coming out for many years to come.

This initiative is headed by Dr. Robert Tian, a renowned researcher and academic, who spearheads our efforts in partnering with foreign authors and administering day-to-day operations of this series. Dr. Tian, a Vice-President with North American Business Press and Editor of this series, spends much of his time in Beijing, Shanghai, and other Chinese cities, focusing on developing and managing our interests with authors and universities. Below is the list for the books we have published:

Enterprise Strategy: New Horizon authored by Zhang Xiuyu
Governance of Private Enterprises in Modern China authored by Zhong Qin
The Art of War and Enterprise Strategy Management authored by Fu Shouzhi
Marketing Issues in Modern China edited by Robert Guang Tian et al.
The Footprints of the Academician authored by Fu Zhouzhi

Marketing and Economics in Modern China (I) edited by Xiaoguang Qi et al.

Marketing and Economics in Modern China (II) edited by Wang Tianjin et al.

An Islamic Heritage in China authored by Ma Zhanming

China Environmental Anthropology authored by Wang Tianjin, Tian Guang, and Ma Jianfu

Can China Rule the New World? Authored by Tian Guang and Chen Gang

Critiques on Pan-marketization authored by Li Cunlin, Liu Hongfei, and Tian Guang

Economic and Business Anthropology in China edited by Xiaoguang Qi and Tian Guang

China-Mongolia Economic Corridor authored by Eerdun Taoketao, Zhang Zhe, Wang Gang and Wei Lisi

Anthropology of Chinese Foodways authored by Tian Guang and Chen Gang

Urbanization of Rural China authored by Li Taohong

ABW Management Theory and Practice authored by Zhang Xiuyu

Preface

An Outstanding Example of Chinese Management Style

This book summarizes the ABW theory in a comprehensive and concrete manner. The said theory with characteristics of Double Star proved to be correct is created by Wang who has led staffs to build Double Star Group and Double Star brand for 40 years. The eighteen tactics described in this book are: (1) the culture is the soul; (2) the theory is the guide; (3) the strategy is the dragon head; (4) the mechanism is the driving force; (5) the leadership is the role model; (6) the innovation is the vigor; (7) the system is the law of heaven; (8) the quality is the life; (9) the cost is the key; (10) the detail is the art; (11) the competition is the lever; (12) the environment is the foundation; (13) The family affection is the bond; (14) the money management is the guarantee; (15) the brand management is the sublimation; (16) the assessment is the essential; (17) the market is the standard; (18) the entrepreneur is the core.

Each tactic includes five parts: pictures, quotations, practices & effects, typical examples, and expert reviews. Quotations with profound meanings are linguistically simple, concise, easy to understand. Practices are easily executed with clear ideas and significantly concrete actual effects. Typical examples are vivid and unique. Lifelike Pictures are lively and impressive. Experts with a long-term vision make profound comments letting readers see things more clearly.

This book is characterized by the highlighted focus, logical rigor, well-defined levels, profound discussions, rich information, accurate data, excellence in texts and pictures, including vivid examples etc. This book as an outstanding monograph adopts an all-round and multilevel approach to expound the Chinese-style management, while with advantages of being useful, readable, practical, and systematic etc.

Founded in 1921, Double Star is the earliest national shoe-making enterprise in China. In the early 1950s, renamed State-run Ninth Rubber Factory by the government, it became the earliest state-owned shoe manufacturer in China. In the past 90 years, with the complicated changes of China's social system and the difficult development of China's national economy, Double Star has gone through many vicissitudes, including those in periods of China being subdued to a semi-colonial and semi-feudal society, adopting thc planned economy, suffering through the throes of the Cultural Revolution (both planned economy and cultural Revolution lasting for 30 years), and implementing the Reform and Opening policy. While experiencing twists and turns as well as tremendous changes, Double Star has obtained tenacious survival and development. Especially in the past 30 years of reform and opening, with China's transition from a planned economy to a market economy having ups and downs, Double Star has taken the lead in breaking through old ideas, dogmas, and system constraints, and completed the transition from a planned economy to a market economy. Previously, Double Star was an enterprise only engaging in the shoe business with a low profit. Now, it has developed into a large-scale group involving in 23 industries including footwear, tires, clothing, machinery, printing and so forth. In the market economy, Double Star has created its own unique system, unique culture, unique spirit, and unique business model. Indeed, Double Star has successfully opened a road for state-owned enterprises (SOEs) to enter the market. Being a bright national industrial banner, Double Star has written a brilliant historical chapter.

In the process from the planned economy to the market economy, how can we combine China's actual conditions and embark on a road of enterprise management with Chinese characteristics? This is an issue that many Chinese entrepreneurs constantly explore in practice.

This new book entitled *Wang Hai ABW Management Theory* is on the Chinese-style management theory created by Wang Hai president of Double Star Group in his long-term management practice. Comprehensively and specifically, it explains the ABW theory under the background of China's reform and opening for more than 30 years during which the outstanding achievements and successful experiences have been achieved in Double Star Group led by said president. In this explanation, theories from political science, economics, military science, history, science of strategy, science of management, science of success, Chinese culture, philosophy, science of ergonomics, psychology, and religious studies so on are taken as the guide.

For a long time, the following public opinions have been circulating in China's business, academic, educational, and government sectors:

"The failure of state-owned enterprises is due to the public ownership of production materials. The only way out is to privatize."

"The traditional processing industry is a sunset industry and has no development prospect. Only the high-tech industry has a good future."

"The meager profit industry has no future. If enterprises want to continue to develop, they must jump out of it and choose the high-profit industry."

The deeds and the laws revealed in this new book are contrary to the above-mentioned opinions. The enterprise led by said president (that is, Double Star Group) is a state-owned enterprise engaging in traditional processing industries, for example, shoes, tires, machinery, clothing, thermoelectric products so forth, of which. These industries, especially the footwear industry and the tire industry, have the longest history, the most complicated technology, the most backward technology, the worst working conditions, the fiercest competition, the least profit, the low quality of employees, and the biggest difficulty of management. In such a tough industry environment, the said president applied his ABW theory in the people's war of management field to transform a state-owned shoe-maker on the verge of bankruptcy into a famous large-scale enterprise group that is cross-regional and cross-sector. Now it has 60,000 employees and more than 140-member units, which directly or indirectly support hundreds of thousands of people. It has achieved huge economic and social benefits: the total assets have increased from less than 10 million Yuan in the early 1980s to 6.7 billion Yuan; the sales revenue from 30 million Yuan to 12.4 billion Yuan; the foreign exchange earned from exports from 1.75 million US dollars to more than 300 million US dollars. In the past 20 years, the accumulated profits and taxes were more than 3 billion Yuan. In other words, while not spending public money, it paid taxes which were more than 300 times that 20 years ago. With travel shoes, travel shoes, leather shoes, and tires rated as famous brands in China, it is the only enterprise in the rubber industry of China to possess four famous brands at the same time. The brand value has reached 49.292 billion Yuan.

Since the application of the *ABW Management Theory* in the people's war of management, 20 changes have taken place in its companies, factories, R&D centers, sales platforms, sales shops and all management services sectors as follows: (1) from "I am afraid to be responsible" to "I want to be responsible"; (2) from "passive" to "active"; (3) from "hate equipment" to "love equipment"; (4) from "perform ordinarily" to "perform ordinarily excellently"; (5) from "being mediocre" to "being capable"; (6) from "being an outsider" to "being a master"; (7) from " state-owned management " to " family management"; (8) from "same big pot" to "four freedoms plus one guarantee"; (9) from "estimate and contact" to "careful budget"; (10) from "aimless youth" to "heroic youth"; (11) from "migrant worker" to "worker who take the unit as home"; (12) from "market that has nothing to do with me" to "market that is my rice bowl"; (13) from "punitive management" to "integrity and self-discipline"; (14) from "institutional management" to "family management"; (15) from "authoritative management" to "cultural management"; (16) from "culture is useless" to "culture is the soul"; (17) from "empty talks" to "four combinations"; (18) from "imitation" to "innovation"; (19) from "indifferent to the famous brand" to "treasuring the famous brand"; (20) from "creating the famous brand" to "developing the famous brand".

Since 1959, due to the flourishing development of the enterprise, Wang Hai has successively won the following honors: national outstanding Communist Youth League member, national excellent management personnel, national May 1st labor medal, national labor model, one of first national outstanding entrepreneurs, one of young and middle-aged management experts having outstanding contributions, one of top ten champions nationwide in poverty alleviation, one of top ten management talents nationwide, one of top ten figures in chemical field, national quality management advanced worker, one of first men of the day in national petrochemical industry, most influential entrepreneur in national apparel industry, one of top ten news figures in China, most concerned entrepreneur and so forth. In 1993, he was included in Five Thousand Personalities of the World. In 1995, he was named World Man of the Year after Deng Xiaoping. Subsequently, he won the International Outstanding Entrepreneur Contribution Award and the World Outstanding Person title. He became the only Chinese diplomatic entrepreneur selected in the large-scale documentary film Diplomatic Records of P.R.C. His personal value has reached 32.142 billion Yuan, being the highest in the community of entrepreneurs in China.

In 1988, 20 outstanding entrepreneurs were selected for the first time in China and cordially met by the party and state leaders in the latter's office room. At present, among these 20 outstanding entrepreneurs, some have risen, some have fallen, some have fled to foreign countries, some have been jailed and so forth. However, as director of Ninth Rubber Factory in Qingdao at that time, now president of Double Star Group, he still works hard in the same unit. He is known as Market General, Long-lived President, and Evergreen Tree in the Chinese business community.

In the management practice of leading Double Star Group for more than 30 years, he has always adhered to the principle of seeking truth from facts. For him, the reality is the norm, rather than the dogmas from any books and theories educed by any ancient or foreign authorities. He is realistic and practical-minded. With adherence to the principles of inheriting traditional excellence, absorbing foreign achievements and creating our own distinct products, he dares to innovate and is good at innovation. He learns from others and creates his own unique *ABW Management Theory*.

For a long time, experts have explored the Chinese-style management. So, what is it? Different from the enterprise management under the highly centralized planned economic system before the reform and opening and from the enterprise management under the highly developed market economy under capitalism. It should be able to adapt to actual environments for the economic, social and cultural development, reflect the socialist nature of state-owned enterprises, promote the superiority of public ownership of production materials, reflect the status of employees as masters, and bring into play the innovative spirit and commanding role of entrepreneurs. This new management model, characterized by a lively and sentimental management, possesses combined advantages and a complete set of functions. The *ABW Management Theory* consisting of 18 tactics is an outstanding example of Chinese-style management.

The eighteen tactics described in this book are: (1) the culture is the soul; (2) the theory is the guide; (3) the strategy is the dragon head; (4) the mechanism is the driving force; (5) the leadership is the role model; (6) the innovation is the vigor; (7) the system is the law of heaven; (8) the quality is the life; (9) the cost is the key; (10) the detail is the art; (11) the competition is the lever; (12) the environment is the foundation; (13) The family affection is the bond; (14) the money management is the guarantee; (15) the brand management is the sublimation; (16) the assessment is the essential; (17) the market is the standard; (18) the entrepreneur is the core.

The basic principle of Marxism is that practice is the sole criterion for testing truth. *Wang Hai ABW Management Theory* is on the Chinese-style management, which, not created on imagination by scholars, is created by Mr. Wang as one of first Chinese outstanding entrepreneurs in reform and management practice for more than 30 years. The ABW theory comes from and guide the practice and is proven to be effective in the practice. The Americans commented that "Double Star has the best-managed factory in the world." The Japanese took the initiative to visit the factory of Double Star, and the South Koreans offered a high salary to hire supervisors from Double Star. Double Star has won the recognition of the market with its excellent management, won the respect of the industry and won the admiration of foreigners! Double Star has not only achieved brilliant achievements, but also won honors for our country and people, thereby being worthy of being a famous brand in China and even the world.

Looking back at the past, we are full of joy; looking forward to the future, we are full of confidence. Today’s Double Star will soon set off a prelude to the turning of history. Today's Double Star, under the leadership of Mr. Wang, under the encouragement of the national spirit and under the impetus of the people's war in the commercial field, will continue to improve the new path of market economy development, create new characteristics of market economy development, and create the new model of Chinese-style management. With the grand goal of building a hundred-year brand and enterprise, Double Star will win a new victory in its way and write a new chapter with glory in brand.

The decision on writing Wang Hai ABW Management Theory came out in May 2011. That year, the great Communist Party of China (CPC) reached its 90th anniversary, and so did Double Star. We celebrated the 90th anniversary of said enterprise by writing a comprehensive, systematic, and concrete summary of successful experiences created by Mr. Wang as its president, including those on management. The leaders of Double Star Group went to Beijing to invite me to help doing this work, and its management experiences were accumulated for more than 30 years. After more than a year of investigation, writing, and revisions, it was officially published by Peking University Press in January 2013.

Zhang Xiuyu
December 2018

Congratulations (In Lieu of Foreword)

All staffs of Double Star Group:

When the 90th anniversary of establishment of Double Star Group, I would like to extend my sincere greetings and congratulations to all staffs of Double Star.

In past 90 years, Double Star has developed from the earliest shoe-making enterprise in China into a comprehensive large-scale enterprise group, which has created its own national brand and achieved remarkable results.

Since the reform and opening, Comrade Wang Hai had led staffs to actively explore and keep pace with the times. Double Star has been successful in the reforms and in the development of the market economy and embarked on a unique development path. Double Star has created a new management model, fulfilled corporate social responsibility, and gained useful experience, which is worthy of being learned by peers.

I hope that in the future, Double Star will continue to innovate, dare to break through, achieve greater achievements, and make new contributions to the development of China's national industry!

Yuan Baohua

September 9, 2011

Table of Contents

Introduction: ABW Theory in Market Economy

A theory is an inevitable result of historical development. Namely its formation has its background and historical origins. Similarly, the ABW management theory created by Mr. Wang is a new practice-based theory with Chinese characteristics, which meets development needs of the era and market. This management theory is proposed in the transition of China from a planned economy to a market economy with the ups and downs of economy fluctuations. It is formed against the background of historical and social changes as well as development of market, industry, and enterprise.

Formation of ABW Theory

Review of economic development in China: In 1978, the Third Plenary Session of the 11th Party Congress was held. Deng Xiaoping proposed the building of socialism with Chinese characteristics, and the party's work focus shifted to economic construction. That china shifted from planned economy to market economy is a fundamental change in the system and mechanism, because in this process, the private ownership began to be accommodated. Although the old system and the old model of the planned economy have been broken, compared with the development speed of the market economy, our market theory has clearly lagged the market development. Although we call for and talk about reform and opening every day, we still adopt the theory of power grabbing in the 1920s and 1930s, still follow the old thinking of class struggle in the 1950s and 1960s, leading to the theory being seriously lagging practice. We should reflect on the huge gap. Since we have recognized the private ownership system and recognized the market economy, we need to explore and summarize a set of theoretical viewpoints that conform to historical development and adapt to the changing market economy, to guide the reform practice of the market economy in the current era.

Current situation of social development in China: Reform and opening not only have brought a take-off and development for China's economic construction, but also have moved people from the empty-talk politics of the planned economy to the money supremacy of market economy. There are three phenomena in society: First, for some people, the money is all-powerful: everything being viewed from money by which all problems can be solved. Second, the economy is over-emphasized. Formalistic politics, politics not reflecting reality, and empty slogans have resulted in a feeling of repugnance among the public and an ideological trend of economy over-emphasized and politics neglected. Economy and politics like two kinds of skin are separated from each other. One phenomenon is the blind faith in foreign things. At the beginning of reform and opening, China came out from planned economy and closed state, and some people fell into blind worship of foreigners and had a wrong idea that everything in foreign countries was better than that in our country, including the moon in the sky and even enterprise management. Under the influence of this trend of thought, the MBA entered China and set off a whirlwind all over the country. Almost every university has an MBA class. Everyone was eager to finish the EMBA degree program, show it off, and take it as a stepping stone in pursuit of promotion. Instead of in-dept studies on Chinese management, the MBA was directly taken as a course of our management school. Although the MBA has entered China for nearly 20 years, how many people after completing the MBA course can guide a company to develop and become strong? Which Chinese entrepreneur has succeeded after studying for an MBA? While not reflecting characteristics, actual conditions, and culture of China, MBAs can't solve the practical problems of Chinese enterprises. China is the country with the longest history and culture with her people being the best in the world. China is also a big manufacturing country in the world and has enormous potential for market development. At the beginning of reform and opening, it is not surprised that such a model of learning from abroad emerged. However, the reform and opening has been over 30 years. Why are we still using Western management theory? Why should we guide and develop the market economy of a socialist country in accordance with the theory of capitalist countries? Are Western countries with economic crises not the birthplace of MBA? Therefore, while developing the economy, we should sum up a set of market theory systems with Chinese characteristics that adapt to market development and have.

Analysis of competition in the international market: In the early days of reform and opening, our country was eager to integrate into the global economy as soon as possible. In the process of global economic integration, some so-called experts and scholars and individual senior officials over-emphasize the economic activities and advocate China to become the world manufacturer, but don't mention the national industry anymore. In the face of blind worship of foreigners, in the face of the lack of national spirit behind economic prosperity, in the face of some officials, theorists, and economists who seem to have abandoned the political economics which is a heirloom for the communists, we should clearly understand that we get technology by market, get the foreign exchange by resources, get political achievements by preferential policies, get the investment by cheap labor, get the GDP by land. Such a high price paid can be understood in the early days of reform and opening, but now with an economic foundation, we should not continue like this anymore. We should be soberly aware that Western developed countries rely on the virtual economy of the financial industry and the real estate industry to drive economic development, but it causes the economic crisis. China having a population of 1.3 billion is a big country and a big market, and her economic development is inseparable from basic industries. For China, it is important to develop financial and real estate industries. However, our real GDP growth must rely on the development of basic industries. We should be soberly aware that to curb China's rapid development, the developed countries have set up relevant barriers: technical limitation, anti-dumping investigation, control over resources by multinational groups, and brand exploitation, thereby intensifying trade disputes and frictions in the international market. In this world, it is always a powerful economy and a powerful military to support power politics. Therefore, our virtual economy should be re-considered, and it is time to solve the development problem in our real economy. At present, there is an earliest and biggest impact in the labor-intensive manufacturing and processing industry with a low entry threshold, and the biggest gap with foreign companies is not in technology but management. If China wants to have a voice in the world, it must achieve a strong rise in the thought while the economy rises. After more than 30 years of reform and opening, we should have our own theory and management in economic development. Instead of going all the way according to foreign theories and methods, we must create our own theories and methods of management, to guide our market economy with Chinese characteristics in developing in an orderly and healthy manner.

Wang Hai as one of the first generation of outstanding entrepreneurs in China and the president of Double Star Group, is the first to realize that China's development of a market economy requires a combination of politics and economy and that we should create a new theory to guide people and solve their thinking problems, including the problem of impetuousness. In the 1980s, Double Star proposed that creating famous brand is the biggest politics in the market economy, that an effective use of money is the best work in politics, summing up its own management method - Double Star Nine Plus Nine Management Method and its own corporate culture concept - known as Wang Hai Quotations. In a sense, this is the embryonic form of China's market economy management theory. When many people crazily developed the virtual economy, Wang Hai always adhered to the real economy and led Double Star to make a great achievement in the context of the collapse of the state-owned 3,000 shoe-making enterprises. Double Star is the earliest to obtain the following titles: well-known trademark in China; famous brands of professional sports shoes, travelling shoes, tires in China, thereby becoming the only company in the rubber industry of China that has four Chinese brand-name products at the same time. Double Star has successfully extended to other 23 industries, e.g., machinery, thermoelectricity, tires and so forth; and has created new miracles: merging a large tire company, merging an enterprise with a slow development pace, and merging a state-owned enterprise (namely Dongfeng Tires Factory). Double Start created the first colorful tire & the first four-mode vulcanizer in the world; the first V-shaped molding line, the first stainless steel belt style shot blast machine, and the largest resin sand mixer in China. Both shoes and tires industries simultaneously realized the technological revolution of the rubber material from cold to hot and filled the technical gap in the process. Moreover, Double Star created the most efficient assembly line in the footwear industry of the world; developed the shoes for astronauts in Shenzhou 6 and 7 and for vogue purposes. In a word, its shoes have been very famous in the high-end market of the world etc.

All these are the concrete practices of Deng Xiaoping's theory - building socialism with Chinese characteristics - in enterprises. Combining the many management theories and the practical experience of creating national brands in the past 40 years, Mr. Wang creates the ABW management theory. His theory reflects the principles of seeking truth from facts in Marxism, Mao Zedong Thought and Deng Xiaoping Theory, and takes as the cornerstone the essence (namely honorable deeds and blessings) in traditional Chinese culture, including Confucianism, Taoism, and Buddhism. The essence of thought is the cornerstone. The ABW theory reflects his spirit to inherit traditional excellence, absorb foreign achievements, and create distinct products. Furthermore, the ABW theory is a result of his constantly summing up the thinking of market economy, the corporate culture, and the other management theory.

Under the new situation of highly integrated global economy, our country needs to promote national spirits, develop national economy and needs many national entrepreneurs, to make strong economy and develop basic industries. Meanwhile, ABW theory created by him is a successful management theory of the real economy. Let us interpret the complete system and rich connotation in ten aspects of the ABW theory.

Basic framework of ABW theory

1. Meaning of ABW theory

The ABW theory inherits Chinese traditional pictographic culture, with the national cultural wisdom and unique national spirit as the connotation.

For him, A is the big shot. A is the first among the 26 English letters, and we Chinese people say that it is the big shot, the first, and the spire. It means that Chinese entrepreneurs and enterprises should stand taller and look farther as well as dare to be the best in the world or compete for the first place.

B consists of two parts: 1 and 3 means a big country and a big market with a population of 1.3 billion. 1 is like a pillar, which means that our entrepreneurs must have the indomitable spirit and three characters under market economy (personality, humanity, and party spirit). 3 is like a person in shape who bends his waist and means that entrepreneurs must be down-to-earth to do an excellent job.

W is like an eagle spreading wings. W is also the first letter of Wang's name. It means that the entrepreneur leads his team to meet the challenge and is never satisfied with what he has achieved.

2. Basis of ABW theory

Seeking truth from facts and doing charitable deeds with blessings resulted.

Building of the socialist enterprise with Chinese characteristics.

Seeking truth from facts is the essence of Marxism, Mao Zedong Thought, and Deng Xiaoping Theory.

Doing honorable deeds with blessings resulted is the essential of Confucianism, Taoism and Buddhism constituting a part of Chinese traditional culture.

Double Star, which seriously implements the theory of building socialism with Chinese characteristics put forward by Comrade Deng Xiaoping according to the actual conditions, has embarked on a successful road for the socialist state-owned enterprises in manufacturing and processing industries. This road has characteristics with Double Star.

3. Main line of ABW theory

New three people's principles of market economy: national spirit, national brand, and national entrepreneurs.

The market economy needs to inspire the national spirit, create national brands, and cultivate a team of national entrepreneurs, to develop the national industry and revitalize the national economy.

4. Core of ABW theory

The core of ABW theory is people. No matter what kind of management, we need people, and our management core is to solve people's problems. "Managing people is a high-end high tech", "managing people is a tricky thing for managers, and culture is very helpful because of soulful involvement", "people's war is as a strategy in the commercial field."

5. Essence of ABW theory

Inheriting the traditional excellence, absorbing foreign achievements, and creating distinct products. Inheriting the traditional excellence: namely, inheriting the clever ideas - doing honorable deeds and accumulating virtues - advocated by in our national culture. Absorbing foreign achievements: namely, learning from all domestic and abroad management experience that is conducive to enterprise development.

Creating distinct products: namely, on basis of inheriting tradition excellence and absorbing foreign achievements, Mr. Wang creates a set of theories with unique characteristics, for example, he puts forward the following cultural ideas: "doing good product quality is the biggest doing-good and gathering of blessings", "not innovating today means a falling behind tomorrow, and not innovating tomorrow means a failure the day after tomorrow", "enterprises can reform everything except the quality" and etc.

6. Features of ABW theory

Political and economic integration. Politics and economy have always been inseparable. The more market-oriented the economy is, the more politics is concerned. "Creating famous brands is more political in the market economy", "creating famous brands is the best patriotism", and "an effective use of money is the best ideological work."

7. Principles of ABW theory

Follow the market, focus on the market, and change with the market. "The market is the top leadership of the enterprise", "the market is the standard for testing all work of the enterprise", "the market is endless, management has no end."

8. Methodology in ABW theory

Adhere to the combination in the following five aspects: leading culture, all-staff innovation, management innovation, system reform, reward and punishment mechanism. Adopt the followings: cultural management, contractual management, strict management, fine management, use of money management, integrity management, emotional management, and competition management; cooperation, and mutual promotion. Create a family consumption style management characterized by self-management, self-work, self-reduction, etc.

9. Purposes of ABW theory

Challenge the market, compete in the market, and win the market. The survival and development of enterprises depends on the market. They can win the market only after bravely challenging and competing in the market which is quite volatile.

10. Strategies and tactics of ABW theory

Five strategies are as follows: brand, diversification, internationalization, differentiation, combination of shoes and tires. Eighteen tactics are as follows: (1) the culture is the soul; (2) the theory is the guide; (3) the strategy is the dragon head; (4) the mechanism is the driving force; (5) the leadership is the role model; (6) the innovation is the vigor; (7) the system is the law of heaven; (8) the quality is the life; (9) the cost is the key; (10) the detail is the art; (11) the competition is the lever; (12) the environment is the foundation; (13) The family affection is the bond; (14) the money management is the guarantee; (15) the brand management is the sublimation; (16) the assessment is the essential; (17) the market is the standard; (18) the entrepreneur is the core. The central content of this book is the interpretation of these tactics.

What is unique for a nation is also precious for the world. When you are unique, the world comes to you. Mr. Wang working as plant manager, secretary of party branch, president, and chief executive in an enterprise for nearly 40 years has experienced various changes and fluctuations in the market economy. He creates the ABW theory based on Double Star Nine Plus Nine Management Method he created earlier and applies the ABW theory in creating and developing the national brands, of which our country and our people feel proud. Moreover, Mr. Wang, who creates and applies his ABW theory, has provided the valuable experience for running socialist enterprises with Chinese characteristics.

Personal Profile of Wang Hai

In 1987, 20 outstanding entrepreneurs were selected for the first time and were cordially met by the party and state leaders in Zhongnanhai. At present, among these outstanding entrepreneurs, some have risen, some have fallen, some have fled to foreign countries, some have been jailed and so forth. However, as director of Ninth Rubber Factory in Qingdao at that time, now president of Double Star Group, he still works hard in the same unit. He is known as Market General, Long-lived President, and Evergreen Tree in the Chinese business community.

Under the leadership of Wang, today's Double Star has developed from a shoe factory that is on the verge of collapse to a large-scale enterprise group involved in the five pillar industries (footwear, tires, clothing, machinery and thermal power) and the eight major industries (including printing, embroidery and tertiary industries). The products have been exported to more than 100 countries and regions in the world, the number of employees has grown from more than 2,000 to 60,000, the fixed assets have increased from less than 10 million to 5.5 billion, the annual sales income has increased from 30 million yuan to 10 billion, the foreign exchange earned from exports has increased from 1.75 million US dollars to 150 million US dollars. The total amount of profits and taxes paid has reached more than 3 billion Yuan.

Since 1959, due to the flourishing development of the enterprise, he has successively won the following honors: national outstanding Communist Youth League member, national excellent management personnel, national May 1st labor medal, national labor model, one of first national outstanding entrepreneurs, one of young and middle-aged management experts having outstanding contributions, one of top 10 champions nationwide in poverty alleviation, one of top ten management talents nationwide, one of top ten figures in chemical field, national quality management advanced worker, one of first men of the day in national petrochemical industry, most influential entrepreneur in national apparel industry, one of top ten news figures in China, most concerned entrepreneur and so forth. In 1993, he was included in Five Thousand Personalities of the World. In 1995, he was named World Man of the Year after Deng Xiaoping. Subsequently, he won the International Outstanding Entrepreneur Contribution Award and the World Outstanding Person title. He became the only Chinese diplomatic entrepreneur selected in the large-scale documentary film Diplomatic Records of P.R.C.

In 2001, the result of evaluation by an intangible assets appraisal center in Beijing showed that Wang as a CEO was worth 3.99 billion yuan. Currently, he is worth is 32.142 billion yuan, becoming the first Chinese entrepreneur. He has been elected as the chairman of Rubber Shoe Branch of China Rubber Industry Association (CRIA) for five consecutive years, concurrently served as the vice chairman of the CRIA and the vice chairman of China Leather Industry Association the like.

In 2000, in the fifteenth joint meeting of the first staffs' congress of Double Star, it was resolved that Wang was appointed the lifelong president of Double Star. According to this resolution, President Wang had followed the wishes of the staff and worked until 2013. After acquiring both success and fame, he gloriously retired when he was 72 years old. President Wang works hard and delivers an excellent transcript to the party, the country, the people, and the staff!

Tactic 1: Culture Is the Soul

"Culture management is an important part of modern enterprise management. Enterprises without culture are destined to be hopeless. Enterprises are like this, and so are countries and nations. Without the support from excellent culture, the future of a country or nation is unimaginable. For enterprises, the market is the root, the management is the foundation, and culture is the soul."

——Wang Hai

On January 6, 2000, Seminar on Reportage Entitled "Bolshevik Thinker" and Double Star Theory sponsored by the People's Daily was held in the Great Hall of the People. The market theory created by President Mr. Wang for the reform and development of current state-owned enterprises attracted much attention and was highly valued by participants.

The slogans reflecting the corporate culture and hanging in the workshop of Double Star play a positive role in educating employees and encouraging them to work hard.

I. Wang Hai Quotations

(I) Significance of corporate culture

☆ Culture management is an important part of modern enterprise management. An enterprise without culture is hopeless. Enterprises are like this and are countries and nations. With the support from excellent culture, the future of a country or nation is unimaginable.

☆ The market is the root, the management is the foundation, and the culture is the soul.

☆ Culture is a high-level thing. Management of culture is the highest level of management.

(II) Connotation and essence of culture in Double Star

☆ Double Star Spirit: Love our factory, seek truth, work hard, gain profit, develop and advance.

Establish national ethos, carry forward national spirit, and create national brands

☆ Double Star Motto: People wear shoes, the key is at work; cars use tires, the key is at work.

☆ Core of Double Star Culture: Seeking truth from facts, doing honorable deeds, and gathering of blessings.

☆ Century Declaration with Double Star: Objectively think, scientifically create, earnestly work, be pragmatic, happily live.

☆ Integrity is the paving stone of corporate culture, and corporate culture is the booster of the enterprise.

(III) Role of corporate culture

☆ Double Star stands out mainly due to its excellent culture and strong spirit.

☆ Culture is not only knowledge and learning, but also the spirit. Culture is visible, which must be paid attention. Culture has a key role in changing people's ideas, promoting national spirit, building national ambition, creating national brands, and promoting social-economic development.

☆ Double Star's unique and intangible corporate culture, combined with tangible innovation and technology upgrade work, employee position and value, plays a role in uniting employees and enhancing cohesion plus combat effectiveness of the enterprise.

☆ What is the key to the success or failurc of a company? It depends on management. Cultural ideas are the top management. It is a main line of political work in Double Star to use cultural ideas to educate people, transform people and unite people.

☆ Use culture ideas of Double Star to create its national brand.

☆ Managing people is a high-end high tech. Culture is very important in managing people, which is an awkward thing for managers. Culture is very helpful due to soulful involvement.

(V) Key to create excellent corporate culture

☆ Inherit the traditional excellence, absorb foreign achievements, and create our own characteristics.

☆ Only rooting in actual conditions of the enterprise, can culture be very vigorous.

☆ Corporate culture constantly evolves and is subject to the impact of the times.

II. Practices and Effects

In March 1995, President Wang gave a speech in Singapore. Speech theme: Essence of Buddhist culture applied by Double Star to modern enterprise management

(I) Main practices

The main practice of corporate culture construction in Double Star can be summarized as four adherences and four combinations:

1. Adhere to the basic principles of cultural innovation and combine with the unique culture of Double Star

(1) Inheriting traditional excellence

Chinese tradition has the three major cultures - Confucian culture, Taoist culture, and Buddhism culture. The precipitation and accumulation of these three cultures have formed the Chinese national culture.

First of all, we inherit the outstanding thoughts of Confucianism, Taoism, and Buddhism (including doing good and gathering of blessings), rule of law strategy of Legalism; we pay attention to the strategic and tactical thoughts represented by Lao Tzu and Sun Tzu etc.

Second, it is necessary to inherit the revolutionary spirit and successful experiences created by the Communist Party of China in leading the Chinese people in the long-term practice of revolution and construction, e.g., Jinggangshan Spirit, Long March Spirit, Nanniwan Spirit, Iron Man Spirit, Angang Constitution, Three Kinds of Honest and Four Kinds of Strict; Care for Masses' Lives, Attention to Working Methods; Two Participations, One Change, Three Combinations; and etc.

(2) Absorbing foreign achievements. It is necessary to learn from the advanced management theory and management experience of Western developed countries represented by the United States, Japan, and Europe.

(3) Create our distinct products. Through the exploration and the combination with actual corporate conditions, Double Star has formed nine major series of corporate culture system with more than 3,000 cultural ideas. It is a grass-roots culture, which is very practical and very suitable for the national conditions. Moreover, in Double Star, employees continue to break old processes, old standards, and old operating procedures, and write the pithy formulas, including three-word type and seven-word type, which are easy to remember, understand, and master. There are 1,892 pithy formulas, which are divided into five categories, totaling 29,000 words and becoming an important part of corporate culture in Double Star. Double Star inherits the essence of Chinese traditional culture - doing good and gathering of blessings, adheres to the principle of seeking truth from facts as a core, absorbs western advanced management achievements, creates a new culture and innovative ideas of socialist market economy, which become an important part of Chinese industrial civilization.

2. Adhere to the national spirit and combine with the creation of a new culture of the Chinese nation.

Mr. Wang believes that the national culture being able to continually discard the dross and select the essence is the root of national progress and the best soil for cultivating national brands. Any successful national brand that is superior to others has a unique cultural connotation. In the development of Chinese enterprises, many brands have been created. These brands of which Chinese businessmen felt proud, adhere to the principles of being honest, quality first, doing good and gathering of blessings, thereby reflecting the essence of the Eastern civilization which is admired by the Western world. The spirit embodied in these brands, which exudes a strong Chinese national culture, should be inherited for the development of modern Chinese enterprises. It should be noted that the national spirit is the soul of the national brand. The national spirit is the deep connotation of the national culture, reflects the outstanding thoughts, noble character, and firm ambition that a nation has shown in its historical activities. The national spirit has an important function to mobile the people and display the national image. The national spirit is a necessary condition for a nation to stand on its own feet in the world's advanced nations. This kind of spirit needs to create a new culture on a basis of combining traditional excellence with the current situation, while the new culture has a role of education, cultivation and guidance. By combining excellent national culture and national dignity with market competition, both the new culture the national brand can be created.

3. Adhere to the spirit of advancing with the times and combine with the new era

Mr. Wan knows that, when culture is combined with humanity, society, and reality, it can generate an immeasurable role. Culture is an idea, an invisible thing, and a soulful thing. Culture is also the most cohesive and driving thing.

Throughout the 5,000-year history of the Chinese nation, each dynasty has a very important culture that determines the dynasty, determines society, and determines the rejuvenation and weakness of the nation. In the 1920s and 1930s, the first Marxist-Leninists in China, represented by Li Dazhao, accepted Marxism-Leninism and created the Chinese Communist Party. Later, the Chinese Marxist-Leninists represented by Mao Zedong developed the Chinese Communist Party. Why we say that Mao Zedong as a representative developed the Chinese Communist Party? A very important one is that Mao Zedong created a new culture through combination with the reality of China and combination with the social phenomenon at that time. Mao Zedong put forward cultural theories, for example, struggling against despotic landlords and dividing up the land, resisting the Japanese to save the country and saving the people, and US imperialism is a paper tiger, which played a key role at that time. Therefore, the whole China was liberated, and a new China was established. In the early days of reform and opening, Comrade Deng Xiaoping put forward the cultural theories, e.g., seeking truth from facts; emancipating the mind; it doesn't matter whether the cat is black or white, as long as it catches mice; these theories reversed the situation of class struggle for nearly 30 years since the Communist Party being in power, enabling us to spend all efforts on economic construction, changing and developing China. In every era, culture plays a very important role. Now, culture should be combined with actual conditions of the new era.

4. Adhere to the goal of corporate survival and development and consider actual corporate needs

In Double Star, the culture is created by Mr. Wang through summarizing his practical experiences in the market, in which he is good at exploration and absorbing the traditional excellence. It originates from the market and guides the practice of Double Star in the market economy. As we know, initially, when the new culture collided with the old ideas, it is a life or death struggle. It was not easy for him to create and promote this culture.

For example, the following words were put forward: people wear shoes with the key being work; do not wait for others to give food, instead, find it for yourself; the market is the highest leader of the enterprise and the standard for testing all work of the enterprise. These amazing slogans, emerging in 1983 as a critical moment when more than two million pairs of yellow rubber shoes of Double Star were rejected by the state-owned commercial system, were strongly opposed by many superiors. However, it is these words that enabled Double Star to successfully break away from the constraints of the planned economy and become the first wave rider in the tide of China's market economy. Another example, in the mid-1980s, when foreign brands successively entering our domestic market caused significant impact on Chinese national industry, Mr. Wang put forward the following words: creating the Chinese national brand; Chinese people are not shorter than foreigners in case of standing or lying. Since then, Double Star has entered the stage of brand development, and it has only taken ten years to create the Chinese national brand. In the process of adopting the brand strategy, Mr. Wang put forward the following slogans: creating a famous brand is the biggest politics in the market; the brand name is the atomic bomb in commercial warfare; innovation is the eternal theme in commercial warfare; not innovating today, we will fall behind tomorrow; not innovating tomorrow, we will be eliminated the day after tomorrow; taking ourselves as the backbone and feeling good about ourselves; despite the gossips, our development is the absolute need. These philosophical words are simple and vivid, giving employees a clear and passionate call, thereby soon leading to a good situation in which all staffs are innovative and results-oriented.

When the Double Star entered the market, its spirit was condensed into these words: "Love our factory, seek truth, work hard, gain profit, develop, and advance", which reflects the philosophy of Mr. Wang and his colleagues to seek truth from facts and keep making progress. With the increasing awareness of the market and the accumulated market experience, Double Star constantly enriched its ideas: e.g., the customer is God with a gold medal won in the market (reflecting its market spirit); there are goods inferior in quality but not poor markets (reflecting its market awareness); compassionate leadership and ruthless disciplines (reflecting its management method); the brand is more famous, the impact is greater, the image is more important (reflecting its brand image awareness); the market is the best development department, the market is the largest sample room (reflecting its market development ideas); more ideas for famous brands and less reasons for mistakes (reflecting its aggressiveness); be an excellent person, be a market capable person, be a new person in the new era, be a good person representing the image of Double Star (reflecting its self-discipline awareness); objectively think, scientifically create, earnestly work, be pragmatic and happy (its century declaration). The above slogans cover all aspects of corporate management, including brand, development, technology, market, and talent etc. These ideas have a clear core, that is, the market. Double Star always insists that "the market is the highest leadership of the enterprise and the market is the litmus test of corporate deeds", effectively unifying the thoughts among employees of Double Star.

Mr. Wang's aphorisms are from his summing up and refining at any time in his practice, which are known as Wang's Quotations and received the affirmation and support from Gu Xiulian former Minister of Chemical Industry. After a visit to Double Star, many enterprises have used Wang's Quotations as a magic weapon for them. Even the bosses of Taiwan and South Korea have done so to educate employees. These popular and straightforward slogans contain the principles of management; regardless of national boundaries, regardless of ownership, and even regardless of industry, they can play a guiding role for enterprises in the market economy.

Excellent culture is an indispensable spiritual pillar in the commercial war. A model is used by Double Star to manage 20 or 30 production plants, more than 20 logistics platforms and 5,000 chain stores across the country, which depends on culture. The cultural management enables Double Star to successfully enter the tire and machinery industry and in a brief time rapidly develop including creating a national brand.

(II) Main effects

Many examples show that the market is the root of the enterprise, management is the foundation of the enterprise, and the culture is the soul of the enterprise. In the industrial expansion of Double Star, management is mainly based on corporate culture. The change of enterprise appearance is also based on cultural management. Therefore, cultural management is at the top level of Double Star. The culture refers to the sum of material wealth and spiritual wealth created by human beings in the process of social and historical development. The corporate culture we introduce here refers to the spiritual wealth of Double Star.

Corporate culture includes unique corporate values, corporate spirit, behavioral norms, moral norms, life beliefs, business operation awareness, business guidance ideas, business strategies and the like, which are gradually formed and developed by an enterprise with certain economic, social and cultural background in the long-term production and management process. For Double Star, the corporate culture is a kind of value. The core of this value is to seek truth from facts and do honorable deeds as well as gather blessings. It is a characteristic cultural system that is produced and gradually formed in the development of Double Star. It is a theory and idea that Double Star sums up according to its own reality. It integrates the essence from Confucianism, Taoism, and Buddhism, uses Marxism-Leninism, Mao Zedong Thought, and Deng Xiaoping Theory as a cornerstone, and reflects the actual conditions in the development of Double Star. The culture of Double Star is an outstanding example in cultural construction of Chinese enterprises. It is the greatest contribution from Mr. Wang. Its effectiveness is reflected in the following aspects:

1. Making four breakthroughs

With the spirit of "dare to be the first", Wang has made four breakthroughs in corporate culture construction:

(1) Breaking through the old standards of political work and finding new standards for political work

The market is the standard for testing all work of the enterprise. Adhering to his development concept embodying in the following slogan: "despite the gossips, the development of Double Star is the absolute need," Mr. Wang has found new standards for political work. In the fierce market competition, people at double Stars always take the market as the standard in the thinking and action, follow the market, change with the market. This is also the only useful weapon for state-owned enterprises to seek development under the conditions of the new era.

(2) Breaking through the old content of political work and finding the foothold of political work

"Creating famous brands is the biggest politics in thc market economy." With the creation of famous brands as the goal of political work, Mr. Wang creatively applies political work to economic construction, to guide the work of Double Star. Thus, he has found the foothold of political work.

(3) Breaking through the old form of political work and finding a breakthrough in political and ideological work

"The effective use of money is the best ideological and political work." People at Double Star have found a breakthrough in political and ideological work. The material things are used to adjust and balance the spiritual things. The attention is paid to both the spirit and the material things, to achieve the best combination plus the enrichment in the political work, and fully mobilize the enthusiasm and initiative with employees.

(4) Breaking through the old methods of political work and finding new ways of political work

"High quality of products is the biggest doing-good and gathering of blessings." Mr. Wang boldly absorbs the essence of the traditional culture in Confucianism, Taoism, and Buddhism to create the moral management suitable for modern enterprises. The moral management is used to educate employees to be self-confident, self-reliant, self-discipline, love work and work hard. Thus, Double Star has found new ways of political work.

2. Creating five highlights

Double Star has a strong cultural atmosphere. In the production plant, aphorisms and slogans are hanged everywhere, which are simple and concise. In the production line, shoes are well-made and beautiful. In the chain store, the 200% value-added service can be enjoyed, by which the essence of the culture with Double Star is revealed. In the resort, there are statues of heroes who are patriotic, and there is a pavilion depicting traditional stories about twenty-four paragons of filial piety. In the headquarters of Double Star, there is a statue of a Chinese lion wearing shoes of Double Star. At the gates of plants and chain stores of Double Star across the country, there are statues of the black cat who works hard and the white cat who indulges in empty talk the like. These tangible cultural carriers make people feel that Double Star are fully vigorous and cultural. You may get in touch with a staff at Double Star, and from his rhetoric and meticulous operation, you can feel the spirit of people at Double Star who work hard and pursue the ideal of revitalizing national industry as well as show great cohesiveness and combat effectiveness.

Here we highlight intangible and tangible cultures with Double Star including service and image etc. In the whole culture system of Double Star, there are five highlights: idea, brand, strategy, marketing, and product.

(1) Idea culture

In layman's terms, the idea is a unique value system formed by the enterprise in the long-term development process and is the fundamental driving force for the enterprise's continuous growth. The idea of an enterprise can be elaborated in an article or a book, such as President Wang's "Market, Enterprise, Innovation", "Market, Enterprise, Famous Brand", "Secret- Double Star" and "Market Is the Root of the Enterprise" and other monographs. These monographs discuss the corporate ideas of all aspects of Double Star in different periods. However, to make the public understand, recognize, and resonate, he often summarizes and expresses ideas with key statements. These key statements have become the basic ideas of the enterprise. These statements are not imaginary, nor based on gorgeous words, but are the enrichment of corporate ideas. Moreover, they are the code of conduct and the goal of employees, while letting suppliers and customers understand the enterprise and enhance their impression and loyalty.

(2) Brand culture

In the market economy, the brand is a corporate logo, which is like the face of a person. The brand is the most lethal weapon of the enterprise in the competition. President Wang said that "brands are atomic bombs in the market economy", which fully reflects the importance of brands to an enterprise.

In today's global economic integration, the competition between countries is reflected in that between large enterprises and between famous brands. The famous brand represents the strength of an enterprise. To a certain extent, the number of famous brands reflects the strength of a country. Every year, some media and statistical departments jointly evaluate the value of brands and rank the most influential companies in the world. On the list there are relatively more companies in the United States, Japan, Germany, etc., and with the development of the market economy for hundreds of years, these countries have cultivated several famous-brand companies that have scaled up and have tremendous influence in the world. The power of famous brands is to obtain priority in the market and easily get customers' favor. The brand value of Double Star has reached 49.292 billion Yuan, and the personal brand value of President Wang has reached 32.142 billion Yuan. These are the huge intangible assets of Double Star.

(3) Strategic culture

As a competitive enterprise, it is necessary to design the future development of the enterprise always, that is, it should not drift along, instead, it should have a clear-headed mind, clearly know at what stage what should be done, that is, it should have goals and solutions. As such, it can deal with unexpected events and overcome countless hardships.

Strategic thinking is a comprehensive manifestation of corporate spirit, corporate values, and moral values. The establishment of strategic thinking has an important impact on the long-term development of enterprises. The formulation of a strategy is a cultural project of great economic significance. It cannot be changed capriciously, nor can it be immutable. It should be a dialectical unity of stability and dynamics, reflecting the overall quality of corporate leaders.

In the past 30 years, there have been experienced three major ups and downs in China's economic overheating and overheating, in which Double Star has not made big mistakes and has not been affected. Double Star has steadily advanced according to market and industry rules, creating miracles in the labor-intensive traditional manufacturing and processing industries. The leaders represented by President Wang have formulated a development strategy plan that conforms to the actual conditions at every stage.

Double Star was the first to enter the market, in which there was national policy as a basis and there was no model to follow. In contrast, this entry was prohibited by government documents at that time. If the leaders of the enterprise did not have fearless courage and keen insight, it would be impossible.

In the early 1980s, President Wang broke through the stereotypes that restricted urban factories from going to the countryside and led Double Star to implement the horizontal economic integration and transfer old products out, solving the difficulties of new product projects without funds, facilities, and equipment, and creating a new development space for Double Star.

In the early 1990s, military factories in the mountains moved to the city exposing to the wonderful outside world. However, President Wang made the decision of going out of town and going to the countryside. "It is necessary to both go to the sea and go to the countryside." It has been proved that the implementation of the strategy of Development in the East and Exploitation in the West is a very wise move, but at that time it was thought that the Double Star was difficult to keep on going in the city before going to the countryside. Luzhong and Hanhai, which were built in the Yimeng Mountain area at that time, were the backbone production bases for which there was a competition between Double Star and so-called "guerrillas" dominated by township enterprises and self-employed households. Now, a lot of state-owned enterprises have successively closed, and it is hard to imagine what would happen today if Double Star did not go to the countryside. The process of Double Star strategic transfer is also the process of Double Star brand operation and low-cost expansion. The brand operation development strategy has expanded the broader space for Double Star. The process of Double Star strategic transfer is also a process of diversification. Uninterrupted strategic transfer and diversified development have made Double Star stand out in the domestic footwear industry and become a famous brand.

In the 21st century, which is a new era of economic integration of the market economy, the members of the Party committee in Double Star Group, represented by President Wang, have formulated two new strategic decisions for Double Star, that is, To Develop into Advanced Stage and Set up New Image in New Era. These two strategic decisions are the program for the development of Double Star in the new era; the goal of the struggle with Double Star in the new era; the strong measure and guarantee that Double Star develops into a strong brand and goes global etc. The correct and advanced enterprise development strategy relates with the survival of enterprises.

(4) Marketing culture

The business is very important in the enterprise, and the business decision-making, means and effects are directly related to the economic benefits of the enterprise. In the past 40 years, Double Star has become its own unique marketing culture. The core of marketing culture with Double Star is the market. With the development of the market, with the changes in consumption patterns, Double Star adjusts the marketing strategy, meets the market and customer needs, so having become a leading provider in the market.

Since its entry into the market, Double Star has established its own marketing network which is quite efficient. Indeed, in the past, Double Star made difficult explorations and went through several stages, including engaging in door-to-door sales, establishing its own operating branches, and setting up chain stores; moreover, Double Star successively adopted mine warfare, positional warfare, and three-dimensional warfare.

The network is only the hardware. If there is no software, the market will be inefficient. Double Star software is a unique 200% service. It can be said that service is an extremely important part of the marketing culture, and it is also a unique part of Double Star culture. It has played an incomparable role incomparable by other strategies in the market.

In the new century, the domestic market is characterized by the influx of foreign famous brands and the increasingly fierce competition in the market, and the issue is how to attract customers and expand the customer base. President Wang proposed the following approaches: psychological promotion, emotional marketing, personalized marketing; and shoe-tire linkage marketing. By these approaches, Double Star can constantly increase the flexibility, diversity, and connotation of services, meet consumer needs, and naturally gain profits. This is the theoretical basis of the 200% service in Double Star.

(5) Product culture

A product is any item that meets the needs of users and consumers. Product culture includes technology, quality, price, packaging and other aspects. Product culture is an important part of enterprise culture and the most essential element that reflects the overall image of an enterprise.

In expounding the theory of the advanced stage of the famous brand, President Wang once said: The representative of the advanced stage is the product. At any time, consumers are familiar with an enterprise by its product. Only by continuously introducing products that suit the needs of consumers, can the enterprise survive for a long time.

The reason Double Star has been at the forefront in this fickle market is that they established the correct product development policy just after elimination of Jiefang shoes (an old fashion shoes made for military men). This policy is below: generations of products co-exist in research, development, production and storage. Double Star always leads the trend of shoe consumption by providing new products with high quality.

Another key factor in the popularity of Double Star products is the quality of the products. “High quality of products is the biggest doing-good and gathering of blessings.” This simple motto is used to educate employees, uniting the wishes of employees with the goals of Double Star achieving a good interaction. The quality qualification rate of Double Star products has been maintained at over 99.99%. The popular motto - “Yield is money, quality is life, Double Star wants both money and life; if there is no choice, Double Star will prefer life to money.”- makes employees to deeply understand the dialectical relationship between output and quality. Quality is always the first. By the activities from the anti-advertising program to publicly burning unqualified shoes, Double Star vividly educates employees to understand the meaning of quality for the survival of enterprises and enables the quality concept deep into the hearts of every employee. With the long-lasting awareness of quality first, Double Star became the first in the same field to pass the ISO 9001 international quality system certification; became the only national-level enterprise with its export products exempt from inspection; became the only state-owned enterprise recognized by PSS the world's largest footwear distributor.

"A wide variety, fashionable style, superior quality, high, middle and low grades" is a good impression left by Double Star products to consumers and is also a comprehensive reflection of Double Star product culture in the market.

3. Highlighting five features

Enterprise culture is the crystallization of corporate wealth. Enterprise culture of Double Star reflects the value pursuit and spiritual outlook of people at Double Star, also reflects the overall level, individuality and development history of Double Star. Double Star culture has five distinct features:

(1) Personality

Enterprise culture is essentially an entrepreneurial culture. Double Star culture is first a reflection of the personalization of President Wang, who, by his creative thinking, refines the practical experience of Double Star in market and form a unique value, market theory, enterprise spirit, and management thought. Mr. Wang influences employees of Double Star with his integrity and exemplary behavior and cultivates Double Star culture in practice. With his novel ideas and rigorous plans, Mr. Wang is committed to the cultural construction by organizing relevant activities and projects. Mr. Wang injects into his work national feelings, fearless spirit and a keen sense of professionalism, thereby creating a unique enterprise – Double Star which dares to be the first in the world, wins the glory for our motherland, creates famous brands, and encourages employees to work hard. Mr. Wang is the soul of Double-Star culture. Whether it is the cultural carrier of hardware or the spiritual innovation of software, it is the crystallization of the wisdom of Mr. Wang who has profound thinking.

At the same time, Double Star culture emphasizes the importance of the realization of human values. Double Star was the first to establish a democratic management committee, and employees participated in the management; Double Star was the first to hold a product design grand prix, Double Star promoted mass education, training and competition; Double Star broke the rigid employment mechanism, advocated paying attention to the talent in the market economy and selecting the talent through multiple channels, and paying attention to the high-level psychological needs of employees, including self-esteem and self-value realization. These are the embodiment of the "people-oriented" concept. His outlook on life and values gradually affects employees at Double Star thus uniting them. Double Star culture strongly reflects the personality.

(2) Chinese style

Double Star culture is rooted in the background of reform and opening. With its formation based on Deng Xiaoping Theory, it absorbs essences of excellent traditional culture of China and has the originality. It is not the copycat of "modern management theory" with characteristics of capitalism. Therefore, Double Star culture has a distinctive Chinese character."

(3) Contemporaneity

Enterprise culture constantly evolves, and its development cannot be separated from the influence of the times. For example, Double Star culture is developed in the practice of China's market economy. The richness and perfection of Double Star culture show the complicated process of transforming the enterprise from a planned economy to a market economy. At Double Star, management, quality, tech, market, talent, mechanism, and culture are inseparable from the characteristics of the market, which reflect the requirements of the era of market economy, and they are also marked by the era of China's reform and opening. Therefore, Double Star culture has distinct characteristics of the times.

(4) Model

Previously, Double Star was on the verge of bankruptcy; now it has developed into a large group of 60,000 people. In the past, it only covered 100 Chinese acres of land in the western part of Qingdao; currently its production bases and marketing networks are all over the country and even international. Double Star, which only produced Jiefang shoes, has been involved in 23 industrial fields such as tires, machinery, clothing, thermoelectricity, printing, and tertiary industry. Although as a group it is involved in many fields with a lot of employees, it adopts the same management mode in all plants and chain stores, where you will not find any significant differences. The management mode of Double Star has penetrated every corner of production and operation. Model management is the reflection of the characteristics of enterprise culture.

(5) Innovation

Enterprise culture should be constantly enriched and improved in the practice of production and management, showing innovative ideas, new looks, and promoting the continuous development of the business. In the previous analysis of the connotation of Double Star culture, it has been able to clearly see its innovative features. People at Double Star gradually understand the laws of the market economy, which is reflected in the following processes: from "love our plant, love the brand, and love our motherland" to "the brand is the golden rice bowl of Double Star" and "creating famous brand is the biggest patriotism"; from "market-oriented" to "market leading the plant" and "the market is a standard of testing all work in the enterprise"; from "200% service to make up for non-100% product quality" to "any industry is a branch of service field"; from "people are first in the plant, management is people-oriented" to "market Endless, management without a period or full stop" and so on. These are the result of constantly seeking truth from facts, self-surpassing and innovating. Due to its culture, Double Star is brave in breaking the restricted area in the reform, takes risks in scientific exploration, and continuously steps forwards. The core and soul of Double Star culture is innovation.

4. Five major roles

The relationship between a company's basic creed, mission, spiritual drive and its achievements is far closer than the relationship between technical plus economic resources, organizational structure and its achievements. To a certain extent, the spiritual strength is more important. Double Star culture has played a very important role in its development mainly including the followings.

(1) Determining the basic characteristics of the enterprise

Enterprise culture determines the direction of a enterprise and determines its personality, making it unique. For example, when making decisions based on long-term development goals, it will consider the relationship between its own interests and national interests and social interests, and consciously create a development environment that benefits the country, benefits the people, and benefits itself, thereby achieving the unity of the interests of the three, thus avoiding unfair competitions that over-emphasize immediate interests, forget all moral principal at sight of profits, and resort to deception. Obviously, diverse cultures will lead enterprises to different development paths and shape different enterprise images.

Since its entry into the market, Double Star has set a goal in creating world famous brands. To achieve this goal, it implements ethical, honest operation, obeys laws, actively uses technological innovation, institutional innovation, management innovation and other legitimate means to enhance its competitiveness. While it won one victory after another in market, while a few other enterprises resorted to deception. They did not work hard, instead, they earned immediate profits by producing counterfeit and shoddy goods. Without the awareness of long-term development, reputation, image and brand, these enterprises eventually were shut down with the development and improvement of the market economy and the intensification of competition.

(2) Guiding the operation decision-making of the enterprise

The success of an enterprise is inseparable from its decision-making. The enterprise culture has a positive function. It not only reflects the goal of the enterprise, but also plans the operation, coordination and development direction of all aspects of different stages. The enterprise culture not only determines the material indicators of enterprise development, but more importantly, it can generate spiritual motivation and encourage employees to overcome all difficulties on the road to achieve their goals. We can clearly see the role of enterprise culture in enterprise decision-making from connotations with Double Star culture.

(3) Motivating employees to be progressive

The values, entrepreneurial spirit, and development goals described in the enterprise culture can appeal to the employees and let them to see the hopes, so enhancing their confidence in the enterprise. Employees also correct their own goals, outlook on life, and values through understanding the enterprise values, to unit them and the enterprise in destiny and pursuit and keep making progress.

(4) Regulating basic behavior of employees

The enterprise has behavioral requirements for employees in each position and has its own standards for the overall image of all employees. Enterprise culture has a positive and effective role in regulating employee behavior. First, it has a guiding role, which is to provide employees with work direction and spiritual motivation. Secondly, it has a binding role, so that employees know how to do, what enterprises advocate and admire; by enterprise culture, employees gradually and voluntarily use constrain and control their own words and deeds. Thirdly, it has a fusion effect, which gradually unifies employees from different regions, diverse cultural backgrounds and different living environments into enterprise behavioral norms and moral standards; moreover, it influences them unobtrusively.

(5) Keeping the same image of the enterprise

Double Star's production plants and chain stores have distinct characteristics, so that people can see that they are belonged to Double Star at a glance and obtain a good impression. This has the visual effect of the uniformity of hardware, and the influence of the unique temperament of Double Star. This is the role of Double Star culture.

Double Star culture is the product of the socialist theory of building the socialism with Chinese characteristics in practice of the enterprise and is the group awareness formed in the development process of Double Star. With its profound thinking level, unique personality charm and strong radiation ability, Double Star culture influences and promotes the development of Double Star; will continue to enrich and improve in the development of the brand and shine with its own charming brilliance in the global shoe industry and etc.

III. Typical examples

(1) An uproar provoked by Wang's Quotations

When mentioning the quotations, people will remember the Quotations from Chairman Mao in Cultural Revolution period. Unexpectedly, after more than 30 years, we see Wang's Quotations in Double Star. Does Wang really develop personal superstition or worship? What kind of key role does his quotations play in the development of Double Star?

The production workshop of Double Star is full of slogans: people wear shoes, the key is work; brand name is the atomic bomb of market economy; creating famous brand is the best patriotism; a good use of money is the best ideological and political work; there is no end to the market, management is without a period; not innovating today will let one fall behind, not innovating tomorrow will let one be eliminated the day after tomorrow... so many slogans are all put forward by Wang. Therefore, people say that they are Wang's Quotations.

On one occasion, visitors from Double Star came to a shoe-making enterprise in South Korea. They even saw in the workshop the slogans: People wear shoes, the key is work; Users are Gods, market wins gold etc. The Koreans were embarrassed to say that they were Wang's Quotations. On May 26th, 2004, Mr. Kristing, a French customer, visited Double Star. The guest greatly appreciated the on-site management, quality management and fund management of Double Star, and even more interested in its culture. At each workshop, the guest asked about and recorded in detail the slogans (in the propaganda board and wall) and their meaning, saying that he would adopt Double Star culture in his company.

However, Wang's Quotations provoked an uproar in China. Some people said that Wang developed personal superstition and personal worship. Gu Xiulian, Vice Chairman of 10th National People's Congress Committee, former Minister of Chemical Industry, and Chairman of All-China Women's Federation, heard the comment and personally went to Double Star to see these controversial quotations. Unexpectedly, she couldn't help but even praise, "These quotations reflect his experiences in management in the market. They are good!" Thus she became a propagandist of Wang's Quotations.

Compass or Beacon of Double Star

The sea sails by the helmsman, and even the best helmsman cannot do without the compass or beacon. Double Star as a huge joint fleet cleaves through the waves in the turbulent market, relying on Wang's Quotations as a pass.

Always at the most critical time, his quotations can point people of Double to a correct direction and enable them to re-adjust the course. For example, in 1983, Jiefang shoes produced by Double Star were rejected by the state-owned commercial system and had a backlog of more than two million pairs; all of employees felt anxious. At a critical juncture, Wang said, "Do not wait for others to give you rice, instead, find rice for yourself." It is this sentence that enabled Double Star to successfully get rid of the constraints of the planned economy and become the earliest wave rider in the market economy of China.

For more than 30 years, every step of Double Star has been guided by Wang's Quotations. In the mid-1980s, foreign famous shoes flooded into the domestic market, which had a great impact on the Chinese footwear industry. Double Star was no exception. At this time, Wang said: "Chinese people are not shorter than foreigners in case of both standing and lying." "Chinese people must have their own famous brands." Then Double Star entered the stage of implementing the famous brand strategy. In 2002, its shoes won the title of China Famous Brand; in 2004, all-steel radial tires were recognized a famous brand of China; therefore, it took only a dozen years to own its own brand products. Wang also proposed slogans: "creating international famous brands, becoming the world famous factory, being celebrities of Double Star", "brand name is the atomic bomb of the market economy"; in 2001, facing the more fierce market competition after China's access to the WTO, Wang said that "we create our Chinese brand", "innovation is the eternal theme of market competition"... So, when putting his quotations together, we can undoubtedly see the most vivid entrepreneurial history of Double Star!

Quintessence of *Wang Hai Quotations*

Wang Hai Quotations are the product of the market. They originate from the market and guide the practice of people at Double Star in the market economy. Therefore, the quintessence of his quotations is to seek truth from facts, do honorable deeds and gather blessings, which is the mystery of the success of Double Star.

One of slogans from Wang is the motto for people at Double Star, namely, "People wear shoes and the key is work." His explanation is that there are 1.3 billion people in China, and 6 billion people in the world. No one cannot be without shoes.

The key is whose shoes are worn? Although Double Star can't make everyone wear its shoes, it must work in this direction. At least it can let everyone who wears its shoes feel that they must wear its shoes.

Wang also says, "Having excellent quality of product is the largest doing-good and gathering of blessings." His explanation is that, at present, the relationship between employees and enterprises has undergone fundamental changes. Many people come to and work in Double Star only for money, so the previous method of education cannot be adopted. Instead, authoritative management should be changed to moral management which has a better effect due to its compliance with the human nature of doing-good and gathering of blessings. Indeed, employees are more willing to accept this new method. Therefore, the product quality of Double Star has always been recognized as on the world-class level.

In 1994, Double Star cancelled all maintenance service stations in a variety of major cities and regions, because Wang said, "Quality is dependent on production other hand inspection." The defect should be eliminated during the production process; otherwise, the brand image will be damaged. Therefore, if the quality problem is found in the product, the responsible person must pay for it and buy it back. Now, people at Double Star have such a consensus: Double Star has obtained the National Quality Inspection Exemption Certificate, but there is never an exemption from inspection within Double Star. As known, Wang is not a philosopher, but he is not inferior to philosophers in the philosophical rationality. Slogans and mottos from him are more realistic and more easily accepted.

The relativism and absolutism of philosophers are so profound that many people cannot understand them. But Wang says, "Price competition is temporary, while quality competition is eternal." which makes people understand at a glance.

Philosophers say that quantitative change can promote qualitative change, but Wang says to the workers that when the daily output of Double Star reaches 600,000 pairs, if one out of ten thousand has a problem, then there will be 60 pairs one day and ten thousand consumers one year who are dissatisfied with shoes of Double Star. In the long run, the brand will undergo qualitative changes. Therefore, Wang says, "The more famous brands are, the more attention paid to quality. The more famous brands are, the more improvements made in quality."

"There are products of inferior quality but are no unreasonable markets", "there are enterprises of poor management but no those which cannot be managed well" ... It is believed that a person without a philosopher's mind can't say such words.

Wang put forward, "The market is the highest leader of the enterprise", "the market is the only standard for testing all work of the enterprise" and "market leading factory". When these words came out, many people were alarmed. Many enterprises have not begun to understand them until now. Mr. Wang believes that if enterprises only seek the help from ministers and mayors, they can't find the market; therefore, enterprises can't rely on governmental departments, instead, they can only create markets by themselves.

His quotations always reflect an innovative spirit. Wang says that an entrepreneur in the market must abandon the old for the new. "Innovation is the source, soul and motivation of enterprise development." Double Star takes the innovate as a standard of testing whether each employee is market-oriented. All of people at Double Star actively carry out theoretical innovation, technological innovation, systemic innovation, mechanism innovation, management innovation, business innovation etc.; are encouraged to break old ideas, old concepts, old traditions, old methods, old patterns or stereotypes and establish new thinking, new ideas, new concepts, and new practices. According to the scientific thinking from him (including "the anti-thinking is the beginning of the success, only the anti-thinking can create miracles"), Double Star has created new, special, and excellent products and famous Chinese brands in the fierce market competition.

In the new century, President Wang proposed the following innovative viewpoints: “The innovation is carried out by leadership, engineering and technical personnel, and front-line employees”, “the position is the market, the competition is on the machine station, all the staffs are innovative, everyone is result-oriented”, “launch the people's war in innovation”. People at Double Star hold up the innovation banner, and with the unremitting effort, all of them carry out innovation programs. Relying on innovation of all employees, Double Star builds its core competitiveness.

A good remedy for people at Double Star

For people at Double Star, Wang’s quotations are a good remedy. When being in difficult, they are encouraged by the following slogans from him: "taking yourself as the backbone", "self-improvement", "solving problems raised by yourself", "even if you are misunderstood, you feel good about yourself". He motivates people at Double Star to "win the glory for our country and their own enterprise"; and alarms them by saying: "Brand without the sense of crisis are the most dangerous, and employees without the sense of crisis are hopeless."

Wang says that his quotations are the crystallization of the collective wisdom of people at Double Star, and a summary and sublimation of the theory and practice of Double Stars over the years. Therefore, his quotations can be deeply loved by staffs, engraved in their mind, understood and applied in practices, and regarded by many people as a treasure...

If our state-owned enterprises and private enterprises can have their own set of Wang’s Quotations, what will happen? It is really hoped that in the market economy, China can have more entrepreneurial quotations like his quotations, so that Chinese enterprises will have great hope.

(2) Double Star culture and Dongfeng —— key to successful acquisition of Dongfeng Tire

State-owned Dongfeng Tire Co., Ltd., which set up a joint venture with Malaysia, did not see the hope. After Double Star Group as a state-owned enterprise cooperating with it, it took only a brief period of more than two years for this tire unit with a great debt to regain vitality. Double Star has created serial classic success stories: for example, acquiring enterprises with slow pace of development, state-owned enterprises, and foreign enterprises. The acquisition of the above-said tire unit illustrates that cultural integration is the key to successful M & A.

In the morning of December 25, 2007, Luo Qingquan, secretary of Hubei Provincial Party Committee, Zhao Bin, secretary of Shiyan Municipal Party Committee, and Chen Tianhui, mayor of this city and so forth, went to the Double Star Dongfeng Tire Ltd for investigation. Everywhere, employees were working with great enthusiasm. After the cooperation with Double Star, Dongfeng overcame the difficulties in 2005 and 2006. In 2007, it developed rapidly with a good result of production and sales. The annual economic indicators were doubled compared with that in 2006; the foreign exchange earned reached 18 million US dollars throughout the year, thereby making a large contribution for promoting the local economy. Luo Qingquan fully affirmed the successful experience of Double Star in transforming a state-owned enterprise on the verge of closure through the culture, ideas, and management; encouraged Double Star to make persistent efforts and accelerate development and strive to build Double Star Dongfeng into a modern star enterprise nationwide and even globally. On behalf of Hubei Provincial Party Committee and Provincial Government, he said that the support would be continuously given to Double Star Dongfeng.

In fact, before being acquired by Double Star, Dongfeng Tire had received a funding of 280 million Yuan when it set up a joint venture with Malaysia in which advanced technology and foreign management methods were implemented. However, it eventually failed. Question: how did Double Star bring it back to life in over two years?

Shared visions and clear directions

In 2005, the reorganization of Dongfeng Tire by Double Star caused a sensation in the society. It also caused a strong reaction inside. The impact of the market economy has caused the source of survival by relying on the government for many years to be depleted. For enterprises and staffs, their eating from the same big pot soon came to an end, and so did their sense of superiority and security under planned economy. Dongfeng people are reorganizing. Facing new things including reorganization, people at Dongfeng Tire felt fear with fuzzy understanding, disagreement and so forth, or even hang the big slogan: Go back, Double Star; Roll back, Wang! In this regard, Double Star used cultural ideas to educate them, transform them, and manage them, leading to their understanding, acceptance, and active integration into the new culture. For them, this is a kind of self-revolution and self-breakthrough.

The reorganization was completed. In March 2005, at the first training mobilization meeting, Wang president of Double Star made a speech lasting two and a half hours on why reorganization was made and how to reinvigorate. He said, "Who can save it? Answer: Only itself." He continuously said that, by the reorganization, Double Star cooperated with it to compete with international brands, won the glory for the state-owned tire industry, and kept this national brand namely DONGFENG which was named by Chairman Mao Zedong personally. His speech made employees to know their goals and see the hope, thereby winning loud applauses.

In the practice, decision makers of Double Star realized that after the merger, most of the employees of the acquired enterprise might feel the uncertainty of the development of the enterprise and their own. The fear and uneasiness might affect the work efficiency and emotion of the employees, which would intensify their boycott against the acquirer's integration. Only when the development vision of the new enterprise is very clear and can be recognized and accepted by the cadres and employees of the enterprise, can the enterprise integration strategy be carried and possible resistance reduced.

Double Star culture and its influence

When the reorganization was made, Wang said with deep feelings, "What is the key to the success of an enterprise? It depends on management. The cultural ideas are the top-level management. The outline of political work with Double Star is to use cultural ideas to educate people, transform people and unite people."

For employees of the acquired enterprise, the planned economy had for a long time banned their thoughts, including the old thinking, for example, they always felt proud of being workers of state-owned and military enterprises and so forth, in which the poor management existed. How can enterprises regain vitality simply by importing foreign capital and so-called model management? Wang analyzed the situation and proposed to initiate a big discussion about for whom it was done and how was it done. Wang hoped that they could completely break with the old thoughts, old habits and old styles.

The reason why the weak can defeat the strong in the war years is the spirit. The spirit and the culture are inseparable. Double Star has infiltrated its excellent culture into the thoughts of employees with Double Star Dongfeng and its reality, which has played a great role. Since their cooperation, Dongfeng Tire has comprehensively carried out employee education and training, organized leaders and employees to visit Headquarters and production plants of Double Star, especially, it has carried out the education about Double Star culture emphasizing the following themes: seeking truth from facts; doing honorable deeds and gathering of blessings; carrying forward national ethos, promoting national spirit, creating national brands etc.

By these measures, employees have understood the management of Double Star as a famous enterprise and made a gradual change in ideological ideas and mental outlook.

After the acquisition, Dongfeng Tire retained almost all previous leaders and managers. The relevant adjustments were made to provide each person with the most suitable position to play a role. The market-oriented thinking prevailed in the mind of all staffs. It can be said that people at Double Star Dongfeng underwent the process of ideological emancipation and thinking changes under the influence of Double Star culture. Dongfeng Tire, previously being on the verge of closure, finally rejuvenated with its staffs working with great enthusiasm.

Market-oriented concept, mechanism, and vitality

The system and mechanism determine the survival of the enterprise. Without the good system and mechanism as guarantee, the enterprise cannot achieve healthy development, let alone grow bigger and stronger.

Double Star Dongfeng Tire Co., Ltd. adheres to the principle of "taking the market as the standard, taking the enterprise development as the standard, and mobilizing the enthusiasm of all employees as the standard." According to the actual conditions, it constantly summed up, adjusted, carried the reform to shift into the market economy from the planned economy, implemented the assessment mechanism (having a clear distinction between reward and punishment) as well as the tendering & contracting system. It changed the market competition of enterprises into the internal competition of all staffs, so that everyone is responsible and supervised. The problem of eating from the same big pot was dissolved, and the lazy attitude changed. As a result, it motivated employees, brought the hope for them, improved the production efficiency, and realizing the spirit of employees; it initially established a staff team having "Three Irons" (iron will, iron discipline, and iron-man style). The profound changes took place in the site management, product development, product quality, employee mental outlook etc. Double Star Dongfeng Tire restored the production of all steel tires regardless of a brief period of time and heavy tasks, with its monthly output reaching the best level in the history; developed a variety of markets; laid a solid step for the market work. Market involved are below: maintenance market, supporting market, foreign market, and licensed market. It broke through the backward situation of innovation and technology development and developed the world's unique and fashionable color tires (please remember that all of tires were black in the past century). It implemented new quality management modes such as on-site Quality Kanban management and let employees have a quality awareness: Pursuit of Excellence in Quality & Service. It assembled four semi-steel car tires for a taxi user in Shiyan; in various complicated roads, four tires could achieve 100,000 km without damage. Therefore, it has achieved a significant improvement in product quality, set up a new corporate image, and enhanced the market competitiveness.

Management Innovation and competitiveness

Management is the eternal theme of enterprise development and market competition. Especially in footwear and tire industries, 30% tech and 70% management has become an indisputable fact. The success of Double Star merging and acquiring other enterprises is mainly due to the strengthening of management.

President Wang told employees of Dongfeng Tire, "All of bankrupt enterprises fail in management, market and culture. We hold the market's bowl and eat the market's rice. Therefore, we must be pragmatic in work instead of indulging in empty talk." Double Star is not the "savior", the "saviors" are employees themselves. Double Star adopts a combination of management modes and market-based contracting systems in Double Star Dongfeng Tire, while management modes involve in culture, money, emotion, and system the like. As results, employees quickly understood Double Star's market management ideas, establish and enhance awareness in quality, market, competition, and development.

As to the on-site management level of a tire unit, the mixing workshop is the most representative. Double Star Dongfeng has made profound changes in the on-site management of production lines and plants (represented by the mixing workshop) by persisting in the basic management. Some retired veteran cadres and veteran employees of the original enterprise visited the mixing workshop in September 2007 and said: "Nobody had ever visited here before. If you came in, you would go out with the whole body blackened. But now it is kept really neat and tidy!"

In the conspicuous position of Double Star Dongfeng office building, a large slogan -"Market Is the Standard for Testing All Work of the Enterprise"- is particularly eye-catching; in the workshop and the plant area, slogans about the market can be seen everywhere, such as "All staffs turn to the market, everyone cares for quality", "Good product quality is the biggest doing-good and gathering of blessings", "Eyes on market, hands on management" and so forth. Double Star Dongfeng started with strengthening management and optimizing staffing, with its leading cadres actively taking the initiative to go deep into the front line, not only being propagandists, but also being commanders and combatants. It fully motivated employees in each branch, workshop, department and post; it linked doing an excellent job with cherishing the future, so greatly promoting management plus production and improving quality.

Nowadays, Double Star has completely penetrated its mature management modes into the management system of Double Star Dongfeng, e.g., process chain claims, factory purchase and supply, contract management, family consumption style etc.

(3) Wang delivered a speech on Microsoft forum

On August 16, 2007 (local time), at the Microsoft Corporation, the world's largest computer software company in Seattle, USA, one hundred personnel from fields of management, technology, and engineering gathered together to meet a famous entrepreneur from China with doubts and curiosity — Mr. Wang president of Double Star Group. A cultural exchange of Double Star and Microsoft organized by the latter officially kicked off.

Wang is China's first Chinese entrepreneur to enter the Microsoft forum. It is a dream of many people to board the Microsoft forum.

With a hat of Double Star on the head, a T-shirt on the body, and travelling shoes or sneakers on the feet, Wang as Shoe King of China entered the pulpit with the other guests filled with amazement.

As one of the world's most successful companies, Microsoft is the world leader in PC (personal computer) software development and brings together the best high-tech talents from around the world.

With the rapid development of the global economy, China has become the center of global manufacturing and processing bases. In the fierce domestic and international market competitions, Double Star stands out in the background that a lot of state-owned shoe-making enterprises fail. With its long-time development, Double Star must have its own unique characteristics. As a state-owned shoe-making enterprise with strong competitiveness and the earliest impact from foreign brands, the survival of Double Star is a special case. The reasons for the success of Double Star are various, but its culture and management theory with unique characteristics play a key role.

It is Wang who created a unique enterprise culture, management theory and philosophical thinking that made Double Star to embark on a road to success for the manufacturing and processing industry from “Made in China” to “Created in China” and let himself go into the forum of the world-class enterprise - Microsoft.

Double Star is the first in the manufacturing industry of China to contact with high-tech enterprise Microsoft. In traditional industries of shoes and tires where there is an intense competition, Double Star has created miracles one after another. "The development of Double Star is driven by numerous factors. The most crucial point is that enterprise culture has played a role. At present, no matter whether it is high-tech industry or manufacturing industry, without their own culture and ideas, enterprises have no hope; only there is a continuous innovation in culture and ideas, can enterprises develop better."

The speech from Wang as an Eastern entrepreneur was very infectious. In his two-hour speech, he used real and vivid examples, humorous language, unique ways of thinking, and profound knowledge to elaborate and analyze relationships between Chinese culture and enterprise management, commonalities and differences between Eastern and Western cultures.

Ethical ideas creatively proposed by Wang ("production of product with high quality is the largest dong-good and gathering blessings", "honesty, 200% service" and so on) are consistent with behavioral norms ("responsibility first, integrity, customer service"). The innovative ideas creatively put forward by Wang (people's war of innovation in the commercial field", "not innovating today, we will fall behind, and not innovating tomorrow, we will be eliminated the day after tomorrow" and the like) coincide with Microsoft's "enthusiasm for new technologies, courage to meet challenges, persistent innovation." His management ideas ("emotional management, money management, system management, cultural ideas management" etc.) coincide with Microsoft "to win people with virtue, motivate employees with money, value and retain talents". His other ideas ("people-oriented; helping employees get rid of worries and overcome difficulties, being eager to meet needs of employees") coincide with Microsoft's "providing employees with a relaxed and comfortable working environment".

Because of the differences between Eastern and Western cultures, the differences in the environment, and the differences in the industries, there are the differences in corporate culture and management forms. Wang said: The cultural concept has played a key role in the development of Double Star in the past forty years. Because of the different nature of the enterprise and the different connotations of the culture, the loose working environment of the high-tech industry cannot be realized in the labor-intensive manufacturing and processing industry. Humanized management represented by compassionate leadership of Double Star does not coincide with the Western procedural system assessment and standard assessment, but whether it is Eastern or the Western, the absolute principle is that management forms and methods derived from cultural ideas should promote the development of the enterprise. Mr. Wang's speech made everyone feel this more deeply.

"This cultural exchange is held between a leading foreign high-tech enterprise in the IT industry and a leading domestic enterprise in labor-intensive type manufacturing and processing industry, that is, both enterprises are from different countries, different fields, and diverse cultural backgrounds. It makes me think about how to better utilize resources of Chinese traditional culture and how to absorb good experiences from foreign enterprises including performance and skill assessments the like, to create our own modern enterprise culture and management ideas." Really, Wang in this trip is like Monkey King who goes on a pilgrimage for Buddhist scriptures.

In a certain sense, the fact that Wang is the first to talk about Chinese culture and enterprise management in the Microsoft forum proves that Chinese state-owned enterprises can run well and that management culture and management model with Chinese characteristics can be created.

Wang said: In the labor-intensive industry, human factors directly affect quality, output and cost. Double Star puts forward the ethical standard ("Production of product with high quality is the largest doing-good and gathering blessings"), grasps the management core ("using cultural ideas to educate, guide, and manage people") , carries forward the dedication spirit of working class ("working hard, working selflessly, and struggling indomitably"), creates Nine plus Nine Management Method and ABW Management Theory, and successfully creates M & A cases, including acquisitions of enterprises with small size or slow pace of development and state-owned ones.

Finally, Wang said: "Culture as a kind of thought, soul, and spirit can educate, inspire, and guide people. Only by creating new cultures, new theories, innovative ideas, can we create new miracles and constantly promote the social and historical development." (Source: *Business Weekly*, 2007, Issue 20, Total 273 Issues)

IV. Expert Comments

It is said that in many occasions at home and abroad, President Wang often meets reporters and listeners who ask such a question: What is the secret weapon for Double Star to stand out in the industry and create brands famous nationwide and worldwide?

Whenever encountering similar problems, President Wang loudly laughs and says, **"Double Star has no secrets. If any, they will be copied away by many people and enterprises visiting us. On the other hand, Double Star is successful mainly due to its culture."**

So, what is the largest contribution of President Wang to China?

Dr. Wang Zhongming, former director of Research Center of State-owned Assets Supervision and Administration Commission of the State Council, after listening to Mr. Wang's talk about the enterprise culture with Chinese characteristics, said with emotion: **"The most important thing for an enterprise is that it contributes to society at the ideological level. The enterprise culture, as the most economically spillover of business management, will surpass the enterprise, surpass the industry, surpass the industry, and surpass the economy. So, it can distinguish the great enterprise from the general enterprise and distinguish real entrepreneurs from business leaders. Why are his views refreshing? A very important point that he does not make a general introduction to experience. He possesses his own characteristics in management thinking. State-owned enterprises have their experience, image and mode, but it is difficult for them to create their own ideas. Why does Wang have a breakthrough in this respect? Because Double Star is not a state-owned enterprise in the traditional sense. Indeed, it has the shell of a state-owned enterprise, but it breaks the stereotypes in business management. Its new ideas in business management contributing to society have become a shared cultural wealth and are worthy of study than the tangible services and products."**

Napoleon Hill as the world's most famous master of success said: **"The power of thinking is the greatest power of mankind. It can build a great kingdom and destroy the**

kingdom. All ideas, plans, purposes, and desires are from the thought which dominates all energy and can solve all problems. Without correct thinking, you can't make great achievements." [1]

Why are the working class and the people of the world able to become the masters from the exploited and oppressed slaves? The most fundamental reason is the Marxism and Leninism created by Marx and Lenin. The most fundamental reason for the Chinese working class and the masses of the people to become the masters of the country and to live a well-off life comes from Mao Zedong Thought and Deng Xiaoping Theory. In the same way, the most fundamental reason for Double Star to create amazing miracles comes from Wang's thinking which is reflected in Double Star culture.

The value of unique Double Star culture is not only the personal intangible assets of President Wang, but also the intangible assets of Double Star Group. More importantly, it will become the common spiritual wealth of Chinese entrepreneurs. As long as Chinese enterprises can master and apply this spiritual wealth, they will certainly create more Wang -style entrepreneurs, create more Double Star-like brands, and create more double-star enterprises, quickly let our motherland become stronger in economic, political, military, and cultural fields, and make a greater contribution to all mankind!

---

[1] Zhang Xiuyu: How to Be Successful, Enterprise Management Press, January 2005, Page 203.

Tactic 2: The Theory Is the Guide

"In every historical period, there should be a guiding theory which considers the actual conditions. The role of theory in social development is immeasurable. Enterprises without theory and thought are hopeless; cadres without theory and thought are hopeless; employees without theory and thought are hopeless. Without good theory and thought, the cause will have no direction; it will fail and even suffer crushing defeat."

——Wang Hai

In 2005, Double Star brand and Wang's market theory intangible assets value conference was held in Beijing.
Value of Double Star brand was 49.292 billion Yuan and value of Wang 32.142 billion Yuan.

In 2008, at the signing ceremony of new book ***Wang Hai's 30 Years***, President Wang Hai explained to the media reporters and readers the meaning of "creating famous brands is the best patriotic act."

I. Wang Hai Quotations

(I) Important significance of market political theory of Double Star

☆ Market politics theory guides market economy practice. If market theory is not updated, enterprises will not develop.

☆ Theory is a crystallization of social sciences and natural sciences. It not only guides the development of natural sciences, but also promotes the progress of history. In every historical period, there should be a guiding theory which considers the actual conditions. The role of theory in social development is immeasurable.

☆ Enterprises without theory and thought are hopeless; cadres without theory and thought are hopeless; employees without theory and thought are hopeless. Without good theory and thought, the cause will have no direction; it will fail and even suffer crushing defeat.

(II) Important role of market political theory of Double Star

☆ Faith is a kind of belief and consciousness. It is the most concentrated and highest form of belief. It is a norm of consciousness that runs through people's world outlook, values, and outlook on life. Morality is an act under the control of faith.

☆ Theoretical innovation is the soul of innovation, the foundation of sustained and stable development of enterprises, and the nuclear power in power.

☆ Market theory of Double Star is the guide of employees, constantly inspiring vitality, passion and fighting spirit. The cohesiveness and centripetal force it produces play an important guiding role in people's thinking.

☆ Theory is the embodiment of culture, representing the trend and development law of an era. Market theory of Double Star is a high-level embodiment of its culture and a major contribution to social development.

(III) Characteristics of market and politics theory of Double Star

☆ Characteristics of such theory: Take the market as the main line and take the famous brand as the core.

☆ Three principles of Double Star's market economy: The market is the highest leader of the enterprise, the market is the standard for testing all work of the enterprise, and the market is the best balance for testing the enterprise.

☆ Cultivate national ethos, carry forward national spirit, and create national brands.

(IV) How to innovate market politics theory

☆ Inherit the traditional excellence, absorb foreign achievements, and create our own distinct products.

☆ Carry forward old traditions, new spirits, and good styles. Only by doing so, will employees be more serious and responsible in the work, and will the enterprise have more synergy and cohesion.

☆ Faith is the fundamental principle of all behaviors and is constantly enriched and upgraded according to the development situation of each period. In real life, in the face of current entrepreneurial spirit and dedication spirit weakening, money worship, hedonism and other ugly phenomena, the primary task of ideological and political work of our enterprise is how to guide the employees to establish a correct outlook on life and values.

(V) How to implement the market politics theory of Double Star

☆ Make effective use of the theory of Double Star, study the politics of Double Star, and encourage the righteousness in Double Star.

☆ The difficulty in production and management is the focus of ideological and political work.

☆ Carry out political work and solve problems on the spot. Four combinations: political work combines with creation of famous brands (which is the biggest politics in the market; political work combines with competition of various posts including technical competition; political work combines with four major factors (namely management, quality, cost, and operation); political work combines with actual conditions of the enterprise (including main contradictions and problems).

II. Practices and Results

(1) Main Practices

1. Adhere to three basic principles of theoretical innovation

Inherit the traditional excellence; absorb foreign achievements; create our own distinct products. (The connotations of these three principles are already stated in the section "The Culture Is the Soul").

2. Follow the basic principle of "seeking truth from facts"

Mr. Wang as a communist believes that ideas, theories, or doctrines, which are recognized socially, promote historical development, and are as a guide to the advancement, follow the basic principle of "seeking truth from facts." Such basic principle also is important for countries, enterprises and individuals.

Therefore, Double Star cannot violate this law. The creation of the market theory is based on the principle of "seeking truth from facts". In other words, the core of the market theory of Double Star is "seeking truth from facts." It is under the guidance of this basic principle that Double Star creates a set of theories according to the actual conditions. Its theories are born under the following backgrounds: no money left on group accounts, wages and loans unavailable in the early stage of entering the market; the transition of the thought (from the spirit representing everything to money being above all else); historical conditions including the loss of faith or spiritual faltering etc. Double Star as a labor-intensive, heavily indebted, and state-owned enterprise in the low-margin industry needed to carry out the construction of spiritual and material civilizations. Under this premise, Double Star needed to create its theories to arm the employees' mind and guide them on their way, to survive and develop. At the same time, private ownership, market economy, value law, capital market, etc., which were not recognized in practice in the past, were now all recognized. The concept had changed, which resulted in the need of the new theory. With this kind of thinking, Mr. Wang bravely carried out the reform and created a set of theories which were not understood and recognized by others at that time. It is these theories that guide and promote the development of Double Star. It can be said that the success of Double Star in the market is due to this set of market theories with characteristics of Double Star, which are suitable for socialist enterprises.

3. Persist in being produced in practice and guiding practice. Practice is the sole criterion for testing the truth of theory.

Double Star's market theory created by Wang is not born out of thin air. It comes from the modern market economy and gradually develops through summing up the experience and lessons in market practices with people who succeed and fail in the market competition. It is the common wealth for people of Double Star. It comes from and is applied in the market. It has been proved to be correct after nearly 30 years of practice. It is in line with the actual conditions of Double Star. Therefore, it has realistic guiding significance and is the most valuable spiritual wealth of Double Star and its staffs. It is precisely due to the market theory that people of Double Star have the spiritual pillar, direction, and enthusiasm in the work. It also made Double Star to quickly complete the entire process of transition from planned economy to market economy.

Wang's theoretical innovation practice demonstrates a truth: an enterprise without theory and thought is without direction; a company without theory and thought is without hope. Therefore, the formation of the market theory with Double Star is the requirement of the macro situation and market development. It can be said that the theory is a product of the market.

(II) Main results

President Wang is an entrepreneur with forward-thinking and innovative courage. He is a successful person who explores innovative ideas and new theories with the lofty sense of responsibility and mission of a Communist in the climate of China's reform and opening. He is a theorist rarely seen in the Chinese business community.

Wang has a lot of business management theories. The theories he created are also edited into thick books. Here, I choose some of his theories for readers. Reading them, people cannot help but admire his wisdom.

1. ABW theory

Many people are keen to choose the MBA degree program. But for Mr. Wang, MBA is not better than ABW. The first among the 26 English letters, A means that we dare to be the best in the world and compete for the first place. B consists of two parts: 1 and 3. 1 is like a pillar, which means that entrepreneurs must have the indomitable spirit and distinct personality. 3 is like a person in shape who bends his waist and means that entrepreneurs must be down-to-earth to do an excellent job. W is like an eagle spreading wings; it means that the entrepreneur should bravely meet the challenge and is never satisfied with what he has achieved.

Why have most of state-owned enterprises collapsed in the shoe industry, while Double Star can survive and develop? The key is in entrepreneurs. Entrepreneurs should consider actual situations of China's society, market, politics, nation, economy, industry, and enterprise itself, especially be considering changes and characteristics of their own situation. Their theories and models about management should not be copied mechanically from the West.

2. Market theory

Being market-oriented and considering the actual management conditions with state-owned enterprises with Chinese characteristics, Double Star creates its modern management theories. One of them is the market theory: namely, the market is the highest leadership of the enterprise and the market is the standard for testing all work of the enterprise.

In the planned economic system, enterprises carried out production while not considering sales and marketing. Double Star eliminated old ideas of planned economy and took the lead in entering the market. It has established the market awareness: for example, "the market is the highest leadership of the enterprise" and "the market is the standard for testing all work of the enterprise". In 1984, it held a press conference and a new product ordering conference.

In the early 1980s, China's institutional transition from a planned economy to a market economy was still in the pipeline. The family-contract responsibility system began in rural area, while no state-owned enterprise in urban areas dared to enter the market. At that time, Qingdao Ninth Rubber Factory as predecessor of Double Star had a large backlog of products which was not concerned by the superior authority and the commercial department. In such a desperate situation, it resolutely entered the market and became the forerunner of Chinese state-owned enterprises to the market economy. It also became an example for a group of pioneering enterprises.

The market theory is an outstanding achievement of theory innovation for Double Star. It is the most valuable spiritual wealth of Double Star and its employees. It is the action guide of employees of Double Star. It constantly provokes vitality, passion, and fighting spirit. It produces cohesiveness and centripetal force. It plays an important guiding role for thoughts and actions of people at Double Star.

3. Theory of rules

Mr. Wang believes that the poor performance in many state-owned enterprises are due to a variety of reasons, including historical and institutional reasons, which very complicated. There has been a long-term misunderstanding, which is mainly reflected in the following three points. First, the principle of scientific socialism is disobeyed. The essence of socialism must be understood. Deng Xiaoping said, "The essence of socialism is to liberate productive forces, develop productive forces, eliminate exploitation, eliminate polarization, and ultimately achieve common prosperity." [1] The essence of socialism determines the characteristics of the socialist economic system. An economic system that conforms to and reflects the essence of socialism and brings the superiority of socialism into full play is socialist; otherwise, it is not. Second, the rules of the market are disobeyed. Practice has proved that the government will inevitably fail to control the market; and the enterprise without autonomy will have no sense of responsibility. The government should also change its consciousness and functions under the conditions of market economy, grasp the market rules, rationalize the relationship between government and enterprises, and combine the macro-control with the market economy. Third, rules of the industry are disobeyed. Each industry has its own rules of operation, but the leadership of many of our enterprises does not really study and master them and does not investigate the market, finally leading to the closure of enterprises. In the

---

[1] Deng Xiaoping, Speech Points in Wuchang, Shenzhen, Zhuhai, Shanghai and Other Places, Volume 3 of Selected Works of Deng Xiaoping, People's Publishing House, October 1993, p. 373. To develop, entrepreneurs must be like "black cats". Double Star Cat is a unique representative of Double Star culture. The competition in mature market is ultimately reflected in cultural competition. Cultural management of Double Star opens its markets, thereby stimulating its business growth.

1980s, he began the production in the suburbs. In the 1990s, he carried out the production in rural areas belonging to poverty-stricken areas. These strategic decisions were based on the rules of the footwear industry at home and abroad, therefore, objectively, it played a role in poverty alleviation and achieved sustainable development of Double Star.

4. Theory of the cat

Mr. Wang said, "I place statues of one black cat and one white cat instead of stone lions at the door of the Double Star Group, at the gate of the production base, at the door of the Double Star chain store. The black cat is holding the mouse tightly with its eyes looking for a new target in front; the beautiful white cat is differently sitting with its words pouring forth like a rushing river. Why? I just want to promote the enterprise philosophy ('it does not matter if a cat is black or white as long as it catches mice; the development of Double Star is the last word.') It can be said that these two sentences vividly show the business development concept of people at Double Star. Double Star insists the above-said enterprise philosophy used to guide the practice of enterprise reform and makes a small factory on the verge of closure develop into the largest multinational group in the world's shoe circle."

"For state-owned enterprises, the key is to solve the problems of the leadership. Entrepreneurs must take the initiative to capture 'mice' and seize opportunities for development. Cadres of Double Star, if not achieving satisfactory results in the work, will be demoted or sacked. Staffs of Double Star, if doing an excellent job, will be regarded as good 'cats'. Double Star creates equal opportunities for all staffs. Truly, in Double Star, even migrant workers can act as directors of factories! "

5. Innovative ideas on development of national economy

Faced with the integration of the world economy, some experts and a few senior officials proposed, "China acts a global processing base, thus the national industry should not be mentioned anymore." They do not understand China's current situation being very different from that of 30 years ago. We are a big country with a population of 1.3 billion, so having a big market. Our people work hard and can endure hardships. At present, we have a certain economic strength with the industrial level greatly improved. Under this circumstance, we should reconsider the development goals of our enterprises and the direction of our national economy with a new point of view. One of first outstanding entrepreneurs, Mr. Wang having a keen sense of national responsibility is a practitioner and winner in the entire process of reform and opening. As president of Double Star Group, he puts forward the motto in this era of change: "national spirit, national brand and national entrepreneur". His dream is to invigorate the national spirit, create national brands, and cultivate a team of national entrepreneurs to develop national industry and revitalize the national economy. The national spirit, national brand, and national entrepreneur proposed by Mr. Wang are called by the media as his innovative ideas on the development of national economy and are believed with profound realistic and historical significance in guiding China's current ideology and long-term economic development.

The national spirit refers to a keen sense of national responsibility and self-confidence. It is the symbol of national dignity and the soul of national progress. No matter in what era, the national spirit is the source of inspiration for the people's struggle, and the soul of a country and a nation. Then, how does the national spirit manifest itself in the current era? Mr. Wang said, "In the market, we should carry forward the national spirit, revitalize the national industry, and create the national brand. Doing an excellent job in these aspects is the greatest patriotism and best reflects the national spirit." Mr. Wang has established the direction of Double Star in the market economy.

National brands are the main force supporting national industry, and national brands are the symbol of national economic revitalization. National brands reflect national spirit, and national brands represent national images. National brands safeguard national interests, and national brands reflect national dignity. Therefore, we must create our own national brands.

National entrepreneurs are the embodiment of the national spirit, the creators of national brands, and the helm of national industry. The revitalization of the national economy requires national entrepreneurs to be leaders. We should fully understand the significant role of national entrepreneurs in revitalizing the national economy, establish a set of institutional mechanisms that are conducive to the growth of national entrepreneurs, protect our national entrepreneurial talents, and cultivate a team of national entrepreneurs. Only under the leadership of national entrepreneurs can we inspire the national spirit, create national brands, develop national industries, and strengthen the national economy.

6. Contradictory theory

In the 1950s, Mao Zedong wrote a famous article entitled Contradictory Theory. Under the conditions of market economy, Double Star applies Chairman Mao's contradictory theory in the market. Mr. Wang believes that:

First, in the market economy, contradictions exist objectively and cannot be avoided. It is a normal phenomenon. All the difficulties we encounter in the competition are contradictions. All the problems encountered in the work are contradictions. These contradictions are different from the class contradiction and the contradiction between ourselves and enemy and so forth described in the theory of class struggle. On the one hand, by the correct handling, these contradictions can be converted into contradictions among the people. On the other hand, if not handled well, they may become worse, leading to a more serious situation.

Second, in the market economy, the manifestations of contradictions are multifaceted and dialectical. There are internal contradictions and external contradictions. There are major contradictions and secondary contradictions. As far as enterprises are concerned, there are following contradictions: between production and management, between quality and yield, between supply and funds, between prices and costs, between managing people and managed people, between market and technical design and R&D. In a word, there are contradictions arising from enterprises not adapting to the market, and there are also new contradictions that emerged after enterprises adapt to the market, but everything has rules, including contradictions. This requires us to distinguish the primary contradiction from secondary ones in enterprises before solving them according to the rules.

Third, in the market economy, the enterprise itself is a small community, and because of factors such as competition, survival, and livelihood, we many have different views. Even for an individual, we may have different understandings leading to different conclusions. It is a normal thing and cannot be considered a contradiction.

In short, in the market economy, there are external contradictions and internal contradictions. Especially when external contradictions and internal contradictions conflict, we must first solve the internal contradictions. In the internal contradictions, there are primary contradictions and secondary contradictions. We must seize and solve the primary contradictions; subsequently, the secondary contradictions can be smoothly solved. If we can't distinguish the primary contradictions from the secondary ones, then any kind of contradiction cannot be solved leading to a more chaotic situation. It can be said that how to solve contradictions is a measure of the ability for our cadres or leaders.

7. Feelings, enthusiasm and passion

Mr. Wang describes the standards and requirements of feelings, enthusiasm and passion under the conditions of market economy for leaders, managers, and employees of Double Star.

He believes that: feeling is the foundation, enthusiasm is performance, passion is sublimation. Only the staff has feelings for the enterprise, enthusiasm for the work, and passion for the position, can the enterprise be stronger and stronger.

Feelings, enthusiasm and passion are the most basic conditions for improving enterprise management, ensuring product quality and reducing production costs; are the most basic standard for measuring whether an enterprise has the righteousness, vitality, competitiveness, and combat effectiveness; and should be strongly promoted by grassroots cadres. If there is a lack of feelings, enthusiasm, and passion, then the enterprise will be without vitality.

The market is like a battlefield and the competition is like war. In the commercial warfare of the market, there must be confidence and determination. Therefore, enterprises must constantly educate leaders, management cadres, and employees, letting them enhance feelings on brands, improve enthusiasm for the work, and passion for the position. As a result, the enterprise will be more vigorous and develop more quickly.

8. Party spirit, humanity and personality

Entrepreneurs should recognize the inseparable relationship between party spirit, humanity and personality, which complement each other.

Personality is the sum of personal ability, temperament, interest, personality and other psychological characteristics; it is gradually formed and developed through long-term social practice under the influence of certain social environment and education. Personality not only has the meaning given by the above explanation, it is also a character and nature that a person is born with, including the tendency to seek truth from facts and be the first in the world, etc., which is precisely the basis for a person to succeed. It is extremely wrong and unfair to confuse personality with disobedience, pride, complacency, reckless or brute action and the like. Personality is a manifestation of one's ability, wisdom, position, and talent. It requires you to not only be forward-thinking, but also have a spirit of adventure. Its purpose is to let a person have an illustrious career, take a new path, and realize his own value. Personality is the key to an entrepreneur's success.

When it comes to humanity, we can't avoid words "self" and "feeling", which are the most mysterious things about which the people are the most unwilling to talk. Entrepreneurs need to involve in personality. Human beings have rich emotions, so the management of people cannot be done with only one method. In addition to the rigid rules and regulations, and the requirements of moral management, entrepreneurs should have the sincere persuasion to give employees warmth and move them. Mr. Wang said, "Ruthless discipline is ruthless, leadership is compassionate." So-called compassionate leadership is to respect people, care for people, understand people, and show consideration for people.

In a wide sense, the party spirit is the highest manifestation of class nature and is a political program and political need of the ruling party. To the Communist Party, it is the highest manifestation of the proletarian class. For example, the Communist Party's "selflessness, fearlessness, dedication, and struggle for communism for life" are all goals set for political needs. Although not everyone can achieve it, it is the direction of all communists. This is party spirit.

Personality can promote human development and social progress; humanity can embody kindness and friendship and unite people's hearts; party spirit is the guarantee to ensure the orderly development of humanity and personality, compliance with law and not exceeding what is proper. As an entrepreneur, we must recognize the complementarity and inseparable relationship between party spirit, personality and humanity, strive to balance and grasp the relationship between the three, and truly reflect our own life value in the struggle for the cause of the party. In this way, the longevity of entrepreneurs can be achieved.

9. Win-win situation

Wang believes that enterprise development must always adhere to the principle of being beneficial for the country, people and enterprise. In the early 1980s, while establishing the enterprise spirit of "love for our plant, truth-seeking, hardworking, prosperity, development, and advancement", Double Star was the first to propose the goal of "prosperity", which brought a shock to the planned economy. When other enterprises successively entered the city, Double Star as the first to open a broad road of "eastern development and western development" entered Yimeng Mountain and successively built twenty or thirty production bases across the country, forming a large framework nationwide. It shares the responsibility for the country's poverty relief. It not only finds its own development space, but also bears the fruits of poverty alleviation. It finds a new development idea for the labor-intensive manufacturing and processing industry and shows that enterprises should enhance a sense of social responsibility to gain their own development and cast national brands etc.

10. Filial piety, loyalty, righteousness in the market economy

"Filial piety, loyalty, righteousness" is the core of Chinese traditional excellent culture (mainly constituted by Confucianism, Taoism, Buddhism), a unique cultural expression of the Chinese nation, and a special emotion for constructing and maintaining blood relations and social relations. For five thousand years, the concept of "filial piety, loyalty, and righteousness" regulates people's behavior and is the foundation of the precious spiritual wealth and moral conscience of the Chinese nation.

The inheritance and development of "filial piety, loyalty and righteousness" is not only the current need to build a harmonious society, but also the need for the healthy development of the market economy. We see that in the process of China's transition from a planned economy to a market economy, due to the lack of filial piety, loyalty, and righteousness, some people's spiritual beliefs and theoretical pursuits are chaotic: being blinded by the lust for gain, and lacking morality and conscience etc. We believe that the development of the market economy requires not only modern technology and management, but also the promotion of professional ethics with "filial piety, loyalty, and righteousness" as the core. A market without good morality lacks fair competition and is full of deception and blackmail. Therefore, the inheritance and development of filial piety, loyalty, and righteousness is a requirement of the market economy.

11. Theory of the tiger

When China joined the WTO, foreign brands flooded in. Many people shouted, "Wolf is coming". Mr. Wang shouted, "I am a tiger and I am not afraid of it." The tiger is the king of beasts.

At China's access to the WTO, many newspapers reported that it means that "the wolf is coming". However, Mr. Wang believed that China's human resources were rich and labor-intensive industries were China's strengths. Joining the WTO was not a terrible thing for China, especially in the footwear industry. Under the premise of improving management, technology and efficiency, domestic products could compete with foreign famous brands.

With the support of tiger theory, Double Star vigorously stands in the domestic and foreign markets. Drawing on Comrade Xiaoping's rural responsibility system, Mr. Wang turns the post into a responsible field for every employee, realizing goals of self-management, self-accounting, self-improvement in efficiency, and self-reduction. Double Star has established a market operation structure, including shares, private and state-owned ownership the like, and forming a strong synergy for participating in market competition.

12. Spokesperson theory

The spokesperson is an effective means of competition among enterprises in the current market economy. In the past few years, there was a trend for enterprises to invite as spokespersons celebrities who occupied the TV screen; Mr. Wang, who was good at reverse thinking, shouted, "I am the best spokesperson for Double Star." When a reporter asked him, "Are you not afraid of young people not wearing your shoes of Double Star?" He replied: "KFC's spokesperson is an old man. Will people all over the world not come to KFC?" Some stars invited by enterprises appeared and disappeared rapidly, why? Mr. Wang told the reporter: "The famous brand comes from the entrepreneur working hard rather than the image spokesperson. The famous brand reflects the struggle spirit of employees in production and marketing."

Entrepreneur is the creator of the brand, why can't he be its spokesperson? In addition to insisting that entrepreneurs are the best image spokespersons of the brand, Double Star has achieved remarkable success in the use of political advertisements and single-product advertisements. Therefore, Double Star subverts the traditional model that enterprises must rely on commercial advertising to create brands.

13. Quality theory

As early as 1986, Mr. Wang put forward the concept of quality involving in a wide range of fields, which included product quality, work quality, and service quality. Product quality, which is related to whether the product can meet the social and people's needs, includes inherent quality and appearance quality; the quality of work, which refers to the quality level of all aspects of the work, is the guarantee and foundation of product quality; service quality means that we should do a good job in services provided in the purchase and use by the user of the product that is designed and manufactured according to the needs of the user.

Quality is all personnel-related and comprehensive. Product quality reflects the overall management level of the enterprise; and is the standard for testing work quality and service quality. Work quality is the core and the key; and with service quality, is the guarantee and foundation of product quality. These three kinds of qualities complement each other and are inextricably linked.

14. Big technology theory

What is big technology? It is the combination of management science, political science and natural science. The three are complementary and indispensable to each other. The concept of big technology also includes industry technology. Each industry has its own different technologies. The technology is used in production plants, supporting factories, secondary industry, and territory industry. Only on the basis of grasping the big technology, can we give full play to the advantages of science and technology and be in an invincible position in the market competition.

The development of technology must be integrated with innovative ideas, new awareness, new thinking, new methods, new management, new processes, and new equipment etc.

In terms of technology in the customary sense, whether it is a process, formula, equipment, raw material, medical work or infrastructure, it is called general technology. In terms of enterprise management, whether it is a method, means, enterprise system, and mechanism, it can be called management technology. In various activities of production, operation, and management, there are technological progresses. A great achievement is achieved in Double Star due to organic integration of the three.

15. Big innovation theory

At Double Star, the big innovation covers all aspects of enterprise development such as theoretical innovation, political innovation, management innovation, technological innovation, operation innovation, market innovation and service innovation.

Double Star broke old ideas in the planned economy, and put forward the innovative ideas (that is, not innovating today, we will be backward tomorrow; not innovating tomorrow, we will be eliminated the day after tomorrow; the post is market, the competition is in the machine station, and everyone is innovative), set up the innovation modes (that is, all-staff innovation, team innovation, joint innovation, high-level innovation, bundled innovation, and infiltration innovation), initiated the people's war of innovation in the market, realized the new change in theoretical innovation, innovation object, innovation mode, innovative organizational form & innovative content, and spurred the creative potential of employees.

All-staff innovation of Double Star: First, it solved the mystery of innovation, realized the goal of post being the market, competition being on the machine station, and all staffs being innovative, and initiated the people's war in the market. Second, it broke the long-standing tradition, old model, and old method. Through innovation, many things that were impossible and that we did not dare to image and do in the past, now can be imaged and done, and we can improve products that are manufactured by foreigners. Third, it broke a routine, especially in old and conventional things that are impossible and that we did not dare to change. Truly, great breakthroughs have been achieved through innovation.

16. 30% plus 70% theory

Under the conditions of market economy, when the technical level of manufacturing and processing enterprises reaches a certain height, then the potential for further improvement is low. In such a situation, Mr. Wang believes that "the market is endless with the brand needing long-time care and the management having no stop" and proposes the 30% plus 70% theory: thirty percent relying on technology and seventy percent on management.

As to actual conditions of management in manufacturing industry and as to labor-intensive manufacturing and processing enterprises like Double Star, Mr. Wang believes that "the object of management is first of all human beings", "people are a key factor in the enterprise and people-oriented management should be implemented"; and proposes the following new theories: "soft rubber, hard management; hard machinery, fine management; small items, cost-oriented management", "internal contracted shareholding system" and "meticulous management" so on. Led by Mr. Wang, Double Star bravely broke through the old management system of planned economy and created a new management model of market economy, thereby being at the front at home and abroad in the overall management level.

17. Both socialist-minded and professionally competent

Being socialist-mined, first, refers to the staff who loves for the enterprise, post, and brand, and dedicates himself to the work. This is the basic standard and condition for a staff being socialist-minded. His salary is taken from and his feeling is closely related with the enterprise. The only choice for him is to be closely linked with the future of the enterprise and its brand, and his obligation is to love for the brand and be loyal to the enterprise. This is the manifestation of being socialism-minded. The core of being socialist in the market economy is the spirit of daring to challenge the difficulty and compete in the market. If there is no such spirit, then nothing can be done well. In the market economy, being socialist-mind is equal to morality. To be socialist-minded, the staff should have good morality. In the work, leaders and cadres in management should uphold justice, establish righteousness, and set up a good style of work, to be reach the standards of being socialist-minded.

Being specialized and being skillful are complementary to each other in the market economy. Only being specialized can create and reflect our own unique characteristics including the superiority and excellence. From a technical point of view, the concept of being specialized mainly refers to: mastering the core technology that others do not have, owning our own unique products or designs; being skilled and capable refers to the standing out in the manufacturing field.

In the world's shoe circle, the reason why the management of Double Star can be admired by the peers is that it is able to create its own characteristics, including its first-class management characterized by carefulness, seriousness and strictness etc.

18. Theory of being plenty

Double Star has a lot of ports, channels, forms, customers, varieties, and methods. In the mid-1980s, Double Star, while actively developing the domestic market, aimed at the international market. It has established more than a dozen overseas companies in the United States, Europe, and the Middle East. The shoes exported can circle around the earth several times. Double Star held its press conference of shoes in New York, demonstrated the Chinese shoe culture in Germany, and made a speech on Chinese traditional culture for enterprise management at the Singapore Forum. In 1995, Wang was named World Man of the Year by the American Celebrity Biography Association and the International Celebrity Research Association.

19. Correlation theory

In the mid-1990s, Mr. Wang understood the broad development space of tires from the development trend of the automobile industry in at home and abroad. Many people proposed to Wang that Double Star should make investments in the electronic network field and the automobile field, but he said that Double Star should carry out the brand expansion and do not involve in the unfamiliar fields, also said that the new growth point of Double Star should be in the rubber manufacturing as a familiar field. With the improvement of people's living standards and the increase in demand for automobiles, the tire market was promising. He decided to invest in tires.

In addition to shoes, Double Star made tires. In a brief period of time, its tires entered the forefront of the domestic industry. The key is to bring into full play the brand, culture and capital, and accurately grasp the opportunities of strategic adjustment. There are complementary advantages between both shoes and tires, and there is a value-added business. This shows that state-owned enterprises in labor-intensive traditional industries should expand the market by entering fields with high tech content high added value, steadily realize industrial upgrading and achieve the goal of rapidly becoming stronger.

20. Two hands theory

Double Star has successfully developed across 23 industries. The reason is as follows: Double Star realized in earlier time that, in the market economy, enterprises should pay more attention to ideology, re-understand political work from the perspective of the market, and organically combine the laws of economic development with the actual situation of enterprises. Mr. Wang masters and applies theories in Political Economics created by Marx, pays equal attention to politics and economy, carries forward the team spirit, and upholds righteousness by relying the enterprise culture. Double Star always adheres to the following mottoes: inherit essence of traditional culture, absorb foreign achievements, create our own distinct products; seek truth from facts, do honorable deeds and gather blessings; understand the knowledge of Political Economics; be market-centered; the more we are unique, the better. By being guided by Marx's Political Economics and bring into full play the political work, Double Star continuously creates new miracles in the fierce market competition.

21. Upgrade theory

Mr. Wang believes that the deepening of management is limited. In the face of a more severe market situation, to gain an advantage in competition, it is necessary to rely on the continuous upgrading of technology.

He also believes that the real technology is from the demand of the market and can solve the problem in the product. It can be said that analyzing and solving product quality problems is the most direct and effective way to improve the technical level, and it is also the best way to achieve technology upgrade.

Technology upgrades should start from four aspects: management technology, process technology, operation technology, and R&D technology. It should be noted that the success of research and development does not mean the success of technology. The final inspection criteria of technology is the product. The inspection criteria of the product is the market. Only with the recognition of the market, is it the real technology. Therefore, we should understand the needs and changes of the market. All research should be carried out around the market. We should carry out research, development, and design according to market demand, and at the same time pay attention to integrating the technical resources of the entire group; apply these integrated technologies to all products.

The market is endless. The technology is endless too. Technological upgrading is never stopped. Moreover, the upgrading can let enterprises achieve the best material, the best structure, the best process, the best design, and the best product.

III. Typical Examples

(I) Theoretical Innovation: Nine plus Nine Management Method in Double Star

In 1988, Double Star proposed its own the management theory — Nine plus Nine Management Method.
It was written by the Chinese Academy of Sciences as The Light of Double Stars and became one of the top ten management methods promoted nationwide.

In the 1980s, when reform and opening began, advanced management methods from abroad had not been widely promoted. Moreover, domestic management methods that were suitable for market-oriented enterprises had not yet emerged.

Enterprises couldn't be with anarchism and a state of no management. To solve the problem of chaos in production, Mr. Wang put forward the fixed-post management, which means that employees must master the work of each post in production. He also put forward the one-stop management method (also named One-Dragon method), which required employees to verify the quantity, performance and location for all kinds of raw materials, uppers, lasts and tools etc., set up the digital tracking card, technology tracking card, and so forth in the production process, and make a mark in relevant parts of the shoe in each production line and each team... There are 255 clauses and 1,561 sub-clauses in the management rules; 42 clauses and 233 sub-clauses in technical standards; requirements in 251 positions, and spirits or mottos in 29 departments... A Taiwanese businessman was amazed after his visit and said that the management was very good in Double Star.

His continuous exploration and summarization made the management to reach a high level. Especially, his unique method – Nine plus Nine Management Method, was finally proposed, which has such rich content:

Three Rings: inherit the tradition, absorb foreign achievements, and innovate our distinct products. With Three Rings being complementary to each other, Double Star has its own road of innovation.

Three Wheels: Refers to ideological education, economic means and administrative measures. The three wheels are turned together to make the development of the enterprise fruitful.

Three Principles: Educating employees to be practical, carrying out active integration, being democratic & open. The three principles require employees to work hard, take care of the overall situation, and unite as one.

Mr. Wang uses Three Rings, Three Wheels and Three Principles as the warp of the management, and uses Three Separates, Three Joints and Three Developments as the weft.

Three Separates: Hierarchical management, layered contracting, and separate accounting. Three Separates clarify the relationship between cost and benefit.

Three Joints: Joint processing, joint sales, and joint stock. Three Joints can make the enterprise unit with external forces for expansion.

Three Developments: Talent development, tech & product development, market development. Three Developments can make the enterprise have more vigor.

This scientific management system is well-organized and complicated. It enables Double Star to have standards and rules in cost management, personnel management, and technological innovation etc. Further it is practical and efficient, thereby enabling Double Star to embark on the track of market-oriented management. Double Star skillfully implemented the modern management, which were not yet familiarized by a lot of other enterprises at that time.

This set of practical and advanced management methods created by Mr. Wang was sent to the Enterprise Management Association for review and competition, but it did not pass the review. The leaders said that it did not absorb the experience from Japan, the United States, and Germany; therefore, it could not be rated as advanced management methods for promotion. When hearing this, Mr. Wang angrily said, "Our country has her own excellent culture, industrial path and business management model. How can they say that our methods are weaker compared with those from abroad? Our methods are better than those from Japan, Europe and the United States so forth. Why must we learn from them?”

Seeing that Mr. Wang withdrew from the competition, the staff of the Enterprise Management Association advised him that he could be selected by adding the experience from Japan. But Wang said firmly, "No! We have no Japanese elements in our management. I only know that Japanese absorb our management methods, for example, one of them is as follows: cadres participate in production, workers in management; irrational and outdated rules and regulations are reformed; the combination of cadres, workers, and engineers is carried. Japanese methods are developed based on this set of methods named by Chairman Mao and the Japanese Bushido spirit. Our methods and our spirit reflect the ambition and morale of the Chinese nation. We disdain for this competition and will not made any change."

In that time, organizing the competition was very bureaucratic. As a result, his set of management methods failed in the selection. However, this event made Mr. Wang firmly determined to carry forward the national culture. He did not blindly worship foreigners. He said that a scientific attitude should be adopted to methods from Japan and the United States. As far as he is concerned, if a nation does not know how to carry forward its own culture and blindly follow foreigners, then does this nation still have hope?!

A few years later, this management system deeply convinced the experts of the Institute of Industrial Economics of the Chinese Academy of Social Sciences who came to investigate. In the special investigation report entitled Double Star Light – Investigation of Management with Qingdao Double Star Group, they highly appreciated the Nine Plus Nine Management Method and considered it to be a business management method with Chinese characteristics, enriching and developing the socialist market economic theory system. The China Enterprise Management Association and the China Entrepreneur Association have included it as one of 22 modern management methods promoted in the enterprise community of China. *(Source:* Zhao Yanbiao, Mr. Wang's 30 Years, People's Publishing House, March 2008)

(2) Mr. Wang's Encyclopedia of Enterprise Management

His experiences in management are written into books.

For more than 30 years, in the practice of leading the reform and management of the Double Star Group, Mr. Wang has boldly and creatively carried out theoretical innovations and put forward many innovative ideas and new theories, which solve new problems in reform and management. Therefore, he has made outstanding theoretical contributions, which are found in his management monographs. Major representative works are below:

1. Wang Hai, Market, Enterprise, Innovation (365,000 words), People's Publishing House, September 1995.

2, Wang Hai, Market, Enterprise, Brand (356,000 words), People's Publishing House, September 1997.

3, Wang Hai, Secrets of Double Star (four volumes, 1.086 million words), Heilongjiang People's Publishing House, September 2001.

4. Wang Hai, Market: Root of Enterprise (477,000 words), Social Science Literature Publishing House, February 2010.

Among them, Secrets of Double Star is the summary of his new theories in enterprise management. This book having over one million words covers the following fifteen aspects: (1) Double Star Forum; (2) Theory of Reform, Development, and Innovation with Double Star; (3) Double Star Market Politics Theory; (4) Double Star Market Management Theory; (5) Double Star Marketing Theory (6) Double Star Technology Management Theory; (7) Double Star Quality Management Theory; (8) Double Star Brand Management Theory; (9) Double Star Talent Management Theory; (10) Double Star International Market Theory; (11) Double Star Financial Management Theory; (12) Double Star Macro Management Theory; (13) Double Star Basic Management Theory; (14) Double Star Production Management Theory; (15) Double Star Management Theory of Tertiary Industry. These monographs are his encyclopedia of enterprise management.

IV. Expert Comments

The great leader Lenin has long pointed out: **"Without the theory of revolution, there will be no revolutionary movement."** (Lenin, What to do? Collection of Lenin's Works, 1956, Vol. 1, p. 328.)

The successful experience of Double Star proves that the revolution cannot be separated from theoretical guidance, and that construction and enterprise-run are also inseparable from theoretical guidance. Mr. Wang said, **"In every historical period, there should be a guiding theory that considers actual conditions. The role of theory in social development is immeasurable. Market politics theory guides market economy practice. If the market theory is not updated, then enterprises will not develop again."**

He also said, "**Enterprises without theory and thought are hopeless; cadres without theory and thought are hopeless; employees without theory and thought are hopeless. Without**

good theory and thought, the cause will have no direction; it will fail and even suffer crushing defeat."

More important, he always does an excellent job. At every turning point in the development of the enterprise, he can advance his own theoretical insights and provide theoretical guidance for the management innovation of Double Star.

Mr. Wang not only attaches importance to theoretical innovation, but also attaches importance to using his new theory to educate the cadres and employees, to unite their minds, unite their will, and unite their actions. This is the most important reason for Double Star to create a miracle; also, this is one of the biggest gaps between some entrepreneurs and Mr. Wang. He is an outstanding example of Chinese entrepreneurs in attaching importance to theoretical innovation and guiding enterprise reform and management with scientific theories

Tactic 3: The Strategy is the Dragon Head

It is necessary to think about how the enterprise will develop after 10 years. Entrepreneurs must be brave and take risks with advanced ideas. It is impossible for an entrepreneur to be like an employee, and it is impossible to decide when all members of the leadership team agree. When everyone agrees, the opportunity has passed; so, it is too late. The market is like the battlefield.

—— Wang Hai

In June 1992, Qingdao Double Star Group Co., Ltd. was established, marking the beginning of the strategic adjustment of the group.

In 1996, Double Star became the first listed company in China's footwear industry. It marks the new development track of Double Star with the combination of industrial capital and financial capital.

I. Wang Hai Quotations

(I) Double Star Mission

I am a shoemaker instead of a researcher in shoes. Research work is difficult for me. Let me see. When man evolved from the anthropoid ape, there were no shoes on the feet. Later, due to the need, shoes emerged. Shoes are one of the first signs of human civilization, which made our ancestors get rid of ignorance. Just as the history of mankind constantly evolving, the shoes constantly change. Bark shoes emerged, which followed by straw shoes, wooden sandals, cloth shoes, leather shoes, rubber shoes... Do not neglect shoes. All of people wear shoes from prime ministers, presidents, nobles, aristocrats to ordinary men. Think again. While being at the lowest level of the human body, shoe have a noble character: bearing a heavy load and being selfless for the sake of people. Then, let us remember one thing: people wear shoes and the key is at work.

(II) Connotation of Double Star development strategy

☆ Rooting in Shandong, facing the whole country, going out of Asia, going to the world

☆ Three strategies with Double Star: Diversification strategy, global market strategy, brand development strategy

☆ Western development, eastern development

☆ Secondary-industry adjustment, territory-industry development, chain store construction; letting Double Star brand bigger and stronger

☆ Famous brand is the atomic bomb of market economy

☆ Enter high-end market, set up the image, and sell brand products

☆ Attention to popularity addition to high-end and brand

☆ Enterprise and bland: built to last

☆ Develop sports and revitalize national brands

(III) How to implement enterprise strategy

☆ Three rules or laws followed in Double Star development: law of processing industry change, law of market economy itself, law of social development and human progress

☆ It is necessary to think about how the enterprise will develop after 10 years. Entrepreneurs must be brave and take risks with advanced ideas. It is impossible for an entrepreneur to be like an employee, and it is impossible to decide when all members of the leadership team agree. When everyone agrees, the opportunity has passed; so, it is too late. The market is like the battlefield.

☆ Working hard to cast brands, never make an excuse for mistakes.

(IV) Significance of creating national brands

☆ Enterprises without famous brands are hopeless. The famous brand is the wealth, the golden rice bowl of people at Double Star, and the atomic bomb in the market economy.

☆ Creating a famous brand is the biggest politics in the market economy; creating a famous brand is the best love for the country, the nation, the enterprise, and the post.

☆ In the modern market, the economic strength is the most crucial factor. whoever has strong economic power will dominate the world and master the right to speak. The brand is also the representative of economic strength, and the national brand can be said to represent the dignity of a nation. Therefore, the more mature the market economy, the more intense the brand competition.

(V) How to create and develop national brands

☆ Establish national ethos, carry forward national spirit, and create national brands.

☆ Treat famous brands with the standard of being a human being and cast famous brands with our own conscience.

☆ Creating a national brand should be a national behavior. It is an act that must be highly valued and taken seriously from top to bottom. No matter which enterprise or industry, the brand created is first national. It requires the care and support of the whole society. National brands created enterprises should be supported by governments, promoted by merchants and reporters, loved by consumers, and studied by experts and scholars.

II. Practices and Effects

(I) Main practices

Wang Hai had a "General's Complex" since he was a child. He decided to grow up to be a general in the army and serve the motherland. However, the fate made him helpless to realize his general's dream. After retiring from army services, he created the Double Star brand, and became a "market general" well known at home and abroad. With his military's career making him familiar with the art of war, he could skillfully apply strategies and tactics in the market competition has repeatedly achieved amazing results. At every turning point in the development of Double Star, he could successfully develop insightful and feasible development strategies.

1. Pioneer of the brand

As early as the early 1980s, when others did not know what a famous brand was, Mr. Wang proposed "creating the Chinese people's own national brand" and took the creation of a famous brand as the main line of all work and the greatest politics. He also established three stages of brand development, namely initial stage, development stage and advanced stage.

For more than 30 years, Double Star has found the best point of combination of politics and economy - creating famous brands; put forward the resounding slogan of "promoting the national spirit, creating national brands, and revitalizing national industries"; and determined to create Chinese own world-famous brands. In the earlier time, it went along the road of applying, promoting, developing brands. As a pioneer in casting brands, Double Star has created its own new culture and new spirit.

(1) First enterprise to propose the brand concept

In the early days of reform and opening, the brand concept was not known among Chinese. Double Star had to enter the market and encountered the experience of "Rubber Ninth Factory" being mistakenly heard as "Banana Winery", thereby realizing a truth: Enterprises need brand names in participation in the market competition. In 1986, Double Star published an article in the "People's Daily" calling for "creating the Chinese people's own brand name", with serial reports entitled "Double Star: Creation National Brands being broadcast on CCTV (the brand name was later collectively referred to as the brand). Double Star took the creation of a brand as the goal of enterprise development, which was linked with the love for the country, the plant, and the post. Double Star is the first to pus forward the brand theory: "creating a brand is the best patriotism, love for the enterprise, and love for the post", "brand name is an atomic bomb of market economy" and "the brand is the Golden Rice Bowl of Double Star". For more than 30 years, Double Star as a pioneer have created a series of new cultures, new theories, new ideas, and new ideas of brands, enriching and developing the theoretical system of socialist market economy.

(2) The earliest use of famous brands

In the early days of reform and opening, there were two extremes. One was the politics characterized by formalism, rigid dogma, detachment from actual conditions, and slogans. The second was the phenomenon of neglecting or lacking political work. Double Star firmly believed that the market economy needed politics and the spirit. It was the first to establish that "creating famous brands is the biggest politics in the market economy". Double Star was the first to inspire the national spirit and unite the workforce through national brands. In 1995, Double Star was the first to let its brand become a Chinese famous brand in the footwear industry. In the rubber industry, Double Star was the first to concurrently receive the following four famous brands: "Professional Sports Shoes", "Tours Shoes", "Leather Shoes" and "Tires"; with a brand value of 49.292 billion Yuan and a personal value of Mr. Wang of 32.142 billion Yuan. Double Star was the first to use brands to solve the problems of neglecting political guidance, spiritual education, lacking goals of political work in the market economy. Double Star also realized its brand strategy with national brands.

(3) The earliest publicity of famous brands

In the early days of reform and opening, Double Star was the first to hold a press conference, with its development and new products being covered by dozens of media organizations at home and abroad. Double Star was also the first to hold a press conference in the United States. Foreign agents still vividly remember that Mr. Wang took off his shoes and showed them to reporters 20 years ago. Double Star broadcast its ads video on CCTV: 18 people danced on a big shoe with a slogan of "wearing Double Star shoes to go around the world". Double Star was the first to hold the national health elderly meeting with fitness shoes given to 100 generals. Double Star was the first to produce professional volleyball shoes for the Chinese women's volleyball team and for the members of a running team led by Ma Junren. Double Star was the first to establish the Chinese professional badminton club and Double Star basketball club. Double Star was the first to enter the sports circle and was the first to promote its products by relating with the sports events. Double Star was the first to do its promotion by cooperating with news media to build a new image as a national brand.

(4) The earliest promotion of famous brands

In the new era of global economic integration, some people, experts and scholars believe that it is no longer necessary to mention the national industry, and that the goal of China is to be the world's processing factory. Faced with blindly worshipping for foreigners, Double Star insisted on promoting the Chinese national brand. In 1995, Double Star held a seminar on "famous brands, famous factories and famous shops", making the following proposal: creating famous brands is a common cause of the whole society; enterprises should create national brands; the government should support national brands; the business sector should promote national brands; the press should promote national brands; nationals should love for national brands. In 1996, Double Star made a proposal for teenagers: Establish Awareness of Domestic Products, Be Promoters and Users of Domestic Products, and Build a Hope Project for Chinese Famous Brands. In 1996, Mr. Wang who attended the China 21st Century Development Planning Seminar organized by the State Council Development Research Center organized clearly stated that "China in the 21st century should plan how many brands to be created." In his speeches at Peking University and Tsinghua University so on, Microsoft Forum, APEC Forum, Davos Forum and Boao Forum, President Wang insisted on promoting the Chinese national culture. People at Double Star determined to push the national brand to the world and won the admiration of the opponent and the recognition of the industry. Double Star won the glory of the world for the Chinese nation with successful practice.

(5) The earliest development of famous brands

The rapid development of China's reform and opening has brought about new changes in the footwear industry. In the face of foreign-invested enterprises entering the Chinese market, in the face of the shoe industry without any entry barriers and with fierce competition, Double Stars was the first to develop in poverty-stricken areas and extend to other industries; and the first to use brands for diversified development, becoming the world's only shoe-making group with the largest production scale including six major types of shoes (vulcanized shoes, cold-bonded shoes, leather shoes, cloth shoes, injection shoes, professional shoes). After being listed, Double Star chose the tires of the traditional industry as a new economic growth point.

Through acquiring Huaqing Tire and Dongfeng Tire, Double Star realized the transformation from shoes to tires and extended to the machinery and thermoelectric industry, thereby creating a new miracle in M & A.

(6) The earliest strengthening of famous brands

Entering the new century, Double Star focuses on the development of three major industries, namely, tires, machinery and shoes. Double Star is the earliest to become more famous by brand name, while transplanting its culture and management of the footwear industry, injecting capital and tech, and bringing into full play the effects of famous enterprise, famous brand and celebrity. Double Star successfully transformed the township enterprises and revitalized Dongfeng Tire which was one of the four top enterprises of China's tires in the past. Today, the Chinese tire industry is almost completely controlled by the world's tire giants, but Double Star has become a "black horse" in the tire industry and created a "Double Star speed" that makes all the Chinese feel proud. From an original extensive enterprise, Double Star Machinery has become a mechanical manufacturing enterprise with theory, culture and going global, and has contributed to the revitalization of the national basic industry.

For more than 30 years, Double Star has been the first to solve the problem of “Two Skins” in the political economy by “proposing famous brands, using famous brands, promoting famous brands, developing famous brands, and strengthening famous brands”, solve the problem of the old concept of culture uselessness, solve the problem of our market economy worldview; has created "Double Star new culture" and "Double Star new spirit".

2. Westward strategy

In 1984, Double Star was the first to implement horizontal economic cooperation and was in Shandong including areas around Qingdao in a brief time to establish 13 joint-venture branches marking the beginning of Double Star going to the countryside from the city.

Double Star entered Yimeng in the west of Shandong in 1992, being ahead of the national development strategy by ten years. The picture shows the Double Star western development seminar.

The production base was transferred from the bustling downtown area of Qingdao to the old revolutionary base - YIMENG mountainous area (the western part of Qingdao) at the inland of Shandong Province - and to the suburbs of Qingdao. Nationwide, the production base was transferred from Shandong Province to the west and southwest of China.

3. Diversification strategy

Relying on the footwear industry, Double Star gradually extends to 23 industries such as tires, clothing, machinery, thermoelectricity, printing, and tertiary industry, and forms a diversified operation.

4. Internationalization strategy

That is, "rooted in Shandong, facing the country, going out of Asia, going to the world." Double Star obtained self-operation import and export rights in 1988. Double Star seized the opportunity of the shoe industry moving from developed world to developing world, vigorously carried out import and export businesses, and won a place in the world footwear market. In 1993, its first overseas branch was established in Russia. In the following years, Double Star set up 8 branches in Poland, Hungary, Brazil, the United States, the United Arab Emirates, South Africa, Iran etc. Now, Double Star has expanded its export business to more than 100 countries and regions around the world and has established trade relations with more than 200 customers.

5. Merger and acquisition strategy

Double Star achieves its goal of revitalize the enterprises on the verge of closure by transplanting the enterprise culture and adopting its merger and acquisition strategy, for example, it acquired Huaqing Tire which was a small enterprise and Dongfeng Tire which was a state-owned enterprise etc.

6. Differentiation strategy

Double Star creates distinctive features or characteristics for its products or services in the competition of target markets in the industry, so that consumers can recognize what the products are used for, what special effects they have, what effects are different from products of other competitors, and what benefits they can bring to consumers, thereby increasing its competitiveness and market share.

7. Competition-cooperation strategy

Both competition and cooperation are carries out. Its goal is to achieve a win-win situation in competition, which is the highest level of competition. It can be said that the cooperation and competition model is an important reason why Double Star can maintain its brilliance under the general situation where other state-owned shoe-making enterprises develop poorly. It is also a great creation from people at Double Star in the transition process the planned economy to the market economy.

8. Shoe-tire linkage strategy

Double Star carries out the sales of both shoes and tires, reflecting its comprehensive advantages of cross-industry operation, multi-channel sale, and strong brands. While selling shoes and clothing, Double Star gives customers tires as a gift. While selling tires, Double Star gives customers shoes and clothing as a gift. As such, Double Star can achieve a win-win situation and expand sales.

This strategy is an innovative marketing strategy with unique characteristics with Double Star, which brings full play its scale advantage.

9. Big Double Star strategy

Under the unified brand of Double Star, it has its own business networks and factories in other places. Its assets are registered locally and form the one-stop pattern of production, supply and sales in the local area. In this way, both the total assets and the operational risks have been expanded, and the goal of losing here and gaining there has been realized.

10. Strategy of famous brand, famous plant and celebrity

The strategy is to create a world-famous brand, a world famous plant, and to be a celebrity of Double Star. Double Star is bravely unconventional, meets the difficulties, encourages employees to create famous brands and plants and be celebrities. With the clear goal, Double Star invigorates the spirit of employees, and brings together national interests, collective interests, enterprise interests and personal interests of employees, making itself enter a new historical stage of the famous brand development strategy.

(II) Main effects

Under the guidance of the strategies formulated by President Wang, Double Star Group has achieved unprecedented and brilliant achievements. Some of main achievements are below:

1. Guaranteeing that Double Star Group as a huge ship always develops along the correct course and is the leader in the industry.

2. Determining a clear goal for each period of the Double Star and encouraging 60,000 employees to be energetic and motivated and from one victory to another.

3. Creating a multi-industry and extra-large manufacturing and processing enterprise group.

4. Creating more than 3 billion Yuan of profit and tax for the country. It is equivalent to providing more than 300 rubber factories for the country without needing no penny from the country.

5. Creating 60,000 jobs for the country and enabling hundreds of thousands of people to live a well-off life.

6. Training an “Iron Army” with high spirit, excellent quality, strong skills, good working style, unity, and hardworking etc.

7. Creating a famous brand namely Double Star for the country, whose value has reached 49.292 billion Yuan.

8. Generating a great entrepreneur – Mr. Wang, whose personal brand value has reached 32.142 billion Yuan.

In 1995, Double Star was the first to obtain the title of National Well-known Trademark in the shoe industry.

III. Typical examples

(1) Implementing the built-to-last brand strategy

In early 1980s, Double Star proposed "creating the Chinese people's own national brand" and created a famous brand as the main line of all work and the greatest politics to educate and guide employees and established three stages of brand development: brand initial stage, brand development stage, and brand advanced stage.

1. Brand initial stage

On July 5, 1983, the successful registration of the Double Star trademark marked that Double Star was the first among Chinese enterprises to have the brand awareness and began to implement the famous brand strategy.

In 1984, Double Star was the first to put forward the brand development strategy. Mr. Wang was the first to publish an article in the People's Daily, calling for "creating the national brand" and insisting that "the more national, the more self-styled, the better.".

President Wang was the first entrepreneur to propose a brand strategy in China. In the early 1990s, he held the Double Star Cup seminar for the national brands.

In 1987, Double Star was the first to participate in the CCTV Spring Festival Gala, and was the first to advertise on CCTV.

In 1992, Double Star was the first to hold a press conference abroad. President Wang made an advertising by taking off his shoes in New York, the United States, showing the world the charm of Chinese entrepreneurs.

In 1992, Double Star was the first to make the shoe culture performance at the World Footwear Expo, which enhanced the popularity of Double Star in the international market.□

From the early 1980s to the early 1990s, Double Star took the elimination of Jiefang shoes as a mark, while constantly updating its products. From the imitation to the innovation, Double Star has become the leader of the national footwear industry by upgrading its products. At that time, through the repeated transformation of process and technology, Double Star realized the production of world famous shoes such as Brooks in China with more than 1 million pairs of shoes sold in European and American markets every year. Through the 4-shoe penetration, Double Star has produced China's first pair of high-grade cold-bonded sports shoes and the first pair of leather-type CVO heat-cured shoes, thereby completing the integration with the international footwear industry. This is the initial development of Double Star brand.

2. Brand development stage

During this period, Double Star established a professional product research and development team, which implemented a policy as follows: generations of products co-exist in research, development, production and storage. Double Star designed and installed China's first high-grade cold-bonded shoe assembly line and created the only national-level technology research and development center in the national footwear industry. Double Star formed the production capacity of six types of shoes (vulcanized-type, cold-bonded type, leather type, cloth type, injection type, and professional type), and won the following titles: the first well-known trademark in the footwear industry and the first listed company in the footwear industry. In the industry evaluation by the former Ministry of Chemical Industry, economic indicators of Double Star ranked first for more than 20 years.

In 1995, Double Star was the first to obtain the National Well-Known Trademark in the footwear industry, marking the creation of the first Chinese brand in the footwear industry. In 2005, Double Star was the only enterprise in China's rubber industry that concurrently received the following four famous brands: Professional Sports Shoes, Tours Shoes, Leather Shoes and Tires.

3. Band advanced stage

From 2000 to the present, Double Star has once again adjusted its development thinking and adopted "specialization, high-grade, and image" as its main targets, and began to compete with world famous brands. Double Star has successively launched high-end professional shoes such as running shoes, basketball shoes, tennis shoes, soccer shoes, etc., and fully realized the transition from low-grade single products to high-grade and serialized ones. The total number of shoes produced by Double Star has reached nearly 100 million pairs. Double Star has been the first in sales volume nationwide for many years and has become one of the first batch of China Famous Brand Products recognized by the state. In October 2005, the latest data were released, showing that the value of Double Star brand soared to 49.292 billion Yuan. While its shoe business (as a core business) is larger and stronger, Double Star has successfully entered the tire and machinery industry by operating brands and operating funds. In just a few years, Double Star Tire has become one of the top five tire companies in China, ranking among the top 20 in the world tire industry. It has been rated as China's "Top Ten National Brands" and has been awarded the title of "China Famous Brand". At the same time, Double Star Clothing has grown from small to large, and Double Star Machine has also moved from the low-grade and low-level to high-grade and high-level. Products of Double Star have entered the high-end market, showing a new image of Double Star brand in the advanced stage.

With the innovation and enterprising spirit of Endless Market, Brand and Management, Double Star has created the Chinese brand and realized the brand dream of the national industry.

The industries in which Double Star engage are almost all traditional manufacturing industries that conform to China's national conditions. Creating famous brands is the greatest patriotism. Creating famous brands is the biggest politics. Creating famous brands is both the need for the survival and development of Double Star, and related with the strength and fate of the country. Double Star always adheres to the belief of independent brands and always adheres to the idea of independent innovation. No matter which industry is involved, no matter how low is the start point, Double Star can quickly become strong, build the core competitiveness, thereby showing tenacious vitality and growth potential of the Chinese national industry.

(2) Western Development and Eastern Development

——Double Star: being successful in creating enterprise brands and making villagers live a comfortable life

In the early 1980s, when many state-owned enterprises were still lying on the planned economic system to make a dream, Double Star Group, which entered the market economy early and made great achievements, made an amazing move: developing eastern and western areas; implementing the strategic change (being out of city and to countryside). After more than 20 years, Double Star has used its own brand technology and management culture to build ten production bases in remote rural areas of Shandong, Henan, Sichuan, Chongqing, Guizhou and the like. Currently, Double Star has its assets becoming 6 billion Yuan from less than 10 million Yuan, has been in the leading position of the industry for ten consecutive years, also mobilized the development of local rural areas in an all-round way, thereby achieving a win-win situation with rural areas, and creating a new socialist a new mode in rural construction.

In the early 1990s, Double Star implemented the strategy of developing eastern and western areas, going out of city and going to the countryside, and established two major shoe factories in Luzhong and Hanhai.

Going out of city & going to countryside is a rule of labor-intensive industry development

Double Star was originally a shoe-making enterprise, which is a labor-intensive industry. In the early 1980s, many enterprises turned their eyes to foreign countries and looked for partners; however, in accordance with the development rules of the market and the industry, Double Star put forward the new idea that going abroad going to countryside reflect the open-minded thinking. Double Star represented by Wang was keenly aware that the rural market was the largest market of Double Star; if doing an excellent job in the rural market, Double Star could establish an advantage in the same industry. The large idle factory buildings and the abundant cheap labor resources in the countryside could create conditions for low-cost expansion of Double Star. Wang said, "In the early 1980s, Double Star began to go out of city. Labor-intensive industries including shoe-making industry should go from developed regions to underdeveloped regions. Really speaking, we had to do so at the beginning. Later, we followed the laws of the market and the industry to take the initiative to transfer." This idea was very advanced and subject to many doubts and criticisms at that time. Double Star resolutely took the first step: with the use of rural dilapidated factory buildings and cheap labor, it moved the production base to the countryside. As a result, it expanded rapidly and far ahead in the same industry across the country about production capacity, scale, and market share. In the new century, Double Star invested another 1.9 billion Yuan and established 14 production enterprises in rural areas across the country. At present, it has annual sales income increasing from more than 30 million Yuan to 10 billion Yuan, being at the leading position in the industry for ten consecutive years and going into the list of top 500 Chinese enterprises.

Cultivating new labor force for construction of new countryside

Double Star has cultivated many management cadres from local farmers. Not only these talents promoted the development of Double Star in the rural area, but also many of them went out of this place to take management positions in factories and markets of Double Star across the country. Yimeng Mountain has become the cradle of talents of Double Star, which is called Whampoa Military Academy.

The first step (namely, being out of city to countryside) was made in the 1980s, and now it is more than 20 years. Double Star has not stopped selecting talents from farmers. Everywhere, Double Star recruits workers from local farmers who are immersed in its advanced ideas and culture, cultivating their qualities, improving their ability to participate in society, and enabling them to grow rapidly into business cadres and experts. Plant directors, workshop directors, section chiefs and team leaders are all selected from local employees. Mr. Wang said, "More importantly, we have cultivated many cadres, who are sent to various factories, forming a mechanism of talent discovery. These people make their contributions after entering Double Star. We have trained local people and promoted the development of the local economy."

Double Star: eliminating rural backwardness and poverty

In the past ten years, Luzhong and Bohai have paid more than 80 million Yuan in profit and tax. While Double Star itself has developed rapidly, its supporting enterprises have been the main tax source for the local government. Jinxing Town where Luzhong is located has jumped into the third place in fiscal income from the last place in Yiyuan County.

Wang Jiayou, secretary of the party branch of Yuhua Village, Jinxing Town, Yiyuan County, where Luzhong is located, said, "It entered Yimeng Mountain in 1992. At that time, Yuhua

Village had a per capita income of 500 Yuan, which was the poorest village in the whole township. After its entry, it consumed the local surplus labor force. Young people worked in it as workers with wages. It quickly built several supporting factories in Yuhua Village. After two years, we became wealthy. At present, per capita income of Yuhua Village is in the forefront of the county, and the per capita income is 6,000 Yuan." Zheng Haihang, famous economist and vice president of Capital University of Economics and Business, commented, "Combination of the business strategy of Double Star with the governmental strategies for poverty alleviation and going to the west has actually achieved a win-win situation. I think this is a path that traditional manufacturing industries, especially labor-intensive ones, must take." *(Source: China Enterprise News, September 20, 1993)*

(3) Not contented ——Double Star: entering the tire field

In 1998, Double Star successfully entered the tire industry, which was a successful leap from shoe-making to tire-making.

In the mid-1990s, Mr. Wang, president of Double Star Group, saw the broad development space of tires from the development trend of the automobile industry at home and abroad. Although many people suggested to him: Double Star should do something in the high-tech field such as electronics and networks, Wang, who often took advice, adhered to his own opinion this time. He decided to invest in rubber tires. He said that the new benefit growth point of Double Star must be a manufacturing industry with strong correlation with the footwear industry. He predicted that with the exponential extension of the highway, the demand for automobiles would further increase and China would be a large tire market.

With a pioneering spirit, Mr. Wang liked to do things without letup. However, in the tire market, he wanted to borrow a boat sailing on sea, and was extremely patient to wait it.

As the saying goes: Opportunities tend to favor those who are prepared always. While looking for a boat, Mr. Wang met Qingdao Huaqing Industrial Group traded at the Qingdao Stock Exchange Trading Center.

Qingdao Huaqing Industrial Group was a tire company in Jiaonan City. In 1998, it encountered trouble. At that time, the authorities began to clean up the illegal stock trading outside the market, Huaqing was suspended from trading.

Huaqing and Double Star complemented each other. The front one wanted to take Double Star as a huge ship for rapid development; the latter one wanted to take a small boat to achieve its strategic goal of entering the tire manufacturing industry. After several rounds of negotiations, on January 10, 2002, Double Star held a press conference to announce the end of its acquiring Huaqing. In this, Double Star, which was like a snake, swallowed Huaqing which was like an elephant, thereby reflecting its spirit of not being contented. Mr. Wang, with his skillful capital operation skills, interpreted a piece of history in M & A for Chinese enterprises.

With its strong brand strength and strong financial strength, Double Star made Double Star Tire enter the fast lane of speeding development. According to the actual situation, Mr.

Wang put forward a new theory: hard management adopted in it; and implemented a new management mode whose essences as follows: considering actual conditions of personnel & things and carrying out work without letup. A German expert who came to debug the equipment gave a thumb up and said in a less fluent Chinese, "I have been to the tire mixing center in many countries for equipment commissioning, but such a first-class mixing center is only available in China. Wearing a white coat to work is a miracle in the history of tires! The management of Double Star is amazing!"

In 2004, a year that all of people at Double Star could not forget, Double Star tires that started late, together with those from other tire companies with decades of development history, won the title of China Famous Brand with unquestionable strength.

On the day of the news coming, employees of Double Star were excited and immersed in a joy. At this time, Wang, who was sitting alone in the office and made reflections without smile which was always on his face previously. He stood up, let the office staff inform the group's vice presidents of participation in a meeting, then drove straight to Double Star Tire.

As usual, when getting off the car, Wang went straight to the workshop. When he completed his inspection on all the factories covering more than 1,400 Chinese acres, it was already 9 o'clock in the evening. Subsequently, he and his colleagues were seated in the conference room of Double Star Tire.

It was thought that Wang summoned them to hold a celebration party. However, he threw "chilly water" on them.

"Don't think that everything is fine since we have created a famous brand. With the approval of the market, it is worth nothing." Looking at the management cadres who gradually calmed down, Wang continued to say, "I hope that everyone starts from this evening to look for the gap with requirements from the brand and look for the difference with the requirements of the market."

Out of the conference room, the management cadres of Double Star Tire Company took a long sigh of relief. They took a steady step and moved to the next goal in their hearts.

Nowadays, Double Star Tire, which is influenced by Double Star culture, has made rapid progress in the domestic tire market with strong capital, management advantages and brand effect of Double Star, and has created a miracle in the tire industry across the country.

Double Star became a tire maker from a shoe maker. In a short period of time, Double Star Tires occupied a leading position in the domestic industry. The main reasons for its success are as follows: Double Star possessed the advantages of brand, culture and capital; grasped the opportunities of strategic adjustment; and understood the close relations between shoes and tires. This indicates that, for a state-owned enterprise in labor-intensive traditional industries, it is necessary to make a large market scale to survive. Once the market is enlarged, it is necessary to identify opportunities to enter the other areas with high correlation, high technology content and high added value, so that industrial upgrading, and goals of rapidly expanding and strengthening of the enterprise can be realized.

IV. Expert Comments

John W. Tiz as a world-renowned corporate strategist pointed out: "**The task of strategists is not to see what the company is like, but to see what the company will look like in the future.**" The so-called "what will the company look like in the future," it means **what the company will look like** after three years, five years, ten years, or even longer.

Sun Tzu as a famous military strategist in ancient China also said: "**The highest form of generalship is to balk the enemy's plan; the next best is to prevent the junction of the**

enemy's forces; the next in order is to attack the enemy's army in the field; and the worst policy of all is to besiege walled cities. The rule is, not to besiege walled cities if it can possibly to avoided." (Works by Sun Tzu; Dao Mingbian: Sun Tzu's Art of War and Thirty-Six Stratagems, Guangxi Nationalities Publishing House, July 1995, p. 31.) In other words, to fight with enemy, the best method is to win them by strategy, the next best method is win them by diplomatic means, and the worst method is to besiege their walled cities. The siege is a last resort.

Wang believes that, to be a successful entrepreneur, he must become an enterprise strategist, strive to be forward-looking and have a global perspective; he must win by stratagems.

So, how can entrepreneurs win by stratagems?

Frederick Gluck, another world-renowned corporate strategist, said, "**Strategists have to make some trade-offs between the breadth and depth of the information they collect. He is like a eagle as a catcher. The eagle must fly high enough to find the prey in a broad field of view, and it must fly low enough to see the details, aim at the target and attack. It is the strategist's task to constantly make this trade-off which is a task that cannot be completed by others.**"

Wang is like such an eagle in market! Therefore, he can always look forward to the future at the critical moment of enterprise development and develop a scientific and correct development strategy for the enterprise, leading the enterprise along the correct course toward a lofty goal from one victory to another. This is the strategy to win!

So, how does Mr. Wang achieve strategic success?

First, he has a clear strategic positioning. Jack Trout as a world-renowned strategic consulting guru pointed out: "**Positioning is the core of strategy. Strategy is how to differentiate enterprises and products to form core competitiveness. For the audience, it is to establish a brand**

clearly." For Mr. Wang, the strategic positioning of Double Star is to make shoes. In his words, it is a shoemaker. In the traditional ideas, this is a very lowly valuable business.

Second, he has a clear enterprise mission. Peter Drucker, the father of modern management, pointed out, "**It is difficult, painful and risky to stipulate the purpose and mission of the company. However, only in this way can a company set goals, formulate strategies, concentrate its resources and proceed. Only in this way can we manage a company and achieve results.**" He also said, "**To understand a company, you must first understand its purpose. The business purpose is so unique that it is the only reason and the most important reason for the failure of a business or organization.**"

The mission of the enterprise is its program, a banner set up by it in front of the public, and its highest soul and commander. The mission of Double Star is to do a decent job in making shoes for people and making tires for cars.

Third, he has a clear, long-term strategic goal. The strategic goal developed by Mr. Wang for Double Star is as follows: Brand and enterprise being built to last; rooted in Shandong, facing the country, going out of Asia, going to the world.

Fourth, he has clear ways and means to achieve strategic goals. There are many ways and means to achieve the strategic goals of Double Star, such as brand, diversification, globalization, western development, eastern development, adjustment of secondary industry, development of territory industry, construction of chain stores, and etc.

Fifth, he can implement the established strategy without letup. Larry Bosidi and Ram Charan, world-renowned strategic management experts and consultants, pointed out sharply in the book entitled Implementation - How to Complete the Tasks, "**The strategy is good. However, if it is not implemented effectively, then the goals cannot be achieved. If ideas cannot turn into reality, then they will be worth nothing. If there is**

no actual implementation, the breakthrough thinking will be a castle in air and the learning will be valueless. If the goals cannot be achieved, the so-called revolutionary changes will only end in the dead." The secret of the success for Double Star is to effectively implement the established strategy.

Finally, he assesses, adjusts, and changes according to the results of strategy implementation at any time. In this regard, the idea of Double Star is the best answer, for example, "Follow the market, turn around the market, and change with the market." "not innovating today means a fall behind tomorrow; not innovating tomorrow means to be eliminated the day after tomorrow."

To be a successful entrepreneur, we should first become an enterprise strategist like Mr. Wang. Confucius, ancient Chinese thinker, politician, and educator, said, "**Those who do not plan for the future will find trouble at their doorstep.**" A man without distant care must have near sorrow. This is also true for an enterprise.

Mr. Wang is clear-headed and well-informed. He often warned his team, "**It is necessary to think about how the enterprise will develop after 10 years. Entrepreneurs must be brave and take risks with advanced ideas. It is impossible for an entrepreneur to be like an employee, and it is impossible to decide when all members of the leadership team agree. When everyone agrees, the opportunity has passed; so, it is too late. The market is like the battlefield.**"

World-famous futurist Alvin Toffler warned, "**For a company without strategy, it is like an airplane flying in a sinister climate, always bumping in the air, going through the storm, and finally it is very likely to get lost. If there is no long-term clear direction for the future, and if there is no guideline for the future, no matter how large or stable it is, an enterprise will fail in the revolutionary technological and economic revolution.**"

The experiences of many successful enterprises including Double Star and the lessons of many failed enterprises have proved from both positive and negative aspects: The strategy is very important!

Tactic 4: The Mechanism Is the Driving Force

"The core issue of state-owned enterprises is, in the final analysis, the system and mechanism. The biggest contribution of the innovation in Dual Star institutional mechanism is to ensure the development of Double Star business in the future ten years and hundreds of years. Under the new institutional mechanism, no matter who is the boss, the enterprise can work well. Double Star will not fall!"

——Wang Hai

In 1987, Double Star was the first to break the big pot from which staffs ate under the planned economy, the first in Qingdao to be successful in the pilot program of profit and tax contracting, thereby laying a fund foundation for its future development.

Each unit of Double Star implements an internal contracted shareholding system. Each line and each machine station are an independent small economic entity.

I. Wang Hai Quotations

(I) Significance of institutional mechanism innovation

☆ Innovation of institutional mechanism is the largest innovation. The institutional mechanism that adapts to enterprise development and adapts to market changes is the key to winning market competition. Today's brilliance of Double Star is due to its constantly adjustment in system and mechanism according to market changes, and its spirit of being never satisfied and never stopping. If the mechanism does not adapt to the market situation, then it will be changed. This is the secret for the success with Double Star in more than 30 years.

☆ Three revolutions of Double Star in market economy: eliminating the conservative and rigid old ideas, adopting new ideas; breaking the old frame of the planned economy, creating a new mechanism; saying goodbye to the passive attitude, and setting up a new model.

☆ The core issue of state-owned enterprises is, after all, the system and mechanism. The biggest contribution of the innovation in Dual Star institutional mechanism is to ensure the development of Double Star business in the future ten years and hundreds of years. Under the new institutional mechanism, no matter who is the boss, the enterprise can works well. Double Star will not fall!

(II) Characteristics of system and mechanism in Double Star

☆ Quick in adapting to market requirements and adjusting the product structure

☆ Our system is the most competitive in the footwear industry today. We bring full play the advantages of the group's economies of scale, namely, American-style economies of scale (which pays attention to the experience of cooperation and overall operations). We adopt a small competitive self-management mechanism, namely, Japanese-style internal accounting unit, which fully enters the market. At the same time, we have established the unique spirit of the Communists, namely, Dare to Fight for the First, thus forming the most competitive operating system in the footwear industry, ensuring the normal operation and growth of the Group's production.

☆ Management is the advantage of Double Star. The internal contracted shareholding system is a unique and effective management model and new method of Double Star. It is the basis for continuous innovation, technological upgrading, improving the overall quality of employees and enhancing employee confidence and determination.

☆ The internal contracted shareholding system is based on the state's management of joint-stock enterprises. It absorbs the management experience of more than 30 years of continuous innovation and combines various forms of management such as market-based contracting, factory-currency operation, and household consumption management. The internal contracted shareholding system, which is new management model and new method of Double Star reflecting its own culture and management ideas, is an effective measure to improve internal management, deepen and refine market-oriented contracting, is an effective means to maximize the enthusiasm and initiative of employees, cultivate talents and enhance the sense of professionalism and responsibility of key employees.

(III) How to do a decent job in system and mechanism innovation

☆ Three means of market economy: system innovation, mechanism transformation, policy adjustment

☆ System innovation is as guarantee and attention is paid to subdivision and management.

☆ Three principles of market restructuring of Double Star: Whether it is conducive to the preservation and appreciation of state-owned assets, whether it is conducive to the development of Double Star brand, and whether it is conducive to the profitability of operators.

☆ Implement the internal contracted shareholding system to realize goals of self-management, self-accounting, self-improvement in efficiency, and self-reduction; provide talents with the platform; and enhance vitality, driving force and competitiveness.

☆ Adhere to the policy of contracting, renting, buying, and recruiting. We must persist in transplanting the great creation of Comrade Xiaoping (namely production quotas contracted to individual households) into modern enterprise management. Through the organic combination of spirit and material, we mobilize the enthusiasm of staffs and adhere to the motto that I put forward (namely, the good use of money is the politics) in political work. In this way, we will be able to uphold the red flag of Double Star and achieve the grand goal of Being Built to Last.

☆ Adhere to the combinations of four factors (namely, factory currency, culture, contracting and execution), integrate economic means, cultural ideas, humanity, and morality, and enhance the market competitiveness.

II. Practices and Effects

(1) Main practices

In the early days of reform and opening, Comrade Deng Xiaoping pointed out, "Reform is China's second revolution." In the market economy, in the face of the constraints of conservative forces, the collision of old and innovative ideas, people at Double Star dared to take risks by breaking the old system, old mechanism, old organization, old habits, and old ideas. This reform is a bold step to create the new system and mechanism of Double Star reflecting the nature of being both state-owned and market-oriented.

1. Breaking the Three Irons

The so-called Three Irons here include both the old Three Irons and the new Three Irons.

The so-called old Three Irons: iron armchair (life-time posts), iron rice bowl (life-time employment), and iron wages (guaranteed pay). These three old iron guys are like a group of political teachers, so that the staffs become stupid and lazy, ultimately causing a rigid mechanism in the state-owned enterprises which have no vitality.

The so-called new Three Irons: iron relationships that is intertwined; iron fences in the old system that hinder the development of productive forces; and iron chains formed by old ideas. These three new iron guys are like a barbed wire net binding people. This wire net must be broken; otherwise, people can only helpless wait for death.

Double Stars took the lead in the reform of the personnel system, cutting off the old three irons and the new three irons. Double Star was the first to break the old recruitment system of the planned economy and began to recruit workers in rural areas in 1986; Double Star said that it had no migrant workers. Double Star was the first to turn iron armchair cadres into blackboard cadres by reforming the old personnel system. Double Star was the first to break the identity boundary of cadres and workers and implement the competitive employment. Double Star was the first to the rigid system in cadre management appointment and dismissal, implement supervision and management by the staff representatives; develop the new system that made those who lost their privilege and interests go to the higher authorities for complaints, and made them revenge against Mr. Wang, including the fabrication of rumors. People of Double Star finally said goodbye to the old system and the old mechanism featuring low efficiency and overstaffing etc.

2. Organizational reform

The organizational overlapping and overstaffing are common problems of state-owned enterprises. Double Star broke through the restricted area of the government agencies and carried out reforms of comprehensive supporting organizations.

Double Star was the first to combine the security department with the armed forces, which even alarmed the Central Military Commission and the Ministry of Labor. However, Double Star insisted on its reform of streamlining operations, with the number of departments reduced from 27 to 13 (including: combining departments of sales, planning, development, supply, statistics, technology and so forth; and establishing its production and operation information company). In Double Star, managers and administrators were reduced from 11.8% of all employees to 7.8%, not only greatly improving the efficiency of the cadre team, but also overcoming the internal wrangling between departments. At present, it has 60,000 staffs, but has only 40 management personnel. There is no director in the production workshop, while the workers become workshop contractors and small bosses. By the organizational reform, Double Star creates a new management system which is unique and efficient.

3. System reform

In mid-1980s, Double Star internally implemented decentralization, layered contracting, and separate accounting; and changed each production workshop and auxiliary department into a branch which was a relatively independent economic entity in which staffs could implement independent accounting and take full responsibility for their own profit and loss.

In the mid-1990s, state-owned enterprises had a common problem of the public property suffering a great loss and the cadres getting rich. Facing the accusation that they would run a family business, Mr. Wang took the lead in the thunder zone. In line with the principles of whether it is conductive to preservation and appreciation of public assets, conductive to the development of its brand, and conductive to getting rich by its employees, Double Star carried out the managerial responsibility system of contracting, the sale of property rights and so forth, and appealed employees to strive together in good faith. By selling chain stores, operating and service companies, people at

Double Star completely changed from selling shoes for the country to selling shoes for themselves, and from asking for money from the enterprise to actively raising money by themselves. Double Star fundamentally broke the old system in which state-owned enterprises did not adapt to the market, thereby letting employees get rich and leading to today's brilliance of Double Star.

Through the system reform, Double Star has created a new mechanism with strong vigor: market-based contracting, namely, internal contracted shareholding system. This is a unique new management model and new method of Double Star. It learns from the management form in the state-owned joint-stock enterprises, absorbs the management experience of Double Star in innovation for more than 30 years, combines various forms of management such as market-based contracting, factory-coin operation, and household consumption, and integrates culture and management ideas of Double Star. It is an effective measure to improve internal management and deepen market-oriented contracting. It is an effective means to maximize the enthusiasm and initiative of employees. It is an effective method to discover and cultivate talents and enhance the employees' sense of responsibility.

4. Income distribution reform

Double Star was the first to abandon practicing egalitarianism with everyone eating from the same big pot under the planned economy and adopt a new system in which workers are recompensed according to their amount of labor expended. Double Star abandoned the iron rice bowl of the planned economy, and adopted the contracting system, the piece counting system and the working hour system, depending on the industry type and the post type, so that the income of employees was closely linked with their effort spent. By reforming the wage system in which new measures were adopted, e.g., rewards (color TVs, houses, and cars awarded for staffs who made outstanding contributions), punishments, transparency (salaries announced on the wall) and so on, Double Star inspired the passion, enthusiasm and affection of the employees. A new miracle of building a cold-stick shoe factory in 99 days was created; a new atmosphere of passionate working emerged; employees successively worked on the assembly line for 48 hours for the sake of completing exported products; orders having only a pair of shoes could be received, and the customer's requirements were taken as standards; young people created the new technology, new process, and high quality. Therefore, this reform solved the problem of the unreasonable distribution system.

5. Getting rid of the old thinking

Chinese enterprises stepped into the market, with many slogans that did not meet actual conditions. When many people did not yet know what enterprise culture was, Double Stars had begun its difficult exploration on cultural management. President Wang deepened into the workshop to investigate and research, put forward a number of famous mottoes: people wears shoes, the key is the work; there are products with poor quality, while there are no weak markets etc. Easily understood, these mottoes were posted on the workshop and called Wang Hai Quotations by the media. At that time, in China, only Chairman Mao's words could be called quotations. Individual leaders saw them and said that Mr. Wang was engaged in personal worship, leading to the quotation storm. But it was calmed by Gu Xiulian Minister of Chemical Industry and Yu Zhengsheng Secretary of Qingdao Municipal Committee who praised Mr. Wang. By eliminating the old thinking, Double Star developed rapidly.

6. Getting rid of the old ideas

Over the years, in the state-owned enterprises, traditional education idea such as "having excellent quality is serving the people and quality is the life of the enterprise" have become slogans. Double Star was the first to adopt Buddhist culture in its management and proposed that "excellent product quality is the biggest doing-good and gathering blessings. This realistic attitude of inheriting essences of traditional culture in enterprise management has been recognized by employees. In 1995, President Wang made a speech in Singapore on the use of the traditional Chinese Buddhist culture for enterprise management, which was highly praised. But for a long time, it was considered the feudal superstition. In the face of irresponsible remarks and social resistance, people at Double Star bravely created a road to the development of enterprise culture in the market economy, while getting rid of the old ideas.

People at Double Star carried out reforms, getting rid of old traditions, old thinking, old ideas, old systems, old mechanisms under the planned economy, and establishing its new market-oriented system in absence of any model as a reference.

Also, Double Star always implemented household consumption management and factory currency operations.

7. Household consumption management

Household consumption management means that Double Star Group applies the concept of household consumption to modern enterprise management and decomposes the goal of saving and reducing consumption into every employee. Each employee is just like living in his own home, calculating and tapping potentials, effectively reducing consumption and improving product quality.

8. Factory currency operation

Factory currency is the internal circulation currency used by various branches, departments, workshops, sections, links, teams, individuals, etc. within Double Star Group. The operation of factory currency is to use the scientific means and modern tools such as microcomputers for currency management with the material flow between the branches, workshops, teams and individuals, to enhance the employees' awareness on quality, capital, cost, consumption reduction. It is a rigorous, complicated and systemic project, thereby being the outline for doing a good job in total management of the enterprise, and being a new management method, which is comprehensive with high tech content etc.

9. Internal contracted shareholding system

As a form of management, the contracting means that the enterprise manager or contractor applies to the enterprise for giving money – spending money – dividing money. It adopts a single form to divide the cost with a limit, provides a commission according to the cost balance, or contracts production and quality in which the commission is provided in accordance with the approved amount.

The internal contracted shareholding system is an economic form in which the employees as shareholders raise their scattered funds for the rational operation and then receive their bonuses. Different from the contracting form (simply applying to the enterprise for giving money – spending money – dividing money), this form lets employees spend part of their money on production and operation, further enhancing the awareness of responsibility, rights and interests between enterprises and employees. It is a new management model combining market-based contracting and internal shareholding system. It is a deepening and refinement of management.

(II) Main effects

Through long-term, continuous, serial reforms and innovations, Double Star Group has created the most competitive institutional mechanism in the footwear industry today, and has created successful experiences for state-owned enterprises. Main performances are:

1. Completing three revolutions in the market economy

Double Star completed three revolutions in the market economy: eliminating the conservative and rigid old ideas, adopting innovative ideas; breaking the old frame of the planned economy, creating a new mechanism; saying goodbye to the passive attitude, and setting up a new model.

2. Twenty novel changes in the group

During its reforms, Double Star always implemented the household consumption management and the factory currency operation. It greatly enhanced the awareness, enthusiasm and creativity of staffs, while there were twenty latest changes in the group.

3. Realizing Marx's goal that "workers are the Master of Enterprises" and raising the sense of ownership of employees

The internal contracting shareholding system created by Double Star realized the goal (namely "workers are the Master of Enterprises") proposed by Marx more than 100 years ago, which improved the sense of ownership of employees and solved the problem of "workers hate machine equipment" proposed by Marx. It let staffs spend money to buy equipment and regard it as their partner, comrade, and weapon of war. It solved the problem (namely, "contradictions between enterprises, leaders and employees under the conditions of market economy") proposed by Marx. Employees regarded enterprises as their homes and regarded leaders as their own reliance in getting rich, thereby enhancing their feelings, enthusiasm and trust. Especially in the context of the labor shortage in the manufacturing and processing industries across the country, the internal contracted shareholding system plays a very important role in stabilizing the workforce, cultivating talents, retaining technical backbones, and maintaining normal production and operation.

4. Ensuring that Double Star is built to last

The new system and mechanism created by Double Star can guarantee its long-term success. Mr. Wang said, "The biggest contribution of the innovation of system and mechanism in Double Star is to guarantee its development in the future ten years and hundreds of years. Under the new system and mechanism, no matter who is the boss, the enterprise can operate normally. Double Star never falls!"

5. Creating successful experiences for state-owned enterprises

The core issue of state-owned enterprises is in system and mechanism. The successful experience of Double Star has a good reference value for all state-owned enterprises, especially those in the manufacturing industry.

III. Typical examples

(I) Old Three Irons and New Three Irons

(Note: Wang - Wang Hai Qi – Qi Yue)

Wang: As the saying goes: The market is the driving force and source of enterprise reform. To face the market, we should innovate the system, introduce a competitive mechanism, and recruit capable people instead of those who are mediocre or bureaucratic. If workers regard a cadre as a dog in the manger, he can't go on any more.

Therefore, I declared that there would be no longer boundary between cadres and workers in Double Star, that the iron armchair would be removed, and the capable people would be appointed, that the working performance of a cadre would be evaluated by the masses.

I think we should deal with different problems in diverse ways, rather than being dogmatic. For enterprises, management talents and technical talents are the biggest resources. Capable people are appointed as leaders despite the age and educational background. Those who are mediocre or lazy are deal with in a proper manner. Cadres who were removed came to me and said, "What is wrong with us?" I replied straightly, "You have no outstanding contribution."

Today, when we are engaged in reforms, we must find ways to appoint capable people as managers. The so-called capable person is nothing more than a person with ideas, insight, ability, and personality. If obedient and mediocre persons are appointed, how can we make reforms? There are a lot of capable persons, but the old personnel system did not create a good environment for them, being unworthy of their talents.

Qi: Now everyone understands that the survival of the fittest is the ruthless rule of the market economy. In the early 1980s, what was the biggest resistance when you broke the Three Irons?

Wang: To implement any reform, it is necessary to impact the vested interests in the existing system. And these people will never give up some kind of "privilege" of their own. They were together and mainly against me.

In that huge pressure, I faced with seven kinds of opposition forces: the first kind was the old cadres, who, after retirement, had nothing to do, felt lost, and stared at your current leader to find his fault. The second kind was the extreme leftists in the Cultural Revolution, who, after dismissal, felt dissatisfied. The third kind was speculators, who, after removal of Three Irons, could not carry out dishonest practices in pursuing promotions. The fourth kind was the opposing persons who used to living in the old model of the planned economy and now could keep up with the times. The fifth kind was those who previously having a backer and acting willfully, now could not do so. The sixth kind was those who were lazy, passive, and not willing to be disciplined. The seventh kind was grassroots cadres who were mediocre and dismissed as well as felt lost. Even in case of a department reformed or a person dismissed, it was like a stone that stirred up a thousand waves.

Qi: Breaking the Three Ions caused a conflict of power and interests, which was often very painful for individuals. It even might lead to a struggle between life and death.

Wang: To what extent was the struggle fierce? I was almost killed. At that time, I rode my bike home from the working unit very late every night, and I had to go through a grove of trees on the road. One night I was particularly tired, slowly rode my bike and thought about my work next day. As soon as I arrived at the woods, I was suddenly alarmed. I felt that the front was dark and there was no street light. Was it dangerous? Thinking of this, I speeded up for the sake of quickly crossing the woods. However, I didn't go far. Suddenly, a stone came out of the woods and came toward me. I instinctively bowed my head. The stone flew over my head and landed on the opposite side of the road. Then I heard a stone fall behind me.

Qi: At this time, you only had to flee.

Wang: Truly. As a saying goes, "Better an open enemy than a false friend." If I did not hurry, I might suffer. Back home, I said to my wife, "You have to be mentally prepared. I don't know which day they will kill me." From then on, at 10 o'clock in the evening, if I did not return home, my wife would be afraid and restless.

From that time, with my enhanced vigilance, I placed the only pistol of our factory on my waist, and on some occasions, I deliberately exposed it from the clothes to show its power. The security chief and activists who supported the reform in our factory also began to protect me in secret.

Qi: So, as a reformer, what do you think is the most unbearable thing for him?

Wang: The most unbearable thing is that you have a single-minded devotion to work for the enterprise, but your superior departments create all sorts of obstacles for you. This is the cruelest thing. At that time, in addition to facing the seven opposing forces within the enterprise, I faced the blame from the competent authorities. The times changed, but they could not yet get out of the old mindset. I upheld the righteousness and did not take part in the power struggle between factions. On many occasions, they were against me.

The head of our rubber company even publicly said, "How can you do it this way in the state-owned enterprise? You ignore the national labor and personnel system and our factory has become chaotic!" Besides this accusation, he punished me. He cancelled all honorable titles awarded me in past years, at which my colleagues were particularly angry. I said, "It does not matter. The fame is just like clouds drifting by. The most important thing is to let our factory stand on the market; otherwise, everything is meaningless."

Qi: What did you mean by breaking the new Three Irons that you later proposed?

Wang: The new Three Irons refer to: iron relationships that is intertwined; iron fences in the old system that hinder the development of productive forces; and iron chains formed by old ideas. These three new iron guys are like a barbed wire net binding people. This wire net must be broken; otherwise, people can only helpless wait for death.

Qi: The old Three Irons existed within the enterprise and new outside it, right?

Wang: You can understand this. In an interview, I said frankly to the reporter, "I am comfortable and happy when I return to Double Star. I am excited when I go to the market. But when I am in official circles, I feel depressed and uncomfortable."

Why do I say so? Under the old system, departments were excessively overlapped. Enterprises might spend much time on going through many procedures before getting a governmental approval. In the 1980s, to enter the international market, we planned to set up an export shoe building. A variety of governmental approvals might take a long time (namely, more than two years) during which a variety of application materials might be needed. If we went through the routine procedures, our export tasks would not be smoothly completed. The Time did not wait for us. We decided to act without prior approval in some links. In this way, we officially started construction in 1989. The construction of the plant and the installation of the equipment were carried out at the same time. The internal installation of equipment is concurrent with the exterior decoration. When the project was completed, the equipment was fully installed.

However, the relevant governmental department in the city rushed to us and said that we did not yet passed the acceptance inspection, and that our equipment was installed without prior approval. The said governmental department prohibited us to use the building.

Qi: The market and the officialdom are often a pair of contradictions.

Wang: I did not obey that order. I said, "We spend our own money to build it. On the other hand, why do you let us take a very long time to wait for your approval? If our production and export are delayed, you will not take responsibility for me." We could not wait for a day. I ordered it to be used. As a result, while quarrelling with the said department, our products continuously were sent to the international market. Our new building was an illegal building for quite some time. When municipal leaders made investigations, I made a report to them and said, "Governmental departments should provide high quality services for enterprises instead of being lowly efficient or even delaying our production. As enterprises, we must timely deliver our products to the international market, which reflects the principle of abiding by the contract and keeping promises. More importantly, there is a benefit. We work for our country too. Now we export our products and should fulfill the contract for the product. Otherwise, we would lose face, and even bring our country into disrepute.

When we planned to go abroad for visit and negotiation and organize delegations for international fairs, the relevant government departments said, "You went abroad last month. Why do you want to go abroad next month again? At least we should obey the rule of rotation!"

Qi: This was the thinking on the officialdom. They regarded a trip abroad as a treatment or honor and formulated a rule of rotation.

Wang: So, I said to them, "Do you think I go abroad for having fun? I have no leisure." They said, "You can go abroad, but we must send someone to follow you." I said, "Are you are a spy or what? Will you spend our money on spying on us? Why can I not be accompanied by my designer?" If we disagreed, they would set up obstacles, which, anyway, always could be found from a lot of outmoded rules and regulations. We organized a delegation to participate in the World Expo. They said, "Ah, at one time, there are more than a dozen people going abroad. Your application cannot be approved." Why? They replied, "According to the relevant government policy, there should not be more than five people going abroad. Furthermore, there was no precedent in the past." I said, "The ancients dared not eat crabs, but now many people eat them. It is also known that there is no road in the world until more people walking. If without this spirit, how can society develop?!"

The biggest harm caused by the new Three Irons is to cause internal friction, letting you look backwards, letting you stand still. If you want to move forward lightly, you have to overcome all the difficulties on the way. Indeed, I spent a lot of time on dealing with these meaningless things.

Qi: What does the Iron Chain mean?

Wang: It can be said that it refers to all means by which the higher authorities or relevant departments control you. For example, in June 1985, our country implemented the factory manager responsibility system, and the higher authorities began to find the new factory director for our Ninth Rubber Factory. The first criterion was that the candidate must be a specialist. As a graduate from a technical school, naturally I was not qualified to be the director of this big factory in their eyes. They sifted through candidates with a college degree or above in the city's rubber system but did not find no right person. They were toward the candidates with a junior college degree. They never paid attention to me who was capable with achievements already made.

Qi: There is now a view that success is the diploma of entrepreneurs.

Wang: In front of these Iron Chains, I thought, for the sake of the enterprise, I should offer myself for this position. For the third time, I knocked on the door of Liu Peng secretary and talked to him about my thoughts. As a result, the higher authorities of the rubber company debated with the municipal party committee and whipped up public opinion against me saying that I was not qualified since I was just a graduate from a technical school. However, this time the municipal party committee did not compromise. In line with the needs of enterprise and the principle of seeking truth from facts, the municipal party committee broke the outmoded provisions and promoted me as the director and party secretary of our factory. At that time, among all the large-scale enterprises in Qingdao, I was the only director who was appointed without junior college degree or above.

The whole life of a person can be summarized in two sentences: "In the tricky situation, you must feel good about yourself, and you must take yourself as the backbone in your work." People like me with such a way of thinking often did not come into favor in eyes of higher authorities. They felt uncomfortable when they faced us. If we compromised, then we would not bring our talents into full play. On the other hand, my character and thoughts always let me feel uncomfortable if I cannot keep my promise.

After being the director, I worked hard. Not only was the competition mechanism be fully introduced, but the channels for the selection, training and appointment of cadres were be widely used. In the whole plant, an unprecedented system reform was made, including power decentralization, stratified contracting, and separate accounting in the enterprise. Various production workshops and auxiliary departments were changed into branch factories, becoming a relatively independent economic entity. In Double Star, dozens of big discussions on emancipating the mind were carried out. While getting rid of old ideas, we accepted the new ideas in line with the development direction of the market economy, for example, the market concept, competition concept, benefit concept, talent concept, innovative concept, management concept, quality concept, new product development concept, ideological and political ideas. We summarize it as three revolutions of Double Star in market economy: eliminating the conservative and rigid old ideas, adopting innovative ideas; breaking the old frame of the planned economy, creating a new mechanism; saying goodbye to the passive attitude, and setting up a new model. (*Source:* Wang Hai, Qi Yue. Market General, Huawen Publishing House 1999)

(2) Double Star and its employees

——Solution of labor shortage: Employees as shareholders

At present, many enterprises in the labor-intensive industry are difficult to recruit, but this problem does not exist in Double Star Group, which is in the labor-intensive manufacturing industry. In some tire companies, the labor shortage is 70%. Double Star Qingdao Tire having 5,000 employees are relatively stable. Other shoe and tire factories near the Double Star Footwear Industrial Park posted the recruitment ads to the gate of said industrial park and promised to provide the preferential treatment. Two employees went out of Double Star and joined one of them. But soon after, both returned, saying, "That company treated us impersonally with its promise not kept."

Under the background of labor shortage, how does Double Star Group enhance its cohesion? According to reports, Double Star Group adopts the following two approaches: the first is family management; the second is the internal contracted shareholding system which is more important. By contracting, it motivates employees to innovate, improve quality, reduce consumption and increase efficiency. In the past, it only gave employees' wages; at present, it gives employees as shareholders wages and dividends. Employees participate in management and truly become the masters of the enterprise. There is a stronger and closer win-win relationship between the enterprise and the employees, thereby enhancing the magnet-like effect of the enterprise and letting the enterprise become more vigorous and dynamic. Through the comprehensive management (that is, enterprise culture, family management and internal contracting shareholding system), Double Star creatively steps out of a new path for China's manufacturing industry to solve the problem of labor shortage and achieve healthy and steady development.

What is the internal contracting shareholding system? According to reports, in branch factories of tires, shoes and clothing, machinery and the like with Double Star, adopt measures to tap the potential of employees, motivate their enthusiasm, enhance their sense of responsibility. Said measures are to encourage employees to pay for their own shares and buy out rubber materials, single products, machine stations, production lines, to realize goals of self-management, self-working, self-reduction, and self-saving. Through dividends and wages, employees become the masters of the enterprise. For example, in Double Star Qingdao Tire, new methods are adopted such as family contracted shareholding system, single-type order-based buyout contracting, and share-stock production and sales contracting, which have stimulated the enthusiasm of employees, with per capita efficiency in production having increased by 8% based on continuous growth for several years basically with no increase in equipment and personnel. Employees use their brains to find ways to reduce costs, engage in innovation, and improve quality. In 2010, the material cost was reduced by 14.8696 million Yuan. In Double Star Dongfeng Tire, different contracting measures are adopted according to the actual situation of the production plant and workshop. In the past, the single rubber material was bought out, but now the whole production line could be bought out. The granulation workshop realizes a profit of 500,000 Yuan for a year, and the employee's income also increases greatly. After the independent contracting of the embroidery workshop in Double Star Printing and Packaging, the contractor as an individual does 5 kinds of work. In the fierce competition in the industry, the external sales income is more than 1 million Yuan, with the income of all employees in the workshop having been greatly increased. So, these employees cherish their jobs with great enthusiasm.

The internal contracted shareholding system of Double Star is a revolution in enterprise management. Its significance is as follows: overthrowing the outmoded mode of the planned economy; activating the vigor, power and market competitiveness of the enterprise; allowing those who are brave, diligent and passionate to bring their talents into full play; completely solving the problems concerning relationships between personal and corporate interests. More importantly, through this method, employees are effectively consolidated, and employees are stabilized rather than having a high turnover rate. By the way of being shareholders, employees and enterprises have common interests. As the income increases due to the innovations and other measures, employees become more and more energetic and hopeful, and really take the enterprise as their reliance to get rich and happy and realize their own value. In this way, the income of employees continuously increases, attracting more relatives, friends, classmates, and fellow villagers to work in Double Star; Double Star really finds a new path for labor-intensive manufacturing and processing industries to solve the problem of labor shortage.

(3) Selling stores

Mr. Wang president of Double Star believes that the implementation of the overall withdrawal of state-owned capital is not only in line with the spirit of state-owned enterprise reform, but also is to achieve better development for enterprises. At the same time, the group can have more funds for expansion in other fields. In the property rights restructuring, Double Star sells intangible assets such as brands, management and technology.

In 2004, Double Star Group took the lead in restructuring the footwear-making state-owned enterprises. Through bidding, more than 200 chain stores in the southwest region were sold to individuals at prices ranging from 100,000 to over one million Yuan. The three operating companies under Yunnan, Shenyang, and Ningxia were also sold to private enterprises. Nowadays, in Double Star, only our parent company (group headquarters) and a thermal plant serving our enterprise and surrounding communities are state-owned, while other enterprises implement a flexible diversified property rights system according to the actual situation, forming a new pattern of property rights (namely, multiple property-right systems owned by an enterprise).

Was the property rights reform carried out passively or actively by Double Star last year?

President Wang believes that the reform is first determined by the law of the development of the footwear industry. A small number of state-owned shoe factories surviving in a highly competitive footwear industry is facing a dark future. Despite the increasing demand for shoes, the footwear industry has not been able to fully automate so far, even if developed countries cannot escape this reality. Prohibitive cost, low profit, large number of employees, and low profitability are the realities of shoe-making enterprises. Especially in recent years, 99% of state-owned large and medium-sized shoe-making enterprises suffer a loss, which is enough to show that it is difficult for state-owned enterprises to establish a foothold in this field, and that it is difficult for state-owned assets to add value in this low-profit industry. Moreover, the state-owned enterprise system is the weak point of Double Star Group, the property rights system is a blocking stone in the reform of state-owned enterprises that cannot be circumvented and is a bottleneck for the continued development of Double Star. It is better to get rid of these obstacles as soon as possible.

Operating companies and chain stores are the link between manufacturing companies and the market. Compared with other economic entities of Double Star, the market pressure is even greater. In recent years, Double Star has invested more than 100 million Yuan to build more than 2,000 chain stores across the country. The sales of chain operations have accounted for half of the total sales revenue of Double Star. However, as the chain stores directly face the market, the drawbacks of the existing property rights system and operating mechanism are more prominent, and it is still impossible to effectively monitor the operation and management of all chain stores and their flow of funds. Before the restructuring, the ratio of chain stores with profits, losses and flats is 1/3 respectively; the main reason for this situation is that property rights are not clear. How to operate? The best way is to sell chain stores to individuals to operate.

In the actual operation, how to sell scientifically and sell reasonably? Faced with this problem, Mr. Wang says that this is too sensitive! If the price is low, it may cause the loss of state-owned assets. If the price is high, the sale may be not successful; in this case, you may be blamed for casting off burden or forsake a ugly girl. By the word “sale", the personal interests are integrated into the interests of Double Star, and the personal fate is tied to the fate of Double Star. How to sell? It can neither let state assets go away, nor can operators make them unprofitable. At the same time, after the sale, they should become the operating tentacles for the enterprise, to obtain its subsequent development.

The three principles for the sale of chain stores: First, it is conducive to the preservation and appreciation of state-owned assets; Second, it is beneficial to the profitability of operators;

Third, it is conducive to the development of Double Star brand. According to these three "favorable" principles, Double Star Group has made regulations: All employees of Double Star and those who are willing to operate Double Star products in the society can buy chain stores. The buyer only pays the rental for one year, the decoration fee (discounted) and the purchase fee of the existing product, then immediately possesses the franchise store with Double Store.

Mr. Wang believes that in the property rights restructuring, Double Star sells intangible assets such as brand, management and technology. If state-owned assets want to break out of the lowly added-value status, they must transform from the production mode to the trade mode, and brand operation is precisely the best ferry boat to achieve this transformation.

The 15th National Congress of the Communist Party of China has clearly put forward the adjustment idea of doing some things and leaving other things undone. Double Star has carried out its own reform in some areas of the low-profit industry according to its own situation, which fully conforms to the general trend of state-owned enterprise reform. The main criterion for measuring the success or failure of state-owned enterprise reform is whether state-owned assets can add value, and the market plays a key role here.

In addition to the restructuring of chain stores in Southwest China and Shenyang and Ningxia, Double Star Garment Ltd, Laser Ltd and Zhongyuan Footwear Ltd carried out joint-stock reforms through extensive absorption of capital from individual employees. The proportion of shares from individual employees is above 50%.

Double Star Zhangjiakou and Chengdu Footwear Co., Ltd. are owned by Double Star Group in the form of intangible assets such as technology, management and brand. In addition, Double Star implements a general agency system for 10 overseas operating companies and domestic operating companies. If they pay interest, pay off the loan, and pay the brand usage fee to the group every year, they can buy out the business. If Double Star can't get through the enterprise restructuring in time, it is very likely that it will be eliminated in the competition. Perhaps three or five years later, people can see the value and significance of this reform through the development of Double Star. (*Source:* China Enterprise News, March 2001)

(4) Double Star will not fall!

Mr. Wang tells reporters that the core issue of state-owned enterprises is, in the final analysis, the mechanism. A labor-intensive enterprise like shoemaking has absolutely no way out, if no reform is carried out. Double Star is brilliant today, but a crisis may be not far away. If an enterprise cannot sell products with a cash flow not smooth, it may go bankrupt in a short time. This pressure was born by the president in the past. This pressure should be borne by all employees of Double Star, and the risk of an enterprise should be taken by everyone. For the sake, a reform of mechanism is needed.

From 1984 to 1985, the first major change of the Double Star mechanism was to introduce the market mechanism into the enterprise, and Double Star thus had the extraordinary development of the first decade. □

From 1994 to 1995, the second major change of the Double Star mechanism was to integrate industry and trade. This laid a solid foundation for the development of the second decade of Double Star.

In 1999, Double Star made a breakthrough in the ownership system and implemented the private ownership of assets, which further adapted the production relationship to the development of productivity. Double Star brand entered the advanced stage and kept up with international famous brands. Therefore, a mechanism guarantee was provided for the long-term development of Double Star.

With the reform and development in the past 20 years, Double Star as a state-owned enterprise has completed the entire process of transition from planned economy to market economy, and gradually established a brand-new system to adapt to the market economy.

Mr. Wang says that the biggest contribution of system innovation in Double Star is to ensure its development in future ten years and hundreds of years. Under the new system, no matter who is the boss, the enterprise can function normally.

Mr. Wang says: For the enterprise, the successor is neither from selection, nor from the appointment; instead, he is created by the market. Selecting successors from a personal point of view will never succeed. I am the result of market choice. A person who understands and controls the market is the leader of the enterprise.

Entrepreneurs are generated from the market. From the very beginning, Double Star had no preferential policy from the government, except the old equipment of the 1930s, the old processes of the 1940s, and the old products of the 1950s... It suffered a variety of difficulties in the early 1980s. In an immature market, a labor-intensive enterprise is like a small boat in the ocean. When a bad wave comes, there is a disaster of overturning the boat. But Mr. Wang has managed the boat steadily and changed it into an aircraft carrier, a fleet, thereby enhancing the ability to withstand risks. The market chooses Mr. Wang and casts him into a great entrepreneur with good qualities such as wisdom, insight, flexibility and strategy.

Mr. Wang insists that entrepreneurs should be generated in the market and be tested by the market. Not long ago, a deputy general of the group, who was a old cadre and worked hard with Mr. Wang for a long time, was dismissed from office and was severely criticized by Wang for his serious mistakes in charge of business. The number of top leaders as old cadres dismissed is not low. At the same time, a capable young man in his thirties is appointed as vice president. Wang says that today' brilliance of Double Star is inseparable from a group of talented people who work hard with me. I hope that all those who work in Double Star will make a fortune. But if you don't do an excellent job and negatively affects our brand of Double Star, I can only deal with it according to the rules.

In Double Star, the senior management structure is consisted of those who were originally workers and those who previously graduates with a college degree or above and just worked as businessmen for a few years in Double Star. We attention to ability rather than academic degrees.

Mr. Wang says that talents are those who can create profits for enterprises and develop markets. Talents are not the ones who always agree with me. Even if people disagree with me or oppose me, if they are beneficial to the development of enterprises, I think they are talents. Talent is not lifelong, not static. He was a talent in the past, but now he does not achieve results, so being not a talent again. The market is the stage for everyone to perform. Those who can adapt to the market will stand out.

Mr. Wang says: As the pioneer of the business in Double Star, I am more concerned about the future of Double Star than anyone else. According to the rules of the market, the brand of Double Star will never fall. When one door closes, God will open another one. Wang's confidence stems from his Big Strategy of Double Star.

Double Star can develop quickly from a shoe factory that is on the verge of collapse to the largest shoe-based enterprise group in the world. It is largely due to the way the assets operate. By the operation of assets, Double Star, in a brief period and with less capital, optimized its product structure and adjusted its industrial structure; attracted and operated each party's assets through state-owned assets, thus obtaining the maximum benefit and reducing the risks of the enterprise. Mr. Wang summarized his business way as follows: **draw on others' strong points to overcome weakness of Double Star and integrate others' resources to develop Double Star**. In other words, Bi Strategy of Double Star include its going out the city and going to the countryside.

In 1996, the strategy was fully implemented. In the southwest, Double Star acquired Chengdu Hongqi (Red Flag) Rubber Factory which was about to close. After the acquisition, the Red Flag flied again. In North China, Double Star acquired Zhangjiakou Wuhuan Shoe Company, which was previously one of Three Tigers in North China and was lifeless at the time of acquisition. Afterwards, it revitalized. Acquisitions also were carried out by Double Star in the Central Plains, in the Northeast... At present, Double Star has 10 operating regions, more than 60 operating branches and more than 3,000 chain stores across the country. The assets of Double Stars in all regions are registered locally, and the one-stop services involving production, supply & sales are provided locally.

Mr. Wang says that Double Star has many operation regions, increases the total assets and reduce operational risks. As a saying goes: lose here, gain there. In case of Double Star in Qingdao falling, Double Star in Southwest and North China still survives. Why? First, its assets have been registered. Although my brand is used, the fundamental problem has been solved. Second, it has its own business network and factory. After operations are carried out in different regions, Double Star has largely reduced its risk. In this way, the problem of the successor, the problem of whether Double Star brand will fall, have been solved. Double Star will not fall! (*Source:* Economic Daily, October 2000)

IV. Expert Comments

The experience of many successful companies at home and abroad proves that an enterprise needs to have many factors to succeed. Among them, five factors are the most important: **system and mechanism; entrepreneur; enterprise culture; development strategy; and scientific management**. Although these five factors are very important, their respective status and role are different. Among them, **the system and mechanism are the premise, the foundation, the motivation; the entrepreneur is the commander; the enterprise culture is the soul; the development strategy is the guide; and the scientific management is the guarantee.**

Among these five factors, although the entrepreneur is in the position of commander-in-chief, it is difficult for him to run enterprises in full accordance with his own will, especially state-owned enterprises. He has complete control over the last three factors (enterprise culture, development strategy, and scientific management), but it is difficult for him to fully control the first factor (institutions and mechanisms). The reason is that the relationship between entrepreneurs and systems & mechanisms is like the relationship between a bird and a bird cage. Entrepreneurs are "birds", "systems and mechanisms" are "bird cages", and "birds" are difficult to escape the constraints of "bird cages." This is an important reason why many entrepreneurs can't bring their talent into full play in state-owned enterprises.

Of course, this is not to say that state-owned enterprises cannot run well, and this must not become "a shield" and "an amulet" for some so-called "entrepreneurs" who exercise poor leadership in state-owned enterprises. State-owned enterprises can run well, if entrepreneurs give full play to their own subjective initiative and reverse-thinking, dare to reform the old system and the old mechanism, dare to innovate, and establish a new system and mechanism that can adapt to the development of the market economy. For example, in the footwear industry, almost all state-owned enterprises have fallen, but Double Star is like the sun at high noon outshining others, realizes cross-industry development and grows into a famous brand at home and abroad. This fully proves **that ownership is not the decisive factor for a good business, and the determining factor is entrepreneurs. If entrepreneurs give full play to their subjective initiative and anti-thinking, state-owned enterprises not only have reasons to run well, but also is certainly be able to run well! Double Star Group led by Wang is one of the best examples**.

Then, with the same nature of the enterprise, the same system and mechanism, why almost all state-owned shoe-making enterprises went bankrupt, but Double Star can stand out alone? Wang says, "**There are many factors for our success, especially, our system and mechanism with unique characteristics of Double Star which adapt to the market play a key role. It can be said that without the reform of the system and mechanism for more than 30 years, there will be no today's brilliant Double Star**."

The reform of the system and mechanism including innovation carried out by Mr. Wang provides a successful example for the tough battle in the process of state-owned enterprise reform – how to correctly clarify the property rights of state-owned enterprises and to maximize the enthusiasm of employees while ensuring the preservation and appreciation of state-owned assets.

Tactic 5: The Leadership Is the Role Model

"Management should start from the leaders themselves. To do an excellent job in the leaders' management, improve the awareness and level of management for the leaders. In all the work, the leadership is the key. The leadership acting as a model is the best method of ideological and political work."

——Wang Hai

In the early 1980s, Wang Hai dismantled the old factory with the employees.

President Wang Hai traveled all over the factory to set an example for the employees.

President Wang Hai demonstrates the new operation method for employees in the production line and urges employees to improve their operation technology.

President Wang Hai goes deep into the market.

In the early 1980s, President Wang Hai learned about the situation at the store of Double Star.

President Wang Hai guides the work at the production site

I. Wang Hai Quotations

(I) Leaders must establish a correct management awareness

☆ Two eyes on the market, two hands on the management

☆ Take yourself as a backbone and feel good about yourself.

☆ No excuses for mistakes, more efforts on the brands

☆ Be responsible, be with a correct attitude

☆ Set a good example, self-discipline for development

☆ Enterprises can run well or be with incompetent leaders

☆ Enterprises may have outdated leaders but without outdated employees. The leaders should earnestly practice what they advocate.

☆ Only the leaders take the lead and set a good example to uphold righteousness, enhance cohesion, and bolster up the morale, can the enterprise maintain healthy and stable development.

☆ In all the work, the leadership is the key. The leadership is the best method in ideological and political work.

☆ Build excellent execution and enhance competitiveness of the enterprises.

(II) Understanding of relationships between reform and management, politics and economy

☆ No matter how good the system is, if leaders can't efficiently implement it (including links e.g., management, inspection & assessment), the enterprise will run poorly.

☆ Leaders at all levels, especially top leaders, should solve the problem of Two Skins in politics and economy. The factory director cannot ignore politics, brands, competition, and the life of employees. The party secretary can't ignore production, business, management, and consumption. The party secretary should also pay attention to production, management, competition, and assessment. While focusing on production and management, the factory director should care about the life of the employees and guide various competitions.

(III) Leaders should take the lead and set a good example

☆ Management should start from the leaders themselves. To do a good job in the leader's management, improve the awareness and level of management for the leaders.

☆ Management is s matter of leadership. Management should start from leaders themselves. Leaders should realize that they cannot stand outside the management circle. Leaders should set a good example in management. With rules and regulations, leaders should pay attention to the implementation, assessment, and reward and punishment.

☆ Market competition requires the leader to take the lead, requires the spirit and passion of Dare to Fight, and requires the courage and style of competition. Only leaders at all levels can make a new improvement, can all industries take a new step. The top leader should pay attention to development, production and market etc.

☆ System and mechanism is not the key to determining the development of an enterprise. The key to determining the quality of an enterprise is people, leaders, especially top leaders.

II. Practices and Effects

(I) Main practices

In Double Star, the leadership team with President Wang as the core, continuously strengthens its own construction. The main leaders are characterized by good ideas, good decision-making, penetration into the forefront of production and market, attention to operation, management, production, quality and development, good skills to manage production and sales. Therefore, the leaders establish their new image.

As the only outstanding entrepreneur still working in the forefront of the reform of state-owned enterprises, President

Wang has set a shining example for all leaders of the group. He has experiences of being a PLA man in the battlefield and a businessman in the market. With a sense of mission and responsibility and bold spirit (dare to enter the market, dare to seek truth from facts, dare to persist, dare to take risks, dare to practice, dare to make decisions), Mr. Wang has made Double Star a winner in each major change (including transformation, adjustment, and so forth) of the economic environment, where there are market competitions among state-owned enterprises, township enterprises, individual enterprises joint ventures and sole proprietorships.

1. Dare to enter the market

For the traditional Chinese, their goal is to be governmental officials with the disparagement of the market. After the entry into market, Mr. Wang found a big world. He was more confident on the road of the market. He was the first to feel the pulse and direction of market development. He was the first to realize the fierce and cruel competition in the market. He was the first to propose that the market was a battlefield where bloodshed could not be seen and that the entrepreneurs in the market were the generals on the battlefield. He was bold in the market. When encountering the obstacles set by his superiors, he did not yield to them. He dared to reform the enterprise with the requirements of the market as the standard; when being complained, rumored and even framed, he never gave up. He dared to make decisions based on the rules of the market, actively shifting, and paving the way into the market. He dared to adjust the product structure to provide the competitive products into the market. While not overstressing products, loans and opportunities or not using personal connections, Mr. Wang always adopted market-oriented operations instead of evading the market. With his insight and heroic spirit, he has become the most successful entrepreneur always at the forefront of the times.

2. Dare to seek the truth from facts

There is no model to follow for us to carry out reform and opening and taking the path of the socialist market economy with Chinese characteristics. In this new and complex era, many enterprises drifted along or were copycats or at a loss. In the reform process (in which an approach of crossing a river by feeling for the stones was adopted), President Wang adhered to the principle of seeking truth from facts -- the core of Marxism-Leninism, Mao Zedong Thought, Deng Xiaoping Theory, with his attitude which was not mechanical, rigid, dogmatic, bookish, and etc. He broke through the old thinking, old ideas, old theories, old frames, old systems, and old mechanisms of the planned economy, and re-established all things according to market standards. When the product backlog led to a desperate status, he resolutely led his staffs into the market. Where there were funds, he borrowed them or used external resources and implemented low-cost expansion. When there were surplus employees in enterprise adjustment, he insisted the path of diversified development. In contrast to the general employment system overstressing education degrees, diplomas, and overseas background, he had his own view of talent: selecting talents without restrictions and entering the market to cultivate talents; he provided opportunities and stages for all people at Double Star. When many entrepreneurs idolized theorists of Western management, he created a new system of management in Double Star with Chinese characteristics;

In the early days of the reform, while a lot of party members did not dare to talk about money, he boldly established the profit-pursuit goal for the enterprise. In the era putting money over everything else, he insisted on the clear view that the market economy should pay more attention to roles of the political work and the spirit. In the era of knowledge economy, while the high technology was worshiped, he calmly insisted that the manufacturing industry is suitable for actual conditions of China, because it can solve the problem of employment and let people get rid of poverty...He was realistic and found a solution in practice, thereby being a pragmatic entrepreneur greatly contributing to the development of national brands.

3. Dare to insist

In the market economy, President Wang put forward the principle of party spirit, personality, and humanity. At that time, the Nine plus Nine Management Method of Double Star was rejected to participate in the evaluation of excellent methods, he insisted on not participating in this evaluation and insisted on constantly improving the Chinese management theory. In the cooperation negotiations with foreign companies, he insisted on the bottom line of national brands without compromise. In the climate of all being adjusted by the interests, he insisted on patriotism education and communist education, constantly looking for gaps, carrying out self-education and self-improvement. In the era of being eager to invite entertainment starts as image spokespersons, he insisted that the entrepreneur is the best image spokesperson. When patriotism education became formalistic, he insisted on set up the statues of national heroes such as Yue Fei, Lin Zexu, Qi Jiguang and Yang Jingyu at the Double Star Resort, guiding employees to learn the spirit of national heroes, and truly integrating the motto (namely the creation of brands is the best patriotism) into the development of the enterprise. In the era of admiring foreign brands and consuming foreign luxury goods as fashion, he insisted that the thing of Chinese style is the best and insisted that we should create national brands that ordinary people can afford. These, reflecting his insight and national spirit, result in the unity, cohesiveness and combat effectiveness in Double Star. Therefore, he is an entrepreneur who insists on revitalizing national industry and developing national brands.

4. Dare to take risks

Reformers are adventurers. We did not recognize the market economy and private ownership in the past. When entering the market, we found everything was new. All the exploration and practice of the reformers were criticized, accused, rumored and framed by others. In the course of more than 30 years of state-owned enterprise reform, President Wang was repeatedly criticized, abused, complained and was given a number of unneeded titles (also called black hats). For example, he was called a lawless man who stealthily sold the shoes; due to the rectification of the enterprise at the beginning of the reform, he was called a gang leader; due to setting up a branch factory, he was called a man who overrated his own ability and wanted to be a senior official; due to leading the developers to go abroad for market investigation, he was called a man who enjoyed the landscape. Due to advocating the creation of national brand, he was called a mad man; due to sending shoes of Double Star to the central leadership to try on, he was called a bootlicker who hoped to get promotion. For more than 30 years, not being afraid of these, he persisted in reforms. Now, he receives a lot of honorary titles (also called red hats), symbolizing the continued prosperity of Double Star. Therefore, he is called an entrepreneur wearing a hat.

5. Dare to practice

In the state-owned enterprises, there are many factory directors or managers working for a lifetime. However, there is a very low number of factory directors or managers in a state-owned enterprise for a lifetime. President Wang serving Double Star for more than 30 years has become a witness, practitioner, pioneer, adventurer, survivor and winner in the entire process of reform and opening. He dares to create and practice, never gives up because of any resistances including accusations and complaints so forth. He never leaves forefronts of state-owned enterprise reform including production and market. He insists on paying attention to all things of the enterprise, taking the lead, and setting a good example. He insists on deployment, inspection, implementation, no matter how trivial they are. Most of his time, he stays in the factory and the market. For example, he often stays in workshop for four or five hours, during which he inspects everywhere, talks about the production affairs, and teaches the staffs. When getting off the car, he directly goes to the shop and the chain store hoping to understand all things taking place there. He sums up his own theories including various management methods in practice. In practice, he proposes major innovation projects, establishes product development goals, adjusts product structures and price systems, and understands employees. President Wang dares to practice, so that his heart and the hearts of employees are put together, forming an extraordinary personal charm and obtaining extraordinary prestige. All people at Double Star have elected him the lifetime president, while he modestly says that he is just a shoemaker. He comments on himself: For more than 30 years, I have cast two votes for myself: one vote meaning that I am an excellent Communist Party member of the market economy and the other vote meaning that I am a professional entrepreneur who enters the market instead of acting as a government official.

6. Dare to make decisions

President Wang dares to make bold decisions based on industry rules and market rules. Despite the pressure including being misunderstood, not recognized and not rejected, he dares to take responsibility and make decisions at every critical moment in development. In the early stage of enterprise development, when the setting of the joint venture was hindered, he decided to go out of town and go to the countryside, and this decision is earlier by 20 years than other entrepreneurs, leading to the development of both Double Star and Yimeng region. When he acquired Huaqing Tire, the local government set many difficulties for him; when he reorganized Dongfeng Tire, some of his superiors laid siege against him. He insisted that what he did was good for the development of the national tire industry and was regardless of personal safety. With the bold deeds, he won the admiration and trust of the employees. When Double Star brand entered the high-end market, he encountered the mad veto of the vested interests and was subjected to the heavy resistance of the old thinking and old habits; but he dared to make decisions and adopted measures conductive for the long-term development of Double Star, including rationalizing the operation and adjusting the structure the like. Therefore, he created a new situation in the high-end market operations. To control China's rapid development, developed countries carried out the technical barriers, anti-dumping sanctions and suppression. Chinese enterprises faced with the competition from multinational groups and suffered brand exploitation. In this case, he dared to make decisions, changed business modes, brought his Double Shoes Linkage into full play, and expanded the domestic and international markets. As a result, Double Star maintained steady growth in the crisis.

In the practice of nearly 40 years, President Wang has his bold spirit to make Double Star (as the old state-owned enterprise in manufacturing field) one of rarely seen long-lived enterprises, while being always active at forefront of the enterprise in the economic transition period as a long-life entrepreneur. The brilliant achievements of President Wang have been widely recognized by all walks of life and international organizations. He has successively won the following titles: national excellent management personnel, May 1 Labor Medal, national labor model, one of first batch of outstanding entrepreneurs nationwide, young and middle-aged management personnel with outstanding contributions, one of top ten poverty alleviation champions nationwide, one of 100 models in Shandong Province in the 60 years of the founding of the People's Republic of China, Fiver Thousand Personalities of the World (1993), World Man of the

Year (1995), and etc. He is only one Chinese diplomatic entrepreneur with most unique characteristics in the large-scale documentary film Diplomatic Records of P.R.C.

He fulfilled the duties of national entrepreneurs with the qualities of thinkers, politicians, strategists, and philosophers. The courage, insight and resourcefulness of entrepreneurs embody the boldness and wisdom of a decision maker, making him indisputably an iconic figure in the representative group in the history of reform and opening of China. It is obvious to all that he has set a banner in the transformation of China's traditional manufacturing and processing industry from a planned economy to a market economy. He has become a model in the development process with market economy and national industries of China.

(II) Main Effects

1. Cultivating an Iron-style cadre team that can win in a hard-fought battle

The most direct effect of leaders taking a lead and setting a good example is that Double Star cultivates a Iron-style cadre team with high awareness, excellent quality, strong skills, and good style. With this team, Double Star becomes a large-scale enterprise group that can produce high-quality products and provide excellent services; also a large school for cultivating excellent management talents. A large number of employees who came out of the countryside, through the education and training in this large school, have quickly grown into the cadres at all levels and embarked on leadership positions at various levels. Some subsidiaries including Luzhong are called Whampoa Military Academy of Double Star Group. The cadres cultivated from Double Star are very capable and invincible at any posts and units, resulting in the fact that the bosses in shoe companies of South Korea and Taiwan want him to give them talents from Double Star.

2. Creating national brand Double Star being famous at home and abroad

Under the leadership team with Mr. Wang as the core, Double Star has become a multi-industry, cross-regional and large-scale enterprise group in the manufacturing and processing industry, which is a shining national brand and winning the honors for the Chinese and the Chinese nation.

III. Typical Examples

(1) Mr. Wang taking the lead and setting a good example

Mr. Wang takes the lead and set a good example, which moves the employees. When coming to Double Star Tire in Qingdao, he stayed in the workshop for four to five hours. He said, "I strive to win the honor for Double Star. With the good spirit, we can realize the goal."

To change the enterprise's appearance as soon as possible and improve the management level, President Wang led the group leaders into the workshop of Double Star Qingdao Tire Corporation. He stayed there for a long time: passing on his management skills to the grass-roots cadres and talking with them about the theories of Double Star. To solve the existing problems, President Wang often worked on the spot and took the lead in proposing ideas on the development of the tire company. He worked day and night, and carried out the in-depth inspection of the workshop, so he was very familiar with every corner of it. Only the speech by him on the affairs of the tire company has been complied into instructional documents of nearly 500,000 words. It can be said that he has passed on all his experiences on working in the market for more than 30 years to Double Star Tire. It is under the influence of him that lets more than 5,000 employees of Double Star Tire appreciate his celebrity style, his courage and enthusiasm, and the great power of his theories created for Double Star, his broad thinking (including reverse thinking in the market), his outstanding ability in making decisions and winning by surprise. It is his personal charisma that deeply influences, guides and encourages the cadres and workers of Double Star Tire, achieving an unprecedented new leap and ushering in a new spring of the development of Double Star Tire brand. Under his leadership, Double Star Tire achieved remarkable results created a miracle only after two years.

Under the leadership of President Wang, Double Star Tire has carried out a few management cadre training courses, which involve in thinking, working style, ideas, theories, and which let trainees recognize themselves and actual conditions, find and analyze problems using theories. Through these training courses, cadres remember the painful lessons in the market, enhance market and brand awareness, thereby firmly establishing the awareness of all work centering around the market in the depths of the mind.

When President Wang went to Double Star Dongfeng for inspection in October 2005. When coming to the bias tire rolling workshop, he found a rolling equipment originally imported from Germany. He carefully examined the details of its process. He climbed the stair. Although it was narrow and very steep, his steps were vigorous and steady. He came to the platform for the second floor. From the platform, he, with other accompanying cadres, observed the upper part of the rolling machine (calendar), which was never so treated in the past. After his careful observation, he pointed out the details to be noted. One of accompanying cadre later said that employees who had worked in this workshop for more than ten years never came to this platform and made such observation in the past, and that Mr. Wang was the first to examine this machine from the platform. It is Mr. Wang who promotes the rapid improvement of various management levels.

With his insight and innovation, Double Star sets up a Chinese-style, market-oriented development path, and breaks constraints of the planned economy, with the change of ideas from Begging for Food to Actively Looking for Food; finally completing the entire process from the planned economy to the market economy and creating the Double Star brand of which all people at Double Star. Thanks to his significant contribution, Mr. Wang always supported and loved by employees. Employees wrote a slogan in the workshop: "President, thank you for your hardworking!" This truly reflects their deep feeling for him.

(2) Leaders of Luzhong: role model

President Wang says that after the group's political and economic work conference, all units have changed in terms of technology upgrading, management innovation, process reform, buyout contracting, and deepening internal shareholding system, all of which are improving. Especially, Luzhong has implemented the deployment of the group in a faster, more comprehensive, and more decisive manner (including some innovative projects). It has summarized some experiences and practices in the reform of system and mechanism (including buyout contracting). Mr. Wang says that we should learn from it.

1. Leader: Being compliant & serious, and taking the lead

Luzhong has the largest scale, the highest number of employees and the biggest adjustment amplitude among our vulcanized shoe factories. As a unit setting a good example for a long time, to keep its larger step forward was an intense pressure for general manager Xing Yifeng. She followed the group's deployment, played the core role of the team, spent a heroic effort on management, led the members of the team to take the lead, fully implement the group's decision-making, set off a wave of all-staff innovation. Therefore, she and her colleagues kept ahead in the group concerning the refinement of the internal contracted shareholding system, innovation, technical upgrading, system & mechanism reform so forth. In the zero-distance transformation of the group, Luzhong was the first to realize a zero-distance suspension line with a length of 2,620 meters and a height of 16 meters. In the management of the internal contracted shareholding system, it was the first to carry out the operation of the factory currency and a buyout of single-type material. In the innovation project (cold binding changed into hot binding), it was the first to adopt the hot binding (instead of cold) in the sponge, foxing, toe cap, and welt strip; this was an innovative technology replacing the old one which had been used for more than 100 years. In particularly, under the grim situation of the shoe and apparel export in this year, the export of some units dropped drastically, but Luzhong did not due to its production development, price adjustment, and increased domestic sales. Why can Luzhong stand out? The reason is that Xing Yifeng is serious, compliant, responsible, and fully implements the policies of our groups.

2. Leader: decisive and strong in implementation

First, the leaders should be stalwart in implementing the strategic decisions of our group which are made after in-depth investigations. For example, Xing Yifeng implemented my decision most resolutely. If she had time, she went to the scene, encouraging employees, teaching how to do, and giving assistance in investigation. As a result, she got a good result. This proves that every job depends on the determination and implementation of the leadership, because large innovation projects will encounter various problems in the implementation process. These problems cannot be solved by simply relying on the vice president, engineers and operator; instead, they require the leaders to do the reasonable arrangement, so that all relevant staffs and leaders work together. We should learn from Xing Yifeng who always does a good job in implementation of the president's decisions.

Second, be efficient in work. To do an excellent job, we should be efficient rather than procrastinate, and we should never give up halfway. Today's success of Luzhong is due to its efficient implementation of the assignments from the president. It realized the hot bonding of top caps and welt strips in a brief time, because I told Xing Yifeng 20 days ago that they should make a breakthrough in this based on the hot bonding in the sponge and the foxing. During the process of making this breakthrough, she and her colleagues faced with hardships such as the narrow space of the workshop in which the large-scale auxiliary equipment could not be used. While debugging, her team run a pilot production. The old process (that is, manually cutting the large sole) was eliminated, at the same time, the new process used, that is, the large sole was directly sent to the molding line for the hot bonding. Therefore, we should follow the example of Mrs. Xing who is compliant, efficient, and innovative in the work.

The third is to be strong in awareness. Awareness is instructive and directional. It consists of two aspects: On the one hand, it refers to humanity's character, morality, and attitude toward work. For example, while being compliant, serious, and responsible, Xing Yifeng does not strain at a gnat and swallow a camel. If she wants to scrape by in the enterprise, namely, if she just wants to retire after a few more years, then could not do an excellent job. On the other hand, it refers to the awareness of taking the initiative to adjust the product structure and price. Different from other factories, Luzhong not only undertakes domestic sales, but also undertakes export sales; not only produces high-grade products, but also produces low-grade products. Xing Yifeng personally manages the product structure adjustment and actively adjusts according to market changes. In this respect, both shoe factories - Luzhong and Zhongyuan - are the best. It is precisely because these two factories actively adjust the product structure and reasonably set prices, the sales of our vulcanized shoes grow rapidly regardless of the following circumstances: the wholesale network being gradually shrunk, and both the retail market product system and price system being unfavorable. Therefore, we should learn from Xing Yifeng who takes initiative to adjust the product structure and price.

3. Leader: attention still paid after a contracting or sale

I proposed that, "The contracting is the best method of management. In 2011, the internal contracting shareholding system will be fully adopted." While actively carrying out it, Luzhong paid attention after a contracting or sale. On the one hand, they specially held an on-site meeting for the problem that the boiler house contracting effect was not obvious. At that time, Liu Yi, the director of the factory, requested that the coal index of the boiler house should be reduced by 0.5 kilograms in this year than the last year. In March and April, 7500 kg of coal was saved, so proving that a good result can be obtained after a contracting which leads to a working-hard cadre. On the other hand, after the upper factory carried out the single-type material buyout, it always insisted on the high requirements on each indicator and insisted on the reward or punishment was accordingly meted out. Cutting worker Li Guangxing abandoned the traditional trapezoidal knife arrangement from left to right, instead, it adopted various forms of knife arrangement according to the actual needs, not only creating benefits for the enterprise, but also increasing personal income. Luzhong promoted timely the use of this new method, which played a better promontory role. Therefore, contacting and buyout are just a management method. If the management is continuously carried out after a contracting or buyout, the effect will be better. The inspection and assessment are as far as the outside world is concerned, and the enterprise is more vigorous.

4. Leader: constantly innovating and adjusting

The success of any innovation project does not mean that it will never change but will be constantly adjusted as the product and market need change. Although Luzhong has created several modern technologies and new processes such as chaining and hot bonding, it is not satisfied. Instead, it constantly improves and adjusts them to be more in line with production practice. In the shoe industry, the glue always was spread by a brush. Luzhong looked for many ways to develop the automatic glue spreader, but it was not yet successful after three years. I dialed a telephone many times to told its people that they should break the old thinking and suggested that whether they could replace the brush with two rollers. They got a good result. They made continuous improvements through different tests, including changes of angle and rollers. Finally, the best result was obtained by the brush removed fully. I don't ask your supervisor to reach my level, but he should follow my intentions to guide the key employee in continuous changes. Further, the adjustment is needed, which depends on our key employee, contractor, and first-line operator. For the key employee, if he wants to do an excellent job, he should be good at thinking, diligent, and intuitive. I appeal to all of you to learn from the people at Luzhong who are never satisfied, constantly surpass themselves. Only all of us, including top leaders, common cadres, key employees and general employees, are highly spirited, can we launch the people's war of innovation in the commercial warfare.

5. Leader: Enhancing the management in various aspects

The implementation of the internal contracted shareholding system leads to the following changes: letting key employees shareholders (who only received wages in the past); letting employees working more passionately; earning money from the external market instead of internal. Practice has proved that from the contracting to the buyout, from the inside to the outside, this unique management mode of Double Star is in line with the development of the market and is successful. We should move it forward and let the units that can operate independently go to the market. I advocate internal invigoration, but it must not be fouled up. For a new company, no matter what ownership structure is adopted, it must be absolutely controlled, because it has a solid backing from Double Star and runs under the Double Star brand. It is necessary to protect overall interests for the group and employees. This is a basic principle. Don't think that the management is no longer needed, and this is a wrong idea. Therefore, the management cannot be relaxed in Double Star Qingdao Tire and Double Star Dongfeng Tire which are bought out.

6. Leader: Feelings, passion and enthusiasm

Luzhong has made great achievements since the leaders and key employees have feelings for the company, the president, and the common employees, work hard and propose clever ideas. For example, it designed a fashionable women's shoes. I heard that Qingdao held a product ordering fair, and shoes not yet vulcanized (due to time being urgent) were ordered. This situation never took place before. We know that manufacturing and processing industry is labor intensive and requires workers to be quite laborious. We need a backbone team with passion, enthusiasm, dedication, not afraid of suffering and tiredness, to lead the staff, so as to overcome difficulties and solve any problems. It is also proved that the direction of combining corporate culture with production and management is correct. If we persist in this way, I believe that Double Star will be always a winner. *(Source: Speech by Wang at Double Star Group's January-April 2011 Work Reporting and Exchange Meeting.)*

(3) Innovative problems solved in 34 hours in a row

From 11:00 pm on June 9 to 9:00 am on June 11, 2011, a group of people at Double Star finally solved all problems of innovation and completed the upgrading of the equipment. These people, who never gave up, totally spent 34 hours a row. Such a brief time (that is, 34 hours) spent on solving innovation issues and technical improvement, vividly reflects the good spirit from people at Double Star who always work efficiently...

At 10:00 pm, June 9, President Wang came to the headquarters of Double Star Qingdao Tire for inspection. He proposed the requirements on the upgrading project of the hot bonding at the side wall and the inner liner. In accordance with his instructions, the leadership team of Double Star Qingdao Tire attached immense importance to this project and went into action immediately. Management personnel and key employees responded quickly and adopted more measures. After working hard for 34 hours without letup, problems were finally overcome, and the new technology emerged. These diligent people marked the 90th anniversary of Double Star with a great result obtained through their innovation spirit.

Birth of modern technology: efficiency doubled

"You carry forward the innovative spirit of the team of Double Star (namely, Four Combinations) and possess the innovative attitude (that is, completing tasks as soon as possible). After 34 hours of working hard, you created a unique modern technology for Double Star. I hope you continue to work hard in the improvement and innovation, so as to create more miracles for Double Star..."

In the morning of June 11, when President Wang came again to No.1 Radical Tire Plant. He delivered the above speech to affirm the innovation and upgrade project completed in a brief period. This project, which was completed in a brief time through the sweat and effort with participators, that is, 34 hours, reflects their wisdom and strength. Behind these are the manifestations of Double Star spirit of Daring to Think, Daring to Do, and Never Give Up. Truly, people at Double Star always unite and work hard toward their common goals.

On June 9, soon after Mr. Wang' visit to No.1 Radical Tire Plant, Bing Liangguang general manager of Double Star Qingdao Tire led Zhang Li and Zhou Shifeng as two deputy general managers to hold an on-the-spot meeting, to discuss the transformation plan. Key employees attended it, innovative ideas and measures were proposed. Plant directors Zhang Guodong, Jin Boguo and Liu Hanjun took the initiative to do an excellent job. The cadres of production, equipment and tech worked together and supported each other. Technician Wang Hongkai and worker Chai Fangshun were responsible for improvement and debugging. Frontline employees Liu Zhaorong and Chen Mingxia were encouraged when seeing leaders at all levels who took the lead; and took the initiative to work overtime, to be helpful in the debugging. In this way, more than ten people cooperated with a joint effort for the sake of solving problems and were busy all the time. This night, no one left the scene. On their tired face was a pair of bloodshot eyes still shining with a spirit of never giving up. In the process of overcoming difficulties, the leaders rolled up their sleeves to help them debug and solve problems one by one, including those occurring in the changes of equipment, processes and operations. After more than 20 trials, two side walls were extruded except 11.00R20 and 12.00R20; which was perfectly matched with the online hot bonding of the inner liner. Therefore, the modern technology finally emerged! This new technology of Double Star has doubled labor productivity.

Improvement to ensure favorable effect

"Every innovation project needs to concentrate on the wisdom and strength of the team. There should be a clear goal for innovation. It is necessary to find problems, find gaps and ensure the best use effect in the improvement process..." In the early stage of innovation, the company appealed all people to write a pledge. Immediately, they went into action and solve the problem as soon as possible. For example, when testing the online hot-bonding project of the sidewall and inner liner, the compaction effect after compounding was not good. Equipment manager Zheng Shibin led Cui Guirong and Liu Jianye and others in solving it by tracking and improving the press fit. While supported by the company and leaders, they were not afraid of hardships, worked overtime for 20 hours. While improving the press-fit direction of the roller, they successively completed several tasks: installation of the roller and improvement of the screw adjustment device etc. After two improvements and four installations, the combination of the sidewall and inner liner achieved a good press-fit effect, which laid a solid quality foundation for the successful completion of the inner liner hot-bonding project.

34 hours of hardworking to solve the innovation problem, once again boost the morale for people at Double Star with the spirit of bravely overcoming difficulties; forges a new team of innovation personnel who are brave, courageous and not afraid of challenges; and creates an innovation miracle. *(Source: Double Star Newspaper in 2011)*

VI. Expert Comments

Mao Zedong pointed out long ago, "**After the political line is determined, the cadre is the determining factor.**" (Mao Zedong: The Position of the Chinese Communist Party in the National War, Selected Works of Mao Zedong, Vol. 2, p. 514). While being aimed at the great cause of the party and the nation, this is applicable for enterprises. As far as an enterprise is concerned, the political line refers to the development. To run well the enterprise, we need the right strategy and cadres. So, how should we properly handle the relationship between the two?

First, it is necessary to develop a development strategy. At this stage, whether the enterprise's development strategy can be formulated properly plays a decisive role in the success of the enterprise.

Jack Trout, a US strategic consulting guru, said, "**I worked at General Electric in the early years and then contacted hundreds of companies in the United States and around the world, so I was fortunate enough to understand the key to**

business success. I have understood more than once that success does not come from the right people, the right attitude, the right tools, the right models, and the right organization. These factors help the company succeed, which must be guided in the right direction. I think, Success is to find the right strategy." ([United States] Jack Trout: "What is Strategy", China Financial and Economic Publishing House, October 2004, "Foreword", page 1) What Jack Trout said here is the focus of the company's work when the company has not yet found the correct development strategy.

Second, after the company has developed a correct development strategy, we should emphasize the leadership role of the cadres. At this stage, whether the leading role of cadres can be played well, and whether the strategies formulated can be implemented, will play a decisive role in running well the enterprise.

World-renowned management experts Larry Bosidy and Ram Charan said, **"The strategy is good. If it is not implemented efficiently, it can't achieve the desired goal. The grand idea not turned into reality is useless. The breakthrough thought not implemented is a cranky thought. The knowledge not applied does not bring real value. If the goals cannot be achieved, the so-called revolutionary change will be not successful."** ([United States] Larry Bosidy and Ram Charan: Execution – The Discipline of Getting Things Done, Mechanical Industry Press, January 2003, p. 16).

In Double Star Group, the development strategy is personally formulated by President Wang. Therefore, for most leading cadres, the main task is to unswervingly implement the development strategy. At this point, the leading cadres of Double Star are not only aware of it, but also have handed over a very good answer in action.

Tactic 6: The Innovation Is the Vigor

Innovation is the eternal theme of market competition, the soul and driving force of the development of Double Star, and the magic weapon of the success in the market. In the market competition, only innovation can lead to development, and only innovation can lead to advancement. Not innovating today, we will fall behind tomorrow; not innovating tomorrow, we will be eliminated the day after tomorrow. Without innovation, we will be put in the passive position of having to receive blows. Without innovation, we will be boxed into a corner.

—— Wang Hai

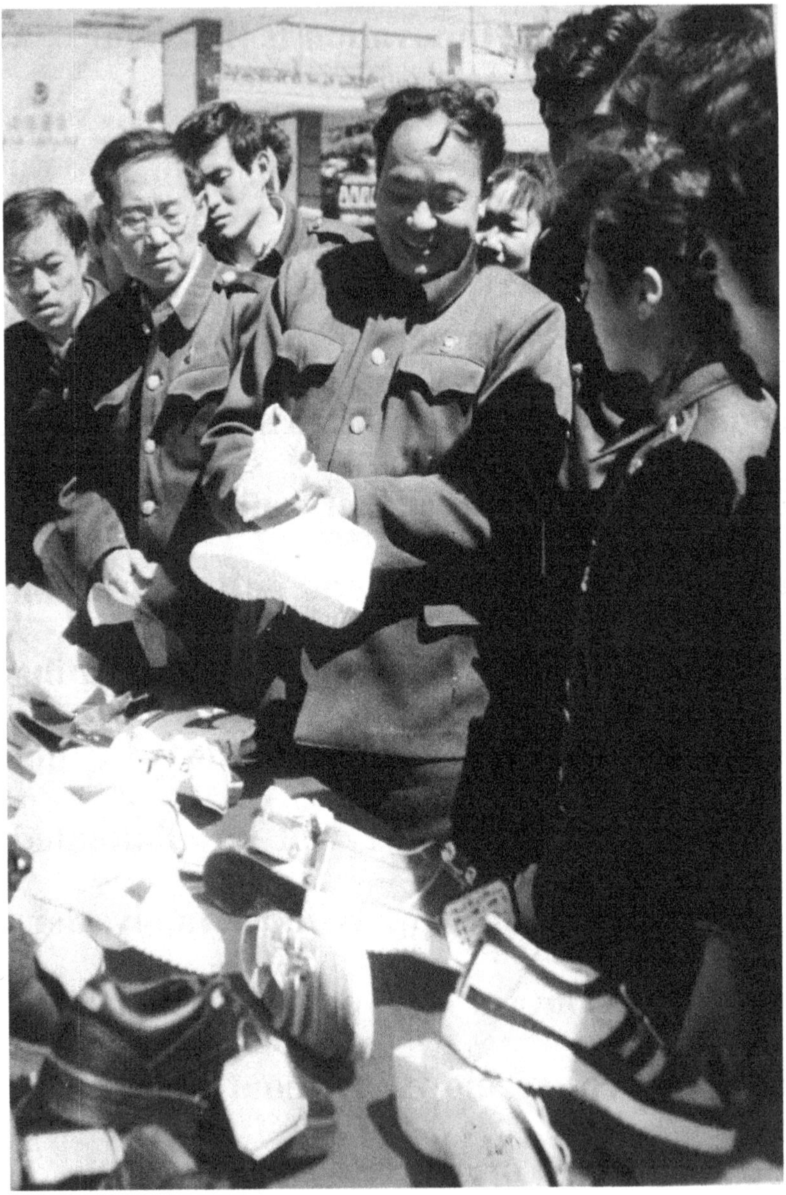

Innovation is the source of the development of Double Star. In the first new product design competition of Double Star in 1989, President Wang, who was director then time, personally participated in the selection and voting.

Double Star Designer Grand Prix

Double Star holds an annual summary and exchange & commendation meeting to encourage employees to constantly innovate.

Double Star has been recognized as the only national technology development center and footwear testing center in the national footwear industry, thereby marking the new height of the shoe technology in Double Star. The picture shows the location of the Double Star Technology Center.

Double Star developed the first colorful tire saying goodbye the history of black tires in the past 100 years, which was released into the market in 2011.

The world's most advanced intelligent automatic hydraulic double-mode vulcanizing machine is developed by Double Star Machinery.

I. Wang Hai Quotations

(I) Great significance of innovation

☆ Innovation is the foundation and guarantee of the success of Double Star. the soul and driving force of the development of Double Star. Without innovation, there is no Double Star brand.

☆ Innovation is the only way for enterprises to survive and develop. Innovation is the most powerful weapon for market success. Innovation is the eternal theme of market competition.

☆ Not innovating today, we will fall behind tomorrow; not innovating tomorrow, we will be eliminated the day after tomorrow.

☆ In the development of the enterprise, we will be in the active position through innovation, and passive without innovation.

(II) Objects and tasks of innovation

☆ Ideas of market development at Double Star: The market is the best development department and the largest sample room.

☆ The position is the market; the competition is on the machine station; all staffs participate in innovation and achieve a result.

☆ The zero defect is achieved through the innovation in equipment, process, and management.

☆ All staffs actively engage in innovation, no matter which position or no matter which field.

☆ Initiating the people's war in innovation

☆ The market is the driving force for technological progress, and technology is the magic weapon for market competition.

☆ Technical types: R & D technology, process technology, management technology, and operation technology

(III) Key to innovation success

☆ Reverse thinking is the beginning of success. Reverse thinking can create miracles.

☆ Innovation is not related with age and education, the key is to be willing to think.

☆ The hardest thing to stick to is seriousness, the most terrible thing is no creativity.

☆ All-staff innovation, comprehensive innovation, whole-process innovation, all-round innovation

(IV) How can we do an excellent job in innovation?

☆ Follow the market, pay attention to the market, and change with the market.

☆ Look at the problem with an innovative perspective and analyze the problem with innovative thinking.

☆ To break the Five Olds and establish the Four News, that is, to break old concepts, old ideas, old traditions, old frames, old methods; to establish new thinking, new concepts, innovative ideas, new practices.

☆ Joint innovation, team innovation, cooperative innovation, innovation together; eliminate the backward production capacity, and embody innovative ideas, new spirits, new looks.

II. Practices and Effects

(I) Main practices

The market economy always changes. For more than 30 years, Double Star has realized its innovation in theory, idea, target, mode, organization, and so forth; created a new phenomenon, thereby being at a leading position in innovation.

1. Theoretical innovation

Double Stars has eliminated the old thinking that did not attach importance to innovation, and has proposed the following mottoes on theoretical innovation: "Innovation is the foundation and guarantee of success for Double Star, and innovation is the soul and power of development for Double Star", " Not innovating today, we will fall behind tomorrow; not innovating tomorrow, we will be eliminated the day after tomorrow",

"Innovation is the most powerful weapon for market success", " The position is the market, the competition is on the machine station; all staffs participate in innovation and achieve a result", "Dare to image, dare to change, and dare to give suggestions". These mottoes are aimed to encourage and promote innovation. Under theoretical guidance, people at Double Star understand that innovation is a key factor in participation of enterprises in competition. With innovation theories, people at Double Star have stepped into a new world of innovation which is soulful and directional.

2. All-staff innovation

People at Double Star breaks the mystery of innovation and eliminates the old thinking (namely innovation has nothing to do with them). They say that everyone can innovate, everyone will innovate, and everyone must innovate. In Double Star, the method of operation in case of being even slightly improved by an operator can be named after the operator. Double Stars has realized the all-staff innovation, including management personnel, engineers and technicians, and operators; this is people's war in the innovation field, and with the innovation spirit, its people dare to think, dare to do, and dare to be innovative so forth, therefore letting the impossible become possible. Every year, several thousands of rationalization proposals are made by the employees, which create economic benefits of 100 million Yuan. This is a new phenomenon in Double Star: all-staff innovation, comprehensive innovation, whole-process innovation, all-round innovation.

3. Team innovation

The cross-industry innovations and those in large-scale projects require team cooperation. Based on the all-staff innovation, Double Star advocates team innovation, joint innovation, cooperative innovation, and bundled innovation to overcome problems in large-scale projects. Double Star Tire and

Double Star Adhesive worked together to develop an all-steel tire film release agent.

Double Star Vulcanized Shoe and Double Star Cold-adhesive Shoe jointly carried out the innovation to overcome the bonding problem of new materials and successfully completed the export task of high-grade vulcanized skateboard shoes.

The innovation of zero-distance in process in Double Star Tire and Double Star Shoe is the result of strong cooperation in different fields such as technology, process and equipment, creating an industry-leading process. The team innovation has brought about a new phenomenon of all units of Double Star working together in large projects.

4. Being brilliant

In the past, Double Star only produced Jiefang Shoes. In more than 30 years later, Double Star has shifted from imitation to innovation, gradually established its own R&D team and created the only national-level technology center in China's footwear industry. In shoes and tires, Double Star has completed its technological revolution from cold to hot in rubber material, saying goodbye to the old process. Double Star has developed shoes for Shenzhou 6, Shenzhou 7, and Shenzhou 9 spaceships.

Double Star Tire has changed the history of One Tire Being Generally Used in China's tire industry by developing specially purposed tires, including Three Kings, anti-puncture tires etc. Double Star Tire provided shoes used for the National Day military parade for the 60th anniversary of the founding of New China. Double Star has changed the history of black tires that lasted for more than 100 years with innovation and strength and created the core technology of color tires belonging to itself and Chinese people. The successful development of color tires and their successful release in the market have led the world tire industry into a new era.

Double Star Machinery has developed the first horizontal type molding machine in China, equipped with special cleaning equipment for shoes used in spaceships such as Shenzhou 6, Shenzhou 7 and Chang'e II. With independent tech R & D and design, Double Star has ushered in a new era with the diversified, specialized, and serialized products and technologies etc.

5. Innovation having penetrative effects

Double Star takes advantage of the coexistence of multiple industries and proposes innovative ideas that various industries should learn from each other and carry out penetrative innovations. The penetration among four processes (vulcanization, cold bonding, leather shoes, injection) led to the birth of a vulcanized anti-static cold-adhesive shoes.

Inspired by industry of shoes, Double Star Tire produces multi-color trademark tires, saying goodbye to the history that Chinese tires could not produce multi-color trademarks.

Double Star Shoe and Double Star Tire promote each other, realizing the zero distance in processes, eliminating unnecessary procedures such as carrying, pulling, lifting and the like, and creating the production line which is most efficient.

Double Star Machinery develops unique four-mode vulcanizers and multi-function molding machines. It can be said that units and departments in Double Star learn from each other, complement each other, and cooperate in innovation.

6. Comprehensive innovation

People at Double Star have created the follows: a new theory of the market; a new concept that brands are the main line for the ideological and political work; new theories, new methods and new models of enterprise management; a new marketing system integrating factory, logistics platform, chain operation as a whole; a new realm of brand marketing, emotional marketing, experiential marketing and cultural marketing; a new standard of 200% service. The innovation ideas of Double Star cover theoretical innovation, political innovation, management innovation, technological innovation, operation innovation, market innovation, and service innovation.

People at Double Star break the old habit of blindly admiring foreign experts and worshiping foreign products and put forward the motto that people at Double Star are as capable as foreigners in the manufacturing field. People at Double Star cracked the secret codes with the computer control procedures from the Germans; changed the single-purpose lathe into a universal lathe; repaired the equipment that was claimed by the Japanese to be repair impossibly; broke the mystery of the Dutch equipment that could not be repaired; boldly transformed the imported equipment(as a result, a Germany-made injector stored in museum could be used again).

Under the grim situation of raw material and labor prices constantly rising, people at Double Star realized the leap from Manufacturing of Double Star to Creation of Double Star: total assets increasing from less than 10 million Yuan to 6 billion Yuan; sales revenue increasing from less than 30 million Yuan to 12 billion Yuan; foreign exchange earned from exports increasing from 1.75 million US dollars to 300 million US dollars; annual income of employees continuing to grow; sustainable development in innovation.

(II) Main effects

1. Innovation lets theoretical culture management reach a new level

The most fundamental thing in market competition is culture. Cultural innovation is the most important innovation. Double Star attaches great importance to theoretical innovation, cultural management, and concept management, and proposes many new decisions, new theories, new cultures, and new targets, new ideas, and new requirements that are distinctive and conductive to the development of Double Star as well as are proven to be correct and effective. For example, in the development strategy, Double Star puts forward a series of new goals and new theories: Five pillar industries and eight major industries should be big and strong, and cast brands; Double Star should be built to last; Double Star should become a large-scale group in the manufacturing and processing field.

2. Innovation brings recent changes in the quality of leadership work

Double Star attaches immense importance to the quality of work of leaders at all levels, and the training of managers. With the change and improvement in their awareness, leaders and management cadres take the lead in innovation. There is a lower number of staffs who are with a passive attitude on innovation; who stand outside the circle of innovation; who are against the innovation work; who make irresponsible or sarcastic comments about the innovation; who are conservative and rigid in ideas. There is a higher number of staffs who take the lead in innovation; who take the initiative to innovate; who support and guide the innovation; who take innovation as the instincts of the leaders. Double Star has formed a good atmosphere: all-staff innovation, encouragement of innovation, being proud of innovation, fault-tolerance in innovation etc.

3. Innovation brings new vigor to system and mechanism

The innovation of system and mechanism determines the development vigor of enterprises. Double Star constantly make changes in its system and mechanism. For example, innovations have been made in the management system of the tire company: separation of tire and machinery; independent accounting of their own profits and losses; machinery company and so forth attached to tires in the past being pushed into market. Another example is that the incentive mechanism is used to let innovation and job competition closely linked, stimulate the enthusiasm of employees to participate in innovation, and unearth the enormous innovation potential in employees.

4. Innovation makes management work leap to a new level

In the on-site management, all units of Double Star have taken a new step. For example, Double Star Qingdao Tire changes the old concept that the tire is dirty and messy and that the mixing workshop is black and dark. A thorough revolution in tire site management is carried out, and the profound change in on-site management of the tire company takes place. Double Star Tire has a new image. These reflect the excellent quality in management and the new spirit of employees. It is highly praised by domestic and foreign customers and leaders at all levels.

5. Innovation brings technological improvement

Mr. Wang puts forward, "The reverse thinking is used to carry out destructive innovation and cause a revolutionary change." According his requirements, Double Star breaks the old rules and regulations: carrying out bold tests and bold innovation in transformation of old formulae, old technology, old equipment etc.; broadening the new horizons and new fields in technology; and achieving new technical results. Double Star has realized innovation of traditional technologies such as bonding (now hot bonding instead of cold bonding), rubber material not passing water, and tire production over floor etc. Double Star represents the level of Chinese enterprises.

6. Innovation brings a new situation in market operations

Each unit of Double Star makes its comprehensive innovation in the management system, operation mechanism, operation ideas, operation methods, and operation policies. For example, according to the market needs, Double Star Tire pays attention to market segments, spends greater effort on the development of supporting market, export market, terminal networks, and spends heroic effort on research and development of special products; thereby obtaining an obvious effect. There is a great adjustment in the market for shoes and apparel: that is, the factory operation is changed into the main area and platform operation. The reform is completely carried out in the apparel unit. In the shoes and apparel operations, a good result is initially achieved in bringing advantages into full play. There is a momentous change in ideas of operation in the machinery market, that is, a change from products alone to brand, technology and service as a whole. At the same time, the scale advantage of shoe-tire linkage plays a key role in promoting the development of domestic and international markets and enhances the comprehensive competitiveness of the market.

7. Innovation makes political work find new ways

Mr. Wang puts forward mottos: Political work is market-oriented, realistic, concrete, and humanized; it is necessary to use market theory to unite people, mobilize people, inspire people, and invigorate people. According to his requirements, the units of Double Star take the problems of production and operation as the focus of political work, explore new ways in the innovation of political work, and create a new situation in political work that is characterized by the broad participation and self-education of workers. All units use comics as a simple education method to show theories, spirits, and achievements of innovation; and make several innovations in combination with the actual discussion, including talks, speeches, knowledge contests, cultural performances and etc.

III. Typical Examples

(1) Adhere to independent innovation & build independent brands

—— Special brands of Double Star

All enterprises that are built to last have their independent brands. Over the past 30 years of reform and opening, Double Star Group cherishes its own brand, pays attention to independent technology, attaches importance to independent innovation, insists on expanding and strengthening its own brand,

and has evolved from a single shoe industry to a five-pillar industry (five pillars being shoes, tires, clothing, machinery and thermo-electrical products). Double Star has four brands famous nationwide (traveling shoes, sports shoes, leather shoes, and all-steel radial tires), the first brand (famous nationwide) in the footwear industry. Double Star exports products to more than 140 countries and regions around the world and are well known in the international market. Its brand value exceeds 49.292 billion Yuan.

Cherishes its own brands

Mr. Wang believes that Double Star brand is the total symbol of Double Star in technology, and the brand is high-tech of high-tech. The technical standard of Double Star is to become the support of the brand, realize independent innovation, have market competitiveness, to be recognized by the market, and to have economic benefits in practice testing.

Double Star has also experienced OEM production in the development process. In the early 1990s, at the beginning of the OEM production, Double Star set the following goals: imitation then innovation; becoming a global leading enterprise; casting its own brands. During the OEM production of PONR and Brooks, Double Star established a high-level and professional R&D team, achieved the co-existence for generations of products in research, development, production and storage; designed and installed the first high-end cold-adhesive shoe line in China; established the first national-level technology research and development center in the national shoe industry. After continuous development, Double Star has gradually acquired ability to compete with the global giants in the shoe industry.

To push its own independent brand to the international market, Double Star has adapted to local conditions and changed from time to time, mainly adopting five strategies. First, in the United States, Germany, the Middle East, South Africa and the like, Double Star establishes overseas branches and overseas agents responsible for overseas sales and maintenance. Second, for small-volume short-time export orders, Double Star directly signs sales contracts with local vendors. Third, Double Star spends a lot of resources (including personnel, capital and materials) in product development, marketing, image promotion, etc., such as setting up the English website, participating in the Las Vegas shoe show, German GDS shoes show and other international exhibitions to enhance brand awareness. Fourth, Double Star Registered Double ★ trademarks in 33 countries, Double Star and celebrity trademarks in 55 countries. Fifth, Double Star cooperates with other channels, for example, letting Double ★ brand enter Carrefour in the Middle East.

After possessing a bigger and stronger shoe brand, Double Star fully utilizes its strong brand influence to continuously expand into other fields, e.g., tires, clothing, machinery, and thermoelectric products. Tires produced by Double Star are very popular in more than 110 countries and regions such as the United States, Australia, Europe, Indonesia and South Korea.

Focus on independent technology

If an independent brand wants to dominate the world, it must be present in the high-end market. To win the high-end market, the core technology is the most important. Double Star always pays great attention to independent technology, especially core technology, and regards it as the primary condition for making its own brand bigger and stronger.

To achieve international standards in hardware, Double Star purchases state-of-the-art R&D equipment from abroad and invests millions of US dollars to build the most complete testing center in China. This is the only national-level shoe testing station established by the enterprise.

In Double Star, the technicians are required to understand the job of developers, quality inspectors, information staffs; go deep into the production and market; familiarize with the latest technology and theory and carry out the independent technology development. In recent years, Double Star technicians not only independently developed a variety of leisure, lightweight, and hygienic mass tourism shoes, but also developed a series of advanced sports shoes. A large number of technologies have filled the domestic gap. Among them, R & D of BR/SBR based multi-phase high polymer blending sole materials, insulation type special leather shoes, air cushion shoes, rubber-plastic blending micro-hole soles has reached the international advanced level.

When entering the tire industry, Double Star faced with a situation of outdated equipment and backward technology. In two years, it invested nearly 10 million Yuan to import the advanced testers and instruments, established a research and development center, adopted the computer-aided design system in the development of all products. To grasp the latest international tech trends and catch up with the international advanced level, Double Star has made visits (a total of 67 people sent in 6 visits) to world-renowned tire companies in France, Germany, Italy, Japan so forth. Also, Double Star has cooperated with experts from research institutes and higher education units.

With the principle of inheriting traditional excellence, absorbing foreign achievements and creating our own distinct products, Double Star mastered the core technology of tire design in the shortest time. Now it has developed 56 new products including tubeless steel-wire tire, tubeless engineering tire and sandstone tires etc. Of which 7 products are still with the advantages of exclusive production and more than 10 have applied for national patents.

Attach importance to independent innovation

Double Star always adheres to independent innovation, especially its unique all-staff innovation. In the employees, independent innovation is not just a matter for technicians, but for every employee. Each employee is the subject of innovation. By maximum stimulation of creativity of employees and relying on the strength of all employees to innovate, Double Star continuously develop its technologies with independent intellectual property rights.

Double Star places independent innovation into institutionalized management. From the plant director and manager to the operator of the machine, the wages are linked to innovation. The soft task of innovation is turned into 184 hard indicators, stipulating that the responsible person should be subject to penalty of 100 Yuan in case of his unit having no innovation in one month, 200 Yuan in two months, and dismissal in three months. On the other hand, innovating staffs with a significant contribution will be rewarded. At an annual group summary and commendation meeting, there are innovators are rewarded with houses and trips etc.

In the process of innovation of all employees, names of frontline workers, together with their invented operation methods become those of which employees of Double Star feel proud. *(Source: Qingdao Daily in 2003)*

(2) Innovation is the eternal theme of enterprise development

In the past 40 years, Mr. Wang with his courage of Dare to Eat Crabs, has led the people at Double Star to continuously innovate and obtain breakthroughs, enhance ability of independent innovation as a strategic basis. He often reminds people around him that innovation is the source and driving force for enterprise development, and the law of the market economy is the change.

Referring to breakthrough innovation, Mr. Wang speaks with fervor and assurance, "Now China's economic development is slowing down, indicating that the model is not sustainable, whereas the market is exchanged for technology, resources for foreign exchange, preferential policies for political achievements, cheap labor for investment, and land for GDP. For sustainable development of economy in China, it is wise to take innovation as the driving force and continue to expand and strengthen the real economy. Now China has proposed a new industrialization strategy, but photovoltaic and wind power equipment and other industrial fields have seriously excessive production capacity. Today's China should be at the beginning of high-degree of processing with Japan. On the other hand, now Japan, South Korea, Germany and so on still focus on manufacturing. Even as an economically developed country, United States, after suffering a heavy blow from the financial crisis and a long-term economic downturn, encourages its multinational companies in industries such as tires to return to the United States, because it knows the importance of developing manufacturing and processing industries. Therefore, China should be down-to-earth, do an excellent job in basic manufacturing industries, and continue to stabilize the low-end manufacturing industries while entering the mid- to high-end industries. This will accelerate the transition from China-made to China-created.

Double Star led by Mr. Wang called Market General who is brave, responsible and highly spirit, takes the innovation theory as guidance. Also, under the joint efforts of all the employees, Double Star achieves a great result in its innovative construction, possesses strong technological strength, and significantly enhances its innovation ability. For example, Double Star develops its unique environmentally friendly tires using low-carbon tech, which are characterized by low noise, fuel saving and long life. Double Star develops its oil-resistant tires breaking the monopoly of foreign tires, which are characterized by unique technology, special rubber design, high performance, and being oil-resistant, acid-resistant, alkali-resistant, corrosion-resistant. Double Star develops color tires saying goodbye to the history of black tires for more than 100 years, which are characterized by cutting-edge manufacturing technology, gorgeous colors and being fashionable. Double Star develops the super-wide tires as high-tech products characterized by strong bearing capacity, small resistance and fuel saving, thereby being quite popular in the European and American markets. For its high technologies, Double Star has its own independent intellectual property rights, with its shoes divided into seven major series: volleyball shoes, basketball shoes, soccer shoes, running shoes, and etc. Its extra large and small shoes greatly expand the scope of its customer base. It accepts an order of only one pair of shoes, which can be customized including specially-shaped. Double Star is the first in the world to develop the four-mode vulcanizing equipment which characterized by vulcanizing four tires at one time, being 1.8-fold improved in efficiency and possessing 8 core technologies...

From the primary stage and the development stage to the advanced stage of brands, people at Double Star, supported by the national spirit, their insight and strict management, never cease to innovate. As the first to create the first national brand, Double Star successfully enters the tire field from the shoe field and wins the glory for Chinese people.

Innovation has enabled Double Star to enhance its core competitive advantage and maintain its vitality. From manufacturing to creation, Double Star has the initiative to compete in the high-end market and be included in the Top Ten Outstanding Enterprises for the first commendation meeting on national enterprise independent innovation. *(Source: Manager Daily in 2012)*

(III) Three-in-one and gold mine in innovation

An ordinary steel plate is worth only 5 US dollars. If this steel plate is made into a horseshoe, it will be worth 10.5 US dollars. If it is made into a steel needle, it will be worth 3550.8 US dollars. If it is made into a needle of a watch, it will be worth 250,000 US dollars. This is an example of innovation that can create a way out and wealth. Innovation is the topic of concern to the whole society; innovation is an inevitable way for enterprises to survive and develop. For different industries, how to find their own gold mine in innovation, is the issue that every enterprise works hard to solve.

Double Star Group standing out in the national shoe industry has found its successful road, while this industry is a labor-intensive processing industry. Its success is due to its innovation path suitable for its own conditions – all-staff innovation, including managers, engineers and operators. Mr. Wang president of Double Star believes that innovation is not mysterious, that everyone has an innovation potential and can innovate despite his position, that managers should be innovative in thinking and encourage all staffs to take part in innovation.

Managers and their innovations

In March 2003, Ying Fengmei inspector of the upper workshop in Double Star Hanhai has no innovative result so being not rated as an outstanding staff. In April, she made careful observations in work and used her brain. She proposed to make a standard port on the fixed position of the two new varieties of uppers, thereby simplifying the process. Her income increased by more than 300 Yuan. She said, "In the past, I was chained by the old idea. I thought that innovation was a matter of leaders and technicians and that as an inspector what I need to do is paying attention to the quality. Now, if I keep my brain ticking over, I can achieve innovative results. Only with innovation can I be qualified for my position. It is a good thing to make innovation in the post."

In Double Star, an innovation atmosphere is formed and recognized by the majority of employees. This is inseparable from the innovation theory of Double Star (that is, leaders, technicians and operators take part in innovation). Innovation is not limited to technological progress. The impact and intangible benefit from the innovation by leaders and managers are invaluable.

In 2003, with the goal of the innovation being up to a new level and everyone achieving an innovative result, Double Star required management personnel to take the lead, stipulating that the responsible person should be subject to penalty of 100 Yuan in case of his unit having no innovation in one month, 200 Yuan in two months, and dismissal in three months. This stipulation, which is humorously called a sharp sword for laziness, not only enables management personnel to establish a sense of innovation, but also gives birth to unexpected management innovations.

The planner of the production plant may have been considered to be comfortable in the office which is not a sun-scorched and rain-drenched environment. But in Double Star, you rarely find planners in thc office. The market changes rapidly, with the orders characterized by small batches and different product types. In the past, a specific product might be produced for several days in one production line, but now there may be a number of products dealt with in it a day. Therefore, the planners of Double Star should always go to the warehouse and workshop to understand the inventory of raw materials and semi-finished products. If the market has feedback information, it is necessary to change the production plan in time. One time, due to the production being not well planned by a planner in Double Star Haijiang, the raw materials were found to be excessive after the production; this planner had to personally pay for the remaining materials. This is a driving force for the planner of Double Star to be do an excellent job under the conditions of market economy, including being innovative.

Similarly, the accountant is innovative in his work. He adopts a new method – Capital Block. In this new method, he calculates the cost spent in a machine station, a process, a workshop, and a plant according to the product type each day, to achieve the most effective use of funds. Thus, the accountant is a good housekeeper of Double Star. In the quality management of Double Star, the responsibility system is adopted. In the past, the inspection was made after the production; but now, the policy of putting prevention first is carried out. The same measure is also adopted in management of tires and castings, thereby effectively controlling the occurrence of quality problems, fundamentally improving the quality and responsibility awareness of managers and employees at all levels and guaranteeing the excellent quality of products in Double Star.

Some people may say that even the worthy Homer sometimes nods. Is this a high demand in Double Star? However, its staffs said, "The market constantly changes. We should always work hard and be careful; otherwise, the market would be far away from us and our market share would be lost." This is not due to people at Double Star who have a high degree of ideological and political awareness; instead, this is due to the market awareness formed in their constant innovation of management after their entry into market.

30% technology and 70% management: The reform and innovation in management has always been the most stable foundation for Double Star to always be at the forefront of the market. In the 1980s, the digital tracking card of Double Star solved the problem of tripping and so forth. In the 1990s, Nine Plus Nine Management Method of Double Star solved the problem in human and material management and was promoted as the national-level enterprise excellent management method. People at Double Star are the first to propose that the effective use of money is the best ideological and political work and reward the employees with outstanding contributions with color TVs, cars, houses, etc., so solving the problem of how to combine the spiritual and material incentives in the market economy and more effectively exert the role of ideological and political work. Double Star proposes that the best product quality is the biggest doing-good and gathering of blessings, which solves the problem of how the fate of employees is linked to the fate of the enterprise and how to let the management concept of

Double Star run through the daily behavior of employees. Double Star develops more than 10,000 management regulations, which solves the problem of how soft content of management becomes a hard indicator.

Management innovation is the eternal theme of market competition. From the history of management innovation in Double Star, it is found that the market is always the standard for effective innovation of Double Star. If it is needed by the market, the reaction from the people at Double Star is "How do I find a way to provide it" instead of "We had never provided it before." Therefore, there are many problems that seem to be impossible to be solved in the eyes of others but be possible in the eyes of people at Double Star. This kind of innovative awareness is the driving force for people at Double Star to move forward forever. With a sense of innovation among managing personnel, management innovations emerge in an endless stream.

Haijiang as a production base of exported shoes with Double Star creates a 3-day work method, which is aimed at adapting to the rapid changes in the international market and meeting the strict customer requirements. This method which can ensure the flawless management stipulates that, on the 10th day of each month, the comprehensive management assessment is made, on the 15th day of each month, the assessment of sales cost and benefit is made, and on the 27th day of each month, the assessment of innovation results is made. The 3-day work method takes the work of management personnel quantified into a hard indicator as the main content, and is supplemented by a strict system assessment, which will involve production and operation such as planning, process, technology, quality, cost, equipment, capital, sales, and efficiency. This method requires employees to carry out self-summarization, self-assessment, and self-improvement, and eliminates the blind self-satisfaction of employees on their work. The following three events aroused strong repercussions among all employees: the development department of Haijiang sent the samples with quality defects to the customer, which damaged the image of Double Star; a technician wrote the wrong compound formula, which led to the re-adjustment of some rubber materials and increased production costs; a supervisor due to work quality problems were exempted from receiving his full-month bonuses totaling 5,500 Yuan. Cao Dunfeng, director of the cloth-scraping workshop, said, "The 3-day work method implements hard indicators and true assessments, which makes us really under pressure. Everyone strives to do an excellent job without mistakes. Now I really understand the meaning of management personnel being in line with the market." Li Xin, a worker of the sewing workshop, said, "The head of our quality inspection department, due to his poor implementation of the supervision process, is subject to the penalty of 500 Yuan with a notice posted. We think that the management on cadres becomes stricter than before. In the past, their work was not strictly monitored. Therefore, we should work harder and strive to realize the goal of the workshop without mistakes." The 3-day work method has brought about a significant boost to innovation of Haijiang in management. Management cadres of functional departments and workshops have changed their work style and created a good situation in which cadres take the lead and all staffs participate.

In Double Star Zhongyuan Shoes, the handover between good and bad teams is set up in the molding workshop. That is, at the time just prior to the work time every Monday morning, the handover ceremony is carried out between the winning team and the team having the worst performance in the innovation competition of the last week. The workshop director presides the handover ceremony, while the workshop staffs attend it. This kind of management method with high transparency can stimulate the collective sense of honor and enthusiasm of the employees. In the workshop, it has created a strong atmosphere of learning, helping, and competing among staffs and cultivated the positive work style of the employees.

In Double Star Machinery, there were many scraps in the sheet metal workshop, but no one was willing to take the initiative to re-use the scraps. The full-time team for blank-cutting was set up; the team leader, who was also the material manager, was responsible for coordinated arrangement for blanking with the workshop and his team, in which the scraps should be first used, if available. In the first four months of this year, the workshop used 27.468 kg of scraps, namely, the materials that could only be treated as waste materials were reused.

The leader of Double Star Casting Machine changes the wooden box (that is used by the tire company to purchase the rubber compound) into the packaging box of the casting machine product, which not only saves the funds for purchasing the packaging materials, but also reuses the waste products from the tire company. Therefore, with attention paid, a good idea is easily capture in innovation.

Not only the grassroots units pay attention to management innovation, but also the functional departments of Double Star Headquarters bravely take the lead in innovation. These functional departments have implemented a management method in which the hard indicators are specified. That is, the soft tasks are quantified into hard indicators. Each piece of work is should be done in specified time with the result assessed, thereby completely solving the problem of the disconnection between the functional work and the market. The person in charge of each office thinks that the hard indicator management method can soon produce results, thus, he does not need to arrange tasks each day. Also, he does not need to arrange visits to the workshop or trips, because he can understand the situation of the workshop in a timely manner and get the latest information. For him, the work efficiency is high, and the results are good. The political and ideological department is responsible for the group's ideological education work. Previously, its job was very simple in a year: that is, it issued an education program at the beginning of the year; and it wrote a summary of work according to the materials from the grassroots at the end of the year. Now this job is assigned to a specific person in charge. This responsible person planned six rounds of inspections in the workshop in a year to obtain the first-hand information, and his goal was to bring a new method into full play in the education work. The second round of inspections was completed, and his good method of education was promoted in the group. He said with deep feelings, "I used to think that the education work was not significant, and I did not feel that I could play a role in this regard. But after having my innovative ideas, I think that the education work can really help the production and management."

Technician and innovation

Technology are primary productive forces. Although Double Star is in the traditional processing industry, it never neglects the power of technology to transform traditional industries. Technological innovation is the magic weapon for Double Star to lead the industry. The reason why Double Star is always brilliant in traditional industries is that it constantly carries out the technical innovations.

After winning the glory of the four major inventions, China has fallen behind in natural sciences. On the other hand, Double Star gets rid of the mode of blind imitation and is against the blind worship of foreigners. For people at Double Star, our Chinese should seek truth from facts and carry out the technological innovation.

In the tire industry that Double Star entered, the formulas of the 1940s and the process of the 1950s had been used for many years, while there was no effort spent on the innovation. Later, with the unique thinking of Double Star, technicians of the tire company carried out their technological innovation.

First, technicians dared to repair the imported equipment. The cutting machine in Double Star Radial Tire was imported from Netherlands. When it failed, it must be repaired by a so-called foreign expert. Now, our technicians boldly carried out repairs to ensure that the market need is met in the timely manner. One time, the repair was successful, thereby avoiding an economic loss of nearly 3 million Yuan. Another machine is called the direct cutting machine from Netherlands. Foreign experts did not allow our staffs to touch it without their consent during its debugging process. After it was put into operation, the operation process was adopted, in which two wires were trimmed in each side (four sides in two sides). In this way, the annual scrap value was 500,000-600,000 Yuan. Led by the innovation theory from Mr. Wang, a staff who was workshop director & equipment administrator used his brain and made bold improvements to the structure of the cutting knife. He let the machine trim 1 wire each side, which met requirements. As such, 14 wires could be saved each day; namely, total about 1,624 wires were saved in the first quarter, equivalent to more than 60,000 Yuan, and so on.

Second, there is a technical improvement. Double Star Agricultural Tire Factory made an improvement to sulphurization tech in butyl capsule rubber introduced from abroad, which greatly shortened the time of sulphurization, saved electricity costs, and increased the number of times of use of each capsule to more than 120 times.

Third, there is a bold change in traditional process. A technician in the radical tire workshop of Double Star Qingdao Tire broke the traditional process and designed a new formula for the tread, which not only reduced the cost, but also significantly improved the wear resistance of the rubber. In the bias tire workshop, the tread process was adjusted to reduce the cut side of the formed tread and reduce the return rate of the rubber material, thereby not only saving the rubber material, but also reducing the waste tread caused by the mixed return material. Currently the return material of each shift is from more than 100 kg to 10 kg and the rubber saved per month can be about 18 tons.

The achievements of these technological innovations are reflected in the benefits. Also, the breakthrough of traditional concepts is an asset for the technicians. Some comrades who have been engaged in technical work for many years say, "The biggest obstacle for innovation is the problem of ideas. I used to take technical experts as an authority and be bound by the stereotype, so I did not do pioneering work. We all say that the technologies advance rapidly. If there is no breakthrough creation by technicians, how can there be a technological advancement? In the market economy, the standard of the enterprise is the market. All the old equipment, old technology, old formula and so forth which are not suitable for the market can be changed. We dare to change, revolutionize, and break, to transform our traditional industry using high tech and promote the continuous development of the enterprise."

For the technicians of Double Star Shoe, this breakthrough innovation has become a habitual thinking, and the awareness of the initiative innovation of technicians of Double Star is also cultivated in the market. As early as the early 1980s, Double Star entered the market. To meet customer needs, Double Star developed the anti-wear and transparent wide-sole shoes which were the first of its kind to appear in the market. Double Star was the first to develop high-end sports shoes, which were popular in the market and became a famous brand. In the 1990s, the technology development center of Double Star was recognized as the only national-level technology center for footwear and ranked 11th among technical centers in various industries, thereby fully demonstrating the technical strength of Double Star. Double Star has long been involved in professional shoes which have the highest technical content. In the 1980s, Double Star developed volleyball shoes, which were worn by members of

Chinese women's volleyball team after taking off foreign shoes. When national table tennis team coach Cai Zhenhua was an athlete, he wore shoes of Double Star to win glory for our country. Based on the principles of human body science, Double Star created a theory of positive power efficiency. With the support of this theory, Double Star developed shoes having the following effect: people want to run when wearing them. With their performance at the international advanced level, these shoes were wearing by runners led by Ma Junren. Currently Double Star has the production capacity of various sports shoes, which are popular among members of many provincial and national professional teams. Double Star has developed high-grade air cushion shoes using exclusively owned technology, which are exported to developed countries such as Europe and America. Airbag type 2-airway sports shoes of Double Star are awarded the first prize of scientific and technological progress by British Institute of Applied Technology. Running shoes and nano-antibacterial and deodorant sports shoes are recognized as national key new products. Double Star has more than 100 national patent projects. Therefore, with strong technical strength, Double Star has created intrinsic quality of its products, which shows its independent innovation spirit instead of blind worshipping the tradition and authority.

In 2008, facing the unfavorable factors such as the substantial price increase of raw materials including rubber, the technicians of each unit took the lead to change the structural design, adjust the process formula, and digest the unfavorable factor of price increase. Under the severe pressure of the first half of the year, the production plants of Double Star all achieved a good start and were not influenced largely. This shows that the engineering and technical personnel of Double Star have formed the inertial thinking and behavior of breakthrough innovation. This also shows the ability of Double Star to quickly adapt to the market.

Operator and innovation

Du Demei is an ordinary employee of Double Star Hanhai. With her upper wrist operation method, she won the championship in the technical competition. Proven to be very efficient, this operation method was promoted in the whole group. In the company sewing workshop, one old process became a bottleneck in production of basketball shoes. To solve it, team leader Ma Ling was boldly innovative by changing the method to cut the sponge strip, which led to the elimination of the three processes: sticking the wrist, turning the wrist and brushing the foam without affecting the quality. Results? The daily output was increased from 1300 pairs to 1800 pairs, with a one-time reduction of 6 people, a reduction in monthly salary, sponge and glue cost so forth of more than 8,700 Yuan, and the monthly salary of operators increased from 600 Yuan to 750 Yuan. One operator of Double Star Shoe created a new method (called Peiyan Operation Method) which could improve efficiency by 30%. In the cutting workshop, operators created two methods, respectively called Wanxiang Heart-shaped Knife Arrangement and Enyun Ladder-type Knife Arrangement. In the radial tire workshop, Yang Jiezhang created a sidewall film padding method named after himself, which led to saving 3,480 hours and 260,000 Yuan. These innovations are made by our common workers of Double Star. Truly, the light of the innovation theory of Double Star has shone in every corner.

Modern business management theory believes that there are only incompetent leaders and there are no incompetent employees. Similarly, for the creative potential of employees, they should be stimulated by leaders at all levels using innovative methods. Mr. Wang president of Double Star believes that innovation is not just a matter with the cadres and technicians but also the responsibility of everyone in the enterprise. He hopes that all staffs dare to think, dare to say, dare to suggest, and dare to innovate. People at Double Star have established the idea below: innovation is in the post, innovation is on the machine station, and innovation is around us.

To form a good atmosphere for all employees to innovate, the units of Double Star have mobilized the enthusiasm of all staffs with colorful technical competitions and labor competition activities. Double Star Shoe organized a labor competition with the theme of Sisters Hand in Hand, Excellence and Win in Market; Li Ling and Li Na two sisters set a record of 161% efficiency. In Haijiang, an innovative expert's competition was carried out in the cutting workshop; in it, the signboard made using funds saved in innovation was hanged on the machine station with the champion, which greatly enhanced the sense of honor of employees. In the printing and packaging unit, a new method was used to create opportunities for all of employees to innovate; innovators could enjoy free meals. Luzhong carried out a labor competition with the theme of Who Was More Skillful in Sewing, Mother or Son? Bohai carried out a labor competition with the theme of proposing suggestions, solving problems, increasing efficiency, and striving to be pioneers. Double Star launched a labor competition with the theme of Three Highs and Three Falls etc. The above-said competitions let employees be highly spirited, stimulate their creative enthusiasm and give birth to more achievements in innovation from them. In terms of equipment and technology, the employees of all units in Double Star dare to take risks, break the old thinking and old habits the like, and achieve remarkable results.

Li Jiwei, a maintenance worker of Double Star Shoe, in his routine change of the bearing in the moving knife of the embossing roller with the extruder, found that the power roller and the reducer were damaged due to the high rotation speed of the embossing roller. This time, he did not plan to change them. Instead, he was determined to solve this problem and reduce waste. He carefully collected the data, made the drawings, changed the circuits. After five days and nights of hardworking, he found that the motor could be directly driven by the motor instead of the reducer, thereby avoiding the replacement of the part and saving a cost for a long time.

In Double Star, in addition to male workers, there are female workers in maintenance of mechanical equipment. These female workers work hard and achieve a good result. Wang Shuling was a famous female worker in this regard in Double Star Shoe. She found that a bolt at the connection site between the semi-lunar rocker arm and the eyelet-maker was easily damaged. If this bolt was broken, the said rocker arm had to be replaced. She enlarged the bolt hole, which was matched with a larger bolt, leading to the fact that the said rocker arm could be re-used. This simple method created by her could save more than 2,000 Yuan a year. In a batch of new products exported, there was a decorative buckle on the upper; its manual operation was time-consuming and laborious. She suggested replacing manual operation with the eyelet-maker, leading to efficiency increased by 33%. When a new method was used (namely 2-knife 2-way processing of clothes), the production efficiency increased by 195%. In the punching and rolling process, the board and the scissors were completely removed. the application of the sole punching machine and the upper machine was semi-automatic, thereby eliminating the knife, scissor, basket and shelf. These are the result of innovation by frontline employees.

All-staff innovation lays the ideological foundation for people at Double Star in innovation. Cadres take the lead in innovation, which ignites the desire for innovation of all employees. Technical competition and labor competition so forth create a good atmosphere of innovation. The timely promotion of some innovations opens the mind of all employees. Employees say, “The theory of all-staff innovation really ignites our energy and creativity. Innovation projects constantly emerge, and innovation is really everywhere. The all-staff innovation is the driving force for continuous advancement of Double Star."

(3) Why does Double Star develop color tires?
——Wang's reply to the reporter's question

On November 16, 2011, the world's first color tire production line was put into operation at Double Star Dongfeng Tire Co., Ltd., and a variety of colorful tires came out. To this end, the Double Star Group held a special press conference. At the conference, President Wang answered questions from reporters on why Double Star develop color tires. His answer is relates to business operation of Double Star, and its history and future. Through his honest and passionate words, readers can even see the development history of Chinese tire enterprises and Chinese national industry since the reform and opening.

Why does Double Star develop color tires?

Why does Double Star develop color tires? There are 3 reasons. First, now American companies are against us, so we are determined to catch up with and surpass them, which requires technological innovation. To restrict the development of Chinese tire enterprises, foreigners set up a variety of technical barriers, including Americans. For example, they set up the limits in the tire noise and the exhaust gas generated by friction; obviously they are barriers. Second, they adopt the anti-dumping policy against us. The most ridiculous thing is that the Obama government imposes special protectionist tariffs on tire imports from China. Americans draft the regulations and act as the judges. Is this fair? Obviously, they are against us in the tire industry. It is our honor to join the WTO, but all the WTO rules are formulated by them, and they can impose sanctions on us at will. Third, domination by multinational corporations. In recent years, tire companies in developed countries have mastered the technology, controlled the market, and manipulated raw materials. The price is controlled by them. It can be said that this is an aggression of them which we can't see. This is the exploitation by multinational corporations through the brands. We make shoes, and it is not easy for us to sell shoes at a price of 200 or

300 Yuan. But, if added with a foreign brand name, they can be sold at a price of 800 to 1000 Yuan. It is a cheating behavior, isn't it? The clothes I wear are priced at one or two thousand Yuan in China and may be one thousand Euros in Europe; they are made in China using Chinese materials and sold at a very high price in case of being added a foreign brand. In fact, this is a kind of invisible exploitation. At the beginning of reform and opening, many of you were still children. I tell you that the necessities of life produced in China are the best and most abundant in the world with the lowest prices. They influence markets and customers through their brands. What is the problem? This is an aggression, isn't it? So, we just want to counter this kind of suppression. We are the first to develop color tires, which deserve a high price. We strive to create a favorable environment for the development of Chinese enterprises and win the glory for Chinese people.

In fact, we began to produce color tires in 2009. A team of South African customers came and wanted to immediately place their orders. We said that this was not possible, because we were still in the experimental stage. Only qualified in parameters, could they enter the market. This shows that color tires are very marketable.

Then its price is more expensive than black tires. A color tire is priced at more than 2,000 Yuan, and 4 tires are about 8,000 Yuan. This kind of personalized, market-oriented tires is definitely not the same as the tires we generally use. This price reflects the technical content and reflects the core technology, which shows that the tires made by the Chinese are as good as those made by the foreigners, and even better. Our color tires are customized to meet requirements in terms of color, time, and quantity. Dear reporters, if you want to buy them, please tell us. What is your opinion on their price? I believe this price is reasonable.

Only an enterprise continues to innovate, can it develop. Moreover, it must always change with the times, the market, and the people's thinking. If it can't keep up with this change, then it will be eliminated by the times and the market. We understood that our people's living standards were improved with the reform and opening, and that younger people had their own demands in the market, so we saw the prospects for this market and decided to develop color tires. We believed that our color tires would be welcomed by our young consumers who were in vogue and attached importance to personality. Of course, it was impossible for a new thing to be accepted by everyone. But I believed that this market was very promising.

Color tires: our own technology

The development and development of color tires is completely different from traditional black tires. It is impossible to produce a colored tire with the old technology. To produce the color tire, we specially renovated an old workshop for doing relevant work. It took us two years. Sorry, you cannot see our technology, because it is a trade secret. The goal of our technical innovation is to show to the global tire industry that our tires are a wonderful thing in the world.

As we all know, Double Star was mainly a shoe-maker in the past with its shoes having a variety of colors. Everyone knows the shoes we wear have soles made of beef tendon; Double Star are the first to make these shoes. At that time, the supply of the natural rubber as a kind of raw material for shoes was insufficient in the chemical industry nationwide. I said that Americans began to control the supply of natural rubber in the World War II. How could we solve this issue? Later, we found an engineer who helped us to develop the sole using the beef tendon. It is a good thing. The beef tendon sole is more beautiful than the traditional black sole and plays a key role in casting our brands. This innovation won a second prize in the national rubber industry and won a prize in the first scientific conference of

China. Currently, this engineer has passed away, after spending a heroic effort on the development of synthetic rubber in China. We have carried forward his spirit. The shoes can be colorful, so can tires. Therefore, we firmly believe that the tires can be colorful and personalized to meet different customer needs.

In Double Star, manufacturing processes for tires and shoes learn from each other and improve each other. We overcome various technical difficulties. From raw material formulation to process formulation, we have conducted thousands of experiments and created our core technologies. This is a major change in the history of tire development in the world.

These tires are brightly colored. In terms of color, black is more contaminant than red. I give an example, which proves that this tire is environmentally safe. I just said that the beef tendon sole is transparent, the shoes using it are better than the black ones in the service life so forth. The engineer takes a year or two to study the color, because how the color changes is very complicated. But we have experience in making shoes. Therefore, it is not accurate to say that we study this colored tire in one year or two. This is the result of our 30 years of experience!

I have always disagreed with the views of some people saying that currently young people are not vigorous. Our R&D engineers for color tires were basically young people born in the 19 70s and 1980s. They worked hard and listened to the superior. To make up a piece of data, they did work day and night. You now see this demonstration apparatus of vulcanization discoloration, which is prepared by them. We have trained them as R & D engineers, the new generation of people represented by them are migrant workers. For example, a migrant worker from the production line of Double Star created a two-color trademark. He had carried out material preparation for more than 20 years, and his creation of the said trademark was supported by an old engineer. Therefore, technology is derived from the first-line practical experience. The workers can do the technical research and development. Due to the change of the market, we should develop core technologies. To develop core technologies, there must be talents. Some of developed countries bully us, but we must keep calm and tell young engineers and technical workers that in the market we compete with foreigners, that we must turn our ambition into our strength to create excellent products and win the glory for Chinese people. If there are dreams, perseverance, and pioneering spirits, migrant workers who do not have high diplomas and high academic qualifications can become senior engineers with professional skills. I am very pleased that the color tires of Double Star have been integrated into the research and development of our young engineers.

Why do we insist on casting national brands?

Double Star is the first shoe-making enterprise listed in China. At the end of the last century, the then mayor of Qingdao said to me that if Double Star entered the car industry, then the government would provide funds of 300 million. I said that the domestically introduced cars were technologies eliminated at abroad and that they had no technical value. Later, said mayor met me again hoping me to acquire and revitalize Tsingtao Brewery (at that time it was going downhill) in case of 300 million Yuan provided by the government. Someone told me at that time that I could spend money to buy technology from abroad. I didn't want to spend money on buying technology. By my experience, I knew that what foreigners would sell to us were not high technologies. On the other hand, I felt encouraged by the government expecting me to revitalize the state-own enterprise and promising to provide a sum of money. I considered that the tire would be better the beer, for I was familiar with the rubber that was the raw material of the tire and the shoe. I said to the government that I would spend 3 billion on the tire industry. Later, the government handed over a tire company that was on the verge of bankrupt, and I used this money in the wire tire business. That's how it developed.

How did we come to Shiyan? Seven years ago, Shiyan Dongfeng Tire could not go on. The Although invested by Malaysian Golden Lion Group for ten years. Because of poor management, it was forced to stop production. Such a large state-owned enterprise on the verge of bankruptcy made the municipal government worried and seek the help from the provincial government. At that time, Yu Zhengsheng secretary of the provincial party committee, who was secretary of the municipal party committee in Qingdao in the past, knew the industrial affairs, supported the tire business, asked me whether I could revitalize Dongfeng Tire. I felt very nervous, because it was a well-known company needing a heroic effort. In case of not running it well, our Double Star would lose face and our state-owned assets suffer a great loss. But why should Chinese people fail to run their own business? Is it necessary for foreign companies to merge it? I gritted my teeth and accepted this task. At that time, local people in that city did not understand or accept it. I came there and just got off the train, I saw slogans: Rolls Back, Double Star; Rolls Back, Wang, with hundreds of local employees protesting at the entrance of the factory. Many people were not optimistic about our management, asking: could a shoe-maker run well a tire factory? I said that I could and that the key was whether we had our own technology, whether we had our own management, or whether we had our own spirit. We had not been scared off and we had persisted. After two years, our tires became one of the top ten national brands of tires.

We paid a high tuition fee and bought the so-called core technologies. Now I think it is all deceptive, for they are not core technologies. A simple example is the cord fabric of the tire. This technology was from abroad. We found that this technology only applies to low-end tires used in tractors. This kind of tire did not run smoothly, affecting the speed. In other words, with this technology, the tires did not run long. We later boldly innovated and solved this problem. Don't think that this is nothing. The car tires often run for four or five hours, and the speed is very fast. If this technical problem was not solved, the tire quality grades would difficultly go up. In the tire performance tests, our tires could run for 54 hours at a high speed (while the national standard is 34 hours). We tested our tires through the taxi whose running characteristics could make us have the best test on our tires.

In recent years, with the development of the world economy, Western developed countries have set up more and more technical barriers to China, especially in the tire industry. The most typical case is the American government imposed punitive tariffs on tires imported from China. So do not expect others to sympathize with and help us! China's tire companies can only stand in the international tire market by constantly innovating and mastering the core technology.

I believe that this colored tire has changed the history of Chinese tires without innovation. It will bring great development and improvement to the tires of Double Star as a national brand. The more crucial point is to let foreigners know that Chinese people are as capable as them. It can be said that foreigners attach importance to the strict compliance with the rules while we attach importance to the more flexible policies. When I negotiated with foreigners, I was so angry that I didn't want to meet them. Instead, I asked my general manager to negotiated them and I slept at the hotel. Our Chinese can adopt flexible measures according to the actual conditions and this is where our Chinese are smart. Of course, this wisdom of our Chinese can be utilized for good or lead to counterfeit and shoddy products, depending on how to guide. Therefore, foreigners are afraid of us and know the power of our nation.

As early as the beginning of reform and opening, we put forward an innovative theory that only the reverse thinking can create miracles, and constantly carried out innovation practices. As a result, Double Star Shoes won China's first well-known trademark. In 2002, while seizing the opportunity of China's tire industry to adjust and reorganize and reshuffle, we actively carried out the strategic transformation, actively involved in the tire industry, and created one of the top ten national brands of Chinese tires in a short time. It can be said that the driving force for our sustainable development is to inherit the traditional excellence, absorb foreign achievements and create products with our own characteristics. The goal of continuous innovation of Double Star is to create the core technology that belongs to our Chinese people. Faced with the increasing resistance of western developed countries to the Chinese tire industry, Double Star changed the history of black tires for more than 100 years and created an innovative technology, ushering in the new era of tire industry development. This reflects the power of our Chinese people. *(Source: China Chemical Industry News, Nov 17, 2011)*

IV. Expert Comments

Comrade Jiang Zemin pointed out, "Innovation is the soul of a nation and an inexhaustible motive force for the development of a country." Mr. President Wang also often said, "The soul of Double Star culture is innovation. Innovation is the foundation and guarantee of the success of Double Star. Innovation is the soul and motivation for the development of Double Star. There would be no Double Star brand without innovation."

Innovation is a concept that is frequently used in society. Its scope can be radiated to party and government organizations, military organizations, economic organizations, science and technology departments, educational institutions, news media, and social services etc. As far as the business world is concerned, many enterprises vigorously advocate for innovation and put innovation in a certain position, but the actual results achieved are not satisfactory. In other words, there are very rare enterprises like Double Star that achieved such remarkable results. We cannot help but ask: why?

The fundamental reason is that many enterprises only regard innovation as a slogan, but do not regard it as a very difficult systemic project, nor even regard it as the soul of enterprise culture. Their work remains quite superficial with their innovation being nothing more than a castle in the air.

Double Star can achieve remarkable results in innovation, because its leadership with Wang as the core attaches immense importance to innovation, regards innovation as a systematic project, places the soul of enterprise culture in a prominent position, and adopts a variety of practical measures. The main measures are below:

1. To provide a powerful driving force for innovation. They intensify the reform of the system and mechanism, consolidate various basic management, initiate the people's war in innovation to provide an inexhaustible motive force. They advocate all employees to innovate regardless of position, constantly improve production and technology. In a word, Double Star is with innovative ideas, new spirits and new features.

2. To form the concept of all-staff innovation. They strengthen ideological education and publicity work, form the concept of innovation with all staffs from top to bottom, and create a strong atmosphere of innovation for all staffs.

3. To pay attention to innovation of leaders and skilled workers. Leaders are the key of innovation, while skilled workers are the main force of innovation.

4. To strengthen the construction of innovative teams. They adhere to a principle of the innovation being carried out by leaders, technicians and operators.

5. To comprehensively plan, highlight key points, and make full efforts to focus on key innovation projects.

6. To conduct market-oriented job competitions and set off a wave of innovation for all staffs.

7. To create an environment and atmosphere that is conducive to innovation; to advocate innovation, encourage success, and allow failure.

8. To advocate and encourage team innovation, joint innovation, and cooperative innovation.

The above eight points are the deep reason why Double Star can achieve meaningful results in innovation, and the essence of innovation experience with Double Star.

Tactic 7: The System Is the Law of Heaven

"The rules and regulations of Double Star are mostly formulated after discussion by the workers congress, so they are called the highest laws of Double Star. Even for a staff who has a long record of service, a great achievement and an outstanding contribution, if he violates them, he will be subject to a punishment. This is also applied to me as a president of Double Star."

——Wang Hai

In 1995, the national conference of learning Jilin Chemical was held in Double Star, where large enterprises across the country absorbed the management experiences of Double Star which was highly praised by Minister JIA of the former Ministry of Chemical Industry.

Strict system is the basis of enterprise management. Since the early 1980s, Double Star has implemented militarized management.

I. Wang Hai Quotations

(I) Significance of management system

☆ Theory is the guide, regulations are guarantees, implementation is the key

☆ Strict management ensures a success, and loose management leads to a collapse.

☆ Management is a magic weapon for enterprises to win in competition and maintain unbeaten records.

☆ The development of Double Star (including domestic and foreign markets) depends on our excellent management at which we are good and for which were are admired.

(II) Characteristics of management system

☆ The rules and regulations are laws of Double Star and no one can violate them.

☆ Iron will, iron discipline, iron style

☆ Enterprises should be operated according to rules and regulations, and their leaders should take the lead and set up a good example.

☆ Style of Double Star: strict, high, meticulous, realistic, fast, and diligent

☆ Systems, regulations and standards under the market economy are changeable with the time, which should be formulated to be compatible with the current development needs and actual conditions. Double Star is with strict regulations, perfect systems, and unified commands.

(III) Goals and requirements of management

☆ The post responsibility system is carried out.

☆ The system is the standard of work quality, the embodiment of comprehensive quality, and the embodiment of the standard of being a person.

☆ Formulate a comprehensive system of regulations and regulations

☆ Go from rule of man to rule of law and promote the development of brands.

☆ Overcome our weakness by absorbing strong points from others, fully utilize the external resources to develop Double Star.

(IV) How to implement a good management system

☆ Double Star is the home for everyone who should obey rules and regulations.

☆ Our rice bowls are from Double Star whose rules and regulations should be not violated, and as its staffs, we should be responsible in work.

☆ In all our work, we should be strict and be not afraid of hurting the feelings of others, to achieve actual results.

☆ Compassionate leadership, ruthless discipline; be strict and fair in meting out rewards and punishments; unified will with ease of individual mind.

II. Practices and Effects

(I) Main practices

1. Staff participation and democratic management

In the beginning of reform and opening, when many enterprises regarded employee representatives as a puppet, Double Star established a staff representative system and established a democratic management committee to allow employee representatives to participate in and supervise enterprise management. This good tradition has kept going on until now.

2. Authority management being temporary

In the development of the enterprise, authority management is needed, but it is temporary. Authority is always associated with an individual who has a life cycle.

3. Management under rule of law

It means a kind of management under a set of rules and regulation plus standards (collectively called laws of the enterprise). After his visit to Double Star, a Taiwanese businessman exclaimed in surprise, "The rules and regulations in management of Double Star is very specific!" In the development of the enterprise, only management under rule of law is lasting and eternal.

4. Individual awareness and moral management

Moral management is a long-term educational problem. It mainly relies on improving the individual awareness and moral level to achieve an effect. This kind of management can make people to control themselves. However, because of being not feasible in most cases, ethical management must be combined with management under rule of law to achieve results.

5. Emotional investment and family management

President Wang often educates cadres, "People are the foundation for the enterprise development, and management is people-oriented." He put forward the following slogans: "Warming employees with family, retaining employees with emotions, and motivating employees with true feelings", "Let employees feel that they are hopeful in our enterprise, and even have a feeling of being at home." This is the emotional investment and the family management he has created.

6. Soul-shaping and cultural management

The management of cultural concepts is a high-level management. This is true for the enterprise. Therefore, it is necessary to use cultural concepts to educate people, transform people, and unite people. The most important thing for the management is the cultural management. The person who manages the people is easily exhausted, and the cultural management is associated with the soul.

(II) Main effects

1. Realization of the staff being the owner of the enterprise

Today, there are still many enterprises to regard employee representatives as puppets. However, as early as the beginning of reform and opening, Double Star set up a system of employee representatives and a democratic management committee to allow employees to take turns to participate in and supervise enterprise management throughout the year. This good tradition has gone through more than 30 years and has been up to now. This management innovation serves the enterprise development, enhance the cohesiveness, wins the praise of employees, and achieves certain economic benefits. Every year, the employees of Double Star put forward nearly 10,000 reasonable suggestions, which lead to benefits of tens of millions Yuan or even nearly 100 million Yuan. Therefore, the enormous energy can be tapped from employees.

2. Greatly improving the modern scientific management level of Double Star

Double Star has formulated detailed rules and regulations according to the actual conditions of all units. Its management method - Nine Plus Nine Management Method with characteristics of Double Star - won the first prize of the national modern enterprise management innovation results. This set of management system deeply convinced the experts of Institute of Industrial Economics of Chinese Academy of Social Sciences who came to investigate; in their special investigation report titled Light of Double Star - Investigation on Management of Qingdao Double Star Group, they highly praised Nine plus Nine Management Method and considered it to be a management method with Chinese characteristics, thereby enriching and developing the theoretical system of socialist market economy. The China Enterprise Management Association and the China Entrepreneur Association have included it into the list of 22 modern management methods that have been promoted nationwide including in the enterprise community of China.

The management of Double Star is not only among the best in the country, but also praised by the international community. The Americans rated Double Star as the best-managed enterprise in the world. The Japanese took the initiative to visit Double Star. The Koreans offered a high salary to request cadres from

President Wang. Double Star has won the recognition of the market with its excellent management, won the respect of peers, and won the admiration of foreigners!

3. Cultivating many leading cadres

Double Star Group is not only a large-scale enterprise group that produces quality products and provides excellent services, but also a large school for cultivating corporate management cadres. Many young men and women who came out of the countryside and cultivated in this large school have embarked on leadership positions at all levels.

4. Guaranteeing the healthy development of Double Star Group and the success of Double Star brand

The world-class management level of Double Star has guaranteed its healthy development and its brand success. With its brilliant achievements, Double Star has won the glory for our country. It is worthy of being a famous brand in China and the world!

III. Typical Examples

(1) Sword of Damocles over the head of people at Double Star

The Sword of Damocles as a phrase is commonly used as a catchall term to describe a looming danger. In Greek legend, Damocles member of the court was asked by King Dionysius to feast and was ordered to sit under a sharp sword that was hung by only a single horse-hair. This idiom means a state of crisis or means that a person should have a kind of crisis awareness. Here, the democratic management committee is considered the sword of Damocles hanging on the head of people at Double Star.

In the early 1980s, the democratic management of enterprises was just a slogan. There was a saying, "Workers are the masters of the enterprise, and cadres are the servants of the people." However, the goals were not realized. Especially, in some of state-owned enterprises, rules and regulations seem to be formulated for workers rather than for cadres, because cadres could be during their work time to drink tea, chat, read newspapers, go shopping, and leave early etc.

On the other hand, how about workers? What was their sense of being masters of the enterprise? - Anyway, with the iron rice bowl in their hand, the workers were irresponsible and passive in their work. Some workers often stole lasts, shoes etc. At that time, Wang took measures to investigate and deal with it. It was found that a total of 28 workers stole things in 3 days. Wang ruthlessly expelled the workers who stole three times in a row. As a result, there were rumors that Mr. Wang violated human rights because he ordered to make a body research and inspect workers bags. Relevant complaints even were lodged to the Municipal Federation of Trade Unions and the Municipal Party Committee.

With a keen sense of justice, Wang retorted, "The worker is the master of the enterprise. I am the servant of the enterprise. The servant watching the gate finds that master steals things. Is it logical?!"

This event was paid attention from Qingdao Municipal Party Committee and a special meeting was held. Liu Peng former secretary of the municipal party committee said after listening to various reports, "It is right for Wang to catch the thieves. Are they caught? They should be dealt with. Should the Standing Committee of the Municipal Party Committee make a resolution to support the thief?" Due to his speech, the matter was settled down.

The concept of masters and servants in the old system is vague, and the relationship between them is even completely reversed.

So where are the master's rights reflected? What kind of obligations should the servant bear? Under the new historical conditions, how should their relationship be properly dealt with? More importantly, how to change it into a positive factor in enterprise management?

Wang has his own creative ideas. "Enterprise reform without the participation of all employees can only be a castle in the air." Wang said, "Our party organizations can't replace the employees for democratic management, instead, should organize and support their work so that the workers can truly understand what the real meaning of is being the master."

He proposes the establishment of a democratic management committee as a permanent body for the workers congress. Members of this democratic management committee are from representatives of the workers congress and involved in enterprise management (being rotated once every six months), with their duty to supervise and evaluate enterprise cadres. Democratic management teams also are established in its subsidiaries and departments, forming a network of supervision from the team leader to the factory director. It can be said that the democratic management committee is the highest authority in the management of Double Star, because it can supervise all staffs from the president of the group to ordinary cadres and workers. The employee representative of the democratic management committee has the right to listen to and review the work report of the group president, exercise the power of reviewing the key issues such as the company's business policy, long-term plan, annual plan and employee benefits, and exercise supervision and appraisal power over the middle-level management cadres. Double Star also clearly stipulates that any middle-level or above cadre who is criticized by the democratic management committee more than three times should be dismissed.

When the democratic management committee was established, its attention was paid to the labor discipline of the management department, especially the middle-level cadres. In the examination of staff attendance for one day, it was found that six cadres arrived late and leave early, and four cadres left the post without the prior consent. These cadres were publicly blamed by the democratic management committee.

Unexpectedly, this stirred up the nest of the hornet. One f the female cadres blamed, nicknamed Queen, rushed to the bulletin board and shred the public notice down. Then, she ran to the trade union and poured out a stream of abuse, "Wang mobilize the masses to be against cadres. Wait and see. It is not good for you to do so!"

Wang gave his support to the democratic management committee, "You are the masters of our enterprise. It is right for the master to supervise the servant. Don't be afraid. If something happens, I will bear it. If she tears it up, you can post it again. I believe that evil can never prevail over good."

On the evening of the same day, the notice was posted on the bulletin board at the gate of the factory for the second time. It attained more and more attention, and public feelings ran high. Since then, the cadres of Double Star have a sense of responsibility. They are also known as blackboard cadres: - if you do an excellent job, your name can stay on the blackboard; if you don't do an excellent job, your name will be erased from the blackboard. Therefore, in Double Star, several cadres have been promoted or demoted several times.

The group has a vice president. One of his subordinate units had a backlog of cartons, causing losses to the enterprise. The democratic management committee found it; due to it, this vice president was punished by the workers' representatives: namely, he could not receive the bonus of that month. In February 1987, because the production plan was not completed in January, the democratic management committee investigated who would be responsible for this. There was a controversy: Some employee representatives suggested that the factory director should be responsible and should be punished (namely he could not receive the bonus of that month); others believed that there were many objective reasons for not completing the production plan, and it was unreasonable to punish the factory director. After discussions, it was finally decided to deduct the bonus from the salary of factory director Wang. This is the only punishment Wang has received since he joined the work.

The democratic management committee is fair and stern, like the Sword of Damocles hanging over the head of people at Double Star. It is not a formal, insignificant arrangement in Double Star. This mechanism allows most workers to participate in the reform and participate in management. It embodies the essential characteristics of socialist enterprise management and enables the workers' self-awareness and their own values to be truly realized. Today, while most enterprises regard employee representatives as puppets, Double Star Group has been for more than 30 years to let employees be masters of the enterprise. This mechanism serves enterprise management, enhances cohesiveness, wins widespread praise from employees and achieves certain economic benefits. This is a major creation of Double Star in implementation of people-oriented and democratic management and has an excellent value of reference.

(2) Discussion on strict management of the enterprise

In September 1990, the Ninth Rubber Factory (the predecessor of Double Star) launched a discussion on strict management. There were three main guiding ideas for this discussion. First, through the special discussion, we seriously summarized the lessons learned from the strict management. Over the years, Director Wang had led the entire staff to explore the development path of China's socialist characteristics and had achieved great success. The most successful experience was strict management and strict requirements. This discussion on the strict management was aimed at summarizing and theorizing these experiences which were supplemented into Nine Plus Nine Management Method. Second, we unified our thinking and understanding through discussion. Some of employees were inconsistent in understanding the principles of strict management. It was necessary to solve this problem as soon as possible.

Through discussion, the cadres and workers could unify their thinking, understanding, actions, and paces, to lay a good foundation in ideas for continuing to adhere to the strict management. Third, through discussion, we could promote the development of Double Star and ensure that the entire management would reach a new level.

This discussion was focused on solving three problems. First of all, we solved the problem of why it is strict, that is, why we should take the strict management as our policy. From the perspective of the internal requirements, the enterprise should be strict and serious in attitude, style, discipline, etc. Second, we should solve how to understand the "strictness" problem and find out what is "strictness". It is necessary to clarify the strict connotation, including comprehensive, conscientious, timely and accurate implementation of various rules, regulations, systems, and resolute implementation of tasks assigned by the leadership. The strict scope is comprehensive. Strictness should be as a principle to go through all the work of the enterprise. The strict content constantly develops. Strictness is a policy and a standard. From the degree and effect of being strict, we can understand the employees' ideological quality and working ability so forth. The concept of strictness is absolute and relative, and strictness is a means rather than a goal. Third, we should solve the problem of how to be strict in the future. This is the most critical issue to be solved in the discussion. Five principles should be adhered to: the principle of strictness of all employees; the principle of strictness of leadership; the principle of being strict and fair; the principle of being strict and educative; the principle of being strict and compassionate. *(Source: Double Star Newspaper, September 17, 1990)*

(3) From rule of man to rule of law

To create and develop brands and do an excellent job in the market, it is necessary to establish a set of perfect systems including rules and regulations that are suitable for market development and are in line with our own actual conditions. This is independent of man's will. Looking back on the development of Double Star, it is not difficult to see that the reason why Double Star is brilliant today is closely related to the implementation of the systems including rules and regulations. With the site management as the breakthrough point, through the digital tracking, capital classification, and through refinement, quantification, deepening of management, Double Star has achieved rapid development, thus creating the brand of Double Star. the old generation of leaders in Double Star represented by President Wang have created a set of management methods and a set of market theories with unique characteristics of Double Star. Double Star has proposed a variety of management styles including rule of man, moral management, authority management, and the rule of law.

Double Star Group has adhered to the principles of being complete, specific, strict, extensive, changing, leading in the formulation and implementation of the systems including rules regulations.

1. The so-called "complete" does not simply manifest itself in tens of thousands of rules and regulations involving in all aspects. It is known that it is only a form. More importantly, the rules and regulations formulated by Double Star cover various aspects such as leadership, functional department, production and operation, logistics support, and market operation. The rules and regulations formulated for management personnel are more strict and detailed.

2. The so-called "specific" refers to the rules and regulations formulated in Double Star covers a post and a person. The post responsibility system is carried out, so that each person is responsible in the work, with standards, guidelines, and goals.

3. The so-called "strict" means that Double Star is strict in implement rules and regulations and strict in assessment. If rules

and regulations which are formulated completely and specifically are not strictly enforced, they will lose significance and become a piece of waste paper hung on the wall and locked in the case. An ineffective or loose implementation also leads to a bad atmosphere of the enterprise. Therefore, a strict implementation of rules and regulations is the foundation and guarantee for the smooth development of the enterprise.

4. The so-called “extensive” means that the rules and regulations formulated in Double Star can be continuously extended and improved. They should be linked with salaries and wages. The meaning of "extensive" is not only embodied in form, verbally or on paper, but more importantly, is linked to relevant interests. By strictly meting out rewards and punishments, the goals of zero defect in management and zero loss in quality can be realized.

5. The so-called "changing" means that the rules and regulations formulated by Double Star can be continuously revised and improved according to the problems and mistakes exposed and the lessons learned in the work. This is also in line with the law of market development and operation. The market and products constantly change, so the rules and regulations should change with them. Rules and regulations which never change cannot not be able to adapt to the requirements of market development, because the market economy constantly changes. Leaders at all levels of Double Star should know actual conditions, formulate and enforce the rules and regulations according to market changes, to keep pace with the rapid and ever-changing development of the market and meeting the requirements of the market. It is necessary to narrow the gap with the market through the rules and regulations. To better complete various tasks and improve market operations, both leaders on the executive level and the management level should be responsible for Double Star and do their own work in a

serious manner. This can be achieved only through the strict implementation of the rules and regulations.

6. The so-called "leading" means that leaders at all levels of Double Star can take the lead in learning, assessment, and implementation of the rules and regulations. When the leaders violate them, punishments will be carried out. That is, the responsibility of the wrongdoer will be investigated. In Double Star, all men are equal before rules and regulations.

As far as rules and regulations are concerned, the four relationships should be properly dealt with:

1. Money linked with rules and regulations: Implementation of rules and regulations should be linked to interests, rewards and punishments. If this is not done, the rules and regulation will be ineffective and become a piece of waste paper.

2. Assessment linked with rules and regulations: If rules and regulations are not effectively implemented and assessed, then they cannot play a due role; in this case, they will be a waste paper hung on the wall or locked in the drawer, leading to the waste of time and effort and leading to the bad atmosphere, including acts of deception from the execution and management level. The effect of rules & regulations depends on the seriousness of implementation of the assessment in the work.

3. The market linked with rules and regulations: Due to a lack of awareness of overall situation and a lack of constraints by rules and regulations, the unhealthy phenomena occur including departmental selfishness and factionalism etc. This is the greatest potential danger for enterprise development and brand promotion. Everyone must establish a sense of the overall situation of the group, strictly enforce the rules and regulations, and completely eradicate bad practices such as departmental selfishness and factionalism. In addition, the implementation of rules and regulations must be strict; anyone who violates them will be punished. In Double Star, all men are equal before rules and regulations.

4. Management of people linked with rules and regulations: Rules and regulations are established to bind, manage, and educate people. If the leaders especially at the management and execution level do not strictly implement them for the sake of shunning problems or pleasing others, they will be bad guys rather than good guys and be finally dismissed or eliminated during the development of Double Star.

The set of rules and regulations formulated by Double Star is a concrete manifestation of the further deepening and refinement of the market theory with Double Star. It is known that the market theory of Double Star is only a concept, featuring a philosophy and a dialectical unity. The viewpoints and theories are more abstract and difficult to implement. To let these theoretical viewpoints, play a better guiding role, there must be a set of rules and regulations acting as a guarantee. Rules and regulations are the concrete manifestation of further deepening and refinement of the market theory with Double Star. This also shows that the rules and regulations of Double Star are not only the most valuable wealth of people at Double Stars in the market in the past 40 years, but also the greatest contribution to the development of Double Star from the new generation of people at Double Star.

"The fact that rules and regulations are used to constrain our behavior and standardize our management so as to cultivate a new generation of cadres with Double Star, who are leading politically, competently workable, and have a fine style of work plus strict discipline, not only illustrates the success of Double Star and maturity of people at Double Star, but also illustrates a political improvement of people at Double Star. If we continue to do so, we will surely take another step in the future development.

VI. Expert Comments

The management basis of Double Star is: "Two eyes are on the market, and two hands on the management." The management belief of Double Star is: "There are enterprises that are not well managed, and there are no enterprises that cannot well managed."

To manage an enterprise well, there is no way out without management innovation. But, if we are not good at institutionalizing, standardizing, and sublimating into theory of the results of management innovation, then they cannot work for a long time and are difficult to ensure a success.

In management, President Wang not only dares to innovate and is at good at innovation, but also can carry out institutionalizing, standardizing and sublimating into theory of the results of management innovation. Also, Wang enables Double Star to go the rue of man to the rule of law. This is a great magic weapon for success of Double Star.

The goal of management using the rule of law in Double Star is: Every staff of every post should be responsible in the work. To this end, based on their own practical experience, they have developed a set of rules, regulations, and management standards, called the law of the enterprise. According to incomplete statistics, there are 255 rules and regulations, 1,561 management standards, 42 technical standards (233 types), 251 positions with their own image standards, and 29 departments with their own spirits... A Taiwanese businessman after a visit to Double Star exclaimed in surprise, "The rules and regulations in management of Double Star is very specific!"

What is particularly worth mentioning is that, while most state-owned enterprises regard employee representatives as puppets, Double Star Group has been for more than 30 years to let employees be masters of the enterprise. In Double Star, the democratic management committee being fair and stern, like the Sword of Damocles handing on the head of people at Double Star, enables the employee representatives to be masters of the enterprise. This is a great initiative for state-owned enterprises to implement democratic management.

Tactic 8: The Quality Is the Life

"Productivity is money and quality is life. Double Star attaches importance to productivity and quality, but quality is always first. Our focus is centered around quality. Everything may be compromised except quality. All efforts should be aimed at solving quality problems."

——Wang Hai

In 1998, Double Star won the national export exemption certificate regarding sports shoes, which was the only enterprise that obtained this certificate in the national footwear industry, marking that quality management of Double Star reached the international level.

Double Star holds three conferences on quality summary and commendation each year, where the advanced teams and individuals in quality work are commended.

I. Wang Hai Quotations

(I) Connotation and core of enterprise quality

☆ Ideas of quality in Double Star: Product Quality, Work Quality, Service Quality

☆ Improve work quality, do an excellent job in product quality and promote service quality

☆ In three qualities, work quality is the core, the key, the foundation, the guarantee, the key, and the nucleus. If work quality is poor, everything else is equal to zero, including product quality and service quality.

(II) Policy, objective and standard for quality of Double Star

☆ Quality policy: Every process is checked, everyone is an inspector

☆ Product quality objective: 100% pass rate of raw materials, semi-finished products, and 100% finished products

☆ Product quality standard: Supervisor satisfaction, user satisfaction, employees' satisfaction

☆ Service quality standard: 200% service

(III) Importance of product quality

☆ Quality is always the trump card of competition. Without quality, there is no market. Without quality, there is no guarantee.

☆ Good product quality is the biggest doing-good and gathering blessings.

☆ Quality is equal to human character, quality is equal to morality, quality is equal to conscience.

☆ Relaxing the quality means giving up the market. Relaxing the quality means giving up the competition. Relaxing the quality means giving up the survival.

(IV) How to treat product quality correctly

☆ The more famous brands are, the more attention paid to quality.

☆ Productivity is money and quality are life. Double Star attaches importance to productivity and quality, but quality is always first.

☆ Our focus is centered around quality. Everything may be compromised except quality.

☆ All efforts should be aimed at solving quality problems.

☆ Ensure brands with quality and create benefits with brands.

(V) How to guarantee product quality?

☆ Employee's quality awareness in Double Star: I want to live, I want to eat, so I want to do an excellent job in quality; I want to do good, I want to gather blessings, so I want to do an excellent job in quality.

☆ Brand is in my heart, quality is in my hands

☆ Quality problems should be prevented rather than found.

☆ All employees turn to the market and cares about quality.

Methods to improve quality are as follows: constant innovation, deepened contracting, factory currency, post competition, strict management, and change in system & mechanism.

II. Practices and Effects

(I) Main practices

1. Propagandize and implement quality ideas, including the all-staff quality management idea.

Strengthening guidance from the ideological level, carrying out various quality education activities, exposing quality problems, propagating and implementing the ideas of product quality, work quality and service quality, and establishing the all-staff quality management concept as follows: namely, productivity is money and quality is life; Double Star attaches importance to productivity and quality, but quality is always first.

2. All staffs turn to the market and care about quality; all staffs are inspectors with each post attaching importance to quality.

3. Strict system, strict assessment, adherence to the veto power in quality.

4. Adopt the three reverse methods and adhere to the bill payment in quality.

Adopt the three reverse methods: that is, quality reverse method, cost reverse method, and planned-zeroing reserve method; and adhere to the quality problem tracking & claim system, quality reverse method, quality bill payment system.

5. Adhere to the principle of focusing on two ends, controlling the middle, and guaranteeing quality in all posts at all levels.

6. Implement ethical management and advocate being trustworthy and best in quality.

The excellent product quality is the biggest doing-good and gathering blessings.

Quality management slogans hung on the workshop of Double Star

(II) Main effects

1. Put forward quality ideas including the concept of three qualities

Three qualities refer to product quality, work quality and service quality, which cover all aspects of quality work and are paid great attention by all staffs. By quality ideas, staffs get rid of the deviations and errors in the understanding of quality. Double Star advocate ensuring quality by great efforts and being trustworthy and best in quality, to improve product quality and service quality. Double Star has formed a good atmosphere of everyone caring about quality, everyone paying attention to quality, and everyone being responsible for quality, with the product pass rate of more than 99.99%... In Double Star, all export products are exempt from inspection and achieve a state of supervisor satisfaction, employee satisfaction, and user satisfaction.

2. Establish a new quality management model of nipping it in the bud

Double Star eliminates the old quality management model in which quality problems were often found in inspection rather than in the process. In its new management model, everyone is an inspector, and every process is paid attention to quality. This new model attaches important to the integrity, in which traditional excellent ethical ideas are combined with work quality, product quality and service quality, thereby eliminating the influx of unqualified products into the market and creating Double Star brand with excellent quality.

3. Solve the problem of disconnection between production, quality, cost, and equipment; realize the four-in-one management pattern

By adopting the three reverse methods, Double Star solves the problem of disconnection between production, quality, production, and cost, and realizes the management pattern in which production, quality, equipment, and capital are integrated. Moreover, Double Star solves the problem of the unreal cost existing, urges the technical, planning, and quality personnel go to the production line, makes the key control on the key processes, enables staffs to enhance the sense of responsibility, pressure, and urgency, which improves the overall management level of the enterprise.

4. Break the old production organization and management model; create three reverse management methods

Double Star breaks the old production organization and management model and creates three reverse management methods. In the three methods referring to quality reversal method, cost reversal method, and planned-zero reserve method, the quality problem tracking system is carried out in the finished tires, so that the responsibilities for people in all posts and processes can be identified, which are linked with personal income and interests and lead to the mutual inspection between staffs of neighboring posts and processes. As a result, staffs are motivated to find ways to improve the pass rate of rubber, semi-finished products, and finished products, and reduce quality problems and losses to the minimum extent.

5. Realize the process control of the product and solve five major problems

By exposing the problem of each department and each process using the tracking method, Double Star realizes the process control of the product, prevents the products with obvious defects in appearance quality from entering the next process and the unqualified products from entering the market. This solves the following five major problems that had long plagued the tire industry:

(1) problem disconnection between production and quality, production and cost, and production and equipment

(2) problem of cost being calculated at all levels and cost being unreal

(3) problem of quality being paid attention at all levels but often unstable

(4) problem of empty talk on production at all levels and issues being not solved in a timely manner, including equipment

(5) problem of management personnel without pressure and responsibility and their work that cannot be assessed

III. Typical Examples

(1) First special advertisement

Reverse thinking is a typical mode of thinking for human success. When it comes to reverse thinking with Wang, we may mention his first special advertising in addition to his going to the countryside and entering the wire field.

When Double Star was in a good situation (including rapid development and good sales of products), Wang received several letters from customers saying that they found problems in their newly purchased fitness shoes for aged people and hoping to replace them with good ones.

特殊广告

In 1991, Double Star was the first to publish a special advertising in the People's Daily.

His mind was in turmoil. He had not received such a letter from the consumer for a long time. He decided to personally investigate it. He met the deputy manager responsible for quality who made the following comment: this batch of shoes had some defects due to raw materials and might be compromised in comfort but was relatively reliable in quality. The deputy manager opined that it was not necessary to replace them.

Wang was obviously dissatisfied with this report. He walked back and forth in the office and still felt upset. He thought, "As people's living standards continue to improve, it is nothing to spend ten to twenty Yuan to buy a pair of shoes. But if a customer happily buys a pair of shoes and finds them uncomfortable and dissatisfied when wearing at home, what kind of mood will it be? Also, there is a tradition that Chinese customers generally do not lodge a complaint except in a desperate situation. Now the customers write letters, which shows that they trust Double Star. How can we bear to see their unhappiness due to spending money on buying shoes? Elderly persons are not particular about the food but pay attention to whether the shoes are comfortable. If a pair of shoes are not comfortable, they must be not qualified."

Wang also thought of the reputation of the enterprise. As a big shoe-making enterprise, Double Star had a total output of 300,000 pairs per day. If one in ten thousand was unqualified, there would be more than 30 pairs of defective shoes per day, in other words, tens of thousands of pairs of unqualified shoes per year. Such a result would make the enterprise's reputation lost in more than 10,000 users! Product quality was the life of the enterprise and so was the after-sales service. Thinking of this, he immediately convened a general staff meeting on which he said, "No one can make a defective product in the market, especially in terms of quality. In an enterprise, everything may be compromised except quality. The focus of the work should be centered around quality. Especially, the behavior in the work and service leading to cannot be ignored and forgiven. quality problems due to poor work and service quality qua for the quality of the work, poor quality of service caused by product quality problems cannot be let go, cannot be forgiven, while wrongdoers must be held accountable and seriously dealt with. Some people told me that among a population of 1.3 billion in China, it is normal to have a few people feeling not satisfied, but I think this opinion is wrong. We may be unable to satisfy all Chinese people, but it must not be allowed that the problems are not solved even in case of knowing that customers feel not satisfied about products."

After the meeting, Wang was still angry. He was not angry because of quality problems. He was angry at some people, especially cadres, who did not treat customers as God and did not try to solve problems.

Good things stay indoors while bad things will go far away. This bad thing made Wang angry and made him ponder over how to deal with this? It is necessary for the solution to not only reach the goal of educating cadres and workers (letting them better understand the slogans: good product quality is the greatest doing-good and gathering blessings, the user is God and so on), but also to let customers get a satisfactory answer and let a bad thing become a good thing.

During the period of Double Star led by Wang becoming from a small enterprise into a national and even world-renowned enterprise, one of the truths he believed in was seeking truth from facts. A mature and honest enterprise must dare to face customers and face its own quality problems. An unusually bold decision was made by Wang.

The next evening, when people turned on the TV, they saw the first special advertisement on the screen since the founding of the People's Republic. The content of the advertisement is below: For any inconvenience due to quality problems, Double Star earnestly apologizes to the customers hoping they immediately go to sales outlets or sales agents to change shoes or repair shoes bought in February.

This apology advertisement quickly caused strong repercussions throughout the country. Dozens of newspapers and periodicals such as People's Daily, Workers' Daily and Economic Daily made their comments, and even foreign media reprinted them. The courage to expose its own problems and be responsible for customers shows his foresight and enables Double Star to be more competitive.

The special advertisement cast a good image of Double Star. Due to his reverse thinking, Wang was highly praised. As an entrepreneur, Wang certainly attached importance to economic benefits, but he paid more attention to the social benefits of the enterprise. By the special advertisement, Wang sincerely responded to customers' complaints and enabled Double Star to become more popular in the market. *(Source: Zhao Yanbiao: Wang Hai's 30 Years, People's Publishing House, March 2008)*

(2). Setting a thousand pairs of shoes on fire to prevent consumers from suffering losses

Double Star burned low-quality shoes worth more than 100,000 Yuan, indicating that its people adhere to the principle of quality first.

In the morning of December 30, 1997, in Qingdao Double Star Group, the largest shoe-making enterprise in the country, more than a dozen production directors fired and destroyed a thousand of inferior shoes worth nearly 100,000 yuan. The move caused strong repercussions among more than 20,000 employees.

China's footwear industry is mostly manual with more than 200 processes from in-coming raw materials to out-coming products. Therefore, Double Star with a daily output of more than 200,000 pairs of shoes, while ensuring that each product is of high quality, felt the pressure from the consumers. Because of this, Double Star was determined to destroy inferior shoes worth 100,000 yuan.

A few staffs thought that although there were quality problems, these shoes could still be worn after all, so it was a pity to burn them. However, most staffs agreed with burning them. With its shoes being a famous brand, Double Star was responsible for customers. If there were unqualified products, they must not be released to the market.

For Mr. Wang, if these shoes burned being only one-fifth of the annual output of Double Star were into the market, there would be profound consequences. He said that Double Star is a famous brand in China and would become a world-famous brand in the future; it could not be imaged that there was no excellence in quality. Without the excellent quality, a brand could not last long. While being not easily created, the brand of Double Star would be easily destroyed. As a big shoe-making enterprise, Double Star had a total output of 300,000 pairs per day. If one in ten thousand was unqualified, there would be more than 30 customers feeling not satisfied per day, in other words, tens of thousands of customers feeling not satisfied per year. Such a result would make the enterprise's reputation lost in more than 10,000 users, not mentioning their relatives and friends! Therefore, these low-quality shoes must be burnt off, to let staffs firmly establish a sense of quality and let the brand of Double Star be synonymous with high quality.

Double Star always follows the principle of quality first. The slogan put forward by him - Superior product quality is the largest doing-good and gathering blessings - has become the motto of employees.

Since 1986, Double Star has been rated as a brand trusted by consumers. Double Star was the first to pass the ISO9000 certification in the same industry and obtain the national product exemption certificate. JCP, one of the largest footwear distributors in the United States, also granted a exemption certificate for Double Star products. In 1995, Double Star won the first well-known trademark of China's footwear industry with high quality and excellent reputation. *(Source: China Chemical Industry News, January 7, 1998)*

(3) Source tracking and quality

What is the source tracking method?

It means that, through the product quality supervision relationship between the neighboring processes, problems are found, and their reasons analyzed. For example, if the upper workshop finds that there is a problem in the cutting workshop, then the latter will be punished. If a problem is not found in the previous process by the upper workshop, instead, it is found in the upper workshop by the molding workshop, then the upper workshop will be responsible. When the product reaches the final packaging process, if the problem that the packager does not find is finally discovered by the salesperson or the consumer, then the packager will be responsible.

In another method of tracking, a contracting unit receives a certain quality-based compensation after a production index taken. For example, a contracting team receives the production index of 1,000 pairs of shoes, and at the same time obtains 200 Yuan of quality compensation; if the rate of unqualified products is 1%, that is, 10 pairs, and if the team produces 2 pairs of unqualified products, then only 40 Yuan of quality compensation should be paid, and the remaining 160 Yuan can be included into the family ledger; otherwise, if there are 20 pairs of unqualified products, then the team, in addition to paying 200 Yuan for quality compensation, has to pay another 200 Yuan to pay for the unqualified products. The tracking method has pushed the quality of Double Star Group to a new level.

(4) Whoever produces a non-conforming product must pay for it

——New measures in quality management of Double Star

"Whoever produces a non-conforming product must pay for it." This is a striking slogan hanging on the wall of the workshop in Luzhong subsidiary of Double Star.

Double Star is pushing the product quality management work to the market in an all-round way and using the method of calculating the loss to grasp the product quality. They cancel the method of simply looking at the product quality pass rate in the past, instead, they also looking at how much the product loses during the production process and circulation process; the less the loss, the higher the product quality; whoever causes the loss must bear it.

Double Star has exposed quality problems since the 1980s to improve the quality awareness of employees.

Double Star has exposed quality problems since the 1980s to improve the quality awareness of employees.

It takes about 200 processes to produce a pair of shoes, most of them are manually operated, so how to ensure the quality of the product becomes a big problem. People at Double Star make out a bill below: If the daily output is 20,000 pairs of shoes for export, if the pass rate reaches 99%, there will be 200 pairs of unqualified shoes in one day. If the loss is calculated at 9 US dollars, then it will be 1,800 US dollars per day. If the pass rate reaches 99.9 %, there will be 20 pairs of unqualified shoes per day and the loss 180 US dollars. If the pass rate reaches 99.99%, there will be only 2 pairs of unqualified shoes per day and the loss 18US dollars.

The method of calculating the loss in quality management is promoted in the group. Each unit launches an educational activity to find the gap and calculate the loss. Each staff makes out his own bill. Some staffs say, "By this activity, we understand more. In the past, we only saw the results: the product pass rate reaching 97% and meeting the national quality standard, and we did not know how much the loss was, which was caused by unqualified products; especially, although the quality of some products reached the standard, their styles did not meet customer requirements. Therefore, they were not qualified.

Now, all units disclose their daily and monthly losses in product quality in their own quality exposure rooms, so that staffs can educate themselves with many words, pictures and objects. In front of the quality loss exposure desk, an employee who produced unqualified products regretted, "A pair of second-class shoes loses more than 10 Yuan than the first-class. This quality management method is very good!" In Double Star, what the quality inspector now is most concerned about is the loss for an order... and is no longer the pass rate. *(Source: Qingdao Daily, June 8, 1999)*

IV. Expert Comments

In the real world, the quality first is almost the slogan of every enterprise. However, the actual situation in the market is below: in most enterprises, quality of products being not very good; in some enterprises, products being shoddy and unsatisfactory; in a few enterprises, products being copied, faked, or with inferior quality. On the other hand, the number of enterprises like Double Star always adhering to Quality First and being very brilliant is very low. So, what are differences between Double Star and above-said enterprises?

First, the difference is in enterprise culture. Quality First is an important part of enterprise culture in Double Star and is the core of its quality culture. "Quality is equal to human character, quality is equal to morality, quality is equal to conscience"; "production is money, quality is life, but quality is first"; "brand is in my heart, quality is in my hands"; "I want to live, I want to eat, so I want to do a good job in quality, I want to do good, and I want to gathering blessings" ; "Good product quality is the largest doing-good and gathering blessings" and so on. These Wang Hai's quotations form the quality concept of people at

Double Star not only being remembered by them but also being consciously implemented by them. This is the deepest reason why Double Star can achieve the goal of quality first and the most fundamental difference between other enterprises and Double Star.

Second, the difference is in the system and mechanism. The system and mechanism are the premise, the foundation, and the motivation. Double Star has developed a unique new system and mechanism to adapt to market changes and has initiated the people's war in quality management, thereby providing the endless driving force for the development of Double Star. Double Star has formed a good atmosphere: staffs regard themselves as masters and adopt an active attitude in in the work including management; staffs strive to be the first and capable; the all-staff management is carried out whereas everyone pays attention to quality at all levels and in all posts.

Third, the difference is in management measures. To ensure product quality, Double Star has developed a set of rigorous quality management measures. Examples are as follows: strict system, strict assessment, adhering to the voting power in quality work; implementing three reverse methods, adhering to the quality problem tracking and claim system, quality reverse method, and quality bill payment system; adhering to the principle of focusing two ends, controlling the middle, and guaranteeing quality in all posts at all levels.

Fourth, the difference is in moral management. Following the basic principle of seeking truth from facts, Wang boldly has adopted the essence of the traditional culture including Confucianism, Taoism, and Buddhism in the management of the modern enterprise. Through the combination with the actual market conditions and the characteristics of the enterprise, Wang has created a new concept of enterprise management with the unique characteristics of Double Star (for example, excellent product quality is the greatest doing-good and gathering blessings), so as to educate employees to be self-confident, self-disciplined, loyal to the enterprise and work hard. Moreover, satisfactory results have been achieved.

It is hoped that other companies can take Double Star as their good example and realize the goal of quality first.

Tactic 9: The Cost Is the Key

"It can be said that every management revolution has enabled Double Star to bring its development to a new level in the historical period from the basic management of stopping up thriftless and illicit drain on funds, fund block management (being as a key factor), cost management (in which there is a significant reduction of production funds) to today's internal contracted shareholding system implemented in the entire group."

——Wang Hai

President Wang personally guided the work in reducing cost, improving quality, and increasing efficiency.

The cost management exchange meeting was held in Double Star.

I. Wang Hai Quotations

(I) Importance of cost management

☆ Cost determines the profit and loss plus competitiveness of the enterprise. While being the most fundamental of enterprise management, the cost management is a revolution.

☆ Under market economy conditions, funds are an important indicator of whether the enterprise is normal and whether it can run benignly.

☆ Do an excellent job in cost management and win a victory in the market competition.

☆ Carry out quality management using methods of accounting and fund management as well as using economic means.

(II) How to do an excellent job in cost management

☆ In cost management, three goals should be achieved: all-staff management, comprehensive management, entire-process management.

☆ Current account, comprehensive account, market account, and management account: all being good.

☆ Cost management is not just the work of financial personnel, but also the work of all people in all posts and all departments.

☆ Everyone must understand cost management and reduce the cost.

☆ Fund management criteria: speak with facts, explain with numbers, and prove with results.

☆ Fund management: deepening, refining and quantifying.

☆ Fund management: fixing in quantity, money, and time.

II. Practices and Effects

(I) Main practices

1. Use the factory currency and deepen the contract management to maximize the enthusiasm of people in innovation etc.

The so-called factory currency is the internal currency used for the exchange of funds between branches, departments, workshops, sections, links, teams, individuals, etc. within Double Star Group. Using computer and other scientific means and modern tools, the management is carried out in exchanges of factory currency in each process, each section, and each link, to realize the flow of materials between the branches, workshops, teams and individuals, and enhance the awareness of staffs in quality, capital, cost and consumption reduction. This is a rigorous, complicated and systemic project; a key part of comprehensive management in the enterprise; and a new method of enterprise management, which is characterized by being comprehensive, systematic and high-tech oriented.

2. Taking the funds as a key factor to realize one-stop management and understanding the cost of the current day

The attention is paid to the two factors (fund management and cost management) to create the highest level of fund management (whereas the cost of the current day can be known), realize the one-stop management, and the special cost model (whereas each order can be analyzed and implemented).

3. Doing an excellent job in meticulous management and stopping up thriftless and illicit drain on funds.

4. Implementing household consumption style management

The so-called household consumption management is to apply the concept of household consumption to modern enterprise management. In it, the goal of saving cost and reducing consumption is decomposed into each staff; each staff is like living in his own home, being with a calculating mind, tapping potential and reducing consumption. In this way, Double Star effectively reduces consumption and improves product quality.

5. Practice frugality and economy and start with small ones.

6. Do an excellent job in weighing and measurement to promote basic management and realize subdivision of cost accounting.

(II) Main effects

1. Strengthening cost awareness and achieving significant benefits

Double Star replaces the old method (namely analysis and calculation after tasks completed) with the new method (namely each order analyzed and implemented with cost known on current day), achieving significant benefits.

The biggest shortcoming of the old method is disconnection with the market. If products do not meet the market need, then a backlog will occur immediately, which results in the precipitation of funds leading to the death of many enterprises. The new method can eliminate this operation risk from the source and ensure the economic benefits of the enterprise.

2. Reducing costs and enhancing market competitiveness

In the recent years, the price hiked rapidly, and the competition was heinous in the market. Some enterprises were poor in cost management leading to its fund chain interrupted and its production stopped or limited. In contrast, the business boomed in all units of Double Star Group.

3. Strengthening the awareness of saving, forming a good atmosphere of practicing frugality and economy which starts with small ones, and creating a new method of cost management.

4. Creating the highest level of management with the best combination of factory currency, culture, contracting, and execution, which is another major contribution to national industry.

III. Typical Examples

(1) Grasping the key link of enterprise management

Double Star began to focus on cost management in the 1980s and is the first to adopt a digital tracking card in enterprise management. This realizes the combination of dynamic management & static management and solves the big problem of management in the global shoe industry.

In Double Star Group, a financial staff said that there was a question that he had thought for several years - should the money from the bank be spent?

At the beginning, Wang as president of Double Star told the financial staff that the cost was the key link in enterprise management and that the production could run with money and had to stop without money. Some financial personnel did not understand his words. According to the traditional theory, the funds serve the production services and it is natural that the funds are reserved for the production; if the funds are insufficient, the loan may be made from the bank. The financial staff had to follow a new fund management method which reflected the ideas from Wang. This new method is below: When the material is taken from the supply department, the requisition form, which is signed by the plant director, the person in charge of finance, and the person in charge of the plan, is faxed to the finance department of the group, which, knowing how much you have, informs the supply department how many materials you can take. Using this new method, Double Star can grasp the key link (namely money) in cost management.

If a production plant has no money, at least it shows it has a problem in its input and output. The product is not suitable for the market and the funds cannot be recovered in time, so it has no money. The market forces you to change your mind, forces your products to be marketable, and forces you make a change with the market. If your product does not adapt to the market and your cash flow does not work, you have to stop production. In this way, the production plant has to be market-oriented, be cautious when planning production, and strive to reduce costs, thereby leading to its booming business again.

Under the market economy, many of old practices become obsolete. In the past, when the supplier sent materials and did not immediately ask to make a payment, the producer felt that it was a good thing. However, Double Star Group as a famous state-owned enterprise does not agree with this old practice. From the point of view of fund management, the excessive materials cannot be accepted even as a gift, because they occupy the warehouse space and need to be taken care of. In other words, there is a problem of cost.

In the past, it could be said that an accountant did an excellent job if there was no difference between the general ledger, detailed ledger and journal when reported to the superior at the end of the month. This accounting was done after the task was completed, which was disconnected with the actual conditions. In the past, the day-to-day account was kept in major production bases of Double Star Group, and the ledgers were based on the original records. These records were based on the premise of ensuring production, so the margin was particularly large, which was quite different from the reasonable funds that must be occupied by the actual production cycle. For example, for an order of 10,000 pairs of shoes, the plan was made according to 15,000 pairs of shoes, so the planned quantity of raw materials was excessive which was the so-called guarantee of the smooth run of the production. On the ledger, this order was profitable, but the cost of the raw materials was not considered. Therefore, the biggest flaw of this accounting system is that it is out of touch with the market, and easily leads to the backlog of the product and the precipitation of funds. The evidence is that many enterprises ran poorly.

Now Double Star Group adopts a dynamic approach in making out bills. Its cost planning is made according to the market need. In other words, its awareness of funds is raised. To do a good job in quality and cost management, Double Star has created a new method of contract management. Under the market economy, each workshop makes a contract for the production process, machine, post and production line. The machine station becomes a responsible field and the contractor a small boss or a housekeeper who has his own decision-making power in management, accounting, consumption, etc. Under the encouragement of this new mechanism, the cadres and staffs work harder and have achieved outstanding results in management innovation, equipment transformation and energy consumption so on. Units of Double Star create more than 100 methods in cost management, e.g., bidding management and special contracting method etc., which have reduced costs. For example, due to the rising price of energy, heat transfer oil boilers are more widely used; and 10 steam boilers in the whole group are replaced. As far as the coal is concerned, the annual cost is reduced by more than 4 million Yuan. Therefore, under the efforts from all cadres and staffs, Double Star does a good job in cost management.

(2) Implementing the operation of the factory currency and deepening the contract management

Labor-intensive industries such as shoes and tires, are characterized by the complicated production process and many raw materials and semi-finished parts. Double Star adopts the currency to buy materials instead of the requisition form, bringing about a change in the staff's mind. This change involves every link and each sector of the production process of the enterprise, which interlock and restrict each other. The problems in a link may affect the overall situation. Double Star eliminates the old the management mode of eating from the same big pot. On the other hand, Double Star adopts a new management mode: cost planning prior to the production and striving to reduce the cost through the entire production process. This enhances the sense of responsibility of staffs and is conductive to the long-term and stable development of the enterprises and the formation of a fair and righteous atmosphere in the enterprise.

Deepening the contract management through the operation of the factory currency is a new management mode of Double Star, which meets the market needs and the actual conditions of the manufacturing industry. This management mode organically runs through all aspects of cost management, funds management, and quality management of the enterprise, affecting every link and every department of the production process of the enterprise, which interlock and restrict each other. The problems in a link may affect the overall situation.

Therefore, the operation of the factory currency should be healthy. It is necessary to find problems and solve them in a timely manner. It is necessary to establish a set of complete operational procedures by setting standards, identifying factors, and doing rigorous assessment, so that each department and everyone can actively participate in factory currency management. This new management mode is aimed to enhance the competitiveness and the overall management level of the enterprises.

(3) Vertical contracting and horizontal contracting

Mr. Wang believes that another crucial point in contracting is to get rid of bureaucratic thinking, be fully market-oriented, and establish a harmonious interpersonal relationship within the enterprise.

Mr. Wang hates the bureaucratic thinking very much. At the same time, he is a leader advocating innovation. He thought for a long time and thought of Luzhong. He came to its cadres and staffs and hoped them to carry out a comprehensive contracting program.

By July 2006, Luzhong had carried out a variety of contracting models, including vertical contracting, horizontal contracting, professional contracting, and joint contracting etc. However, vertical contracting and horizontal contracting achieved better results.

What is vertical contracting? It is a kind of contracting made by cadres at different levels including the top-level leaders.

What is horizontal contracting? It is a kind of the same-level contracting, which is based on the working relationship. For example, the maintenance personnel contract for the machine station, the receiving and supporting auxiliary personnel contract for their own process, the operating personnel contract for the operation process.

After the implementation of vertical contracting, the enterprise's leaders work with financial, equipment, quality and other functional departments to refine the contract management indicators, not only develop the new management goals in human resources, output, quality, material consumption, power maintenance, and safety management so forth, but also developing new standards, including how many needles, how many sheets of paper, cards, how many brooms, brushes, how many pairs of gloves, the number of violations of labor discipline, etc. Thus, there are more than 6,000 regulations in contracting, achieving the refined management effect.

After the implementation of vertical contracting, leaders and cadres take the lead in innovation and deepen the management of the production organization. Based on rational task assignments for operators according to technical levels, the enterprise carries out the fixing system of workshops, production lines, equipment and personnel in different processes such as cutting, sewing, vulcanizing, rubber processing, and molding so forth, thereby further improving efficiency and ensuring product quality.

After the contracting of the upper workshop, funds were reduced by more than 300,000 Yuan with a reduction of 18 quality inspectors in sewing and cutting. In the case of 70 staffs reduced, the output in the sewing exceeded 8,000 pairs per day. In the case of eliminating two supporting subsidiaries, Double Star still could guarantee timely supply.

After the implementation of vertical contracting, the company's leaders and management cadres to find out the power consumption and coal consumption of the heat transfer oil, stayed all day in the boiler room to determine the thickness of the coal seam, coal delivery interval time, and weight of coal delivered each time and so forth. The boiler room had a hot temperature, but they worked hard there. Based on the measurement data, they set the consumption indicators for each season for the sake of saving energy. After the heat transfer oil boiler room was contracted, the four boilers saved 120 kg of coal per day.

After the implementation of horizontal contracting, the enthusiasm for all staffs to participate in equipment and quality management was firstly stimulated. The operator no longer was slavishly dependent on the maintenance personnel when there was a problem with the equipment. To prevent and reduce the occurrence of equipment problems, the maintenance personnel took the initiative to remove the small oil bottle from the equipment and returned the power of oiling the equipment to the operator. The knowledge of the equipment was used for inspection and maintenance in time to better ensure the normal operation of the equipment. Before contracting, an average of 20 air pressure solenoid valves was used per month, but after contracting, 15 solenoid valves, thereby saving more than 1,400 Yuan per month. It is because of the innovation of contracting form that the monthly maintenance cost of Luzhong was reduced from 40,000 Yuan before contracting to less than 27,000 Yuan and the quality first-class product rate was increased by 0.002%. In 2006, the output of shoes in Luzhong exceeded 15 million pairs, creating the highest record. *(Source: Zhao Yanbiao: Wang Hai's 30 years. People's Publishing House, March 2008.)*

(4) Three Reverse methods to increase efficiency

The three reverse methods are as follows: quality reversal method, cost reversal method, and planed-zeroing reversal method.

The operation procedure of the three reverses is below: the quality problem of the finished product is taken as the source of the reversal to identify the responsibility according to the process flow and the post settings. In other words, the responsible person should be identified. In the management, three reverse methods are used, that is, quality reversal method, cost reversal method, and planed-zeroing reversal method. After a quality problem occurs, it is directly linked to the individual's income, responsibility, and interests, and the relevant staff should bear the responsibility. In this way, neighboring processes can be inspected and supervised mutually, and employees strive to improve the pass rate of raw materials, semi-finished products, and finished products as well as minimize quality problems and losses.

Through the three reverse methods, the problem of disconnection between production and quality, between production and cost, and between production and equipment is solved, and the management pattern of production, quality, equipment and capital as a whole is realized; the problem of unreal cost is solved, and the technical, planning, and quality personnel is encouraged to go to the production line; the key processes are controlled, the sense of responsibility, pressure, and urgency is enhanced, which leads to the improvement of the overall management level of the enterprise.

In the upper workshop of the shoe industry industrial park with Double Star, Sun Xuedong leader of the line-4 team took out a passbook from the pocket of the overalls. The reporter opened it and saw the following records: 252.33 Yuan deposited on February 25 and 492.22 Yuan on March 24... The deposit balance is 3,005.12 Yuan. Sun said, "This is our team's account. The deposit is our disposable income after our contracting of the production line, which means a great saving in material cost and utility fee and a commission from completion of tasks over-scheduled."

The above-said contracting refers to the internal contract management system in which Double Star Group turns its position into a responsible field for each staff and encourages employees to be a small boss who has his own decision-making power in management, accounting, consumption, etc.

Nowadays, there are a lot of contractors like Sun in Double Star Group. They have become a housekeeper of Double Star and become a small boss of the contracted entities. The cost management goes from the plant and workshop in the past to the machine station and production line now. Moreover, at present, the segmented accounting is made with the cost calculated daily and the cost known on the current day.

Mr. Wang said, “In 2009, all the workshop teams of Double Star achieved good results in energy saving and quality improvement. Management is the foundation of the survival and development of enterprises, and staffs should benefit from enterprise management."

In 2009, the cost of single-tire materials of Double Star Qingdao Tire Corporation decreased by 11.16 yuan, and the electricity, water and gas consumption decreased by 3.06%, 35.48% and 0.66% respectively; the fluctuation of single-tire weight tolerance decreased from 4 kg to 1 kg; there were 175 projects for research and development and innovation of equipment, a profit of 38.6 million Yuan and production efficiency being increased by nearly 40%.

IV. Expert Comments

Improving economic benefits is not only a major issue repeatedly emphasized by the party and the government, but also a fundamental starting point and a foothold for management of enterprises. Under the conditions of commodity economy, the economic benefits of enterprises mainly refer to the operating income (after taxes paid to the authorities) from the products produced and sold at a certain cost in a certain period. To improve economic efficiency, **it is essentially to strive to obtain more income at the same cost, or to obtain a certain income with relatively low cost**. Therefore, the cost of enterprise products not only affects the accumulation of state property, but also is closely related to the interests of the enterprise itself and its employees. To do an excellent job in cost management is a key to the success of business operations, or, as President Wang said, is the key link of business management. If enterprises want to achieve good economic benefits, they must do an excellent job of cost management.

However, in the actual management, the effect of cost management between enterprises is very different. For example, in recent years, the price hiked rapidly, labor costs and loan interest rates roared, anti-dumping intensified, rose, polices were tightened by the government and the competition was heinous in the market etc. Some enterprises were poor in cost management leading to its fund chain interrupted and its production stopped or limited and even bankruptcy. In contrast, the business boomed in all units of Double Star Group. So, what is the secret of the cost management of Double Star Group?

First, it has a good mechanism. It uses the factory currency and the deepened contract management to maximize the enthusiasm including innovation of people. In it, everyone is a housekeeper and a small boss; everyone is an accountant paying attention to the cost. Goals are achieved: namely, fewer personnel, higher efficiency, lower cost, and better quality.

Second, it has a good method. It seizes the key links (that is, fund management and cost management), realizes the one-stop management, and achieves the highest level of fund management (in which the cost is known on the current day). Moreover, it replaces the old method (namely analysis and calculation after tasks completed) with the new method (namely each order analyzed and implemented with cost known on current day), achieving significant benefits.

Third, it has a good model. It implements the internal contracted shareholding system and realizes family-style consumption management. In its cost management, three goals should be achieved: all-staff management, comprehensive management, entire-process management

Fourth, it has a useful tool. It uses the factory currency to realize the purchase and sale in each process, each section and each link.

Fifth, it has a good team. It not only is led by Mr. Wang who is an outstanding entrepreneurial, but also has a leadership core and a team of staffs who are loyal, dedicated, serious, and disciplined. This is the fundamental guarantee for Double Star to do a good job in cost management and the like.

Sixth, it has a good system. In it, everyone attends to his own duties and does his best. Leaders and cadres work hard and take the lead. With the finance as the center, the relevant departments are coordinated to make predictions of prices.

Through the use of microcomputers and other modern tools, it smoothly carried out the operation of factory currency.

Finally, it has a good culture. Wang Hai Quotations are a key part of the culture of Double Star, including its cost management culture. His quotations are catchy and easy-to-understand with profound meanings. Some of them are words originally from the mouth of employees, which are refined by Mr. Wang. The quotations about cost management are not only deeply imprinted in the minds of employees, but also become a guide for employee behavior, thereby being a successful source of cost management with Double Star.

Tactic 10: The Detail Is the Art

"Details lead to victory or defeat, small matters lead to development or stagnation, and seriousness determines success or failure. Only the attention to detail is paid especially by leaders and cadres of all levels, can be there improvements in the work quality, service quality, and product quality. It is necessary to carry out management from details and small matters; be serious without dead ends in management. Moreover, it is necessary to combine the details management and strict punishment. If it is not strict, there will be no attentiveness or attentiveness will become a mere formality. "

—— Wang Hai

In the early 1990s, Deputy Minister Li Shizhong of the former Ministry of Chemical Industry visited Double Star and personally weighed an item.

Wang gave guidance on meticulous management in Machinery Corporation.

I. Wang Hai Quotations

(I) Significance of grasping details

☆ Details determine victory or defeat, small matters determine development or stagnation, and seriousness determines success or failure.

☆ Only the attention to detail is paid especially by leaders and cadres of all levels, can be there improvements in the work quality, service quality, and product quality.

☆ Strictness means determination, high spirit means ambition, and meticulousness means a sense of responsibility

(II) Requirements for fine and meticulous management & operation

☆ From a literal point of view, this kind of management refers to a striving for perfection. With the goals of being professional, bigger and stronger, the attention is paid to details or small matters; there is a good sense of responsibility and a working style of being serious and steady; and there is a culture and mechanism adapting to diversified operations.

☆ Different from the extensive operation model in the initial stage, the fine and meticulous operation model has the following features: different markets, different channels, different series, different specifications, different prices, different trademarks, and different packages; goals of being professional, bigger, and stronger; attention paid to details, small matters, and so forth; working style of being serious and steady; getting rid of being outdated (in agency, network, personnel, operation model and method, competitive thinking and so forth) through innovative and diversified operation to improve the marketing ability.

(III) How to pay attention to details

☆ All units should pay attention to small matters and details and follow ambitious standards to make the best products.

Data comparison and case analysis so on should be carried out to meet strict requirements.

☆ Fine and meticulous management as a brand-new business philosophy and business model, puts forward higher standards and requirements for us. It requires leaders at all levels to take the lead and pay attention to details and small matters, including those on product types so forth. It also requires for us to spend efforts on solving the key problems.

☆ It is necessary for us to carry out management from details and small matters; pay attention to details and small matters; be serious and meticulous without dead ends in management. Moreover, it is necessary to combine the details management and strict punishment. For management details, there should be provisions formulated. If a person violates them, he must be punished. Detailed management is carried out through punishment. Attention paid and punishment are complementary. If it is not strict, there will be no attentiveness or attentiveness will become a mere formality.

☆ Zero emission, zero leakage, zero pollution, and zero fault; inspection always made by the leadership.

II. Practices and Effects

(I) Main practices

1. Deepening the reform in system and mechanism

Deepen the reform of the system and mechanism, implement the internal contracted shareholding system, foster the innovative spirit and mobilize the enthusiasm of staffs.

2. Grasping the key link in enterprise management

Grasp the key links in enterprise management - funds management and cost management as revolutionary fields.

3. Grasping fine and meticulous management & operation

Grasp the fine & meticulous operation and management to completely get rid of the old methods and stop up thriftless and illicit drain on funds.

4. Doing an excellent job in energy saving, emission reduction, efficiency improvement

Do a respectable job in energy conservation, emission reduction, and efficiency improvement; develop a new way of economic growth; and create a green and harmonious enterprise.

5. Doing an excellent job in detail management

Do an excellent job in detail management and strive to get the maximum effect of saving.

(II) Main effects

1. Minimal input and maximum benefit

Complete the transition from static to dynamic accounting in financial management, with the least investment yielding the greatest benefit. In the recent years when raw materials have risen sharply, and market competition is extremely cruel, in the case that some enterprises are not in place due to cost management and the funds are not moving, **the business boomed in all units of Double Star Group**.

2. Sustainable development with energy saving and emission reduction

Double Star has been a resource-saving and environment-friendly enterprise and have embarked on the road of sustainable development of energy conservation and emission reduction benefiting our country, our society and ourselves.

3. Building a resource-saving enterprise has become an important development goal

Through the people's war in the market, Double Star constantly carries out innovation, transforms old equipment, and solve the problem of waste of energy in old equipment. To build a sustainable resource-saving enterprise (which is characterized by low input, high yield, low consumption, low emission, and recycling) has become an important development goals for the enterprise.

4. Transformation and innovation of old equipment and old technology; old enterprise gaining vitality again

As an old enterprise with a history of 90 years, Double Star not adhering the traditional concept has boldly transformed old equipment and old crafts, optimized and upgraded products and technologies, and vigorously promoted its tires and machinery products so forth to the high-end market where there are strict requirements in energy conservation and environmental protection. Double Star has become vigorous again.

5. Completely solving the problem of thriftless and illicit drain on funds

For example, in thermal power plant, the said problem was very serious. By adopting strict measures, paying attention to the details, now it has realized the goals of no leakage and zero emissions and realized the considerable economic benefits, including annual recovery of exhausted steam being nearly 11.000 tons, a saving of demineralized water being worth 97.000 yuan, and a saving of heating power being worth 350,000 Yuan per year.

6. Being mindful of both small and large matters and cultivating a good habit of saving and reducing consumption

In Double Star, to be mindful of both small and large matter and to save water, coal, fuel, and power is not a slogan, instead, has penetrated the hearts of every employee and become conscious action. In 2010, a saving of water, coal, oil and power was remarkable, thereby reducing the production cost and bringing advantages to the development of markets at home and abroad for Double Star in the case of skyrocketing raw material prices.

III. Typical examples

(1) Being mindful of details and reducing costs

President Wang often goes everywhere in the workshop and emphasizes that every detail cannot be ignored in production management.

The work should start from inconspicuous and seemingly insignificant places. For example, weighing should start from the details. No matter a needle, a line, a gram of glue it is, the weighing should be made. For some items, weight, length, and number should be known at the same time. Originally measured by the number of points, it is also necessary to use the weight assessment to measure, so that the weight can be used to assess the calculated quantity. In Haijiang, the length of the stitch, which was previously measured from the scraping case, is directly calculated by weighing each meter of the stitch. The quality of the cloth, which was previously determined by measurement and laboratory inspection, is determined more precisely by weighing (this new method improves the overall management). Another example is that, by weighing, the standard weight and standard quantity per kilogram of eyelets with shoes can be accurately obtained. For assorted brands of eyelets, under the conditions of same weight, same specifications, and same price, it is found that there is a deviation in quantity: 897 eyelets at most, which can be used to make 44 pairs of shoes. Since the use of weighing the eyelets, it has saved 66 kilograms of eyelets worth more than 2,000 Yuan; thereby solving the problem of raw material suppliers taking the opportunity to cheat and reducing the production costs.

(2) Giving instructions on a piece of paper

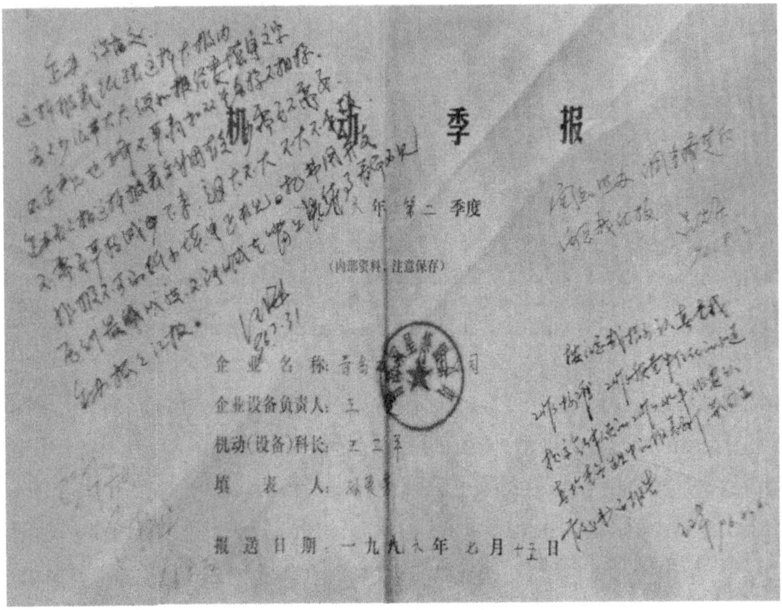

President Wang gave instructions on the wasted report paper at the equipment office.

One piece of paper is of little value for most of us and even less in a large enterprise value system. Therefore, wasting a piece of paper arbitrarily in life and work is everywhere, and many people turn a blind eye to this phenomenon. They think this is a trivial matter and not worth mentioning. Nonetheless, Wang gave instructions on one piece of paper and treated it as a serious matter. This is thought-provoking.

For the phenomena of a supervisor signing on a blank paper, Mr. Wang gave an instruction to the supervisor, "You has proposed to build a money-saving culture. Today, the last page of your report for me has nothing except your signature. This is a behavior of wasting resources." Seeing the instruction, the supervisor carried out self-criticism and took the initiative to punish himself by not taking one month's bonus.

As a president of a well-known enterprise, Mr. Wang blamed the behavior of wasting a piece of paper. In the eyes of some people, he made a fuss. If we look at specific circumstances and social background, we will find that he is right and his instruction is very necessary.

At present, our government calls for the construction of a conservation-oriented society, requiring the entire society to implement economic savings, and most enterprises have begun to formulate conservation plans. On the one hand, in many enterprises, there is a savings plan is not effectively implemented, especially some small matters are often ignored. On the other hand, Double Star Group takes the lead to carry forward the saving spirit and build a money-saving culture. In this background, the said supervisor signed his name on a blank paper of a written report. Obviously, this is inconsistent with the spirit and culture advocated by the enterprise company, whereas there is a humorous irony; just like some people who make fake and shoddy products while blaming the behavior of making them. Wang was keenly aware of this phenomenon and gave serious instructions. He did the right thing. Actually, he fought against two evils existing for a long time in some enterprises: what supervisors say not agreeing with their action; and being careless in their work.

In the enterprise, some supervisors often were reliable, because their words did not coincide with their action. For example, they adopted double standards in their work (setting strict requirements for subordinates but loose ones for themselves); they require subordinates to strictly abide by the rules, but they go beyond the rules; they are strict with others but lenient with themselves. Their working style is very harmful. For example, it undermines the management's prestige and image and leads to the fact that all kinds of measures are difficult to implement effectively.

His fight against the phenomena of wasting a piece of paper is precisely to correct this bad habit. The responsible persons at all levels who have certain powers should take the lead in strictly implementing the rules formulated by the enterprise. Doing so will help to create a good atmosphere. At the same time, it also eliminates the excuses of ordinary people to violate the rules. Wang asks all subordinates to start from saving one piece of paper, to let the concept advocated is in perfect harmony with the behavior, get rid of the above-said bad working style, and help the implementation of rules of the enterprise.

In short, his deed reflects his attention to details and his pursuit of excellence and perfection as well as Double Star culture. Truly, subtleties are tinged with his spirit which should be actively carried forward.

(3) Story of ninety-seven needles

On one occasion, Wang accompanied the customers to visit the factory. When walking to a custodian, Wang picked up a bag of needles and asked, "How many needles are there in this bag?" The custodian replied, "There were originally 100 needles a bag. Now, 3 needles are taken away, so 97 needles are left in it." Wang said, "Please count them." The custodians began counting with composure, one, two, three... Result: precisely 97 needles. The customers were very surprised at what they saw.

Wang believes that management needs to be an ongoing effort. No matter a small thing (for example, a needle) or an important thing it is, the strict criteria should be adhered to.

Being down to earth and attentive to detail is a path to the success.

Management needs to not only be strict, but also be scientific. In making shoes, there are more than 200 processes, and how to deal with defects occurring in these processes or after delivery into market? This problem, which had plagued the world shoe industry for many years, is solved by a small digital tracking card invented by Double Star. Therefore, no matter where the shoes are sold, if there is a quality problem, the responsible person can be found in the factory. Double Star sets up the control points in each production process and enter the data into a computer, thereby realizing the one-stop management, including its system of calculating each order, sector accounting, and knowing cost of current day.

Double Star implements the quality standards of international famous brands and establishes a set of quality supervision and guarantee system for this purpose. Double Star carries out strict inspection and assessment on product quality and is the first enterprise in the domestic shoe industry to obtain the ISO9001 certificate which is a pass for products to the international market. *(Source: A Bird's-eye View of Double Star, 2000.)*

(4) Job number on the plate

Customers who eat at the canteen of Double Star Machinery often see a small plate which is pasted with the job number of the chef. The company's leader says that through the job number the customer can know which dish is cooked by the chef and give advice to him. It is said that a customer based on this point to place an order, even if he did not enter a workshop and that the customer felt assured by what he saw in the canteen.

In today's increasingly fierce market competition, to be successful, the enterprise must start with details to improve product quality. However, in daily management, some companies often consciously and unconsciously ignore the details. It is necessary to understand the relationship between details and the wholeness as well as details and strategic-decision. In other words, the existence of the large thing depends on the small thing; the wholeness is made up of small things; strategic decision is the result of analysis of various situations. With the rapid development of high technology and the rapid development of economic globalization, with the increasing division of labor and the increasing degree of specialization, an era of needing fine and meticulous management has arrived. Details become a powerful expression of product quality and service levels. How to deal with the details, from the perspective of enterprise leadership, is the artistic embodiment of leadership ability; from the perspective of enterprise style, it is the embodiment of the company's seriousness and responsibility; from the perspective of enterprise development, it is the way for enterprises to achieve their goals. Strong companies pay attention to the details in the competition. In the past, staffs of Double Star Machinery did not attach importance to the details, resulting in the frequent occurrence of problems and a poor sale. Later, Mr. Wang President required them to adopt the fine and meticulous management, which made them become serious and meticulous. As results, the products gradually gained a good reputation and a good sale in the market.

Only by pay attention to the details and pursuing perfection in all details, can the enterprise comprehensively improve market competitiveness and ensure the long-term success. *(Source: China Chemical Industry News, August 23, 2006.)*

IV. Expert Comments

As we all know, in the domestic book market in recent years, two books have been quite popular, whose views held are opposite to each other.

One book is entitled Details Determine Success or Failure. (Wang Zhongqiu, Xinhua Publishing House, 2004). The author of this book discusses the importance of details in management in many cases. This book is intended to remind companies and even the community that the era of fine and meticulous management has arrived. There are too few people who can do remarkable things. Most people can only do some specific things, maybe dull, maybe trivial, maybe monotonous, but this is the basic tone of the work and life and is an indispensable foundation for doing wonderful things. China does not lack strategists but lacks the executor of excellence. China does not lack various management systems but lacks the effective implementation of the rules and regulations.

The other book is entitled Strategy Determines Success or Failure." (Yu Laiwen, Blue Sky Publishing House, January 2005). The author of this book points out in a tit-for-tat manner, "The details do not necessarily determine success or failure, and the strategy really determines success or failure. If without strategy, there will be no details. Only with a right strategy, can there be right details. There being a strategy leads to a plan which determines success or failure."

Five years later, another book was published with the same name: namely, Strategy Determines Success or Failure (He Xuelin, Beijing Higher Education Audiovisual Press, October 2010). The author of this book points out, "There is a popular view that the details determine success or failure. It finds favor in many people's eyes, because it caters to a certain need. Bosses attach importance to details and execution, but the popularity is not necessarily the truth. For this saying that the details determine success or failure, there is a premise that the strategy is correct. This book proposes that the strategy determines success or failure. Only the strategy is correct, can the details make sense, and can the execution make sense. The wrong strategy leads to a generation of Chinese enterprises fallen. The right strategy can make the fallen enterprises stand up again. Following the 21 strategies proposed in this book, enterprises will be built to last; not following these strategies, they will surely die."

Obviously, as the title suggests, these three books propose two viewpoints: the first viewpoint is that details determine success or failure, and the other viewpoint is that strategy determines success or failure. So, for an enterprise, what determines success or failure?

The successful experiences and failure lessons of many enterprises prove that if an enterprise wants to succeed, it needs both the right strategy and the solid details. The two are closely related and complement each other and are indispensable. However, the important role of the two is reflected in the different stages of enterprise development, and it is necessary to emphasize their important role according to the different stages of enterprise development.

In the strategy-formulation stage, the strategy determines success or failure. At this stage, the central task is to formulate a scientific, innovative, correct and feasible development strategy for the enterprise. At the same time, it is necessary to highlight the strategy, rather than prematurely emphasize the details. The reason is that, if the strategy is wrong, the best details are not only worthless, but also cause huge waste, and even have a serious negative effect.

In the implementation strategy phase, the details determine success or failure. At this stage, the central task is to put the correct strategy of the enterprise into practice and effectively implement, so it is necessary to highlight the details. Larry Bosidy and Ram Charan said, **"The strategy is good. If it is not implemented efficiently, it can't achieve the desired goal. The grand idea not turned into reality is useless. The breakthrough thought not implemented is a cranky thought. The knowledge not applied does not bring real value. If the goals cannot be achieved, the so-called revolutionary change will be not successful."** (Larry Bosidy and Ram Charan:

Execution – The Discipline of Getting Things Done, Mechanical Industry Press, January 2003, p. 16).

Therefore, to ensure the success of the enterprise, we should formulate a good strategy, then carefully pay attention to the details in implementing it.

Tactic 11: The Competition Is the Lever

"Through technical competitions and job competitions, we have done many things which we dared not or could not to do before. We have been successful. The competition itself is by no means a formality. Carrying forward the good traditions of our party, we enhance the sense of the righteousness, invigorate the spirit of the staffs, and mobilize the enthusiasm of everyone, enhance the cohesiveness of the enterprise, and be together to work hard to make the enterprise bigger and stronger."

——Wang Hai

President Wang was together with leaders of the Qingdao Municipal Government and leaders of the trade unions in the scene of the sewing skill competition of the shoe factory.

The forklift competition was held at Double Star Group Production.

The scene of the cooking skill competition

Cooking show

I. Wang Hai Quotations

(I) Significance of carrying out job competition

☆ Job competition is a concrete manifestation of the actualization and humanization so forth of ideological and political work.

☆ Job competition is the best means and measure to invigorate employees' spirit and inspire their enthusiasm.

☆ Job competition can best reflect the power and role of political work and reflect the creativity and innovation of political work.

(II) Role of job competition

☆ By job competition, we can find management and market talents and excellent technicians.

☆ By job competition, we can improve quality, reduce costs, and promote management

☆ By job competition, we can improve overall quality of our management team, our ability to adapt to market economy and our employment mechanism.

☆ Job competition stimulates the enthusiasm and passion of the cadres and staffs, enhances the cohesiveness and combat effectiveness of the enterprise.

☆ Job competition improves the process and equipment, reduces labor intensity, and improves technical level and production efficiency

☆ Job competition is a powerful guarantee to strengthen enterprise management, promote production and operation, and participate in market competition.

(III) Relationship between job competition and ideological & political work

☆ Under the market economy, to achieve the highest level of the field, we must strengthen political and ideological work, which can unify the thinking of staffs, enhance the sense of righteousness, invigorate the spirit of staffs, and create a good environment. Especially, the job competition can best reflect the power, role, creativity, and innovation of political work.

☆ Our leaders at all levels, especially the political leaders, must solve the problem of politics and economy as Two Skins. We must study people, educate people, inspire people, and motivate people considering the actual conditions of production and operation.

☆ The job competition is by no means a formality. This way can invigorate staffs' fighting spirit, and tap their potential in innovation, including technological innovation.

(IV) How to do an excellent job in the job competition

☆ The difficulty of production and management is the focus of the job competition

☆ The job post is the market, and the competition is on the machine station; all the staffs are innovative and achieve results.

☆ All the staffs participate in the market and participate in the competition.

☆ Job competition can polish the skills, improve the quality, and create the brand name

☆ Job competition should be combined with production and operation.

☆ It is necessary to grasp the post competition around production and the construction of two civilizations. Everyone has the spirit of striving for the first class.

☆ It is necessary to engage in post competitions around the construction of the team to make the team management more distinctive.

☆ It is necessary to carry out job competitions in every position, every process, including management positions and the tertiary industry. This is a good form of combining material and spirit.

☆ It is necessary to combine job competition with Three Qualities. The political work team should attach importance to it and integrate it all work.

(V) How to do an excellent job in innovation of job competition

☆According to the actual conditions of the enterprise, the job competition is held in the weak links of management to tap the potential and reduce the cost.

☆ The competitions are regularly held, with making regular summaries, strict assessments, and meting out rewards and punishments, to mobilize everyone's enthusiasm and promote the improvement of three qualities.

☆ It is necessary to continuously carry out various forms of competitions, motivate employees to participate in management, and form a good atmosphere of competing, learning, catching up, helping, and exceeding.

II. Practices and Effects

(I) Main practices

1. Combine job competition, technical competition and ideological and political work

Take the job competition and technical competition as an important means of ideological and political work, and as the best combination point of political and economic work, carry out various forms of competition activities around innovation, quality, skill and efficiency to stimulate employees' enthusiasm and cultivate their feelings for the enterprise.

2. Combine the job competition as an effective method with the incentive mechanism

Adhere to the use the job competition as the most effective and direct working method; while considering the internal shareholding system of buyout contract, continuously innovate the incentive mechanism of competition, and extensively carry out various forms of wonderful innovative competitions to cultivate a large number of talents.

3. Often carry out Five Goods competition

The so-called Five Goods refer to: good family, good husband and wife, good brothers, good sisters, good relatives. The Five Goods competitions are often held lively, so that staffs can respect each other and help each other in their work. Many staffs have received the titles of good families, good couples, good brothers, and good sisters, which have become important forces that cannot be ignored in the development of Double Star.

4. Carry out job competitions with the theme of Double Star Youth Pioneer among young staffs

These competitions are carried out among post-80s and post-90s to enhance the sense of responsibility in the work of youth staffs and invigorate their spirit of working hard and actively participating in innovation. The activities of discussion, education and brand creation are also carried out with the following themes: Let the youth shine in the enterprise; have better skills, pass on skills, improve quality via innovation; talent show, innovation by youth to improve effectiveness, young model at the post, and young master at the post.

5. Carry out job competitions among female staffs with the theme of Double Star Heroine

In response to the recent changes in the employment situation and the fact that female staffs are more and more in number, these competitions are carried out to inspire the enthusiasm of female staffs.

6. Carry out job competitions among old staffs with the theme of Willing Ox

Old staffs are the backbone of the development of the enterprise. They are selfless in important posts, serve the enterprise heart and soul, and dedicate themselves to the work in management, technology, production, etc. These competitions are carried out to build a platform for them to show their value and invigorate their spirit of being diligent, dedicated, earnest, and persistent, and set up a Willing Ox team who can add luster to the Double Star brand.

(II) Main effects

1. Established a competitive mechanism of employment

Through competition and elimination, Double Star has established a competitive mechanism of employment, in which talents can be chosen and give full play to their abilities. At the same time, it can improve as soon as possible the overall quality of the management team and their ability to adapt to the market economy.

2. Create a high-quality & high-skilled leading staff team

The job competition inspires the enthusiasm and passion of the leading staffs, activates their innovative potential, improves their operational skills, and lets many of them receive various honorary titles, for example, Double Star Youth Commando Member, Double Star Youth Pioneer, Double Star Post Model, Double Star Willing Ox, and Double Star Heroine etc. Therefore, Double has trained a team of high-quality & high-skilled leading staffs.

3. Improve the technical level and production efficiency, improve product quality and reduce labor intensity

Through competitions, Double Star constantly innovate its process, technology, equipment, boldly transforms old equipment and old technology, improves old technology and old formula, changes old standards, old parameters, and old operating methods (in which various difficulties are overcome), thereby greatly improving the technology level and production efficiency, achieving automation and mechanization, and improving product quality and reduce labor intensity.

4. Guarantee stability of personnel and production, improved quality and increased output

The family-style competition plays a very important role in ensuring the stability of personnel and production, the improvement of quality and the growth of output. According to statistics, there are 160 families, 800 couples, 260 pairs of brothers, 250 pairs of sisters and more than 700 relatives in all units of Double Star. Staffs having the family relationship account for 24% of total staffs, and those having fellowships, comrades and classmates account for near 50%, thereby becoming the main force of the enterprise. Moreover, their ideological steadiness, quality improvement, skill improvement and loyalty to the enterprise are very important to the development of the enterprise.

5. Cultivate good character and morality, and continuously enhance the cohesiveness and combat effectiveness of the enterprise

Through the Five Goods competition, Double Star has cultivated good character and morality of staffs and constantly enhanced the cohesiveness and combat effectiveness; also cultivated good character and morality leading cadres and let employees with family members and relatives so forth respect each other and help each other, which become an important force that cannot be ignored in the development of Double Star.

III. Typical Examples

(1) Job competition to let staffs as stars shining

To fully mobilize the passion and enthusiasm of leading staffs pursuing skills, create a stage for staffs to show themselves and their value, and enhance the vitality of the enterprise development, Double Star Group launches job competitions with the theme of achieving results and shining in the post. These competitions have stimulated the enthusiasm, feelings and innovation potential of leading staffs, promoted innovation to improve quality and reduce consumption, and the rapid development of the enterprise.

Strive to be the Willing Ox and further improve quality

Wang says, "The difficulty of quality management is the focus of the job competition." According to his instruction, the units of Double Star Group carry out a series of job competitions with the theme of achieving results and shining in the post. In this way, they have created a good atmosphere of everyone being an inspector and attention paid to quality in every post and cultivated forging a team of experienced and skilled staffs who serve the enterprise heart and soul.

Double Star Qingdao Tire carries out various quality competitions such as rubber identification, rubber inspection and semi-finished joint quality examination so forth, whereas it extends the requirements of being even in rubber mixing to the whole production process. As results, it improves quality of rubber, semi-finished products and finished-products. Dong Junjie of the mixing workshop is a charcoal black worker, has been successively recognized as an innovation pioneer and a quality model worker. Since the start of Willing Ox Competition, he has worked harder and obtained greater results. With his honest attitude and high spirit, he has worked in the current post for 13 years and delivered more than 100,000 tons of carbon black without errors, thereby creating a new miracle.

Establish a unique machine station in which staffs work hard

Double Star Qingdao Tire and other units make a thorough investigation, and on the basis of respecting the wishes of staffs and considering their different abilities, readjust job posts and set up different machine stations, such as fellowship machine station, comrade machine station, brother machine station, post-80s or post-90s machine station, couple machine station. Among these unique stations, there is a new round of competitions in terms of unity, skills and dedication.

At present, Double Star Qingdao Tire has 18 comrade machine stations, 17 fellowship machine stations, 22 college graduate machine stations, 71 pos-80s or post-90s machine stations, 26 brother machine stations, 23 couple machine stations. There are more than 130 machine stations winning in the competition. Its technical team dominated by post-80s, through the competition, has successfully developed new professional formulas including formula meeting requirements of EU in environmental protection, long-distance wear-resistant formula, mine-specific formula and the like. Therefore, Double star tires are better adapted to market requirements.

In Double Star Hanhai Sports Shoes, Zhang Zhaozhen, his wife Gong Peiqin and his son Zhang Mingwen work in the workshop. In it, a family machine station for them who are together to take part in the competition. Zhang Zhaozhen is in the boxing step to create a side-boxing method whose efficiency is 17% higher than the other method. His wife is a shoe inspector; due to her fairness and selflessness, her team is always in the leading position in working quality. His son continuously pulls the uppers in 250,000 pairs of shoes and there is no quality problem in any case. Three people from the same family are granted titles such as Double Star Post Model and Youth Post Pioneer.

Female staffs of Double Star to hold up half the sky

With the increase of female staffs in number, the female staffs of Double Star have become a new main force in production. Among them, Double Star has launched competitions with the themes such as Heroines of Double Star and Double Stars and March Eighth Red Flag Lines. Female staffs' unit and spend efforts on technical research. A lot of them receive honorary titles such as Husband and Wife as Working Partners, Sisters Machine Station, Elder Sister Machine Station, and Heroine of Double Star.

Chen Lifei is a staff at 2#255 final rubber mixing post at D Zone in Mixing Workshop of Double Star Qingdao Tire. Her output in the first half of 2011 was 23,841 vans. Born in 1980s, she is highly spirited and granted honorary titles several times such as Model in Quality and Innovation Pioneer. Liu Yanhong is a staff at vulcanizing machine station of Double Star Dongfeng Tire. While not being inferior to male staffs, she is always among the best in terms of output and quality. Sun Xuedong is the leader of line 4 in the upper workshop of Double Star Footwear Industrial Park and led more than 50 staffs to take part in the job competition named Double Star Record Challenge, whereas, with her unique non-stop operation method, she achieved the best results.

Strive to be a skilled staff

In Double Star, a unique skill will be named after its creator, and this can tap the potential of its staffs. The reporter learns from the Double Star Group that Double Star has built a stage for staffs by actively carrying out technical competitions of skilled workers and developing technical evaluation and promotion mechanisms for them. To motivate staffs to learn technology and improve skill levels, all units offer a series of incentives, for example, staffs who win the championship are rewarded, and unique skills are named after creators who are granted rewards in spirit and material.

In Double Star, every staff regards the post as a stage and turns technology into art. Luzhong implements incentives for middle and senior technicians who achieve excellent results in key positions or special positions to better stabilize the backbone team. Ma Tao as a staff in outsole vulcanizing who is awarded the title of vulcanizing champion is recognized as a middle technician to receive a subsidy of 200 Yuan per month. He says happily, "Leaders give me high pay as technician and my family members are very supportive of my work. I will work harder to keep this honor!"

Double Star Haijiang launches activities of selecting the Star of Innovation and Gold-level, Silver-level, and Copper-level technicians. The rear and front uppers of the diving shoes have 14 eyelets with a diameter of 4mm. The production of these eyelets is quite troublesome. It takes 8 people to produce eyelets in 400 pairs per day. In the molding workshop, Liu Bin and others actively made explorations in the competition and made a self-made eyelet machine, which can produce eyelets in rear and front uppers at one time. Due to it, a production line only needs 2 people to complete the production task of Nissan 800 pairs per day; now this modern technology completely replaces the manual operation in eyelet production.

Mast and apprentice: pursuing technical perfection

Each unit of Double Star actively carried out the competition in which masters and apprentices participate. It enables the staffs to understand that technology plays a key role in the survival of the enterprise and the embodiment of personal value and stimulates them to be very skilful.

Ji Xia at the vulcanization station of A Zone in the radical tire workshop of Double Star Qingdao Tire passes on skills to five apprentices without any reservations. With her guidance, all her apprentices have become quite skillful. For example, apprentice Ding Peiqin at the beginning felt timid when seeing the huge steam room. But seeing her master made a skillful operation, she immediately relaxed; she also read jingles composed by her master which reflected the working experiences. In this way, Ding Peiqin quickly became an independent staff with her skills improved; and with his master, received an honorary title in the competition.

Double Star Machinery carries out similar competitions. More than 30 young staffs have grown into skilled staffs, and 6 young technicians have grown into technical leaders. There are 21 unique skills created in the competition, including defect-free fillet welds, no-stop air cutting of flanges and so on.

Pioneer in reducing consumption and enhancing competitiveness

The various competitions carried out by the units of Double Star are centered around the posts and machine stations, and truly fulfilled the requirements of posts being the market and all staffs being innovative, thereby uniting staffs, invigorating the spirit of staffs and stimulating them to do the best.

In the cutting workshop of Double Star Footwear Industrial Park, each contracted machine station carries out the competitions with the theme of Pioneer in Reduction Consumption and Double Star Youth Pioneer. Zhang Zhangjie is a cutter. There was an order of shoes which were high-grade sandals (Model No.153) which were required to be shipped as soon as possible. The Green Space leather was only 27.4 meters in the workshop with 1.1 meters in short under the need of this order. To ensure the supply, Zhang took the initiative to contract the cutting of the leather. With his skills, he not only made up for this lack of 1.1 meters of leather, but also saved 0.2 meters. He has received the title of pioneer in reducing consumption with the workshop.

In Double Star Zhongyuan Shoes, after the steam boiler is replaced by the heat oil boiler, there is a saving of more than 8,000 kWh in the 5-roll calender, 3-color machine and foxing plate. Considering that there is a high temperature in the region and that water can be heated to 70℃ using solar energy, Dong Junyong proposed a scheme of heating water with solar energy. As results, this scheme has greatly reduced the time of steam generation and saved electric energy by more than 30% or 12,000 kWh per year.

Through the job competition, Double Star Group has stimulated the enthusiasm and affection of the leading staffs, invigorated their spirit, tapped their innovation potential, enhanced the cohesiveness, creativity and combat effectiveness of the enterprise, and promoted the development of Double Star in all fields.

The cultural and sports activities were held by Double Star Group.

Art and cultural show to celebrate the 90th anniversary of Double Star

(2) Let youth shine in the enterprise

——Giving full play to talents of post-80s and post-90s

Youth is the main force in enterprise development. In recent years, units of Double Star Group carry out the relevant competitions among post-80s and post-90s to enhance the sense of responsibility in the work of youth staffs and invigorate their spirit of working hard and actively participating in innovation. The activities of discussion, education and brand creation are also carried out with the following themes: Let the youth shine in the enterprise; have better skills, pass on skills, improve quality via innovation; talent show, innovation by youth to improve effectiveness, young model at the post, and young master at the post.

Under the guidance of cultural ideas with Double Star, young staffs work hard, passionately carry out innovation, and make outstanding contributions. It is them who enable the enterprise to overcome all kinds of difficulties and obstacles on the road ahead and achieve innovative development. Therefore, young staffs play a key role in promoting and guaranteeing the vigorous development of the enterprise.

Improve skills by practicing and let the youth shine

Through in-depth analysis of young staffs in the new era, units of Double Star Group understand that young staffs receive a better education with broad vision, rich knowledge, strong ability to accept modern technologies and innovative ideas, and quickly master new technologies. All units of the Group organize the skills training and job competitions with themes such as Youth Demonstration Post. In this way, the Group forms a strong atmosphere of competing, learning, catching up, helping, and exceeding, while young staffs passionately pursue skill perfection and let their youth shine in the post.

Wu Dan as a staff in the mixing workshop of Double Star Dongfeng Tire works hard to possess super skills in examining rubber sheets. He defeated an old master who had worked for more than ten years and obtained the first place in the competition. He has been awarded the title of Excellent Quality Model by Double Star. Zhang Dongji as an operator of Luzhong created a unique operation method of square grid cloth and a method of quick rubber delivery, so being recognized as Innovative Pioneer.

By the activities of improving skills and letting the youth shine in the post, young staffs of Double Star embark on the road to success.

Master and apprentice: making progress together

For post-80s and post-90s, there is a process of technical adaptation after entry into the enterprise. Double Star vigorously implements the projects to help young staffs rapidly master skills. For example, it adopts a master-apprentice system. For the newly-entered employees, they will be guided by masters or instructors with excellent ideological quality and strong ability. Moreover, a letter of responsibility on instruction is signed to ensure the guidance role played in ideological work and passing-on of skills. The masters are conscientious and diligent and diligent, letting young apprentices feel greatly touched and gain the encouragement and strength. Accompanied by masters, these apprentices not only learn the skills and the spirit of working hard from them, but also establish correct world view, outlook on life, and values.

Meng Xiangshuang, born in 1991, was a newly entered operator in vulcanization at a workshop of Double Star Luzhong and felt afraid when seeing a heavy mold for the vulcanized outsole. Luckily, he was selected as an apprentice by Tian Xianghua an operational expert who had been rated as the quality model of Double Star Group. Tian passed on his experience of vulcanization work for many years to the apprentice and actively looked after him in the life. As a result, the apprentice could quickly carry out independent work only in a week. Yao Jiaguo a master of the EVA workshop in Double Star Footwear Industrial

Park adopted the hands-on approach to teach his apprentice Han Xilong. When the apprentice debugging equipment encountered a problem, he always encouraged him. The apprentice was very touched and spent more efforts on learning. Under the guidance of the master, the apprentice's operational skills were improved very quickly. The master-apprentice system lets young staffs of Double Star embark on a road of unity, harmony and common progress.

Competition in quality and innovation among young staffs

Young people in the new era have a higher level of knowledge and literacy with broad horizons and are good at thinking. When entering the society, they are eager to achieve success and glory and look forward to being recognized. Through the implementation of the internal contracted shareholding system, Double Star carries out a full-staff innovation competition for the following purposes: namely to build a stage for young staffs to show their ingenuity and reflect their own values; discover and cultivate innovation models among them in a timely manner; grant rewards for young staffs who are good at study and innovation; and fully mobilized the initiative and enthusiasm of young staffs in quality and innovation.

Yan Fangke, born in 1980s, is a plastics worker in Zone C of the mixing workshop with Double Star Qingdao Tire. He adheres to the behavioral principles of gratefulness, passion, hardworking, and innovation, and hopes to repay the enterprise with conscience. In a night shift in November 2010, he was in 1#270 production line to change ABN with ANN. With his rich experience, he found a problem in the first van of ABN. He immediately stopped the operation to find the reason. Finally, he solved the problem, thereby avoiding the occurrence of quality accidents.

Huang Junchao working in the mixing workshop of Double Star Dongfeng Tire led a team of 7 young people to achieve a good result in successive competitions in terms of quality and competition. In the past year, the team has achieved satisfactory results in the quality competition. In Double Star Zhongyuan Shoes, Xu Hongyou of mixing workshop led a team of uncles to be teachers for young staffs in a classroom after work for innovation. and uncles to open up a "small class after class" for innovation. Since the beginning of this year, he has led them including young staffs to make more than 10 innovations, for example, rubber sheet automatic delivery, rubber material automatic drying, and automatic powder sweeping, which not only reduce the labor intensity and improve the cohesiveness of staffs, but also improve the on-site management level and production efficiency. Furthermore, the quality of semi-finished products has reached more than 99.8%. Competitions in quality and innovation let the young staffs embark on the road of development and improvement.

IV. Expert Comments

The socialist labor competition is originated in the former Soviet Union and is derived from the Voluntary Labor on Saturday. On Saturday, April 12, 1919, 13 Communists and two other workers on the Kazan Railway in Moscow repaired three locomotives after a night of voluntary labor, attracting a lot of people to participate in voluntary labor nationwide, which was praised by Lenin as a great pioneering work. This is also considered to be the original form of the socialist labor competition, which has gone through more than 90 years.

A campaign of Learning from Comrade Zhao Zhankui was initiated in Shaanxi-Gansu-Ningxia Border Region in the 1930s and has now gone through more than 70 years. At that time, it was the hardest time of China's anti-Japanese war. Mao Zedong put forward the call of getting ample food and clothing by working with our own hands, and our revolutionary people overcame all difficulties using their own strength. As a fire watcher of the boiler, Zhao Zhankui worked hard under extremely difficult conditions and became a role model for the working class. Yan'an Liberation Daily published an editorial calling for learning from model worker Zhao Zhankui. In the period of the War of Liberation, it developed into a campaign of production & contribution-making. After the founding of new China, many advanced experiences were summarized and promoted, for example, working method created by Wang Chonglun in the industrial field, working method created by Hao Jianxiu in the textile field, and rapid excavation method created by Ma Liuhai in the coal field. of the horses in the coal industry, etc. A strong atmosphere of competing, learning, catching up, helping, and exceeding was formed across the country. Later, due to the influence of the Cultural Revolution, the labor competition was stopped for more than a decade. Since the Third Plenary Session of the Eleventh Central Committee of the CPC, it has been carried out again. In 2006, the National Federation of Trade Unions decided to carry out the competition among staffs nationwide with the theme of being a good main force, making contributions in the period of the Eleventh Five-Year Plan, and building a harmonious well-off society.

From the historical context of the above-mentioned labor competition, it is clear that the labor competition is to fully explore the ingenuity and improve the skill level of the staffs through the platform of the competition, and to guide the enthusiasm and creativity of the staffs to the economic construction. This is an excellent tradition created and persisted for a long time by the Communists and the working class.

President Wang has inherited and developed this outstanding tradition of the Communists in the 30 years of reform and development of Double Star Group. He has attached importance to and organized labor competitions in which he has made many innovations. In Double Star, its job competition is unique and has main characteristics below:

(I) Leaders attach importance to and take the lead in the competition

President Wang points out, "Competition activities can best reflect the power and role of political work and can best reflect the creativity and innovation of political work." Each year, the group establishes a competition leading team with the president as the leader of the team. Each year, the president gives instructions on the enterprise newspaper, briefings, information reports and so forth, and personally guides the competition. The attention of the president and the party committee of the group to the job competition broadens the mind of the leaders who recognize that job competition is an effective way to achieve political goals and a powerful measure to create an economic foundation. Therefore, the leaders take the lead to participate in the competition.

(II) Full-staff participation and invigorating competition

In recent years, the full-staff job competitions have been held, in which all the staffs participate, from the production personnel to the market personnel, from the leading staffs to the common staffs, from the technical personnel to the logistics. Their roles are to promote the production, management, innovation; reduce costs; and eliminate unfavorable factors for the development of the enterprise. After participation in competitions, all staffs have enhanced their enthusiasm and improved their qualifications and skills.

(III) Considering actual conditions and innovating competition

President Wang says, "Political work should be market-oriented, realistic, concrete, and humanized." According to this theory proposed by him, Double Star carries out innovative forms of job competitions which can invigorate the spirit the staffs and improve the cohesiveness of the enterprise. If there are job posts, there will be competitions; and as long as there is a competition, there will be results.

These characteristics of the job competition are unique to Double Star Group. Around these characteristics, the organizers of Double Star have created several new forms and new contents during the organization of competitions.

These new forms and new contents are embodied in the following Eight Combinations: combination of job competition with leaders as an example; combination of job competition with cultural ideas innovation; combination of job competition with pursuit of skills perfection; combination of job competition with integrity & quality; combination of job competition with bidding plus tendering; combination of job competition with post innovation; combination of job competition with family management; and combination of job competition with equipment management.

In short, the most essential feature of the Double Star Group's job competition is its market competitiveness. As President Wang points out, **"The labor competition in the planned economy is not the market competition. On the other hand, our job posts and machine stations are directly or indirectly connected to the market and have the competitive relationships. The competitions are around job posts and machine stations, thereby really fulfilling the requirements of the job post being the market and all staffs participating in innovation etc. Therefore, in the future, the labor competition under planned economy should be changed to the job competition under market economy."** What he says is the essential feature distinguishing the job competition of Double Star from the labor competition under planned economy, and the fundamental guarantee for the excellent results obtained in job competitions of Double Star.

Tactic 12: The Environment Is the Foundation

"We should change the production environment and enhance the feelings and trust of staffs for the enterprise. For example, if the carbon black workshop is as dark as before, the staff is not willing to work there. He will say, "I would rather work in other units with a salary of 2,000 Yuan than work the carbon black workshop with a salary of 3,000 Yuan." As far as the semi-steel tire vulcanization workshop is concerned, the temperature was 70 degrees two years ago with all workers being male and stripped to waist while working. Now this workshop is no longer hot with more than half of workers being females. This shows that our environment has changed, which has increased the feelings and trust of staffs for the enterprise and enhanced affinity, attractiveness and cohesiveness of the enterprise."

—— Wang Hai

Since the early 1980s, Double Star has paid great attention to on-site management

In Double Star Group, the shoe workshop is clean, spacious, bright and comfortable.

I. Wang Hai Quotations

(I) Importance of environmental management

☆ Change the production environment, enhance the feelings and trust for the enterprise, and enhance the affinity, attractiveness and cohesion of the enterprise.

☆ Grasping safety means grasping production, doing-good and gathering of blessings; it is responsible to staffs and the enterprise. The concern for workers is actually the biggest concern for production. To be love with workers, it is necessary to take safety as the focus of the work with leaders, reach the height of relating with staffs' family happiness, whether leaders really have conscience and morality, and do a good job of implementation.

☆ The zero-distance process helps us to change the backward situation (in which the cumbersome labor methods are adopted) and completely liberate staffs. At the same time, it improves the living and working environment of staffs, and enhances the staffs' feelings for the enterprise. Under the macro situation of labor shortage in the country, we are the choice for many people in their employment, including our factories in Yimeng Mountain and Qingdao. This shows that our management is excellent.

(II) Requirements and objectives of environmental management

☆ On-site management is standardized with workshops being clean and tidy, and a new brand image is established.

☆ Love the factory like a home, manage the factory like a home.

☆ The equipment should be well managed without dead corners.

☆ Strengthen basic management and beautify the production environment.

☆ Processes are inspected and sites are cleaned up daily.

☆ The maintenance is the key in equipment management.

Taking the on-site management as a breakthrough point, strengthen basic management in a comprehensive manner.

(III) Environmental management of Double Star

☆ From the 1980s to now, we always pay attention to the improvement of the production environment, with the lowest requirement of letting it is free from toxicity, harm, and odor.

☆ From planned economy to reform and opening, we always pay attention to the improvement of staffs' production and living environment, with the following measures adopted: decorating with flowers, grasses, hills and pavilions; beautifying factory zones; building basketball courts; providing air-conditioning & ventilation for equipment (meeting the requirements of environmental protection); providing entertainment facilities. Therefore, the current production and living environment is environmentally friendly.

☆ By the combination of dynamic management and static management and the combination of scientific management and strict requirements, Double Star achieves a virtuous cycle of on-site management and ensures steady improvements in product quality.

II. Practices and Effects

(I) Main practices

1. Strengthen on-site management and do an excellent job in on-site civilized production

Strengthen on-site management, including fixed-position management, and do an excellent job in on-site civilized production.

2. Optimize the production environment to let it be comfortable

Improve and optimize the workshop environment, such as expanding the work space, adjusting the layout of machinery and equipment, improving ventilation, lighting, lighting and other conditions to create a comfortable labor space for employees.

3. Strengthen equipment management and innovation to achieve production safety and automation

Strengthen equipment management and equipment innovation, transform old equipment, make better use of new equipment (including imported equipment); eliminate old technology and equipment; rely on equipment transformation and innovation to improve labor efficiency, reduce labor intensity, and gradually realize automation of production processes.

4. Reform the production process to achieve zero-distance as possible

Reform the production process and strive to achieve zero distance and fully get rid of heavily physical labor (including manual moving, pushing, pulling, lifting and so forth).

5. Beautify the production environment to let it be comfortable

Beautify the workshop environment by being decorated with flowers and green leaves and by choosing harmonious colors, letting staffs feel comfortable and reducing their psychological tension.

6. Production zone is decorated with propaganda materials to create a strong cultural atmosphere

Properly hang or post propaganda materials including quotations and slogans or mottoes so forth, to create a united, upward, relaxed and harmonious labor atmosphere.

(II) Main effects

1. Improve the level of on-site management and solve problems of being dirty and chaotic in the industry

Improve the level of on-site management and solve the problem of being dirty and chaotic so forth. The problem includes the placement in a disordered manner of the spare parts, molds and tools etc.

2. Change the production process and reduce the labor intensity

Through technological innovation, the process achieves the zero distance, which gets rid of the backward situation (in which heavily manual moving, lifting, pushing, pulling and so forth are needed) and reduces the labor intensity, therefore completely liberating the staffs from heavy physical labor.

3. Guarantee safety of staffs and their family happiness

Let staffs safely operate without accidents and achieve the success in both equipment management and safety work to ensure staff safety and family happiness.

4. Three Zeros machine stations and Five Nos equipment

There have been many Three Zeros machine stations through the month (Three Zeros refer to zero maintenance, zero consumption, and zero emission), and there are many Five Nos devices (Five Nos refer to no oil leakage, no air leakage, no wind leakage, no water leakage, no electricity leakage. Even the boiler room has reached this standard. Therefore, Double Star has solved the big problems in on-site management of tire enterprises.

5. Enhance the attractiveness and cohesiveness of the enterprise

Due to changes in the production environment, staffs' feelings and trust for the enterprise have been enhanced. Staffs work in a comfortable and decent environment, therefore promoting stability, health and development of staffs and enhancing attraction and cohesiveness of the enterprise.

6. On-site management win orders

Customers held a wait-and-see attitude before visits to Double Star. When being at Double Star, they were stunned by standardized and strict on-site management. As a result, they immediately placed orders with Double Star. Many customers seeing the strict management continuously placed orders and established a long-term relationship with Double Star.

III. Typical Examples

(1) Strive to reduce the labor intensity

Machining workshop of Double Star: clean and tidy

The new generation of migrant workers are reluctant to be common workers, instead, they pay attention to whether the job is decent and easy. Many units of Double Star recognize this situation and transform the technological process to achieve the effect of zero distance. Also, these units continuously introduce and transform equipment, improve the level of equipment automation, reduce the labor intensity of staffs, create a good working environment and conditions for them, and promote the stability of staffs.

Double Star Qingdao Tire carries out the process transformation (with the zero-distance goal) in natural rubber, rubber sheet, tread, wire ring and apex so forth, which reduces the labor intensity and enables some female staffs to work. Double Star Dongfeng Tire last year carried out the transformation of the vulcanization workshop equipment (including the roof fan), so improving the working environment and reducing the labor intensity. In the sole-making workshop of Double Star Footwear Industrial Park, the manual roughing work had a low salary and easily caused fatigue and monotony. Since the roughing process becoming automatic, the working environment has been clean with a high salary, high efficiency, and low labor intensity. Roughing staff Hao Jiawei says happily: "Double Star is a big enterprise with standardized management. Through innovation, our work becomes easy with a high salary. We must do our best in Double Star."

(2) Factory investment generates effect of poverty alleviation
——Luzhong becomes a garden-style factory

Luzhong is a garden-style factory located in Yimeng Mountain.

Double Star Luzhong is located in Yimeng Mountain which is an old revolutionary base area. Due to resources shortage, geographical remoteness, inconvenient transportation and so forth, this base area was poor for a long time. Since the establishment of Double Star Luzhong, it has produced a momentous change.

In 1992, Double Star Luzhong was completed and put into operation. Located at site of former Yuhua Machinery Factory, it is supported by the Yiyuan County Government on the principle of mutual benefit and common development.

After its establishment, Luzhong combines the advanced management experience of Double Star and the actual situation of the local area; relying on the integrity and innovative management, it rapidly develops.

Based on its rapid development, Double Star Luzhong actively repays the society. Since its establishment, it has invested more than 60 million Yuan to help build roads, develop hospitals, and so forth in the local area. It also has continuously enhanced the environmental construction of the plant, including Double Star Garden, Double Star Zoo, Double Star Green Plaza, Double Star Tower, Double Star Business Center, and Temple so forth. Now it has become a garden-style factory with several attractions: water flowing out in a trickle and wavelets rippling in a lake; winding path leading to a secluded spot, arched bridge, and high tower; white goose with its neck upwards and green bamboos; lake fish happily chasing; groups of magpies, sparrows, and turtledoves passing by. This scenic spot is also a good place for local people to relax and have fun. In addition, every spring, the company holds a temple fair for the purpose of sharing happiness with and benefiting the people, which is highly praised by local people.

Its development not only creates benefits for itself, but also promotes prosperity of the local economy and eases the local employment pressure. The annual output value of its carton unit, weaving unit, sponge unit and manufacturing processing unit can reach more than 20 million Yuan, solving the employment problem of more than 1,000 people. In the commercial street derived from Double Star staff market, the number of stores has reached more than 80 with their business booming.

As the local people say, the mountain villages which were poor in the past now have become prosperous and beautiful.

(3) Let flowers speak

A corner of production workshop of Double Star Tire that is equipped with central air conditioning

The flowers in the workshop are in full bloom. Even in the boiler room, workers wear clean white coats. While visiting Luzhong in Yimeng Mountain old revolutionary area. most people would not believe that this is a Chinese shoe factory. 98% of the workers here are local farmers, and the first-class shoes they produce are shipped to international markets such as the United States on the other side of the Pacific Ocean.

Over the past 20 years, Double Star has been constantly adjusting itself according to the change of the situation including the market. Since 1984, it has successively built more than ten production plants in Qingdao, Chengdu, Guiyang, and Zhangjiakou. Most of the staffs are from the backward areas, which brings certain difficulties to management. However, President Wang says, "There are enterprises poorly managed and there are no enterprises that cannot be well managed." He adopts the international management model which is combined with the essences of traditional military and family management, and leads all staffs climb to the highest level of enterprise management. For example, he develops the on-site management standard: workshop management being without dead corners, material management being without wastes, surface management being without dust; equipment being well managed and maintained.

Regarding how to manage, he says, "Leaders should pay attention to management and take the lead in it. If management is not strict, the enterprise will die. In the most difficult place, it should be managed to be the best. In the dirtiest place, it should be managed to be the cleanest. If an effort is made, a factory in the remote mountain area can reach the international level." To create a good environment and promote on-site management, Double Star places flowers in the workshop and boiler room. The state of flower growth and cleanliness is used as a standard to measure the cleanliness of the workshop and boiler room. Every day, the inspection is made. If there is a lot of dust on the leaves, it proves that the workshop is not clean; in this case, the team leader on duty will be punished. Using the method of letting flowers speak to manage the working quality has greatly promoted the overall management level of Double Star.

The export staff represents the image of the enterprise; in case of contacting with foreign customers, also represents the image of Chinese people. To improve the qualifications of exporters, according to the actual situation, Double Star Group has established a staff image standard: attention to appearance, courtesy, teamwork and etc. Double Star is very strict from raw materials to production to sales management and has won the trust of international customers.

Wang said at the press conference in New York, "Foreigners say that our hardware is not good, it means that the quality of the products is not good; that our software is worse, it means that our management is worse. But I can proudly tell you: Double Star is the best-managed enterprise among the world's shoe-making enterprises." With words reversing the opinion of foreigners that Chinese state-owned enterprises are poorly managed, Mr. Wang won the glory for Chinese people. It is the excellent management that has solidified the cornerstone of Double Star built to last. star "longevity enterprise." (Source: People's Daily, November 2002.)

(4) Works in mixing workshop put on white coats

Neat and spacious tire warehouse in Double Star: tires being kept in good condition

With its strong brand strength and strong financial strength, Double Star has made Double Star Tire as its subsidiary enter the fast lane of development. According to the actual situation, Wang puts forward a new theory of soft rubber and hard management. With adherence to management essence of paying attention to details, the management work has quietly changed. The German foreigner who came to debug the equipment gave a thumb up and said in his not so fluent Chinese: "I have been to the mixing center in many countries for equipment commissioning, but such a first-class mixing center is only seen in China. Staffs can wear white coats to work. This is a miracle in the history of tires! The management of Double Star is really amazing!"

IV. Expert Comments

Ergonomics is an emerging discipline. This term is coined from ergo (meaning work) plus second element economics. Therefore, its meaning is the scientific study of the efficiency of people in the workplace. In other words, this subject is to study the question of the reasonable and moderate labor in the workplace. Ergonomics is a branch of mechanical engineering to study the relationship among workers, machinery, and environment according to psychological, physiological and physical structures to ensure that they work safely, healthily and comfortably and achieve satisfactory results.

This study is made in human-machine-environment system. Ergonomics has passed through several stages: human adaptation, machine adaptation, mutual adaptation of human and machine. Now it reaches the stage of the harmony of human, machine, and environment. In the said system, the study goes from individual physiological and psychological characteristics to the method for improvement of social factors. With the intensification of market competition and the improvement of production levels, ergonomics will be more used in the entire manufacturing and processing industry including the design and manufacture of mechanical products.

The main concepts of ergonomics are:

1. Human ability. This includes the basic size of the human body, the ability of the person to work, the limits of various organ functions, and the influencing factors. Only by understanding the human abilities can these factors be considered

in the design of the system, so that the load on the human body is within the acceptable range.

2. Human-machine interaction. Machine here not only represents the machine, but also represents the physical system in which the person works, including various machines, computers, offices, various automation systems, and so on. The motto of ergonomics is: Making the machine suitable for people.

3. The impact of the environment on people. The physical environment of people has a profound influence on people's work and life. Therefore, naturally, the impact of the environment on people is a key content of ergonomics, which includes: the impact of lighting on people's work efficiency, the harm of noise to people and its prevention and treatment methods, and the impact of music, color, air pollution, air temperature and humidity on people etc.

There are three main goals for studying ergonomics: first, to make people work more effectively; second, to make people work safer; and third, to make the work more comfortable. These three goals are sometimes consistent. For example, a new machine may be more efficient, safer, and more comfortable than the old one. But in many cases, these three goals are contradictory. A safer, more comfortable method of operation may be less efficient than the old method. A new machine can make the work more comfortable, but the added efficiency can not be enough to compensate for the increased investment. The resolution of this contradiction obviously depends on the relative importance of people and machines; the era in which people live, the environment, and so on.

Western society is more developed than us with its standard of living being higher than ours, so its ergonomics emphasizes the importance of human beings. The purpose of their textbooks is: Fitting the task to the man. In China, living standards are still relatively low and productivity is relatively backward, so, in many places, people adapt to the machine. However, with continuous improvement of the level of social productivity and the continuous improvement of people's living standards, the value of people will become higher and higher and ergonomics will be more and more valued as a subject. Ergonomics plays an increasingly important role for the work and life of people.

In the past, due to our overpopulation and high employment pressure, people did not pay much attention to labor efficiency and did not pay attention to ergonomics. However, with the rapid improvement of the living standards, people will pay more and more attention to the quality of their work and life, and people will gradually realize the necessity and importance of ergonomics for doing an excellent job. In addition, China has entered the international market. To improve the competitiveness of our products in this market, we need to improve labor efficiency and reduce labor costs. Therefore, ergonomics has broad prospects for development in China. With the occurrence of labor shortage in recent years, enterprises are required to attach great importance to ergonomics, to scientifically improve the labor environment, reduce the labor intensity, ensure physical safety of staffs, and enhances affinity, attractiveness and cohesiveness of the enterprise.

Under the leadership of President Wang, Double Star Group has long paid attention to the application of ergonomics in enterprise management. It has taken various measures, such as strengthening on-site management, improving the workshop environment, strengthening equipment innovation, reducing labor, reforming production processes, trying to achieve zero distance of work-piece movement, beautifying the workshop environment by placing flowers and so forth. These measures have achieved remarkable results. Under the background of labor shortage across the country, Double Star has attracted a lot of people to ensure normal production and let the staffs satisfactory and work hard. So, Double Star has strong cohesiveness and competitiveness, with its business booming, which is inseparable from their persistence and emphasis on ergonomics. Under the situation of labor shortage becoming more and more serious in the country, the experience of Double Star Group has important practical significance and far-reaching significance for all enterprises.

Tactic 13: The Family Affection Is the Bond

"Staffs are the main force of the enterprise on which the production, market competition and development of the enterprise are dependent. The development of enterprises depends on their efforts. We should care for staffs, including helping them in when they have difficulties and supporting them when they have a need. When you need it, you should support them. Insignificant things of staffs should be paid attention by leaders. Only leaders respect and care about staffs, can their loyalty to and willing to continuously work in the enterprise be enhanced."

——Wang Hai

Apartment of staffs in Double Star

Double Star is always committed to creating a comfortable environment for working and living of staffs. This is the ribbon-cutting ceremony for the staff to move into the new apartment in Double Star Footwear Industrial Park.

Double Star focuses on enriching the cultural life of staffs by providing them with cultural and entertainment facilities including e-reading rooms, clubs and etc.

Cultural and sports activities are held by Double Star Group.

I. Wang Hai Quotations

(I) Significance of family affection management (also known as family-friendly management)

☆ People are a foundation of enterprise development with management being based on them.

☆ People are the most valuable resources of enterprises and talent competition is the first competition.

☆ Staffs are our partners, colleagues, comrades-in-arms and relatives; a main force of our production; our combat capability for our mission; and the first element of our sustainable development.

☆ Enhance cohesion and combat effectiveness of the enterprise.

(II) Carrier of family affection management

☆ Logistics is an important carrier of family affection management.

☆ Logistics service guarantee and family affection management are important contents of enterprise management and are a powerful guarantee for doing a good job in production and operation and market competition.

☆ Paying attention to the life can promote the quality, innovation, and political work.

☆ Logistics as a guarantee is important and should provide a considerable service.

(III) How to do an excellent job in family affection management

☆ The enterprise cares about staffs, while staffs love and are loyal to the enterprise.

☆ Warm staffs with family affection, retain them with emotions and motivate them with true feelings

☆ Care for, influence, and move staffs with love.

☆ Management is made via reason, emotion, money and system.

☆ Image what it is like to be in the staff's position. Attract, recruit, and retain staffs with sincere feelings.

II. Practices and Effects

(I) Main practices

1. Empathy, respect, and care for staffs

Managers must know that leaders and staffs are people at Double Star who are all equal in different job posts. It is necessary to feel real empathy, eliminate the old thinking, old ideas and rude management methods that discriminate against and look down on staffs. It is necessary to care about them in work and life, which is the basic standard for managers of Double Star.

2. Mobilize staff enthusiasm and enhance staff confidence

It is necessary to consider the abilities and levels of each person to make the best use of their talents, provide them with suitable posts to play their talents, build a communication platform that can show their own value, and mobilize their enthusiasm through various competitions and cultural activities. As this way, staffs are hopeful and more confident.

3. Strengthen communication and make friends with staffs

It is necessary to communicate with them sincerely, timely know and adjust their emotions, become friends with them; set up a helping and supporting team, establish a visit system and staff files, care about and help them from small places; produce subtle influences, and increase their loyalty.

4. Adjust and improve the production organization mode and carry out people-oriented production

All units should improve the production organization and production environment, so that staffs can get a reasonable rest, such as two breaks and one non-stop for tire workers, so that staffs have more flexible working hours, reduce their resistance to the management system of the enterprise. Thus, the production mode of Double Star is people-oriented.

5. Improve working conditions and living environment

Double Star improves the production environment, innovates the process (realizing zero distance), reduces the labor intensity. Double Star builds staff apartments (including college graduates) with floor heating and supporting facilities, builds the staff canteen and the staff service unit, and provide rooms for couples. Double Star establish cultural facilities such as kindergarten, e-reading room, video room. Double Star has perfect sanitation facilities, provide laundry facilities, convenience stores and other living facilities. Therefore, Double Star provides staffs with a safe, healthy, stable and comfortable working and living environment, including first-class logistics management services.

6. Strengthen training and provide staffs with continuous education opportunities

Through the launch of the education video, discussion activities, skills and management training courses, Double Star provides staffs with continuous education opportunities to improve the overall quality and technical ability. This enhances loyalty of staffs, especially core talents.

7. Build a stage to show values

By transforming the business operation mechanism and implementing the good form of market-based bidding and contracting, we build a large stage for staffs to display their talents and give full play to their abilities. By continuously improving wages and an open competitive stage, we retain staffs. We also carry out knowledge contests, speech contests, basketball games, table tennis competitions, calligraphy and painting competitions, skills competitions, job competitions, and other activities, to enhance abilities of staffs and discover talents.

(II) Main effects

The process of creating and developing famous brands fully proves that the family affection management created by President Wang has strong cohesiveness, supporting and driving forces. Specifically, the family affection management of Double Star plays a key role in the following aspects:

1. Enhance cohesiveness, combat effectiveness and competitiveness of the enterprise

By harmonizing feelings, communicating ideas, and coordinating work, the enterprise becomes a big family. The team is full of family affection, which guarantees quality, innovation and other work, and enhances cohesiveness and combat effectiveness of the team and the enterprise.

2. Enhance effectiveness of ideological and political work

The meaning of ideological and political work is quite extensive, including greetings, solving practical problems for staffs, raising the level of welfare, etc. These are all areas of ideological and political work in which family affection management is a good form.

3. Activate employment mechanism & promote human resource management

Double Star vigorously advocates the concept of people-oriented and familial-affectionate management. With the principle of retaining talents from policy, cultivating talents from work, caring for talents in life, and retaining talents from treatment, Double Star establishes perfect personnel training and employment mechanism, formulates a number of preferential policies, and strives to lean toward professional talents in the treatment as well as create a relaxed environment for them in life and work.

4. Improve the logistics management

"Caring for the staff in the life is the best ideological and political work." Starting from the insignificant things such as clothing, food, housing, and transportation, Double Star cares for everyone in daily life with a sincere attitude. This promotes the logistics work and the family affection management.

5. Promote the harmonious development of the enterprise

Management by meticulousness and family affection has created a strong atmosphere of harmony, enhanced the sense of unity and cooperation among staffs, changed the attitude of staffs who were indifferent to the enterprise, and made them have deep feelings for the enterprise, thus letting Double Star have high quality of products and establish a good image at home and abroad.

III. Typical Examples

(1) Three special holidays of Double Star

In the early 1980s, Double Star implemented family-friendly management. The good practice of celebrating birthday for staffs, giving a day off, sending a birthday cake, and making a reasonable suggestion can enhance cohesion of the enterprise. The picture shows President Wang giving the staff a homemade birthday cake.

President Wang took the lead in implementing family-friendly management. In Qingdao, Double Star is the first to provide the special holidays: Lantern Festival, Mid-Autumn Festival and employee birthday.

In the early 1980s, it was found that the defective rate of products was higher in the Lantern Festival, because the workers were eager to return home. At that time, President Wang thought that instead of letting the staffs be absent-minded and inefficient in work, it would be better to let them go home early to reunite with their loved ones and have an appropriate time. In this way, Double Star began to provide the first special holiday.

There is a more thing that contributes to providing the second special holiday of Double Star. At a Mid-Autumn Festival in the mid-1980s, Mr. Wang made a visit to the workshop. A worker named Zhao told Wang that his daughter made a special trip from Beijing to see him and asked Wang for a half-day holiday. Wang did not agree. But when this worker said that he had never taken a holiday for personal reasons in the past, Wang immediately approved his request decided that Double Star began to provide a half-day holiday on the Mid-Autumn Festival. At that time, hearing the news, all the staffs rejoiced. In this way, Double Star has another special holiday. Later, President Wang decided that the worker would receive a birthday cake as a gift from the unit and enjoy his birthday as a holiday. On the birthday of an old staff, Wang personally celebrated his birthday. He said excitedly, "The enterprises celebrates my birthday, so I pledge to work hard." This is the third special holiday of Double Star.

(2) Special visitor at the construction site

The construction of the building for the plant for export shoes were concurrent with the equipment installation. In the winter, one night, President Wang was meeting with other leaders. Suddenly chilly wind blew. President Wang stopped the meeting and led colleagues to visit the workers who worked on the construction site. There was no window in the construction site, and the wind ran wild. When Wang appeared on the construction site, the workers looked flurried. The reason was that they drunk wine during working hours. In the face of this situation, Wang did not criticize them, instead, he had a sympathetic understanding of them in this special situation. Wang instructed the office director to go out and buy five bottles of liquor, and instructed the logistics director to prepared hot soup and hot meals. After a while, the wine was delivered, hot soup and hot rice were also delivered, and the workers were moved to tears. They said, "Leader, your wine warmed our body and warmed our hearts." In this way, in the process of completing the project, the logistics department gave the workers daily wine and hot meals as well especially sent a cotton vest to each person. Workers' enthusiasm was even greater. As a result, the 15-day project was completed in 9 days. In the administrative management, Wang often says to the leaders at all levels, "In case of being ill, the worker needs the comfort in spirit. You should take time to visit him. Your visit is the best treatment. From the emotional point of view, it works better than any medicine."

(3) The car stories

Double Star is the earliest enterprise in Qingdao to purchase shuttle buses for staffs. Previously, President Wang said, "You should let the staff get on the bus. If not, I will not take the car."

In the early 1980s, the factory office bought a new car, but President Wang did not take it. He still rode bicycles to work every day. His reason is very simple He said that the staffs had not yet their own shuttle bus. As a result, He took the car after the staffs had it. On the other hand, he did not think that this car was only used by himself. One time, a worker suffered a work-related injury. At that time, the plant had no other transportation means except this car. But the supervisor of the factory office did not let the driver of this car to carry the injured worker to hospital, because in his eyes, workers were not qualified to take such a car. Wang knew it and angrily said, "You always want to flatter me. Now the worker is very injured, but you still want to keep a car for me. Are you still a man?" In this way, this car was immediately used to send the injured worker to the hospital. It can be said that what Wang has done is to increase the cohesiveness of staffs and promote the development of productivity. This is also a concrete manifestation of people-oriented.

(4) New path to retain staffs in Double Star Group

Double Star as a labor-intensive manufacturing and processing enterprise actively explores the new path to retain staffs. Under the background of the labor shortage across the country, Double Star adopt its unique measure: in other words, giving high salaries, caring for staffs, and giving full play to the abilities of staffs etc.

This spring, the labor shortage emerged once again. Many enterprises had to suspend production or reduce orders; while being not able to retain old employees and recruit new employees. As a labor-intensive manufacturing and processing enterprise, Double Star Group faced with a more severe situation in terms of employment. However, due to its effective measures, Double Star attracted a lot of people and had a smooth production. Wang said that after the Spring Festival, Double Star had a high return rate of staffs and recruited more than 1,400 new people to ensure production needs.

Double Star has a history of nearly 100 years and involves in 23 industries including footwear, tires, machinery, clothing, printing, and so forth, and now has 60,000 staffs. In recent years, under the background of labor shortage across the country, it is always the choice for people seeking employment and retains staffs. So, how does Double Star solve the problem of labor shortage?

President Wang points out that Double Star always adheres to the principle of being people-oriented, regards human resources as the first element of the enterprise development, especially in the manufacturing and processing industry. Double Star attaches importance to the talent work and establishes the concept of employing people: in other words, giving high salaries, caring for staffs, and giving full play to the abilities of staffs, therefore, solving the problem of labor shortage, which is a widespread problem across the country.

Effective treatment to be without worries

On February 12th, in the Double Star Community of Double Star Footwear Industrial Park, Zhang Dexin from Taian of Shandong as a worker in the molding workshop drove a newly bought van on which his wife and parents were seated together. Later, they came to the supermarket to buy many foods including meat, fish and cakes so forth for a sake of having a good weekend.

He told us, “The environment here is very good and so are relevant facilities. We live in the couple’s house with my daughter going to the double star kindergarten of Double Star. In addition to the fixed holidays, there are flexible vacations. During the peak of the Spring Festival, our company helps us book tickets for us or charters buses to send us home, while the train tickets are fully reimbursed. We have dignity, hope and happiness in Double Star."

Sun Zengyong from Liaocheng in the same community told us, "Many staffs living in couples' houses have also introduced their parents, sisters, classmates, etc. to work in the Double Star Footwear Industrial Park."

Double Star adopts the policy of building a nest to attract phoenix birds. If the problem of houses is not solved, the talents will not be retained. Before the Spring Festival this year, the Double Star Footwear Industrial Park provided additional 30 sets of couples' houses, so totaling more than 80 sets and retaining 160 migrant staffs in key job posts. Moreover, more friends and relatives were attracted to work in the enterprise.

Each unit of Double Star implements the internal contracted shareholding system. The leaders and management personnel at all levels not only ensure the output, quality, and stability of the personnel, but also ensure a satisfactory income for staffs and attention paid to insignificant things in the life of staffs. For example, there are a number of students in township middle school 20 Chinese miles from Double Star, who were received personally by their parents as workers of Double Star into home every Friday afternoon. Hao Yuanhua as a factory director now uses his own private car to pick up these students, so eliminating the worries of the staffs who happily says, "The leader really cares for us. We are all moved."

By improving employee income and creating a good working and living environment, Double Star allows staffs to decently work and live a comfortable life. Therefore, staffs are very loyal to Double Star.

My acquaintance introduces me to Double Star

Double Star adopts a recruitment policy of introduction by the acquaintance. That is, in the recruitment, the referees of staffs are relatives, friends, fellow townsmen or villagers and those who previously were classmates or schoolmates. The acquaintance-chain recruitment is a new path explored by Double Star in recent years to solve the problem of labor shortage and ensure the talent reserve.

Only when enterprises regard employees as partners and give enough respect, can employees be loyal to them. Double Star accelerates the pace of technological process upgrades, improves the working environment, reduces the labor intensity, and continuously carries out mechanism innovations in which staffs having good skills can earn more money. Double Star implements new methods: free choice of posts and two-way post choice. Double Star carries out new staff training and practical operation training, implements the master-apprentice system, and carries out the relevant competition, to let new staffs, master the skills in a short time, increase the yield, ensure quality, promote production safety. Double Star adopts an innovative approach to rotate days-off. Double Star continues to carry out various job competitions, and improve the evaluation mechanism for chief technicians, gold medal technicians, young technicians, and golden blue collars. Double Star sets up farms to plant contamination-free vegetables and sell them to staffs at a low price. Double Star adopts serial measures to respect, care for, and motivate staffs, including greetings to staffs in festivals and so forth, so that staff can work and live happily with peaceful mind. This is the unique advantage in solving the problem of labor shortage of Double Star in the new situation. The good image of the enterprise is more effective than the recruitment of talents in the talent market. Therefore, Double Star introduces a number of policies to encourage cadres at all levels to be responsible for recruitment and encourage staffs to introduce their relatives, neighbors, friends, classmates or schoolmates to Double Star. While being in addition to the traditional recruitment mode (for example, introduction via government departments, talent markets, and intermediaries), the new mode of acquaintance-chain chain recruitment is created which has a very good effect.

In Double Star Qingdao Tire, Tian Shipeng as a molding worker of the radical tire workshop was with his fellows and classmates during the Spring Festival holiday to watch the CD-ROM of Brilliant 90th Anniversary with Double Star and told them about the development and welfare treatment so on of Double Star. As a result, nine people followed him to work in Double Star Tire.

Through the classmates' chain, Double Star Machinery recruited 43 technicians with certain theoretical knowledge and practical operational skills.

Zhang Yunxia a worker at line 5 in the upper workshop of Double Star Footwear Industrial Park recommended her aunt to work at it. Then, her aunt brought six fellow villagers back, all of whom were skilled sewing workers. One of new staffs named Jin Yunyun said, "I trust my fellow villager who introduced me to Double Star." After the Spring Festival this year, Double Star Footwear Industrial Park recruited 135 new staffs through the acquaintance chain, including relatives, friends, friends and fellow villagers.

Zheng Fujuan, a new employee of Double Star Hanhai Sports Shoes, signed up to work in the packaging workshop, and introduced his father Zheng Yuhai to the company. Seeing the effective treatment, Zheng Yuhai introduced his sister and the latter introduced her cousin.

Some staffs mobilized almost all their family members to work at Double Star. According to statistics, after the Spring Festival of 2012, all units of Double Star recruited 1,483 people. Among them, 1,108 people were recruited from the acquaintance chain, accounting for 74% of the newly recruited staffs. This shows that staffs have feelings for and confidence in for the enterprise. Family-friendly posts in the workshops also enabled new staffs to work in a familiar environment and found the warm feeling of home, thereby enhancing cohesiveness and combat effectiveness of the enterprise.

The culture takes root

There are activities everywhere, and there is entertainment every day. The variety performance of Double Star is dominated by the staffs instead of popular film & TV stars. Each unit has its own art and cultural performance team. Cultural activities have become a part of the happy life of staffs.

"Culture does not rely on the input from the outside. The important thing is to rely on our own effort. Double Star forms its own culture, which, while enriching the staff's spiritual and cultural life, plays a role to attract, educate, and motivate people." said the leader of Double Star.

In Double Star Qingdao Tire, the music-loving staffs spontaneously forms a band named Celebrity. Its members are full of passion, and really like stars, so having many fans. They actively participate in variety shows.

Double Star Dongfeng Tire sets up a military band, a contemporary music band, a dance team, a sports club so forth as platforms for many music and sports enthusiasts, and their members have repeatedly represented the company in various cultural and sports activities held by the group and socially.

Double Star Footwear Industrial Park establishes cultural and entertainment facilities such as painting and calligraphy room, e-reading room, billiard room, and table tennis room. Its leader says with emotion, "Through the enterprise culture, we retain staffs. Some foreign companies poached talents from us but suffered failure. It can be said that talents cannot be retained without the enterprise culture."

The enterprise culture plays a key role. Through the Internet cafe, movie bar and KTV, birthday party, dance party, talent competition, and cultural performance etc., Double Star strives to meet the spiritual needs of staffs. While enriching the spiritual life of staffs and letting them more vigorous, the enterprise culture enhances the loyalty of staffs.

The competition of human resources is more severe and more intense than the competition of the market including products. Double Star regards the relationship with staffs as a win-win relationship rather than an employment relationship. Through various innovative measures, it improves staffs' salary and treatment, adopt the form of acquaintance-chain recruitment, cares for staffs, and unites staffs via the culture. Therefore, while attracting more and more people, Double Star has no problem of labor shortage. President Wang says, "The labor shortage exists now across the country. However, through subjective efforts, we can create a decent work and living environment and play an internal role. We overcome the unfavorable factors and change the negative influence of the objective environment." His words may provide some useful reference and inspiration for the labor-intensive manufacturing and processing industry of China in overcoming labor shortage. *(Source: Shandong Workers' Newspaper, March 5, 2012.)*

IV. Expert Comments

The so-called family affection management is to combine strict standards with emotional investment and strive to convince people via strict implementation of rules and regulations and promote the concept of family-friendly in the enterprise, namely, create a family atmosphere in which a good relationship is built on mutual respect in the enterprise. In enterprise management and operation, we mainly rely on people. Only when the enterprise is a harmonious and cooperative enterprise, can we fully mobilize the talents of staffs and give full play to their potential.

Family affection management requires that enterprise cadres treat staffs as much as they care about their loved ones. Staffs are the main body of our enterprise, who spend most of their time in it. The joys and sorrows directly affect their work status and results. Therefore, as the management personnel, we must pay attention to the ideological dynamics of staffs and regard their small things as big ones, so that they can be thankful, regard the enterprise as their own home, cherish the working opportunity, give full play to their abilities to promote the continuous development of the enterprise.

The so-called family affection management model of the enterprise is a people-oriented management model. Only by doing a good job of family affection management can we ensure the healthy and steady development of the enterprise.

Family affection management is a modern scientific management method that President Wang creates from his management practice of the past 40 years and is proved to be effective. Its connotation is extremely rich, and its effect is extremely remarkable.

Through the analysis of the connotation of family affection management, we know that it contains the following contents: elements of Confucianism, Taoism, Buddhism; effective management concepts and experiences in modern ideological and political work (for example, caring for the masses' lives and paying attention to working methods); advanced management sciences in developed countries (for example, behavioral science, interpersonal relationship, psychology, ergonomics and so forth); needs-hierarchy theory proposed by Maslow; innovations in productivity categories (such as beautifying the production environment, improving working conditions, innovating production equipment, and reforming production processes, realizing the zero distance of work piece movement, reducing labor intensity, and realizing a civilized, healthy, easy, pleasant, and decent production); and reforms in production relations (such as implementing small accounting units, personal responsibility system, market-oriented contracting, internal buyout shareholding system, factory currency operation, and militarized management and so forth. With the family affection management, Double Star cares for staffs in their work and life, including their health, marriage, and children; pays attention to their working time and spare time management etc.

Seriously studying the experiences in family affection management from Mr. Wang, we will find that it has four characteristics:

First, the core is clear. That is, everything is centered around people. "People are the foundation of the factory, and management is based on people." "Employees are the main force of enterprise productivity, the indispensable combat force for us to complete our tasks, and the first element of continuous development of enterprises. Without their work, we would accomplish nothing." Therefore, the enterprise should make staffs to feel hopeful and even have a feeling of being at home. If the enterprise gives staffs meticulousness and arouses their enthusiasm, they will be loyal to the enterprise.

Second, significant importance is attached to family affection management. Starting from President Wang, Double Star attached immense importance to it, raises it into the important content of ideological and political work, upgrades it to the same important position as production and management. President Wang pays attention to it, takes the lead, and set a good example in implementation of it. In the market competition, the family affection management plays a key role in stabilizing the workforce and enhancing the competitiveness of the enterprise.

Third, the content has a wide range. As mentioned above, family affection management contains the follows: ancient and modern successful management concepts and experiences of China; advanced management theories of developed countries; innovations in the scope of productivity and reforms in production relations. In short, all problems relating to production, work, life, health, marriage, children, and so forth of staffs are paid attention by leaders of the enterprise.

Fourth, methods are diverse. They have both in-depth and meticulous ideological and political work as the forerunner; they have the advanced machinery and equipment as the material basis; they have both advanced systems and mechanism to bring power and vitality; they have good economic benefits and high wages as a gugrantee; they have the great effort from full-time political, logistical, management and technical personnel; they initiates the people's war of family management in which all staffs participate.

Fifth, effects are remarkable. The market is the standard for testing all work of the enterprise and the standard for testing the work of family affection management. The effect of family affection management is first manifested in the fact that under the current situation of labor shortage in which Double Star has no such problem. Even in case of recruitment ads pasted in the factory gate by some manufacturers, Double Star remain stable in the staff team and attracts more people, thereby ensuring the production needs. Secondly, in the context of the slowdown of the domestic and international economy this year, Double Star has further spurred the enthusiasm of staffs to overcome the crisis and overcome difficulties by strengthening family-friendly management. Several new products have been successfully introduced to the market. Double Star is the typical representatives of state-owned manufacturing and processing enterprises achieve export growth in the unfavorable environment.

As President Wang points out, "Human resources are the most valuable resources of enterprises and the talent competition is the first competition." Leaders of all units of Double Star consciously and actively apply family-friendly management to attract and retain staffs through the affection, mechanism, environment, development, and salary so forth, thereby ensuring a booming business. The valuable experience of Double Star is worth learning.

Tactic 14: The Money Management Is the Guarantee

"The effective use of money is the best ideological and political work. The leader who does not pays attention to money management is not a qualified market leader. Political work needs economic guarantee. The people at Double Star having the spirit of dedication also need money. Management and employment of people are carried out through the money, which can maximize their enthusiasm. This is the best way in the current market economy. Double Star should let the staffs become rich by working hard and sweat, and finally realize the brand development.

—— Wang Hai

In 1989, President Wang, after winning the National Ideological and Political Work Innovation Award, was in the national enterprise seminar on ideological and political work to put forward, "The good use of money is the best ideological and political work."

I. Wang Hai Quotations

(I) Significance of money management

☆ Political work needs the economy as the foundation, people at Double Star having the spirit of dedication also need money.

☆ Emotion is the foundation, strictness is the key, money is the catalyst.

☆ Double Star should let staffs become rich by hardworking and sweat. There should be a good balance between spirit and material. The development of the enterprise benefits the country and the individual.

☆ Whether it is conducive to the development of productive forces is the fundamental criterion for testing all work, and also the standard for testing political work. It is necessary to promote the development of productive forces and improve economic efficiency as the starting point and the foothold of ideological and political work.

(II) How to play the role of money management

☆ The good use of money is the best ideological and political work.

☆ Management and employment of people are carried out through the money.

☆ Rely on wisdom, hardworking, and sweat to become rich.

☆ Develop the brand, bring the fortune, and let staffs have a good life.

II. Practices and Effects

(I) Main practices

1. Do an excellent job in ideological and political work via good use of money

Do an excellent job in ideological and political work through the good use of money to solve the problem of Two Skins (politics and economy).

2. Straighten out various distribution relationships via good use of money

Straighten out various distribution relationships through the good use of money. The distribution is based on contribution with proper gaps kept in wages and incomes. Give more pay for more work, less pay for less work and no pay for those doing nothing; give up the practice of eating from the same big pot. Use money to measure the level of ability and the size of contribution, promote the position, and raise the salary.

3. Use money to recognize contributions and performance

Use money to measure results of labor and innovation, give more pay for capable staffs who work hard without professional titles. Encourage staffs in different fields to actively innovate, encourage new staffs to actively learn skills, and encourage staffs in production and operation to become models or examples, skilled persons and star mechanic technicians. Grant rewards for those having achievements, and great rewards for those having great achievements. Let staffs work hard with goals.

4. Use money to improve staff welfare

Use money to improve the welfare of staffs, fore example, solving problems that are closely related to interests of staffs (including housing, canteen, hospital, kindergarten, bus shuttle, bath, vacation, and travel).

(II) Main effects

1. Solve the problem of Two Skins (politics and economy), and achieve the best combination of spirit and material

Double Star broke through the restricted area where political work in the planned economy period did not dare to talk about money. It completely solved the problem of Two Skins (politics and economy) and achieved a good balance between spirit and material. It enriched the connotation of political work by putting forward the theory "the good use of money is the best ideological and political work", granting rewards such as TVs, houses, and cars to those who make outstanding contributions, and proposing a slogan "Let our staffs become rich through wisdom, work hard and sweat." These have become goals of staffs of Double Star, greatly stimulating their enthusiasm and creativity, guiding them in the work, and encourage them to create miracles in Double Star.

2. Find the foothold of political work

Double Star gets rid of false promises and empty words in ideological and political work during the planned economy period, sincerely treats and really cares for staffs starting from trivial things. Double Star is people-oriented and let staffs able to see what it wants and does so forth. With the principle of being open and fair and paying attention to details, Double Star is supported by more than 60,000 staffs in the distribution (including honors, positions, wages, rewards, bonuses, benefits and the like). Therefore, Double Star has found the foothold of political work under the market economy.

3. Reward those who have a contribution and mobilize enthusiasm of staffs

Through the effective use of money, Double Star reward those who have made outstanding contributions in innovation, quality, management, etc., with the prizes being from TV sets in the 1980s to now houses, watching the national flag, and traveling abroad. Through the money management, Double Star has greatly mobilized the enthusiasm of staffs. Every year, more than 1,000 staffs in the Group receive group-level rewards and more than 80% of staffs rewards of the workshop level or above.

4. Inspire the enthusiasm and passion of staffs and enhance their cohesiveness

Through the effective use of money, staffs can really feel the meaning of no pain no gain, and really feel hopeful in Double Star. This is an affirmation of the value of staffs, stimulating their enthusiasm and passion and strengthening their cohesion.

5. Promote the basic management of the enterprise

Rewarding those who have less important innovations or improvements can encourage staffs to actively carry out innovation and improvement activities, and constantly promote the improvement of all basic management of the enterprise.

III. Typical Examples

(1) Management via money is a unique feature in ideological and political work of Double Star

In the spring of 1991, Wang Zhongzhi, the former Minister of the Propaganda Department of the Central Committee of the CPC, made a visit to Double Star. President Wang hurried back from his trip and made a report to Minister Wang. President Wang started to say, "Would you like to hear the truth or the lie?"

Minister Wang could not help feeling surprised and said, "Of course, I want the truth!"

"But the truth may let the hearer feel unpleasant." President Wang said.

Minister Wang said, "The Communists adhere to the principle of seeking truth from facts and naturally we should tell the truth."

President Wang said bluntly, "We rarely pay attention to and implement the policies from the propaganda department at municipal, provincial and national levels."

"You pay attention to what?" asked Minister Wang.

"We adhere to the principle of one central task and two basic points. We do what we want at the premise of not violating the party's basic line and basic principles." President Wang said, "Our enterprise has its three loves: love Double Star, love being part of the collective, love the post. Workers who are patriotic should love the enterprise and those who love the enterprise should love the post. Realizing the above-said three loves means to love our party, love our country and love our socialism. Therefore, we propose that the image consciousness of Double

Star is to win the glory for our enterprise, our country and our nation. In the new situation, ideological and political work must be strengthened and must be innovated. We think that our goal is to let everyone believe that we tell the truth, that it makes sense, and that they are willing to do it. If we just read documents and newspapers here and there day and night, then he will feel that this is meaningless. Thus, such political work is vain and effortless. For example, in the current era of market economy, our ideological and political work should turn to the market. In other words, it is closely related with the market. If the upper is sewn poorly, then its quality will be poor. In this case, the image of Double Star will be affected, causing a backlog of products and an elimination of jobs, not to mention the other matters···"

In the face of a central leadership, not all of us dared to tell the truth. Wang Hai is such a person with a noble character. After a visit to Double Star, Minister Wang said to him, "I have visited fourteen coastal cities and you is the first person I meet who dare to tell the truth."

President Wang uniquely put forward the idea of market politics. That is, we should guide the behavior of enterprises in the market economy with market politics. The connotation and extension of the concept of market politics proposed by President Wang: market politics is the superstructure of enterprises under the market economy; and is guiding ideology and core concept of all the work of enterprises. market politics includes the ideological and political work of enterprises, enterprise management, enterprise culture and related institutional aspects, and is the dialectical unity of matter and spirit. In short, it is enterprise politics in a market economy.

The reason why Double Star can take the lead in the market is that the idea enters the market first. The advanced thinking forms an advanced theory in practice, and then guides the development of the business, so that the double star can be under the conditions of the internal and external environment of the enterprise. Highlighting the encirclement and constantly developing and growing, and embarked on a road of their own, and created their own corporate culture.

Looking back at the development path of Double Star for more than 20 years, there have been no major mistakes in every historical stage, and it has always stood on the forefront. In the final analysis, it is because of the correct market politics theory.

It can be said that the soul of his market politics theory is to seek truth from facts. For it, the guiding ideology is Deng Xiaoping Theory, reform and opening, and emancipation of the mind. Under this banner, we can creatively embody and implement enterprise politics.

The so-called market politics of Double Star has a large component about political and ideological work in the market economy. Many people think that market economy enterprises do not need political work. In fact, this is a misunderstanding. This view has a lot of damage to enterprises, especially state-owned enterprises. President Wang always believes that the more active the market, the more pragmatic political theories and the more flexible political work. The political work should be strengthened rather than be weakened. If there is no correct thought and theory and there is no good political style, then we cannot creatively play your own role in the market creatively.

In 1984, President Wang determined the spirit of Double Star. One point is to pursue the profit, which many people did not understand at the time. In the public opinion environment of that era, the distinction between righteousness and profit was very strict. In that era only paying attention to dedication and spirituality, to concern about the profit was not in conformity with Marxism and and was regarded as a vulgar philosophy and a matter concerned in the capitalist society. Therefore, the public opinion struggle was fierce. But how could enterprises be not concerned about the profit when engaging in economic development? If we do not proceed from reality and do not seek truth from facts, then the ideology and politics would be dogmatic, and the political work would be empty and boring, which would be more and more rejected by people as a negative effect on economic construction. President Wang started from the profit pursuit to emancipate the staffs' mind.

Later, President Wang proposed that the effective use of money be the best political and ideological work. In the market economy, for state-owned enterprise under certain historical conditions, a problem to be discussed was how to have the effective use of money to let it maximize its benefits and mobilize people's enthusiasm to contribute to the enterprise and create value. This problem had existed for a long time, involving in the relationship of politics and economy. Later, Double Star solved it. It carried out serial competitions with themes such as cost around me and saving money; in-depth management centering around funds and focusing on reduction of six major costs; and discussions on three reputations. These activities were aimed to the organic integration between spiritual and material and between politics and economy. Political work also requires economy to be a guarantee instead of ignoring the interest. In 1992, he also proposed that people of Double Star should become rich by working hard and sweat. That is, there should be a good balance in the relationship between spirit and material and between individuals and enterprises. In a word, the development of the enterprise should benefit the country and the individual.

At a theoretical seminar of the Central Propaganda Department, President Wang said that money is the general equivalent of goods; that it does not represent personality, but it circulates in society; that, without it, the food cannot be bought in the restaurant; that the use of money in the enterprise is worth an investigation. As a result, his views caused a heated debate at the meeting. The person who agreed with him said, "The effective use of money is the best political and ideological work."

It is proved that units having an effective use of money can do a good job in the construction of spiritual civilization and material civilization.

In addition, market politics is also democratic politics. The Double Star Workers' Democratic Management Committee has been involved in enterprise management since 1983. The staff representatives have a face-to-face and realistic evaluation of the specific people and specific matters of the enterprise, and have supreme authority, which is called the model of enterprise politics. Management is also politics. Double Star proposes to manage people, educate people, and liberate people in practical work, advocates adopting the deep and meticulous attitude in political work and paying attention to specific people and specific things. This is a more important and better political work, and a manifestation of success in the political work.

There was a time when the party and government were required to separate from each other, d, and some enterprises even canceled its party committee. It seemed that enterprises would no longer need political and ideological work. President Wang had his own unique idea, "The party committee cannot be canceled. Under the new situation, the factory director should pay attention to political work in addition to economy, and the party committee should pay attention to economy in addition to political work. Now our party shifts the focus of work. All the work is around economic construction, that is, both the party and the government attach importance to it, is it possible to separate the two from each other?" Later, the new spirit was conveyed from superior authorities: the party and the government could not be separated from each other; and the party's work should be strengthened. Some enterprises rebuilt the party's organization which was configured with party cadres. But Wang did not blindly follow suit and said, "No trouble making. Two sets of teams may cause a conflict between the party and the government. " While good at the reverse thinking, Wang consistently adhered to one principle: everything starts from reality and the truth is seek from facts.

Wang says that an entrepreneur should not only be a general on the battlefield, but also a politician with his own thoughts. If he does not understand politics, especially if he does not understand Chinese politics, then it is difficult for him to win in the market. What Wang says often is thought-provoking, but no one can deny that he is very politically minded. This is a higher level of wisdom.

(2) Rewarding talents for scientific and technological innovation

In the early 1980s when the color TV appeared, Double Star had already granted color TV sets as rewards to talents for innovation.

Li Youcai, 52, is a capable person. He graduated from Zhengzhou Industrial School in 1961 and came to Qingdao Ninth Rubber Factory. In the past 29 years, everyone knows that he loves the innovation. Whether being young or old, he actively participates in the innovation.

Li is good at thinking and loves to make suggestions. From the early 1960s to the present, he has made a lot of innovation proposals. Although the factory leaders are changed a few times, Li is still passionate about innovation.

In 1963, Li created a last remover which could improve efficiency by 30 times and was used to replace the manual operation. The Ministry of Chemical Industry specially held a meeting to promote this modern technology. Li said, "When I made this invention, I proposed a few ideas. The leader adopted them and provided the relevant help for me. I thank them for their support." In 1964, with the support of the factory leader, Li also invented a punching machine for the rubber sole sponge according to the principle of the cutting machine, which improved the work efficiency by nearly 40 times. Through these two things, everyone said that Li was talented.

He is a man of few words. When having an innovative idea, he will come to the leader and tell him about it. He says, "Doing so proves that I am loyal to the enterprise."

In 1985, Wang became the director of Qingdao No. 9 Rubber Factory. The first thing that he did was to call on employees to make rational proposals. One day, after work, Li came to Wang and put forward the idea of automatizing the molding of rubber shoes. Wang felt happy. Their discussion ended after pm 9:00. Li finally said, "I hope you give me two helpers in completing this task." Wang answer, "OK. You are free to choose them." The next day, Li selected two young people who were willing to learn more.

There were two small rooms in the west of the factory, which were quite cold. But Li felt that it was quite good to carry out this innovation project there. Li worked with his two helpers. Wang often visited them and asked whether there were problems. This encouraged them greatly.

Li began his research. In the past, the color strips on the edge of the rubber shoes were hand-applied, having the poor quality and being very laborious. With a heroic effort, he invented a 2-color foxing machine. Soon after that, he invented a foxing machine of multiple colors, which could automatically apply strips of four distinct colors on the edge of the shoe at the same time. Experts believed that this equipment filled a technical gap in the production of rubber shoes in China, and its performance was comparable to that of similar equipment in Japan and South Korea. Therefore, Li received a color TV set as a reward, which created a great stir in Qingdao. *(Source: Popular Daily, June 14, 1990)*

(3) A prize of a trip abroad granted for innovative experts in Double Star

—— A prize of a trip to enhance confidence and overcome difficulties

The departure ceremony of 34 staffs who were granted a prize of a trip abroad was held at the headquarters of Double Star Group. President Wang attended it.

Due to the financial crisis in the United States, the global economy experiences a decline. Some enterprises in China attempt to survive through reduced wages or layoffs. On the other hand, the other enterprises unite and motivate staffs to enhance their confidence and competitiveness. In the afternoon of December 18, 2008, Double Star Group held a departure ceremony of 32 staffs who were granted a prize of a trip abroad was held at its Qingdao Headquarters. It was a 9-day trip including Hongkong, Macau, Singapore and Malaysia. President Wang shook their hands and congratulated them, encouraging them to create new achievements in the future and make unremitting efforts to overcome the impact of the financial crisis. These staff who had made outstanding contributions worn red star hats, sports clothes, and shoes (all made by Double Star), with a red ribbon on the body, a high-grade red luggage on the hand, a smile on the face, and a feeling of being proud. ", all smiles, it is filled with pride and glory.

Over the years, Double Star Group has granted a prize of a trip to outstanding staffs in innovation and quality and other model workers every year. Most of them are from the production, technology and management posts. Trips include climbing Taishan Mountain, Qingcheng Mountain, Wudang Mountain; climbing the Great Wall; watching the flag-rising ceremony; visiting the Forbidden City and Longmen Grottoes in Luoyang etc. Through these activities, Double Star has created a good atmosphere of striving to be pioneers, stars, and models, with a solid talent foundation for continuous development and advantages in human resources.

Double Star organizes outstanding staffs in innovation and quality and other model workers to travel abroad for free of charge every year. While having a high cost, this practice has become an important part of its incentive mechanism for the enterprise. President Wang said, "This is a good form in which Double Star adheres to the combination of spirit and material for many years and pays attention to the details in of ideological and political work. Through this form, the staffs are indeed well educated and motivated. This practice is very valuable. They are our stars in posts and have contributed to the development of the enterprise. These talents are the most valuable assets for our enterprise to participate in market competition and overcome the unfavorable factors in development. We grant them a prize of a trip abroad, which can let them see the outside world to be more knowledgeable (including the overseas market) and which will make them more enthusiastic in their future work. Especially in the current financial crisis, it is necessary for enterprises to rely on core technology, give full play to talents, have a new idea, and initiate a people's war in innovation, to overcome difficulties."

Sun Aiqin, director of the upper workshop in the shoe industry park of Double Star, who was about to embark on a journey abroad, could not help but feel excited. She said happily to the sisters in the workshop, "I never dreamed that the group would give such a high treatment to me as a common cadre at the grassroots level. Now it really comes true. We should work harder in the future to make outstanding contributions." The picture shows the staffs who went to Qingdao Liuting Airport. *(Source: Western Leather, February 15, 2009)*

IV. Expert Comments

In the era of market economy, including the primary stage of socialism, man lives as an economic man. That is, he must have a certain economic income as the basic condition for survival, then can engage in other activities, for example, political, legal, moral, artistic, educational, philosophical, religious etc. In this circumstance, if there is an unbalance between the labor and the income for a long time, that is, he can't make ends meet, then his enthusiasm will be frustrated. However, for an extended period of time, especially in the era when the ultra-left trend of though prevailed, we always wanted to solve the basic problem of historical materialism with the way of thinking such as attaching importance to righteousness but ignoring the profit. The results obtained were always counterproductive.

As a high-level animal, the manifestation of their own value is an instinct for human beings. There are two manifestations of this instinct of human beings: one form is spiritual pursuit, such as honorary title, certificate, and medal, etc.; the other form is material pursuit, and its concentrated expression is the pursuit of money. This is something that spiritual encouragement cannot replace. The reason is that in the market economy, currency is the most important premise and guarantee of commodity exchange. Currency is circulated socially; without it, people cannot survive. Therefore, no one can shun money.

President Wang recognized this earlier, and he often said, "**People at Double Star who have a keen sense of dedication also need money.**" Therefore, as early as the early 1980s, when he was talking about the entrepreneurial spirit, he included the profit pursuit as a very important content in it. It can be said that the idea of the profit pursuit produced a strong impact socially on the mind of party members who were ashamed of talking about it at that time. This caused a debate for a long time, but made Double Star firmly establish the economic benefits concept in the earlier time. Later, he expanded the above concept by boldly putting forward the theoretical viewpoint: "The effective use of money is the best ideological and political work", and rewarded those who made outstanding contributions, with prizes including color TV sets, houses, and cars, thus mobilizing the enthusiasm and initiative of the whole staff to a greater extent. He also proposed that his staffs should rely on wisdom, hardworking, and sweat to become rich. This is not only a good combination of spirit and material, but also serves as the standard and career pursuit goal of people at Double Star, and the guide for them to advance in the market economy.

Revolutionary leader Engels pointed out long ago, "**Mankind must first eat, drink, have shelter and clothing, before it can pursue politics, science, art, religion, etc.**" (Engels: "Karl Marx", In "The Collection of Marx and Engels"

(Volume Two), Volume 2, People's Publishing House, 1958, p. 162.) The basic principle of historical materialism described by Engels, that is, material being first and spirit second, should become the fundamental policy of enterprise management, especially enterprise salary and compensation management.

So, does this mean that the role of spirit is completely denied? No. Historical materialism believes that spirit is in the second place when compared with material, but this does not mean that spirit is useless. Instead, spirit has a counterproductive effect on matter. Under certain conditions, spirit can be transformed into matter and have a powerful action on matter. So-called "certain specific conditions" mainly refer to specific people (such as revolutionary leaders, fighting heroes, labor models and other elites), specific environments (such as extremely lack of material conditions, continuous cruel wars, such as Struggle in Jinggangshan, Long March by Workers' and Peasants' Red Army, earthquake-relief work, fighting flood and providing relief, and fighting with gangsters), specific time (such as the sprint phase of various competitions, time to the peak in mountaineering). Under such specific conditions, it is necessary to emphasize the role of the spirit and promote the transformation of the spirit into a powerful material force. This does not violate historical materialism. Instead, this insists on materialist dialectics, thereby avoiding mechanical materialism.

For the principle that **spirit has powerful action on materia**l, President Wang not only understands its essence, but also perfectly applies it to his management practice.

Tactic 15: The Brand Management Is the Sublimation

"I hope that the typical representatives who are commended will continue to work hard, play the role of the main force in the production at the grassroots level, continue to keep ahead in innovation and quality the like, assist the leaders to carry out all production and management, invigorate the spirit of the staffs, unite and cultivate more people to be pioneers, form a good atmosphere of catching up and overtaking one another, receive more advanced collective titles on the workshop and plant levels, and develop the enterprise with one heart and one mind."

——Wang Hai

More than 100 model staffs were rewarded with a trip to Tiananmen Square to watch the flag raising ceremony, so fulfilling their dreams.

Double Star always insists on rewarding the excellent operators in the first line of the market.

I. Wang Hai Quotations

(I) Outlook on honor for people at Double Star

☆ Be proud of Double Star and proud of working in it.

☆ I and the brand add brilliance to each other.

(II) Honorary goals for people of Double Star

☆ Five Loves: Love the motherland, love Double Star, love the brand, love the field, and love the job post.

☆ Strive to be famous: global brand, famous global enterprise, and celebrity of Double Star

(III) Attitude to honor for people at Double Star

☆ Let the past be the past; work harder to create a brighter future.

☆ Cherish your honor and treatment obtained.

☆ Cherish the conditions and opportunities created by Double Star.

☆ Cherish the power, status and value of your own

☆ retain the honor and guard against arrogance; constantly innovate and improve.

(IV) Hope for people commended at Double Star

☆ Catch up with and overtake one another; invigorate the spirit of all staffs.

☆ Be modest and prudent; never complacent.

☆ Be sober and not afraid of finding the gap; be wiser and good at asking questions.

☆ You will lose face if you damage the image of the enterprise.

II. Practices and Effects

(I) Main practices

1. A prize of a trip

For pioneers in innovation and quality, there are a number of prizes. One of them is a trip to Taishan Mountains, Great Wall, Forbidden City, to Sichuan Qingcheng Mountain, Hubei Wudang Mountain, Luoyang Longmen Grottoes and other attractions.

2. Flag-raising ceremony at Tiananmen Square

The model workers in each unit of Double Star Group are organized to watch the flag-raising ceremony on Tiananmen Square for carrying out patriotic education and linking the patriotism with the love for the plant and the job. This enhances the ability of Double Star as a national brand to compete with foreign brands.

3. Let outstanding staffs become protagonists of the book and become TV stars

The typical deeds of the outstanding staffs are collected into books which are released sent. The books already compiled include Stories of 100 Honesty Staffs, Shining Stars Here and so forth. The touching stories of staffs are also complied into the TV column of Education Video to let them become stars, thereby greatly encouraging them.

4. Operation method named after the staff who is its creator

The staff brand initiative is an upgraded version of Double Star's staff qualifications project. By naming the operation method after the staff as its creator, Double Star fully recognizes his value. This is the best incentive for him and can encourage the staff to create a greater value.

5. Family members of a commended staff is proud of him

A staff who has an outstanding contribution will be commended. The enterprise sends the good news to his family members and invites them to the venue of the commending conference. Therefore, family members and acquaintances are proud of him.

(II) Main effects

1. Enhance the enthusiasm, sense of honor, and loyalty of staffs

In addition to material rewards, outstanding staffs are granted spiritual rewards, which can enhance their enthusiasm, sense of honor, and loyalty.

2. Build a team of passionate and motivated staffs

Through striving to be brand staffs, their enthusiasm and creativity are continuously mobilized. The team of passionate and motivated staffs has become a new competitive force in the new development stage of Double Star. Double Star has created a good atmosphere of striving to be pioneers, stars, and models, with a solid talent foundation for continuous development and advantages in human resources. There are more and more staff brands, which are the core competitiveness of Double Star in the new development stage.

III. Typical Examples

(1) Watching the flag raising ceremony in Tiananmen Square

Since the 1980s, Double Star has insisted on selecting the model workers, not only giving material rewards to them, but also giving spiritual rewards, such as trips including trips abroad.

In the early morning of September 4, 2006, more than 100 model workers wearing red hats and red clothes watched the flag-raising ceremony in Tiananmen Square. "We want to use this form of activity to motivate staffs' patriotic enthusiasm and passion for their job." President told reporters excitedly at the scene of watching.

Along with the national anthem of the People's Republic of China, the five-star red flag rose slowly. The model workers of Double Star Group solemnly saluted it until the end of the ceremony. After the flag-raising, model worker Sai Guiping of Bohai as a subsidiary of Double Star was still excited and said, "It is my dream for many years to watch the flag-raising ceremony. Today, my dream finally comes true. I deeply feel proud of our great country and hopeful about our future. Chinese people deeply love their nation."

Subsequently, more than 100 model workers boarded the Tiananmen Gate. As a symbol of the founding of New China, Tiananmen Square has become an integral part of China's national emblem, witnessing the changes in China's modern history and the rise of the Chinese nation. All of this has inspired the enthusiasm of the Double Stars to grow and develop national brands. "Now China is still too lacking in national brands. This has already sounded the alarm for the people of the whole country. It is imperative to create a national brand!" Wang Hai said.

In this regard, he pointed out that the development of the national economy requires the support of national brands. The enterprise casts a national brand, which should be supported by the government, researched by experts, promoted by merchants, and loved by consumers. "Only if the whole people work together to develop national brands, can we make our country more prosperous and strong." said Wang.

By watching the flag-raising ceremony on Tiananmen Square, Double Star carries out patriotic education and links the patriotism with the love for the plant and the job. This enhances the ability of Double Star as a national brand to compete with foreign brands.

(Source: Manager Daily, September 2006.)

(2) Staff brand of Double Star

Recently, Luzhong officially sets up several staff brands: Meng Yun Team, Sewing Gold Technician Liu Binghua, Foxing Technician Wang Lei, Innovation Little Doctor Liu Fangjun etc. These names shine on the billboard of the post. There is a also an official naming ceremony held in it: that is, Cutting Process Innovator Li Guangxing, Upper Machine Maintenance Expert Du Yicheng, and Packaging Little Housekeeper Wang Chengdong. This ceremony marks that the project of Double Star has been fruitful. The staff brand has become the core competitiveness of Double Star in the new development stage.

The staff brand initiative is an upgraded version of staff qualifications project in Double Star. Since the launch of the project, the units of Double Star have set off a wave of striving to become a model staff and a staff brand. President Wang says that understanding the value of staff brand and cultivating the staff brand is the core competitiveness and the talent strategy of the enterprise.

The initiative of staff brand in Double Star, which is a new highlight of management, further stimulates the enthusiasm of staffs to improve quality and reduce consumption, enhance the sense of honor and pride of staffs to show their own value. The initiative plays an active role in improving the quality, reducing costs, reducing the labor intensity, deepening family affection management, improving work efficiency and promoting safe production. Moreover, the initiative establishes the new image of Double Star and enhances its brand awareness.

The creation of the staff brand enables the staffs of Double Star to have new directions and goals, which has greatly promoted advancement, innovation, quality improvement and cost reduction and has played a key role in overcoming unfavorable factors such as skyrocketing raw material prices.

(3) Operation methods are named after workers as their creators, which achieve remarkable results

Double Star relies on independent innovation to accelerate technical progress, including the process and equipment. This not only improves production efficiency, reduces energy consumption, but also overcomes the unfavorable factors brought about by rising raw material prices, and cultivates many skilled workers having innovative ideas.

The practice of the operation method being named after the staff has become an important way for staffs to improve their operational skills and has played a huge role in improving production, improving efficiency, and reducing consumption so on. Double Star maximizes the use of the talents, lets everyone do their best, and puts forward "the first-line staffs are the main force of innovation", "posts are the market, competition is in the machine station, all staffs are innovative and achieve results". In the shoe industry industrial park of Double Star, the upper workshop names the knife arrangement method after the staff, which provokes the enthusiasm of staffs for innovation. There are more than 10 methods for knife arrangement, which are named after staffs, such as Wan Guo Method, and Xin Tao Method. Since the beginning of this year, the workshop has saved more than 24,000 Yuan of raw materials. In Luzhong located at Yimeng Mountainous area, each worker in the sewing line team for fitness shoes for females provided materials for 500-600 pairs of shoes (no more than 800 pairs in maximum) per day in the past; but after the use of the method created by Wang Anxiang, each worker can provide materials for 1,050 pairs of shoes. After this operation method is promoted in the whole workshop, the average production per person per hour is increased by 5 pairs. In Double Star Machinery, the operation method is named after the staff, which has mobilized staffs to initiate the people's war. One of achievements is that a knife becomes four knives and that the ordinary lathe becomes a universal lathe, with the efficiency increased by 3.5 times. Double Star combines the use and cultivation of talents, adheres to various forms of education and training. Double Star runs its education institute in which young workers are carefully selected as students and well-known experts from the rubber industry and colleges are hired as teachers. In addition, some self-taught experts have published their own monographs.

In the sports shoe factory of Luzhong, the molding team create economy benefits, through a learning and promotes the development through innovation, achieving a total of 26 innovations in management and technology with an economy benefit of more than 700,000 yuan. In 2006, this team received the honorary title - National Learning-oriented Advanced Team. In Double Star Bohai, all kinds of shoe-upper cutting knives were outsourced, which had a negative impact on rapid product delivery into market. Wang Cunjun as a former carpenter took the initiative to contract the task of making knives, which provided enough time for new products into market, thereby bringing benefits for both himself and his unit. In Double Star, the talent training model of learning in classroom, applying knowledge in practice and taking achievements as the test criteria has built a stage for the staffs to fully display their ambitions and reflect their values. Double Star has carried out the rationalization proposal activity among all the staffs. In its Golden Ideas project, all the staffs are the main force of innovation. *(Source: Double Star Magazine, 2006)*

IV. Expert Comments

American behavioral scientist Maslow's hierarchy of needs theory is one of the theories of behavioral science. This theory was proposed by him also as an American psychologist in 1943 in his paper entitle A Theory of Human Motivation.

This hierarchy of needs theory divides human needs into physiological needs, safety needs, love and belonging needs, self-esteem needs, and self-actualization needs. The five categories of needs are ranked from lower to higher levels, like a ladder. But this order can be changed, and there are exceptions. When the needs of a certain level are relatively satisfied, they will develop to the higher level, and the need to pursue a higher level becomes the driving force for the behavior of the people. Correspondingly, the need to obtain basic satisfaction is no longer an incentive force.

The five needs can be divided into two levels, in which the physical needs, the safety needs and the emotional needs are all low-level needs, which can be met by external conditions; the self-esteem needs, and the self-actualization needs are high-level needs, which can meet through human internal factors. A person's need for self-esteem and self-actualization is endless. Especially the need for self-actualization is the highest level of human needs; it refers to a need for those who realize their ambitions or for those who exert their personal abilities to the maximum extent and achieve the self-actualization. For example, a composer must compose music, an artist must create works, a poet must write poetry, an entrepreneur must run a business. . . such need is a need for self-actualization. Therefore, people must perform the task competently, to feel the greatest happiness. The need for self-fulfillment can motivate people to work hard to fully tap their potential and make their dreams come true.

President Wang creatively classifies people's needs into two categories: spiritual needs and material needs. In short, people live by pursuing reputation (spiritual needs) and profits (material needs). He often says, "People must have a spirit, and the power of the spirit is endless." This is the fundamental difference between man and animal and is also the highest pursuit of man.

Based on his deep understanding of people's needs, in addition to materially meeting the needs of staffs, he pays special attention to meeting their spiritual needs by adopting a variety of innovative methods, such as selecting advanced models, awarding honorary titles and brand staffs, naming innovations after staffs, letting staff deeds into books and TV columns, letting staffs into the Hall of Fame, let staffs wear red flowers and red ribbons. This practice has achieved very good results. This is a management method that is simple, effective, and small in costs. Therefore, Double Star is worth learning.

Tactic 16: The Assessment Is the Essential

"If a complete set of rules and regulations are not strictly enforced (instead, just written on the paper, hung on the wall and locked into the drawer), they will be a piece of waste paper - becoming not effective. This will also let the rules and regulations be no more than a formality resulting in a bad atmosphere. Therefore, their strict implementation is the basis and guarantee for the successes including smooth development, consolidation and improvement.

——Wang Hai

"Enforcement of rules and regulations should be strict." "Compassionate leadership, ruthless discipline." Strict assessment and strict enforcement of rules and regulations are an effective guarantee for management in Double Star.

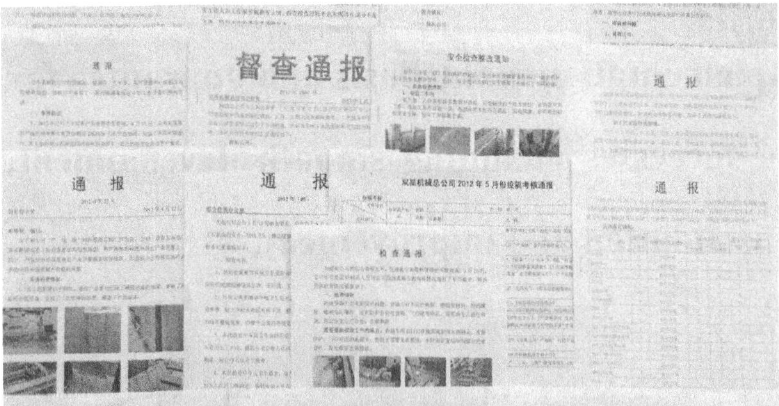

In Double Star, everyone is responsible, and assessment made in every post, with rewards and punishments meted out.

I. Wang Hai Quotations

(I) Significance of strict assessment

☆ Theory is the guide, regulations are guarantees, implementation is the key.

☆ Rules and regulations not effectively implemented equals zero.

☆ If a complete set of rules and regulations are not strictly enforced (instead, just written on the paper, hung on the wall and locked into the drawer), they will be a piece of waste paper - becoming not effective. This will also let the rules and regulations be no more than a formality resulting in a bad atmosphere.

☆ Strict implementation rules and regulations is the basis and guarantee for the successes including smooth development, consolidation and improvement

(II) Standards for assessment in Double Star

☆ Management policy of Double Star: strictness, lofty standards, and attention to details

☆ There is responsibility for every post; also, there are rules and regulations.

☆ Everyone is responsible with assessment made in every post.

☆ The work must be completed excellently without resorting to deception.

(III) Measures for assessment in Double Star

☆ strict discipline, strict standards, strict requirements, strict rules & regulations, and strict enforcement

☆ Super-strict inspection and assessment, and microcomputer management

☆ Be strict, be fair, be just, and be result-oriented.

☆ It is necessary to handle the relationship of rules & regulations with the money, strict assessment, market, and personnel management.

II. Practices and Effects

(I) Main practices

1. Establish and improve assessment standards

Establish and improve the assessment standards, so that there is responsibility for very post with rules and regulations as a guarantee.

2. Establish and improve the assessment system

Establish and improve the assessment system, so that everyone is responsible with assessment made in very post.

3. Establish and improve the assessment mechanism

Establish and improve the assessment mechanism, and make a strict assessment, with rewards and punishments meted out.

4. Establish and improve the assessment organization

Establish and improve the assessment organization and carry out comprehensive assessment at all levels.

5. Establish and improve the assessment system

Establish and improve the assessment system, includes assessment of leaders and staffs. A people's war is initiated in the assessment which is made by not only departments and but also most staffs so forth.

(II) Main effects

1. Establish a set of rules and regulations

For more than 30 years, Double Star has created a new management model, whereas there is a responsibility for every post and there are rules and regulations. Double Star has carried out in-depth continuing education on rules and regulations which are constantly revised and perfected. According to its complete set of rules and regulations covering all aspects, there have been hundreds of persons dealt with in various stages of enterprise development. It is precisely because of its management policy (featuring strictness, high requirements and attention to details) that Double Star becomes a first-class enterprise group.

2. Establish the highest authority of rules and regulations

The rules and regulations of Double Star are mostly formulated after discussion by the workers' representative congress. Therefore, they are called by the staffs to have the highest authority. If a person violates them, no matter who may be, he will be punished.

3. Create a powerful incentive mechanism

The incentive mechanism includes the property rights system, welfare system, reward system, etc. of the enterprise, which determines the rules for the distribution of wealth in the production process. Double Star Group has established and perfected a set of incentive systems, e.g., various forms coexist, including contracting, leasing, share-holding, and selling so forth. Therefore, the internal incentive mechanism has been mobilized. The various forms coexist, and the chain stores of Double Star across the country were sold out, which became private-owned units from state-owned, thereby fully mobilizing the enthusiasm of the operators. The production units of Double Star often carry out various forms of technical competitions and labor competitions, and give them prizes in a timely manner, including money, color TVs, cars, and houses, which greatly stimulates the enthusiasm and creativity of staffs.

4. Create a powerful and stressful restraint mechanism

Double Star Group not only attaches importance to the formulation of various rules and regulations, but also pays more attention to assessment and implementation of laws and regulations. For example, through understanding and keeping up with the change of the external market, Luzhong continuously supplements and improves the quality management system, including 367 specific quality management regulations and quality assessment regulations, e.g., Three Inspections in Quality, Three-level Supervision, determination of production yields and salaries according to actual conditions so forth. These regulations are strictly implemented with relevant assessments made. As a result, in the process, there is a good atmosphere: in other words, everyone pays attention to quality; an excellent job is done in quality in all posts; everyone is an inspector with inspection done in each process. Therefore, the product quality level has been greatly improved.

5. Create a new model of performance appraisal

To respond to the long-standing problem of merely contracting or selling instead of management in the society, Double Star has created a new model of management still needed after the contracting or selling. In the management, the attention is paid to the assessment and inspection. Double Star forms a new atmosphere: uniting together as a family, working hard; strict but not rigid & flexible but not chaotic in management. Double Star implement the responsibility system as a major feature in the quality management. Through the above-said measures, Double Star has improved the meticulous operation level and achieved satisfactory results.

III. Typical Examples

(1) Strict rules and regulations

The rules and regulations of Double Star are mostly formulated after discussion by the workers' representative congress. Therefore, they are called by the staffs to have the highest authority. If a person violates them, no matter who may be, he will be punished.

A vice president who once contributed to Double Star was punished due to his violation. Namely, his mistake was to sell a truck of shoes to a self-employed person, and this was prohibited by the provisions of Double Star. He was required to self-criticize in the group-wide cadre meeting, with one of his yearly salary being confiscated according to the decision made in the staff's democratic appraisal.

The son-in-law of an old comrade-in-arms of President Wang repeatedly violated rules and regulations. For fear of hurting the feelings of the old comrade-in-arms, the supervisor only gave him a slight punishment. Later, President Wang knew it and required the supervisor to punish the violator strictly according to the rules and regulations. As a result, the punishment was to expel him from the enterprise. The old comrade-in-arms met Wang and begged for his pardon, but the latter said, "The rules and regulations of Double Star are formulated after the discussions in the staff representatives' congress and represent the interests of staffs throughout the company. Except for the said congress, no one has the power to change."

The fierce market competition has made decision makers of Double Star realize that the market is like a battlefield. Therefore, from the battlefield filled with smoke to the dazzling market, the strict discipline must be adhered to, with the strict implementation of rules and regulations. Also, we must never give up. Only in this way can we win. In June of this year, Double Star Group decided to build a large shoe city in the Yimeng mountainous area and required an assistant to the president to complete it and put into use as soon as possible. As a result, 99 days later, a large-scale shoe city with an annual output of 10 million pairs of shoes stood proudly, creating a miracle in the history of the development of Double Star. Therefore, the assistant to the president who received the award said with emotion, "If there were no firm determination, it would be impossible to complete the task anyway."

For people at Double Star, the rules and regulations have the highest authority. Also, Double Star always adheres to the strict assessment. Since its establishment, due to its authoritative management, Double Star has developed stably, continuously and at a high speed. The total assets have increased by more than 180 times compared with ten years ago, and the sales revenue has increased by more than 50 times. While not spending public money, Double Star has paid taxes which were more than 33 times that years ago and has found a path for our national industries to become strong. *(Source: Central Radio Station - Double Star Series Report 2, 1995)*

(2) Rule of law management

In the early 1980s, staffs did not understand strict management, and there were public debates about strict management of Double Star. But President Wang realized that to eliminate the backwardness of the enterprise, it was necessary to thoroughly break the stereotypes rather than make a slight change or a small repair. During this period, due to the vested interests damaged, some people made the criticism, some people made the complaint, some people made the intervention, and so forth. However, Wang bravely got rid of old ideas and old traditions and moved forward with courage.

For more than 30 years, Double Star has created a new management model, whereas there is a responsibility for every post and there are rules and regulations. Double Star has carried out in-depth continuing education on rules and regulations which are constantly revised and perfected. According to its complete set of rules and regulations covering all aspects, there have been hundreds of persons dealt with in various stages of enterprise development. It is precisely because of its management policy (featuring strictness, high requirements and attention to details) that Double Star becomes a first-class enterprise group.

(3) Management still needed after the contracting or selling

President Wang said, "Contracting is the best mode of management. In 2011, the internal contracted shareholding system will be fully implemented." While actively implementing the contracting system, Luzhong has achieved the goal of management after contracting and selling. On the one hand, they specially held on-site meetings for the problem that the boiler room contracting effect was not obvious. At that time, the director of the upper workshop requested that the coal index of the boiler room should be reduced by 0.5 kilograms this year than the last year. Through the careful management, 7500 kg of coal was saved in March and April of 2011. This proves that the management still is needed after the contracting. On the other hand, after the buyout of the single-product material, the upper workshop always insists on the seriousness of each indicator with rewards and punishments being meted out. Cutting worker Li Guangxing replaced the traditional trapezoidal left-to-right knife arrangement method with the new method of adopting various forms of knife arrangement. This new method not only created enterprise benefits, but also improved personal income. Later, this new method was promoted in Luzhong, achieving a good result. Similarly, with the shoe industrial park of Double Star implementing a buyout restructuring of 3 subsidiary companies 5 years ago, Double Star has formulated a series of management and assessment measures. The three subsidiaries developed rapidly using their own advantages (including scale advantage and brand advantage) and the absorption of management experiences of Double Star. This year, they contributed 590,000 yuan to the shoe industrial park.

Therefore, contracting and selling are just a kind of management method. The management is still needed after contracting and selling, including the assessment work. Only in this way, can an enterprise form a new atmosphere: uniting together and working hard.

(4) Whoever causes quality problems should bear the responsibility

The fact that whoever causes quality problems should bear the responsibility is a major feature of the unique management of Double Star and a quality requirement that has been adhered to for many years. This provision has played a good role in promoting the sense of responsibility of operators, improving the level of meticulous operation, and creating quality products.

In the sports shoe workshop of Luzhong, Duan Youqiang is an air pressure operator in the molding process. When producing high-end business casual shoes (1102), due to his carelessness, a defective shoe went into the next processes and finally found in the packaging process. Due to this accident, he not only lost the qualification to be selected as a star mechanic technician, but also had to buy this defective shoe for himself by spending 20 Yuan.

In his introspection, this worker had a deep understanding of the quality of the products and greatly improved his sense of responsibility. Later, the team contractor found that Duan had a substantial change in the quality management. To improve the overall quality management ability of the team, Duan was assigned to the last process. In the new post, Duan Youqiang actively carried out quality inspections based on excellently completing his task of hanging shoes, solving the problems within the team. With his effort, his team was continuously rated as the company's integrity quality team from April to June 2011. He stood out in job competition and was named Double Star Youth Pioneer and got rewards from the company leader. He also was one of staffs benefiting from the implementation of the responsibility system.

IV. Expert Comments

The experiences of many successful enterprises and the lessons of failed enterprises have proved that, to receive results in implementation of the management systems, enterprises must do an excellent job in performance appraisal. Otherwise, all the management systems are ineffective and useless. Gerstner, former chairman of IBM, said, **"If you just inspect something**

which is emphasized, then the fact that you do not inspect the other thing means that you do not pay attention to it."

Therefore, "doing an excellent job of performance appraisal" has almost become the pet phase of each business leader, and almost every enterprise carries out performance appraisal. However, in many enterprises, results of actual performance appraisal are not satisfactory, because it is a merely formality. There are quite a few enterprises like Double Star to do an excellent job in the performance appraisal.

The reasons for the excellent results in performance appraisal of Double Star are as follows: unique corporate culture, god system and mechanism, strong leadership; a set of successful experiences including good standards, systems, organizations, and mechanisms of assessment, and full-staff participation in assessment etc. Especially Double Star is worth learning in its strict attitude and spirit in assessment with rewards and punishments being meted out.

President Wang emphasizes, **"If a complete set of rules and regulations are not strictly enforced (instead, just written on the paper, hung on the wall and locked into the drawer), they will be a piece of waste paper - becoming not effective. This will also let the rules and regulations be no more than a formality resulting in a bad atmosphere. Therefore, their strict implementation is the basis and guarantee for the successes including smooth development, consolidation and improvement."**

Tactic 17: The Market Is the Standard

"The market is the highest leader of the enterprise. The market is the standard for testing all the work of the enterprise. The market is the best balance for testing the enterprise. Follow the market, turn around the market, and change with the market."

——Wang Hai

Double Star has four famous brands in China.

⊙ **Double Star Professional Sneakers**

⊙ **Double Star Travel Shoes**

⊙ **Double Star Leather Shoes**

⊙ **Double Star Tires**

Double Star is the only enterprise in the domestic rubber industry that has four famous brands in China at the same time.

* Double Star Brand Value

49.292 billion yuan

*Wang Hai's Entrepreneur Value

32.142 billion yuan

I. Wang Hai Quotations

(I) Important value of the market to enterprises

☆ The market is a driving force and source of enterprise development.

☆ The market is the highest leader of the enterprise, the market is the standard for testing all work of the enterprise, and the market is the best balance for testing the enterprise.

☆ The customer is king, and the success is obtained in the market.

☆ Gold and silver cups are not as good as praises from consumers and markets.

(II) Attitude of people at Double Stars to market

Follow the market, turn around the market, and change with the market.

☆ People wear shoes, the key is at work.

☆ Cars use tires, the key is at work.

☆ Do not wait for others to give food, instead, find it for yourself.

☆ Follow the market, turn around the market, and change with the market.

☆ There are goods inferior in quality but not poor markets.

☆ Product + feelings = market

☆ Take yourself as a backbone, feel good about yourself, and go your own way.

☆ It doesn't matter whether the cat is black or white, as long as it catches mice; the development of Double Star is the last word.

Do not seek the help from the major, instead, aim at the market.

Get rid of planned economy, go to the market (including mountainous areas), cast the brand through the market.

(III) Market awareness of people at Double Stars

☆ The market is a driving force and source of enterprise development.

☆ The market is the highest leader of the enterprise.

☆ The market is the standard for testing all work of the enterprise.

☆ The market is the best balance for testing the enterprise.

☆ Market is like battlefield, competition is like war.

☆ The post is the market, the machine station is the market.

☆ All staffs turn to the market, all members participate in the competition

☆ The dazzling market is a battlefield filled with smoke. The entrepreneurs in the market are the generals on the battlefield. The market is a never-ending battlefield. We are always students in the market. We are always soldiers in the market.

(IV) Important value of management for the market

☆ The success of Double Star in the market for more than 30 years is first of all the success of management. The management determines the success or failure of market competition. It should be recognized that management is the secret weapon in market competition. Management is the core competitiveness of market competition and the magic weapon for market competition.

☆ Without excellent management, enterprises have no future and hope. Management determines success or failure. For some enterprises which fail, the root cause is still in management.

☆ Those who do a good job in management is excellent and always pay attention to management can take the lead in the market and be the winner of the competition.

☆ Double Star has entered the advanced stage of brand development. The goal of this stage is to build a century-old brand and build a century-old enterprise. Only by doing a good job in management which is the most difficult thing in the enterprise, can it be at the advanced stage with the above-said goal being achieved.

II. Practices and Effects

(I) Main practices

1. Dare to be the first and dare to overcome six obstacles

People at Double Star dare to be the first, dare to reform, dare to break through the restricted area, dare to innovate, and strive to do an excellent job in marketing. In the early stage of reform and opening, under the planned economy, the enterprise was only concerned about the production. At that time, there was a contradiction in the production and sales in Double Star, leading to a great backlog of Jiefang shoes. Double Star had no money to pay wages with staffs losing confidence. It is on the verge of bankruptcy that Double Star dared to be the first and dared to be a pioneer. After overcoming major obstacles, Double Star has become the forerunner of the market among state-owned enterprises.

(1) Going to the market

As early as the early 1980s, people did not hear about the market, did not understand the market, and had no concept of the market. Jiefang shoes of Double Star, because of being refused by the state commercial agency to go into its sales channel, had to be sold by Double Star itself. Why did it refuse them? Because it wanted to punish Double Star for breaking through the restricted area. In the market economy, people of Double Star insisted on the principle of being market oriented instead of seeking the help from the major. Double Star bravely took the first step into the market.

(2) Self production and self-sale

After getting rid of the circulation system of the unified purchase and sale, Double Star began to self-produce and self-sell. Double Star is the first to give up the long-time fixed price system under the planned economy. Double Star is the first to hold a meeting for placement of orders on its own name, which caused strong opposition from the commerce department and caused great resentment in the circulation. The boycott caused great resentment in the circulation system. Double Star had to successively establish 36 self-operated units at home and abroad, including Shenzhen (1984) and Beijing (1986). Its sale was involved in malls and wholesale markets. Later, Double Star became the first to set up its own chain stores. Double Star successfully made a change from the state of not waiting for others to give food to the state of actively finding food for itself.

(3) Funds

To get rid of the backwardness (old technologies, old processes, old products, old factories), in the dilemma of the competent authorities not accepting plans and bank loans not being available, Double Star is the first to carry out horizontal economic integration and is the first to utilize its advantages in brand-name intangible assets and management technology. In 1984, Double Star began its joint operation in Shandong, Xinjiang, Zhangjiakou, Chongqing, Chengdu, Guiyang and so on, and carried out its OEM production in Guangdong, Fujian, Zhejiang and etc. By external resources, external funds, and its own intangible assets, Double Star has set up its subsidiaries in the shoe industry: Zhongyuan (Central Plain) Double Star, Xinan (Southwest) Double Star, Huadong (East China) Double Star, Huanan (South China) Double Star. Double Star actively implements its low-cost expansion and is the first to give full play to the role of intangible assets. Therefore, Double Star solves the problem of funds.

(4) Media and advertising

In the early 1980s, the social concept was still that good wine needed no bush. If an enterprise made an advertisement in the social media, it would be regarded to blow its own trumpet. In the market, after encountering difficulties, Double Star felt the importance of propaganda. In 1984, Double Star made a surprising move: becoming the first to hold a press conference in its own name. This move attracted various stinging criticisms. Luckily, the Secretary of the Qingdao Municipal Committee, Liu Peng, bravely brushed aside all objections and defended this move. Therefore, Double Star took the lead to cooperate with the social media under the market economy.

(5) Job transfer

In the process of product adjustment and industrial transfer, Double Star encountered the problem of job transform for 7,000 urban workers. However, Double Star did not seek the help from the government, instead, carried out the internal placement of staff by developing the tertiary industry and establishing the labor service company. Double Star is the first to build a night life city in Qingdao, where the night market and the eating street were opened. Double Star also built the first large-scale tourism and leisure resort in Laoshan Scenic Area of Qingdao. Due to the involvement in more than 30 industries, such as catering, tourism, liquor, taxi, gas station, real estate, and advertising, Double Star was regarded to not engage in regular fields, which caused strong repercussions in state-owned enterprises. Therefore, Double Star took the initiative to involve in the tertiary industry and successfully carried out the job transfer for staffs.

(6) Export of products

At that time, only the state's foreign trade department had the right to export. However, in 1987, Double Star became the first pilot unit in the industry to possess import and export rights. In 1988, Double Star became the first company participating in the Canton Fair in its own name; and became the first company participating in the US International Footwear Fair. In 1992, Double Star became the first company to hold an international press conference in the United States; and became the first company participating in the international shoes industry fair of Germany. In 1995, by the export, Double Star earned more than 50 million US dollars (reversing the situation that it earned more than 1 million US dollars for nearly 30 years). This caused a strong opposition from the old foreign trade system at that time. However, Double Star resolutely entered the international market and broke the old system of foreign trade export. At the time, Minister Gu Xiulian of Ministry of Chemical Industry sent a congratulatory letter to Double Star which achieved the success in the export of products.

Double Star dared to break the old system, and dared to follow the market, turn around the market and change with the market. This has become the new feature of Double Star in its market work.

2. Marketing channels with 30 marketing strategies

After more than 30 years of practice, Double Star has created 30 marketing strategies leading to an opening-up of up marketing channels.

(1) Channel marketing

In the face of a broad market, enterprises need to take the initiative. Only by the marketing channels, can the enterprise be unbeaten in the competition. With the expansion of its scale, Double Star has begun the practice of chain operation in the country. The marketing network of shoes, tires and outdoor products has blossomed all over the country. It has played a good role in establishing a new image of Double Star, enhancing brand influence and driving market sales.

(2) Cultural marketing

Now consumers pay attention to the reputation of the seller and hope to have the peace of mind after a purchase; the market enters the advanced stage of selling culture. Brand companies sell not only a product itself, but also their image, service, and culture. For example, Double Star wins the order with the culture. One time, the tire market development team of Double Star in Beijing, Tianjin, and Hebei found in its investigation that a tire shop in Cangzhou could sell a certain amount of tires every month. The team took the initiative to visit the manager of this shop and present a DVD disc to him, which was a promotional material depicting the history, culture, management and so forth of Double. While being attracted by the strong culture, strict quality management and excellent production environment of Double Star, the said manager decided to cooperate with it. Now this shop sells tires of Double Star with the monthly sales amount being more than 1 million yuan.

(3) Sales promotion using psychology

In the environment of fierce competition with the oversupply in the market, enterprises will be successful if there is a deep understanding of psychological factors, including how to sell products, adjust prices, make discounts and etc. Business psychology is a deep-level marketing concept, which has a more persistent effect and better popularity than any promotion method. With the business philosophy of product + feelings = market proposed by President Wang, the psychological promotion plays a important role. For example, customers pursue a living environment being comfortable & healthy, Double Star promotes its patented shoes which is antibacterial and breathable by using psychological measures such as two-for-one deals on Mother's Day and Father's Day, respectively.

(4) Knowledge marketing

Knowledge marketing is to promote and introduce products, so that consumers know, need, buy, and be loyal to them. Each production unit of Double Star has compiled product brochures which are sent with products to various chain stores, where the salespersons introduce the products to the customers. For example, in Double Star, Outdoor Products Department has compiled the training manual and the shopping guide card, which are used in the knowledge marketing training for the shop staff, thereby playing an important role in the sales work.

(5) Time and space marketing

In this form of marketing, there is the most effective use of time to create the selling points and obtain advertising effects.

This form can turn time into a business advantage. To put it plainly, it is a marketing at suitable time. Double Star adopts two methods. One is to set the target time, seize the opportunity of the densest people flow, and use the golden time for promotion. For example, in many chain stores of Double Star, the limited time promotion is carried out to stimulate the consumer's desire and produce a good advertising effect. The second is to carry out promotional activities in holidays. For example, Double Star promotes the lovers shoes on Valentine's Day and promotes the fitness shoes for elder people plus shoes for fathers and mothers on Double Ninth Festival.

(6) Weather marketing

Weather management is based on changes of weather to adjust business strategies including products. Double Star is doing an excellent job in weather management. First, Double Star carries out cross-season ordering, cross-season production, and cross-month listing. Second, Double Star launches products in a targeted manner according to the weather characteristics of various places. Third, the operation units of Double Star pay attention to the weather forecast as an important work. In the summer of 2010, Double Star was in many regions to send beautiful umbrellas which could be folded to customers each buying goods worth 100 Yuan on a rainy day. These umbrellas as a gift were printed with a slogan of always comfortably being with Double Star, thereby enhancing the reputation of Double Star brand.

(7) Service marketing

Service marketing is a series of activities that the company takes in the marketing process to fully meet the needs of consumers while fully understanding such needs. Service marketing is not only a new trend in the development of an industry, but also an inevitable outcome of social progress. Double Star proposes a 200% service concept. Staff education, which is helpful in solving the problem of after-sales service and product quality, relates with the brand image and customer loyalty of Double Star. In Double Star, a staff drove thousands of Chinese miles to solve the problem in quality of a pair of shoes, winning the praise from the user; a staff made a good reply in a letter to the user, showing our commitment; Technology Development Center, Haijiang and other units always thought of customers to provide specially large-sized shoes and special-shaped shoes to meet their special needs etc. These established the good image in service and the emotional link with customers.

(8) Emotional marketing

Emotional marketing is to take the consumer's personal emotional differences and needs as the core of the corporate brand marketing strategy. By means of emotional packaging, emotional promotion, emotional advertising, word of mouth, emotional design and so forth. Emotional marketing is better than ruthless competition. Double Star uses emotional marketing and has achieved good results. For example, in August 2009, during a visit, an operator of Double Star Rubber Machinery learned that a company in Shanxi planned to purchase a batch of conveyor belt equipment, but due to being not familiar with Double Star, this customer did not include it into the list of candidates. In such an unfavorable situation, the operator, who believed that handwringing pays off, made 18 visits to the customer. When the Mid-Autumn Festival came, the operator not going home once again visited the customer who was deeply moved and promised to go to Double Star Rubber Machinery for a field trip. After the Mid-Autumn Festival, the customer's boss took their management staff as scheduled, and conducted a detailed inspection of the production capacity and product performance of the Double Star Rubber Machinery. During the inspection process, the customer not only recognized the technical strength of Double Star Rubber Machinery, but also was convinced by its unique corporate culture and management philosophy. As a result, an order worth more than 10 million Yuan was signed successfully.

(9) Entertainment marketing

With the continuous development of the economy and society, the level of people's needs has gradually improved. While paying attention to the material enjoyment provided by products, people pay more attention to the spiritual enjoyment brought by them. How to carry out entertainment marketing is becoming a trend for the new round of competition. Double Star has won the market via entertainment marketing. Double Star has statues of black cat and white cat in front of image stores; has the color TV, VCD, leisure seats, books and newspapers the like; holds cultural performances, award-winning knowledge contest, and special shopping etc. Rich entertainments can make consumers feel relaxed and happy, thereby stimulating their desire for consumption and letting them closer to the brand of Double Star.

(10) Experiential marketing

Experiential marketing is to let the target customers experience the products or services provided by the enterprise by letting them to observe, listen, try on, and use on the trial basis so forth. By this method, the customers perceive the quality or performance of the product or service, thereby promoting their cognition and preference. In Double Star, salespersons are also ingenious in promoting waterproof shoes, insulated electric shoes, air-conditioned cushion shoes and etc: that is, immersing the waterproof shoe in a basin with a certain depth of water to show their waterproof performance; putting the air-conditioned cushion shoe on the ear of the customer, pressing the sole to let them know the breathing effect. It is these novel and promotional strategies that are experiential, which make Double Star's high-tech professional shoes quickly become popular in the market.

(11) Personalized marketing

While pushing the personalized needs to an unprecedented center, the enterprise gradually establishes a new type of relationship with the market and a more personalized relationship with consumers in which the personalized sales and services are provided. At the celebration of the 60th anniversary of the founding of new China, a number of military vehicles in the parade used tires from Double Star. To meet the needs of the rapid maneuvering in troops, General Armament Department proposed the design requirements for all-steel cross-country tires (namely, generous size, light weight, good maneuverability, and high cross-country performance). For this purpose, technicians of Double Star were in two months to deliver the design plan which was successful in the bidding. Double Star strives to meet the individual needs of consumers. For example, it customizes the extra-large shoes for customers. One of its agents in Nanchang said, "We can meet your needs, no matter how large it is. We are good at and famous for designing & producing the extra-large shoes."

(12) Customized marketing

Customized marketing refers to a method, in which, based on mass production, each customer is regarded as a separate market segment with a marketing mix being adopted according to specific customer needs. Customized marketing can make the enterprise to take the initiative to sell products to better cater to consumer needs. In Double Star, the tech development center and production units often receive some letters from consumers and some consumers personally go there to request them to custom extra-large or large shoes, including Double Star Celebrity Sportswear Ltd.

(13) Sports marketing

Sports marketing is to use sports activities as a carrier to promote products and brands. It is a means of marketing. There are two types of sports marketing: the first type is the sports industry marketing that sells sports as commodities, and the second type is the marketing of other industries that is carried out by means of sports activities. The sports marketing usually mentioned refers to the second type. For more than 30 years, Double Star has been participating in a series of events and activities organized by the sports and literary circles. For example, it is a sponsor of followings: International Women Volleyball Invitational Tournament in the 1980s, sports activities of athletes coached by Ma Junren and National Games in the 1990s; events of Sudiman Cup in the 2000s, Mount Everest climbed by National Mountaineering Team of China, Clipper Round the World Yacht Race and so forth. Also, Double Star establishes its basketball team. By supporting the sports industry of China, Double Star has enhanced its visibility and influence. Its agents actively cooperate with local schools and governmental departments to sponsor sports games, to promote sales and improve the brand image.

(14) Differentiated marketing

Differentiated marketing means that enterprises develop different product and promotion strategies in the face of segmented market, and then fully implement them. Since 2008, the entire global economy has been cold, and China's traditional footwear and other export enterprises have been seriously affected. Double Star Haijiang timely adjusts its product structure and intensified product innovation, and successively develops a series of products that leads the consumer market. For example, its new foxing technology leads to a variety of patterns and colors, beautifying the products that are highly appreciated by customers. It also develops fashionable casual shoes that can emit the light in the dark environment and exude the scent from their soles. Its vulcanized shoes are sold in the high-end market at home and abroad.

(15) Brand marketing

Future corporate competition will definitely be competition at the brand level. In the market, a famous brand image can make the enterprise to achieve an advantageous position in the relationship with retailers and other market intermediaries. Double Star enhances the quality and service of the brand to meet the needs of consumers, highlighting the external image of the brand, the emotional image of the brand, the functional image of the brand, the social image of the brand, the cultural image of the brand, and the psychological image of the brand. As a result, its good image in the minds of consumers greatly enhances the competitiveness in its the product market.

(16) Event marketing

As a kind of public relations communication and marketing promotion method, event marketing mainly creates news events that can be spread to achieve the marketing effect. Double Star makes effective use of event marketing. For example, in 2009, the United States imposed special protectionist tariffs on tire imports from China. In response to the unequal treatment of the Chinese tire companies in the United States, the major domestic news media paid close attention to it by conducting real-time reports. As the first generation of outstanding entrepreneurs in China and the representative of the Chinese tire industry, President Wang was connected on the CCTV economic channel live broadcast program, and talked about his opinions on this event, including its impact on the Chinese tire industry, and response measures adopted by Double Star etc. The response measures taken and the attitudes and opinions on the whole incident were connected on the spot. Double Star timely notified its agents, customers, cadres and key employees of the tire company to watch this news program, which enhanced the confidence of the tire agent in cooperation with Double Star and achieved good publicity and promotion effects.

(17) Implantable marketing

Implanted marketing, also known as soft advertising, is embedded in a variety of media, including movies, TV programs, newspapers, online games, text messages in mobile telephones, and even novels. Double Star's big shoe advertisement in the past, tire advertisement on Spring Festival Gala, celebrity logo and product advertisement in the Qingdao TV channel in recent years, are all good implantable marketing practices, greatly spreading the brand image.

(18) Internet marketing

Internet marketing is the application of marketing in online e-commerce, that is, it is a kind of marketing through Internet. The Internet has become a new way of marketing and has become a high-speed road for marketing of Double Star. Double Star has established a website from which customers can see its new products. Units of Double Star actively carry out online sales, contact with overseas customers through some well-known domestic websites, on which the vigorous promotion is made. In this way, Double Star makes friends from all over the world, attracts more and more customers and quickly develops its business.

(19) Relationship marketing

Relationship marketing means that, through long-term and continuous satisfaction with needs of customers, the enterprise establishes a solid & long-term mutual trust relationship and friendship with customers, to achieve the customer satisfaction. For example, remembering the teachings of President Wang (that is, treating customers as relatives and moving them), Double Star Tire Import & Export Corporation always establishes a close relationship with a customer in Egypt, which leads to the decision of this customer that it cancels the partnership with other enterprise and takes Double Star as a sole partner. Especially in 2009, one thing made this customer more confident in cooperation with Double Star brand. It turned out that this customer urgently needed a small number of tires of the 12.00R24 DSR188 specification in this year. When there was a conflict in the arrangement of orders between the old customer and the new customer, the Double Star Tire Import and Export Company would have the right to delay the delivery of the goods for the new customer. However, while ensuring that the old customer's order was not affected, Double Star overcame difficulties to adjust the production plan, finally meeting the needs of the new customer from Egypt and being deeply trusted by it. In May 2010, this Egyptian customer resolutely established the first Double Star Tire Store in Hungary after its continuous communication with relevant business personnel.

(20) PR marketing

It refers to the social marketing through special public relations (PR) activities. It is both a short-term investment and a long-term investment. E.g., Double Star Rubber Machinery wins orders using this method. In 2009, its salesman met a customer manager in Iran at the exhibition and learned that they were preparing to expand the production. To seize the opportunity, both parties communicated with each other in a timely manner and established a good relationship. Later, the customer made a visit and invited several companies including Double Star Rubber Machinery to conduct business negotiations in Iran. In the case of unstable political situation in Iran, some domestic companies decided to postpone the negotiations, but the staff of Double Star Rubber Machinery went to Iran as scheduled. Our staff moved the customer with his professional spirit and sincere attitude and eventually won the order.

(21) Creative marketing

When compared with the conventional marketing, the creative marketing is like a lever, which is long enough and together with a strong fulcrum to be able to be used to move the world. Double Star is very good at winning the market with innovative thinking. In June 2009, Double Star Rubber

Machinery received a congratulatory message from a user in Henan. The user said that the equipment worth more than 40 million yuan had been used normally, so expressing deep gratitude and hoping to receive the next batch of equipment from Double Star in the future. According to common sense, sellers should thank users for purchasing their equipment. Why did this user thank Double Star as a seller? It turned out that due to the financial crisis, this user as a tire company intended to launch a radial tire project, but it was lack of funds and was not able to purchase the equipment. Seeing that the big order was near, the salesman of Double Star Rubber Machinery thought that if the user mortgaged the equipment to a third party, would the funding problem not be solved? Double Star sold the equipment to the third-party financial institution, which was leased to the said user. In this way, these three parties received benefits.

(22) Green marketing

Green marketing pays attention to the environmental protection as the guiding ideology of the enterprise, the green culture as the value concept, and the green consumption of consumers as the center and starting point. Green marketing includes the concept, method, and strategy. With the tenet of low carbon economy and green manufacturing, and with the purpose to further adapt to the requirements of the EU market, seize the anti-dumping opportunities in the international market to expand the influence of its products, Double Star Qingdao Tire Headquarters has developed 8 specifications, and 21 patterned tires which are environmentally friendly. The first domestic rotary Vacuum moulding line equipment developed by Double Star Machinery not only saves more than 50% of space, but also increases the efficiency by more than 1-fold. The second-generation dual-mode vulcanizing machine developed, which adopts the latest nitrogen vulcanization technology, can shorten the vulcanization time by nearly 20% and improve the overall vulcanization efficiency by more than 15%, thereby being well received by the market.

(23) Concept marketing

Conceptual marketing focuses on the combination of rational cognition and positive emotions of consumers and promotes products by introducing new concepts of consumption. For example, Double Star is based on the EVA big-sole casual shoes to develop weekend shoes and soft-sole dance shoes so forth which are ultra-light, comfortable and relaxed, and their sales are very satisfactory. The garment industry is moving towards a low-carbon economy, and it is a breakthrough revolution. The Double Star Celebrity Sports Goods Company has produced a new low-carbon series of conceptual clothing using plant fibres as raw materials, including fibers from bamboo, corn and soybean, not only considering the environmental friendliness but also meeting the full range of needs of customers for clothing performance, comfort, aesthetics, and health. These products are very popular on the market.

(24) Public welfare marketing

In the public welfare marketing, with the concern about people's survival and development, social progress as the starting point, the enterprise communicates with consumers through public welfare activities. While generating public welfare effects, this kind of marketing enables consumers to form a preference for products or services of the enterprise, thereby increasing brand awareness and reputation. For example, Double Star actively carried out the activity of buying our products and bringing back warmth, carrying out May 1 activity of giving model workers shoes, July 1 activity of giving shoes to old party members before the founding of new China, August 1 activity of giving shoes to military personnel, Teacher’s Day activity of presenting gifts etc. Through these activities, Double Star not only satisfied the consumers' desire to purchase products, but also won gratitude and trust from the customers.

(25) Bundle marketing

Bundled marketing means breaking the traditional marketing mindset, avoiding individual combat and leveraging the synergies of assorted brands and products. For example, Double Star sells its shoes. In the domestic market, since 2009, Double Star Tire has continuously enhanced the reform of sales system, formed the strategy, increased the integration of agents across the country, eliminated outdated agents that are not suitable for market and development, and accelerated the construction of logistics platforms; accelerated the development of the supporting market, utilized its advantages (including shoe-tire linkage so forth) and its wide-ranging influence to promote market sales.

(26) Word-of-mouth marketing

Compared with traditional telemarketing, TV advertising and other marketing methods that require human labor, word-of-mouth marketing has extremely low costs and plays an irreplaceable role today. Customers are more inclined to trust referees than the formal traditional marketing methods. For example, in April 2010, the news came that the environmental protection unit of Double Star Machinery Ltd successfully won a bid on a 3-ton electric arc furnace dust removal system at a large machinery factory in Guangxi; at the same time, the 5-tone dust removal system provided by it had been successfully operated in a customer in Guiyang for one year, and the same type of system in a customer obtained an approval from the environmental protection bureau of Zhuzhou (Hunan Province). At the end of 2009, after knowing that a large enterprise in GUANGXI planned to purchase a set of electric furnace dust removal system, the said unit contacted the person in charge of the project. This customer was more inclined to cooperate with relevant enterprises with many years of experience. However, when hearing that a 5-ton dust removal project of a customer in Guiyang was also from Double Star, this customer was very surprised and showed great interest. He contacted the customer in Guiyang, and the latter praised this equipment for being good in performance and steady in run, and recommended it to him. The customer in Guiyang not only praised the performance of the double-star environmental protection arc furnace dust removal project, but also actively recommended them to the double-star environmental protection equipment. Finally, the responsible person in this customer from GUANGXI took the initiative to contact the business personnel of the said unit and decided to purchase the equipment from it.

(27) Festival marketing

Manufacturers with the ability and foresight will always be bold in innovation in marketing for specific festivals. While spending an effort on understanding the consumer's psychology behavior and realistic needs in the holiday market and considering characteristics of related products, they formulate an effective product mix strategy, launch new products suitable for consumers' life, leisure, and learning during the festival, so as to take a different approach and seize the opportunity to obtain a success in the festival market. For example, on the Children's Day (June 1) in 2010, the Zhengzhou Logistics Platform of Double Star Celebrity Shoes did a good job in the festival market with innovative thinking, including the June 1 promotion. It carried out the Children's Day Talents Competition with the theme of Caring for the Future. In this event, there were a lot of participants and onlookers, which improved the popularity of Double Star and increased its sales.

(28) Color marketing

In color marketing, the enterprise incorporates color into the brand theme and introduces it into product R & D and sales. The product may change from a single color and multiple colors to attract consumers' attention, in other words, a visual feast can be created through color changes to stimulate the purchase desire of consumers. In the design and packaging of products, Double Star uses a color marketing strategy. By evolving the color of a product from a single-color system to a combination of multiple color systems, the designer attracts the eye of the consumer and motivates them to purchase. On the morning of November 16, 2011, the world's first batch of colored tires was launched at Double Star Dongfeng Tire in Shiyan, Hubei, whose colors includes red, yellow, green, blue, and so forth. Double Star created the color tires, breaking the pattern of all tires being black in the past 100 years, which means that the future cars will become more dazzling: red family cars with red tires, green taxis with green tires, blue business buses with blue tires, white sports car with yellow tires etc. Color tires from Double Star have attracted great attraction from customers with high popularity in the market. In terms of shoes and clothes, Double Star has paid attention to information of popular colors for many years, and there are right colors in products, packages, clothes, settings, store decoration, and shopping bags the like, which become a bridge to communicate with consumers. Especially in product R & D, special attention is paid to the color application, which has always been at the leading position, achieving a good result - products are popular among consumers all over the world, such as the United States and Germany. Fluorescent casual shoes for women developed by Double Star Haijiang have the beautiful patterns in the upper and represent the latest market trends, thereby being favored by young girls.

(29) Conference marketing

Conference marketing refers to the way in which products are sold to specific customers through affectionate services and product briefings in an affectionate atmosphere. For example, the 2010 UK Financial Times Qingdao International Financial Summit was held on May 20, 2010 at Wanda Le Meridien Hotel Qingdao. W-HAI Outdoor Products Department at Double Star Dengfeng set up an image booth at conference venue, which attracted the attention of participants. With a warm atmosphere, the staff of the said department gave a detailed introduction to the product features. Ms. Gillian-Tett deputy editor-in-chief of Financial Times expressed her strong interest in climbing shoes. While looking at the shoes carefully, she said in Chinese, "Double Stars begin to manufacture outdoor products whose quality and style are very good." At the tea break, the on-site sales amounted to more than 8,000 Yuan.

(30) Tourism marketing

A shop opened by an enterprise at a tourist attraction is like a live advertisement. The prices of tourist attractions are generally high, so the shop there can earn more profits for the enterprise. The most important thing is to make the enterprise better establish the brand image. In June 2009, Yangzhou Logistics Platform with Double Star Celebrity Shoes and Clothing accelerated the construction of chain stores in scenic areas of Yangzhou; this, with the help of shooting TV dramas, not only enhanced the popularity of Double Star, but also brought real benefits. Beginning in May 2009, China TV Drama Production Center started to shoot the TV drama series Fragrance in the famous Phoenix Island Scenic Area in Yangzhou. The supervisor of the said logistics platform in Yangzhou timely seized this opportunity and decisively decided to open a shoe and clothing store in the Phoenix Island Scenic Area to let Double Star have more exposure to the public attention. Since its opening, the store has attracted many tourists and TV drama shooters, and driven the sales of travel shoes, hiking shoes, outdoor sportswear and other products, greatly enhancing the popularity of the celebrity brand of Double Star.

(II) Main effects

From March 26 to 27, 2010, the China General Chamber of Commerce and the China National Business Information Center released the latest monitoring statistics of commodities of China key retail enterprises in 2009. Among them, Double Star brand travel and sports shoes produced and sold by Double Star

Celebrity Industrial Ltd won the first place in the market for similar products in 2009. Since 1998, by absorbing and merging, Double Star has achieved a leap from making shoes for people to making shoes for cars. Through brand and capital operation, high-end orientation, and innovative marketing, Double Star has rapidly expanded into footwear, tires, clothing, machinery etc., thereby enhancing competitiveness in domestic and foreign markets. In just a few years, Double Star Tire has developed into one of the top ten national brands in the tire field of China, that is, it has jumped to the fifth place. In the ranking list of the global top 75 tire enterprises of 2011 from the US Rubber & Plastics News Weekly, Double Star Tire was in the 21st place in terms of sales revenue, while 18th place in 2010. According to the statistics of the European rubber authority magazine European Rubber Journal, Qingdao Double Star Rubber Machinery ranked 11th in the global rubber industry in 2012. Double Star now has annual sales income of more than 12 billion yuan and exports earning 300 million US dollars.

III. Typical Examples

(1) Being forced into the market

In 1983, Wang and his staffs secretly sold shoes marking that they began to enter the market (Wang: second from the right)

In November 1984, Double Star was the first to hold a press conference in the name of a company. It marks that Double Star fully carried out the reform with all of its staffs entering the market.

In 1986, Double Star was the first to hold a national shoe trade fair in the name of a company.

Just when Wang began a comprehensive reform, his suddenly faced a severe test of survival!

The news that the commercial department stopped buying more than 2 million pairs of Jiefang shoes produced by Ninth Rubber Factory was like a thunder shocking worker. This undoubtedly mean that there was a backlog and the company faced a survival problem.

China's reform and opening began in 1978 when the Third Plenary Session of the Eleventh Central Committee of the CPC was held. However, at the beginning of the reform, it was limited to the implementation of the rural contract responsibility system. After the rural reforms were widely promoted for four or five years, the industrial enterprises still were like a pool of stagnant water beneath which there were surging waves and billows. The mode of operation of enterprises according to the plan system had been repeatedly impacted by the undercurrent of the market, though this surge of waves has not yet found a vent. Actually, his move at Ninth Rubber Factory was an ice-breaking move.

In the past, as a large-scale rubber shoe manufacturer in the country, Double Star ran in a planned economy mode: the supply of raw materials and the sale of finished products being planned and implemented by the country; it was only responsible for shoe-making without no pressure of sale and payment collection. In 1983, all of this ended suddenly. The commercial department refused to continue to accept the its products, and its superior department did not render any help. It had a backlog of more than two million pairs of Jiefang shoes piling up in warehouses, workshops, and even office buildings, and the production line still ran according to the plan issued.

As a new leader, Wang felt very anxious. Seeing that the day of paying wages was coming, he did everything to overcome difficulties.

Wang, who was always lofty in character, humbled himself. He personally went to the commercial department, but the latter said, "We do not want to sell your shoes, and we do not want to suffer a loss." Wan met the leader of the superior department (namely rubber headquarters). This leader, who was challenged by Wang in the past, retaliated on him by saying, "The commercial sector does not sell them, and we are willing to help you but unable to do so."

Wang finally couldn't bear it. He yelled at him, "Whom is this factory belonged to? Who issued the production plan? Now we have completed the production task with products not received by you. Is this a responsible behavior? Does this comply with the national policy?"

But this effort was useless. Instead, the leader was secretly glad when the other people encountered difficulties.

When returning and seeing that the warehouse, courtyard, corridor, and even the office was full of shoes, he thought of the story about Robin Hood and his men heard in childhood. These heroes were deprived of the right to survive and had to rebel against the ruler. Wang felt like them to have no way out. In such a situation, he and his enterprise were forced to fight to win or die.

Thinking of this, Wang suddenly became more cheerful. It is said that there is no road in the world, but so many people walk on the earth, making a lot of road; also, where there is a hen, there are eggs. He immediately convened an emergency meeting of the party committee, on which he said excitedly, "Our enterprise must survive, our staffs must be paid salaries. For this purpose, I decide to sell the shoes by ourselves."

In this way, regardless of the ban on restricting the private sale of products at the time, Wang led his staffs to take the first step into the market. To avoid unnecessary troubles, they were often in the dusk to secretly transport products out of their factory for sale.

Unluckily, the commercial department knew it becoming furious and vengeful. This made Wang braver to lead his salesmen to sell products in the daytime. With the one year's effort, more than two million pairs of backlogged shoes were fully sold out. This made Double Star the first to be market-oriented among state-owned enterprises in the city where it is located.

Later, Wang became a celebrity. In an interview with reporters, he often said, "At the end of 1983, we took the first step to sell products by ourselves and we are the first enterprise in the same industry to enter the market and directly participate in market competition. It does not show how insightful I was, instead, it shows a harsh environment that forced us to enter the market."

In the market, Wang felt that the state-owned enterprises under the planned economy were a combination of the giant in the production and the dwarf in the sale. On the one hand, the production process was large and comprehensive; on the other hand, the sales information was seriously congenitally insufficient. When our country used the planned economy as a crutch to support the balance between the two, the contradiction was not very prominent. However, once this crutch was withdrawn, an unbalance immediately occurred with the enterprises which could not move forward normally. .... Therefore, to survive and develop, the enterprise has only one way, that is, to be market-oriented. He says, "We should take the market as the top leader of the enterprise; let the market be the standard for testing all the work of the enterprise." In the 30 years, while leading his enterprise to the market, he has firmly believed in a truth: the fate of the enterprise depends on in the market.

After realizing the decisive role of the market, Wang decisively pointed out that the biggest function of the enterprise management department is to serve the market. There is no reason for existence in a department that does not serve the market. After the reform of the security department, Wang also realized that the enterprise reform was the human problem in the end, and that the brave reform in the personnel system could bring more advantages to the enterprise in the market. For these two reasons, Wang began to vigorously implement mergers and reductions enterprise-wide and reorganized the management department around the market.

Through the above-said reform, he reduced the number of departments from 27 to 17, number of administrative staffs 350 to 200, greatly improving the working efficiency for the departments and cadres. On the other hand, he expanded the sales department of only four people in the past into a production and operation information company, in which he introduced a competition mechanism, recruited talents and established a special sales team.

At that time, the establishment of this information company caused a sensation in the enterprise. First, in the propaganda column, a recruitment notice was posted, saying that 100 salesmen would be recruited from the workers. Those young people who worked in the production line all the time realized that this was a good opportunity to change their own destiny, so they rushed to the recruitment site for registration. The atmosphere of the enterprise is like water boiling after being heated up to 100 degrees.

To be just, fair, and market-oriented, Wang formulated three provisions for this recruitment: first, the best would be chosen; second, the system of the lifelong tenure would not be adopted; third, the personal connection (also known as the practice of pulling strings and abusing influence) must not be used. The first batch of salesmen receive a short-time training then were sent to all parts of the country to develop the market.

Wang attended their ceremony of departure. He said to these 100 salesmen with emotion, "Today, you will be on the road with shoes in the heart. Think about it. When the primitive people went out from the forest, where were the shoes? They put shoes on the feet for the convenience to walk and work. Shoes are one of the first signs of human civilization, which made our ancestors get rid of the ignorance. Just like the history of humans is constantly evolving, the shoes worn by them are constantly changing. Historically, there are bark shoes, wooden shoes, straw shoes, cloth shoes, rubber shoes, and leather shoes etc. Everyone needs shoes from the royal family and the prime minister to common people. The shoes on the ground bear the burden which have noble characters such as being endurable and selfless. We must remember that people wear shoes and that the key is in the work. You will have to travel all over the world, so let us send qualified shoes to the feet of all kinds of people..."

These salesmen lived up to expectations. In just one year, they increased the number of sales outlets from zero to hundreds and achieved more than 60% of the enterprise's self-sales ability.

It is his never-give-up spirit that makes him bravely take this step and become the first person to enter the market. It is also because of his determination that the enterprise gains a new life and enters the list of the first successful companies to enter the market.

(2) New York press conference and entry into the overseas market

In August 1992, Double Star held a press conference in New York, the United States. Wang took off his shoes on the spot and introduced shoes of Double Star to the media, which made a sensation in the American business community.

In the summer of 1992, Double Star Group held its first press conference in New York, USA. Faced with one question from American reporters, Wang having no piece of information at hand smile and responded well with his wonderful speech winning applause.

However, a reporter from Sing Tao Daily in the United States could hardly wait to grab the microphone and raised the most sensitive topic, "I would like to ask you as a shoe king of China, if the United States cancels the MFN status for China, instead, implements Special 301 Clause, then will your Double Star have a current prosperity? What is your attitude towards this?"

Wang calmly said, "First, the MFN status means reciprocal treatment and reciprocal interests. The United States can let China unable to get benefits, and China can also. Second, we may lose here and gain there. The United States has a population of 200 million people, China 1.2 billion, and the world more than 5 billion. It does not matter if the US market is lost, because we still have a market of 4.8 billion people worldwide. Third, our high-quality shoes have already taken a place in Europe. American consumers are also fond of high-quality and low-priced shoes from us. Today's market is free and open, rather than dependent on which person and which government. One clause can't stop our products from entering the US market."

A senior reporter from the New York Times, stood up, with a cunning look, said with a sneer, "Mr. Wang, you are the celebrity in the shoe industry of China. So, I took the liberty to ask, are shoes of Double Star on your feet?" This reporter noticed the beautiful shoes on his feet and wanted to let him become a laughing stock by asking such a question.

Wang smiled, "I am very grateful to you as a reporter for asking this question. You give me a good opportunity to promote our products. I know that taking off shoes in public is a very uncivilized act, but..." He started to take off his shoes.

His voice became louder, "Look, CHINADOUBLESTAR, the authentic shoes from us. Truly speaking, I wear our shoes all the year round, and so do all our staffs. We have more than 20,000 staffs. We put our shoes on feet to travel the world."

The spotlights flashed again.

The next day, his photo with a smile and a shoe in hand was published in a prominent position in many newspapers in the United States.

The press circle of the United States commented, "In our memory, there are only two communists from socialist countries who took off shoes in front of the American public. One is Khrushchev who was the United Nations headquarters in New York, took off his shoe and knocked against the table with them. The second is Wang who stood at the forefront of the state-owned enterprise reform in China, smiling and promoting his own products in the US market with their own products, so embodying a heroic spirit!"

Enterprises not only represent a group that creates wealth, but also represent a spirit that represents the soul of the country and the soul of the nation. Double Star creates the Chinese national brand, dares to enter the international market. Double Star successfully goes to the world, indicating that the spirit, ambition and conviction are very important to win the victory in the market competition.

(3) Brand and culture promote the product sale

Faced with many powerful competitors, Double Star Rubber Machinery actively explores domestic and foreign markets by relying on Double Star brand and adhering to the business philosophy of selling the culture before selling the product, which is proposed by President Wang. In 2010, Double Star Rubber Machinery won the favor from customers in Thailand by Double Star culture and won orders of more than 30 million Yuan.

The contact between Double Star Rubber Machinery and a certain user in Thailand began in June 2008. During the negotiations, the exchanges between the two parties had been very harmonious. Double Star Rubber Machinery finally beat many competitors. However, when the two parties officially signed the contract, because of the differences in payment methods, the user would like to abandon cooperation with Double Star Rubber Machinery and sought a new partner. Knowing it, a few famous domestic enterprises contacted the user. A fierce competition occurred again.

In the face of this passive situation, after an in-depth analysis, Double Star Rubber Machinery believed that the user lacked a good understanding on its strength and integrity. Seeing that the specified contract-signing time was less than one month, if the good understanding could not be obtained, the opportunity would be taken away. Therefore, Double Star Rubber Machinery set up a special PR team to go deep into the user company for in-depth exchanges. The team members distributed promotional gifts such as compact disks, watches, and ornaments to its employees and managers at the user's office and introduced them to Double Star brand. They also rented audio equipment to disseminate the information (already translated into Thai language) in the living quarters for employees, including the promotional CD, Wang's interview videos, and Double Star workers' evening party videos etc. This activity attracted a lot of employees of the user... in just 15 days, Double Star of China and president Wang as a shoe king became known to more than half of its employees.

Hearing it, the 80-year-old chairman of the user company couldn't help but be curious and personally went to see two promotional activities. After watching the video for the interview with Wang, he was impressed by his celebrity and took the initiative to meet the sales representative of Double Star Rubber Machinery. After listening to the comprehensive introduction, he became interested in Double Star and insisted on personally looking at it. Subsequently, he led a team of 8 members to Double Star Machinery. After the visit to the production site, the sales staff specially arranged for them to see the use of the equipment in the end user sector. Looking at the smooth operation of equipment at Double Star and listening to the praise from on-site workers, the chairman smiled. Shortly after returning to Thailand, the chairman agreed to cooperate with Double Star Rubber Machinery and accepted the full cash wire transfer request. He said, "Double Star is a famous brand with high reputation, so it is very reassuring to cooperate with it."

The enterprise culture is productivity, competitiveness, and a driving force of economic and social competition. Cultural management is a kind of top management. Double Star

Machinery uses a unique culture in management and development of the market and has achieved excellent results.

(4) Distributor's overseas conference to create a global logistics platform

Double Star has always adhered to developing markets at home and abroad.

On March 8, 2011, the first distributors overseas conference of Double Star Tire was held in the Atlantis Hotel in Dubai called the Pearl of the Beautiful Gulf and the world trade capital.

At the conference, Wang as the president of Double Star Group delivered a warm speech. He said, "Since the financial crisis in 2008, the competition in the European and American markets has been extremely fierce. To cope with the challenges, Doublc Star has accelerated the promotion and development of the Middle East and Africa markets. In the Middle East and Africa market. Double Star Tire has developed rapidly in the past two years. This shows that the development potential of the Middle East and Africa markets is unlimited and the most promising. It is necessary further strengthen cooperation and achieve a win-win situation." He also introduced the latest shoe-making technology of Double Star Shoe to the participating customers and representatives.

In the past two years, the prices of raw materials soared, and the United States imposed special protectionist tariffs on tire imports from China. Facing with a grim situation in the international market, Wang led Double Star Tire to continuously adjust its business ideas and adopt its tire-shoe linkage strategy. While exploring the European and American markets, Double Star Tire had increased its efforts in the Middle East, Africa, Russia, and North Asia etc. It had established tire stores in Egypt, Sudan, and Dubai, enhanced the popularity of Double Star brand, and driven the sales of tires and shoes with Double Star. At the conference, participants watched the promotional videos of Double Star Group including technology and new products the like, and jointly discussed the new year sales plan of Double Star Tire.

Managers of tire stores of Double Star in Sudan and Dubai expressed their confidence and determination to cooperate with Double Star Tire as a world's leading company.

On the spot, Wang personally presented the world-class fashion casual shoes to general agents in Sudan, Dubai and Egypt, which were printed with map, logo and trademark of Double Star map as well as the agent's own portrait in 2010. These agents were very excited after seeing such shoes. Especially, when they saw that their portraits were clearly printed on the scented shoes, they all praised Double Star for its technology and process of shoes and tires, which further strengthened their confidence of cooperation. Many agents in regions such as Iraq presented gifts to President Wang with their high-profile ceremonies and expressed their determination to make Double Star brand the first choice in their regions.

The number of agents in the conference reached more than 40 with the order amount reaching more than 10 million US dollars. In the conference, Mr. Ye Hong from the commerce chamber of Consul General of China General Consulate in Dubai spoke highly of the quality of products in Double Star and the wisdom of its president - Wang. Mr. Ye said, "The Chinese government encourages enterprises to go out. Double Star Group has good products and reputation and been famous at home and abroad. I hope that through this annual conference Double Star can achieve a better promotional effect and expand its influence and market share in overseas markets.

IV. Expert Comments

Is the ABW theory (created by Wang in the management practice of more than 30 years) scientific and effective? can it be called Chinese-style management theory? This is not a theoretical issue, but a practical issue. In other words, this problem cannot be solved by debate, but can only be solved by practice, because practice is the sole criterion for testing truth.

The said theory was created under the conditions of a market economy. It is an important part of Wang's market theory. The core and essence of his market theory is: **"The market is the highest leader of the enterprise, the market is the standard for testing all work of the enterprise, and the market is the best balance for testing the enterprise."**

The brilliant achievements of Double Star in the past 30 years have proved to the world that the BW theory created by Wang is not only scientific, effective, but also a Chinese-style management theory.

As Wang pointed out, "**The success of Double Star in the market for more than 30 years is first the success of management. Management determines the success or failure of market competition. The development of Double Star, including its development of domestic and foreign markets, depends on our management which is our best means and most admired by the outside world. Management is the most secret weapon in market competition. It is a magic weapon for us to defeat the other competitors and maintain unbeaten competition**."

Tactic 18: The Entrepreneur Is the Core

"The most basic thing for entrepreneurs is to regard the enterprise as their own home and to devote themselves to the enterprise. As a national entrepreneur, we must have the minds of politicians, the thinking of philosophers, the vision of theorists, the strategies of military strategists, the romantic style of the poets, the hardworking spirit of the doers, the graceful bearing of the diplomats, the passion and the talent of the agitators, the courage of the adventurers. At the same time, more importantly, we must have the following traits: first, we have our unique management theory created based on our national culture; second, we have a keen sense of national responsibility and a national spirit, representing the soul of the country and the soul of the nation. The entrepreneur rather than the ownership system that determines the fate of the enterprise in which the entrepreneur is its core."

——Wang Hai

Wang Hai, President of Double Star Group & Man of the Year

President Wang is the only person in China who was named World Man of the Year of 1995 after Deng Xiaoping.

In 1987, President Wang won the National May 1st Labor Medal.

In 2000, on the fifteenth joint meeting of the first staffs' congress, President Wang was elected as the lifelong president of Double Star Group.

I. Wang Hai Quotations

(I) Entrepreneurship is the embodiment of national spirit

☆ Three Principles in the new era - national spirit, national brand, and national entrepreneurship.

☆ Carry forward the national spirit, build national brands, and cultivate national entrepreneurs.

☆ The creation of national spirits and national brands must rely on national entrepreneurs. The development of international markets must rely on national entrepreneurs. National entrepreneurs are the helm of national industry and the embodiment of national spirit. Therefore, to achieve the goal of being China-created, we must vigorously develop a team of national entrepreneurs. National entrepreneurs are the creators of national enterprises and the defenders of national brands.

☆ Entrepreneurs should always remember Deng Xiaoping's words, "We must have our own competitive products, we must create our own national brands, otherwise we will be bullied."

(II) Entrepreneurs should be generals in the market

☆ Dare to be the first in the world, striving for the first

☆ The dazzling market is a battlefield filled with smoke. The entrepreneurs in the market are the generals on the battlefield.

(III) Entrepreneurs should be like black cats

☆ Entrepreneurship is not an official title, but a profession.

☆ It does not matter whether the cat is black or white, as long as it catches mice. Despite of gossips, development of Double Star is the last word. Double Star Cat is a unique representative of Double Star culture.

(IV) Ownership is not a determining factor for the fate of enterprises

☆ Ownership is a very important factor, but it is not the determining factor for the fate of an enterprise. The determining factor is people, including entrepreneurs and operators.

☆ Be an entrepreneur with personality, humanity, and party spirit.

☆ Have a developmental mind in the market, but don't be rash.

(V) Qualities that excellent entrepreneurs should possess

☆ Entrepreneurs should have the reverse thinking which can create miracles.

☆ The entrepreneur should be market-oriented. He is optimistic no matter the market is prosperous or poor. He can let the enterprise survive in the poor market and develop in the prosperous market. He has a strong leadership; he bravely breaks the routine and always does things that others think are impossible; he can keenly predict risks and has a strong determination.

☆ To become an outstanding entrepreneur in China, you must have eight qualities: the mind of a politician, the thought of a philosopher, the strategy of a strategist, the romance of a poet, the hardworking of a doer, the graceful bearing of a diplomat, and the passion of an agitator. The most basic thing is to treat the company as your own home and to devote yourself to the enterprise.

(VI) Mentality, position, heath and character that entrepreneurs should possess

☆ Ignore fame and fortune, pursue dreams.

☆ Take yourself as a backbone and feel good about yourself.

☆ Follow the CPC leadership, try our best to do the work, and be harmonious in the family.

☆ Career, health, and family are complementary. The healthy body is necessary for a complete success.

☆ Do not flatter the superior, do not look down upon the subordinate.

☆ Think, create; be earnest, pragmatically, and happy

(VII) Entrepreneurs should be the image spokespersons

☆ Entrepreneurs should be the most true and best image spokespersons for the enterprises.

☆ Entrepreneurs are the pillars and core of the national economy. The social value and economic value they create are not inferior to any movie star. Only they are the most qualified people acting as the image spokespersons.

II. Wang is the soul of Double Star

History proves that a great political party must have a great leader; a long-distance ship must have a wise helmsman; an outstanding enterprise must have an outstanding entrepreneur. Under the leadership of President Wang, Double Star has overcome many difficulties and created a brilliant world. No one can deny that Wang has made great contributions to Double Star. As the first generation of outstanding entrepreneurs in China, Wang is the creator of Double Star brand, the core and soul of the Double Star business, the spiritual leader of the staffs in Double Star, and the outstanding representative of national entrepreneurs.

In state-owned enterprises, there are a lot of people who have been managers for a lifetime —three years in one company and five years in the second company and etc. However, Wang is one of a few managers who have worked in a state-owned enterprise for a lifetime, and one of a few long-lived entrepreneurs. He is a pioneer in the reform of China's state-owned enterprises, a pioneer in the creation of national brands, a witness to China's reform and opening, an outstanding entrepreneur in China etc.

Among the first batch of 20 outstanding entrepreneurs in the country in 1987, some were promoted, some were removed, some fled abroad, and some went to jail... However, Wang still works in the same unit (which was previously called Ninth Rubber Factory and now Double Star Group). Therefore, he is called a general in the market and a long-lived president. What is the reason?

(1) Entrepreneur with clear positioning and great goals

The experience of many successful entrepreneurs at home and abroad has proved that to be a successful entrepreneur, you must have a clear positioning and great goals and always focus on them (in other words, never give up). This is the primary condition for entrepreneurs to succeed, and Wang is a successful example.

In the practice of leading the reform of Double Star into the market for more than 30 years, for various reasons, there were 30 malicious labels that were put on Wang below: disregarding the organizational discipline, being lawless, being opposite with the central cadre, being ambitions, wanting to be promoted, looking down on local leaders, forming a faction or a gang, being a gang head, being worse than Japanese invaders, emphasizing the importance of productive forces but ignoring political awareness, making a pig of himself and squandering public money, cultivating a cult of personality, propagating feudal superstitions, boasting about himself, occupying a hill to act as a lord, establishing underhand connections to exploit them for personal gains, being indulged in various activities of sightseeing and amusement, having improper relationships with females, being a thief of selling the factory, exploiting people, violating human rights, being patriarchal, letting state-owned assets lost, being mad, being a bumpkin, ignoring the role of the enterprise culture, acting blindly, and gaining private profits the like.

The brilliant achievements of Double Star in reform into the market for more than 30 years prove that new ideas, new decisions, and new strategies from Wang are all correct and meet requirements of the new era. Therefore, Wang has won 10 honorary titles: one of the first batch of outstanding entrepreneurs, market general, geek, entrepreneur, man of the year, lifelong president, red hat, shoemaker etc. Among them, his most favorite titles are both shoe-maker and professional entrepreneur.

Wang often says, "**I am a shoemaker, so I am dedicated to the shoe culture. Shoes are one of the first signs of human civilization, which made our ancestors get rid of the ignorance. Just like the history of humans is constantly evolving, the shoes worn by them are constantly changing. Historically, there are bark shoes, wooden shoes, straw shoes, cloth shoes, rubber shoes, and leather shoes etc. Every needs shoes from the royal family and the prime minister to common people. The shoes on the ground bear the burden which have noble characters such as being endurable and selfless. We must remember that people wear shoes and that the key is in the work. You will have to travel all over the world, so let us send qualified shoes to the feet of all kinds of people...**"

He also says, "**I position myself as a professional entrepreneur.**" Moreover, at many occasions, he publicly announces, "**I don't want to be a governmental official, in stead, I want to go into the market**." When someone recommended him to be the deputy mayor of the industry, he refused it and said, "**I hope to work in the enterprise.**" The market goal he set for Double Star **is to root in the province he resides, face the country, rush out of Asia, and go to the world**. His brand goal for Double Star **is to create a Chinese brand and a world-famous brand as well as to let the brand and enterprise be built to last**. He says, "**As an entrepreneur, if he does not want to let the enterprise become the world-famous brand or the world's first, then he will be not qualified.**" It is these clear positioning and ambitious goals that provide a great driving force for Wang, which fundamentally guarantees his success.

Napoleon Hill, the master of world success, said, "**You must know what you want to pursue in your life, and make up your mind to get it. Focusing on your goals with one heart and one mind can ensure success. Think and plan what you want to pursue, and ignore other irrelevant things at all. This is the formula that all successful people follow.**" Wang is a good representative among these successful people.

Wang not only has a clear positioning and ambitious goals, but also always focuses on them. Under the grim situation where there were 99% of the state-owned shoe-making enterprises in the country going bankrupt or being transformed, Double Star led by him vigorously developed and achieved excellent results. From a shoe factory that was on the verge of bankruptcy, Double Star has become a large-scale enterprise group involved in 23 industries including footwear, tires, machinery, clothing, printing, real estate, and tertiary industries the like. Now it has 60,000 staffs and more than 140 member units, which directly or indirectly providing hundreds of thousands jobs, creating huge economic and social benefits as follows: the total assets increasing from less than 10 million yuan in the early 1980s to 6.7 billion yuan; the sales revenue from 30 million Yuan to 12.4 billion Yuan; he foreign exchange earned from exports from 1.75 million US dollars to 300 million US dollars. In the past 20 years, the accumulated profits and taxes were more than 3 billion Yuan. In other words, while not spending public money, it paid taxes which were more than 300 times that 20 years ago. With travel shoes, travel shoes, leather shoes, and tires rated as famous brands in China, it is the only enterprise in the rubber industry of China to possess four famous brands at the same time. The brand value has reached 49.292 billion Yuan.

Napoleon Hill said, "**It is necessary to spend all efforts on the things that give you the greatest return; don't waste time**

on things that are not good for success. Only concentrate on one thing at a time, devote yourself wholeheartedly to doing it and actively hope it succeeds. Don't let your mind slip into something else, other needs, or other ideas. Focus on the important project you have decided to do, give up everything else. Successful people will focus on one thing at a time, rather than distract attention. Never be jack of all trades and master of none." This has been proved by **the success of President who started from the shoe industry having a meager profit and gradually created the kingdom of Double Star**.

(2) A hero in new China

In 1992, Mr. Allan, the president of a company in the United States, insisted on hiring Wang as the general manager of his company, and proposed to give him three-tenths of the share capital and a monthly salary of 3,000 US dollars. Wang refused it, and said, **"I am a Chinese and work for my motherland!"**

Wang said, **"An entrepreneur should first of all be a politician. He should have his own thoughts, theories and views, which are implemented in the enterprise. In the market activities, he should be with a spirit, specifically, a national spirit. It is known that the spirit is the soul of a person, a company, a country, a nation, and without it, he would get adrift without clear goals and directions."**

While delivering a speech at annual APEC meeting held in Shanghai and speeches in higher education institutions such as Peking University and TSINGHUA University, DAVOS Forum, BOAO Forum, and Microsoft Forum, Wang clearly pointed out that all of contradictions in the world can be resolved except ethnic contradictions. During the development of the economy, the political work cannot be ignored. In today's world, no one can give up national interests and national interests. This is an indisputable fact. We must not continuously exchange market for tech, resources for foreign currency, preferential policies for political achievements, cheap labor for investment, and land for GDP. Indeed, with his thoughts and insights, Wang won the glory for our motherland.

The three principles proposed by him under the market economy are: **To invigorate the national spirit, create national brands, and cultivate a team of national entrepreneurs**. Wang says, "**On this earth, no matter how integrated the economy is, national interests will always be the bottom line that a country cannot give up.**" He also says, "**National entrepreneurs should be patriotic with a keen sense of responsibility for their motherland. National entrepreneurs are like generals and marshals on the battlefield, while representing the interests of the nation in business activities.**"

Wang says, "**I don't believe that Chinese people are shorter than foreigners in case of standing or lying. Chinese people are as capable as or even more capable than foreigners.**" Encouraged by self-confidence and pride, he dared to say "no" to foreigners, dared to take off the shoe for advertisement in New York, and dared to challenge world famous brands such as Nike, Adidas and Reebok.

In the 1980s, when most of Chinese people unheard of the concept of the brand, Wang proposed that **"creating famous brand is the biggest politics in the market economy", "creating a famous brand is the best patriotism", and "The brand is the atomic bomb of market economy"**. He also published an article in the "People's Daily" calling for "**creating the Chinese people's own brand name.**" Thus, he is the first entrepreneur to propose the creation of a brand in China.

After this, he was like a general in the market to go out of China while wearing shoes of Double Star. In 1992, in the first overseas press conference held in New York, USA, Wang took off his shoe to make an advertisement in the international market. Double Star is the first to hold an oriental shoe culture performance at the German World Expo, with the Double Star brand causing a sensation in the world shoe industry.

Double Star has amazed the world with its road to create a brand. In early 1980s, Double Star went from imitation to innovation and produced the first pair of high-end cold-bonded sneakers, and the first pair of CVO heat-vulcanized shoes with the leather upper, thereby being at the leading position in the global footwear industry. In the 1990s, it achieved the strategic development goal of generations of products co-existing in research, development, production and storage, and established the only national-level technology research and development center in the footwear industry; its products had new features: lightweight, being suitable for a special field, comfortable and sanitary, healthy, environmentally friendly and casual etc. Double Star is the first to consider the occupational characteristics to introduce the following shoes: air-conditioning shoes, ventilation shoes, journalist shoes, nurse shoes, driver shoes, teacher shoes, and so on; and consider the needs of diverse groups of people to induce the shoes for the elderly, mothers, fathers. Double Star introduced the especially functional shoes: insulated shoes, safety shoes, waterproof shoes, etc. Double Star also designed and developed the spaceflight shoes for Shenzhou 6, Shenzhou 7, and Shenzhou 8. Therefore, it contributed to the national rejuvenation.

The most convincing and proud thing is that in the winter of 2001, Nike's president, Knight, took the initiative to extend the olive branch to him, inviting him to talk about the general trend of global footwear industry development. Wang thought that this proposal was very good, and that the competition could promote development. He also hoped to have a chance to talk with Nike's boss about it. Wang said he had been waiting for this day.

The news that Wang was going to have a dialogue with Nike's president on CCTV was spread. Many media were eager to report on it. However, when the satellite O.B. van of CCTV traveled halfway from Beijing to Qingdao, Nike's president, Knight, planned to let the vice president talk with Wang. Wang heard it and said, "I am going to let my vice president talk with him. If he appoints his assistant, then I shall appoint my assistant too. I am the president of the China Rubber Shoes Association, and our products of Double Star are very popular in the world. We should adhere to the principle of reciprocity. I have been dealing with the Americans for 20 or 30 years, and I have never bowed my head to them. There is no exception this time."

CCTV reporters were very familiar with his personality. Due to the temporary change made by Nike's president, Knight, the dialogue between both world-class shoe kings had to be canceled. Later, Wang knew that, in the abortion of this dialogue, a person as the scum played a role.

During the War of Resistance against Japan, there were many traitors in China who helped the Japanese devils, pushing the Chinese nation into the abyss of disaster. After the reform and opening, some people were bent solely on money and left the national interests behind. At that time, a Chinese who knew Wang was a deputy manager of Nike and said to Nike's president, Knight, "I suggest that you should not talk to Wang, because dialogue with Wang can only enhance the popularity of Double Star, being not good for Nike. Wang is active in thinking with wonderful words. The dialogue is in China, and more public attention will be paid to him, thereby adding luster to Double Star and bringing a business risk to Nike." Then, Knight decided to cancel it.

Today, in the global economic integration and market competition, the national integrity is becoming more and more important. As a leader in the footwear industry of China, Wang bear the responsibility and mission and never bows to foreigners. He says, "**As an entrepreneur, if he does not want to let the enterprise become the world-famous brand or the world's first, then he will be not qualified**."

What is gratifying is that Chinese consumers support domestic brands with their own practical actions. After ten years of hardworking, by 2000, Double Star's sales in the China market not only exceeded Nike, but also exceeded the total sales of Nike, Adidas and Reebok there.

2000 China Market Quality Survey from China Trade Center shows that Double Star was ranked first in five indicators in the footwear industry, such as brand awareness, service satisfaction, quality reputation, market share, and market preference in 2000. Eight years ago, this honor was belonged to Nike. From that moment on, Wang wanted to defeat Nike one day. Why was the China market always occupied by foreigners?

More than 30 years of practice has proved that Double Star led by Wang is the best in scale, management, quality, and service in the global footwear industry, which has gained the glory for our Chinese people and nation. So, he is a new national hero of contemporary China!

(3) Clever politician

As Chinese entrepreneurs, especially those from state-owned enterprises, how do you view the Four Kinds of Modernization, how to do a good job in modernization, how to view and cast the brand, and how to view and deal with the economic and political relations under socialist conditions? This is also an unprecedented major issue. In the practice of solving these problems, Wang adheres to the principle of seeking truth from facts and makes creative contributions.

Comrade Deng Xiaoping said, "**What are the main tasks in our current and quite a long historical period? In a word, we are engaged in modernization. Whether we can achieve the four kinds of modernization determines the destiny of our country and the destiny of our nation. Under the actual conditions of China Under the conditions, to do a good job in the four kinds of modernization of socialism is to uphold**

Marxism and hold high the great banner of Mao Zedong Thought. Not grasping the four kinds of modernization and not paying attention to this reality means that you are away from Marxism or make empty talk about Marxism. Modernization is our biggest politics at present, because it represents our people's greatest and most fundamental interests." He also said, "**We must have our own competitive products and we must create our own national brands**." For these teachings of Comrade Xiaoping, Wang understand and resolutely implements them.

Wang said, "**Creating brands is the biggest politics in the market economy**." This sentence is the core of the market theory of Double Star and the cornerstone for people at Double Star. As a product of the market economy, a brand is often a symbol of a country's economic strength. There is almost no political struggle that is irrelevant to economic problems. Therefore, the political struggle between countries, between nations, and even between groups, from ancient times to the present, is ultimately an economic conflict. In the past, to plunder our wealth, foreigners relied on the cannon to invade us. We bled, but they were not necessarily able to beat us. In today's market economy, foreigners use the brands to erode our belief, occupy our economic field, achieving the effect that they could achieve with the cannon. The current market competition without bloodshed or smoke is crueler and accompanied by the more complicated globalization, where whoever can create brand advantages will win the market and will be the ultimate political winner.

It is based on this sober thinking that Wang led Double Star in the early 1990s and put forward the theoretical viewpoint, namely, **creating a brand is the biggest politics in the market economy**. He took the creation of a brand as the goal of political work, and creatively applied political work to economic construction. Creating a brand is the best love for the enterprise and the job. Also, creating a brand is the best love for the country and the for of the nation. Isn't it the biggest patriotism for an enterprise to create its own brand? The brand is the atomic bomb in the market economy. We should be on this height to view and develop the brand. Otherwise, it is very difficult for us to win in the global market.

Double Star has just used 10 years to complete the creation of a brand Nike used 30 years and Adidas 70 years. It has also gotten rid of the backward situation of China's footwear industry for forty years and occupied the leading position of Double Star in the domestic footwear industry. In 1995, it was the first in the same industry to obtain a national well-known trademark. For the first time in the China market, it surpassed Nike, Adidas and other foreign brands in terms of market sales, market share and market influence etc., thereby really creating a brand belonging to China. While occupying the domestic market, Double Star has expanded to foreign markets at an alarming rate since 1993. By 1995, foreign exchange earned by export reached 50 million US dollars, and the total sales in the United States reached 17 million pairs. According to a sample survey conducted in a high school in the United States, one in every 15 Americans ever wore shoes from Double Star. In the world's number one powerhouse - United States and the most competitive US market, it is rare for a developing country's products to achieve such high market impact. Meanwhile, various measures are used to expand the popularity of Double Star in the international market. In addition to the United States, Double Star has established 10 overseas branches, and its products have entered more than 100 countries and regions, with more than 200 customers successively establishing a trading partnership with Double Star, making Double Star a well-known shoe company in the international market. It can be said that for more than ten years of brand strategy, people at Double Stars have brought the pride to our national industry with their own beliefs and courage.□

As an old state-owned enterprise, Double Star can develop in the increasingly fierce market competition; and can have a superior performance in the economic crisis and the situation where the US imposed special protectionist tariffs on tire imports from China. An important reason is that Double Star always carries out the political work in the market economy. With leaders as a good example, Double Star carries discussions and education activities with different themes, and various competitions, enhances feelings of staffs towards Double Star and its president, stimulate the passion and enthusiasm of staffs, constantly proposes cultural ideas, and create new systems and new models in management. Focusing on the difficulties in production and management, Double Star has achieved the organic combination of politics and economy, solved the ideological problem on purpose a method of the work, solved the problem on which contributions staffs should make. In Double Star, staffs are grateful to their president and hold an active attitude in the work, which is reflected in innovation, in management, and in results. In these, the political work plays the important guaranteeing role. In other words, the political work of Double Star is not an empty talk. The experience of Double Star proves that politics and economy are objectively existed in the market economy, inseparable from each other. Only with the organic combination of politics and economy, can a huge promotional role can be played.

Wang emphasizes, "**Politics and the economy cannot be separated from each other, and the equal attention should be paid to both**." Political and economic work are aimed at people. Enterprises should give full play to abilities of staffs and equipment. With the correct ideas as a guide, we must maximize the potential of staffs and stimulate their enthusiasm. With thoughts and consciousness determining their direction of action, people need spirit and need interests. Politics and economy should work together. Only when both are well combined, can we be invincible.

Wang not only took the lead in political work, but also required all levels of leadership to do an excellent job in political work. He often says, **"Leaders at all levels, especially top leaders, must play the core role of the team, pay attention to management, and lead team members to set good examples. There behaviors themselves are belonged to political work**." For the enterprise, where there is the difficulty, there is the leader to act as a director at the scene; where there is the hurdle, there is the leader to lead the staffs and set an example; where there is the problem, there is the core of the team to immediately come to the scene and help solve it. It is the biggest political work to lead the staffs to do an excellent job. Political work is invisible and intangible, but it plays a subtle role. The economic achievements we have achieved have political work in play. If the leaders implement decisions of the Group, the political work will be effective.

(4) Wise theorist

Napoleon Hill, the world-renowned master of success, said, **"The power of thinking is the greatest power of mankind. It can build a great kingdom and destroy the kingdom. All ideas, plans, purposes, and desires all stem from thought. Thought is the dominance of all energy and can solve all problems. If you don't learn to think correctly, you can't achieve outstanding results.**" For him who can continue to succeed, there are many reasons, but the main reason is from his thoughts and theories, especially his entrepreneurial thinking and market economy theory.

In more than 30 years of work, President Wang has closely integrated Marxism, Mao Zedong Thought, Deng Xiaoping Theory with the practice of China's reform and opening, and closely integrated with the reform, development and management of enterprises, thus proposing a series of innovative ideas, new views and new theories. Examples are as follows: (1) Three Principles in the socialist market economy, that is, we should invigorate the national spirit, to create national industrial brands, and to cultivate national entrepreneurs; (2) entrepreneurs must have the correct personality, humanity, and party spirit; (3) Chinese-style Nine plus Nine Management Method and ABW Management theory; the contradictory theory on market economy; (4) both socialist-minded and professional competent, as well as loyal and fair so forth in the market economy. It is these thoughts and philosophical views that guide the reform and management of Double Star for more than 30 years. All the glory and success of Double Star are rooted in his thoughts and theories.

As a theorist, Wang dares to be the first and crosses the river by feeling the stones. In the constant exploration and practice, he answers many problems in the forbidden zone. He is the first to point out the values of the market economy and the direction of the enterprise; the first to say that the effective use of money is the best ideological and political work. He is the first to put forward that the market is the standard for testing all work of enterprises and is the first to enter the market; the first to propose that to create a brand is the biggest politics of the enterprise; the first to say that the high quality of the product is the biggest doing-good and gathering blessings; the first to apply the excellent traditional culture of Buddha, Taoism and Confucianism in modern enterprise management; and the first to create our Chinese own management philosophy.

A thinker's ice-breaking journey is a practice that leads the national enterprise to find a path from one victory to another. What needs to be specially introduced here is his Double Star market theory, whose birth corresponds to the requirement of market development. This theory is from the market.

Among the many entrepreneurs in China, there are two types of thinking modes that are more common: one is to act according to the stipulations or ed-headed documents in which enterprises have no spirit of innovation. The second is to be based on personal experience or even based on personal feelings. In these two types of thinking modes, the former one is mostly in state-owned enterprises, and the latter one is mostly in private enterprises.

Though being a leader of the state-owned enterprise, he dares to make the reverse thinking and make a new difference. He emphasizes that the theory has an important guiding role in doing an excellent job of reform and doing an excellent job in state-owned enterprises. In his practice, he has created a set of unique theories (also known as Double Star Market Theory) meeting actual conditions of Double Star. Under the guidance of these theories, he has created the miracle of the kingdom of Double Star.

Highlights of the Double Star Market Theory:

- Market is the driving force and source of enterprise development
- The market is the highest leader of the enterprise
- The market is the standard for testing all work in the enterprise
- The market is the best balance for testing enterprises
- The user is God, with the gold medal won in the market
- Products from enterprises should meet the market needs
- People wear shoes and the key is the work
- Do not wait for someone to give food; instead, it is better to find food for yourself
- The market is always right, and products may be poor in quality
- Follow the market, turn around the market, and change with the market
- Do not look for the mayor but find the market

- Going into the market, going to the global market, expanding the market in the rural area, and wining the market via the brand
- Aiming at the market, variety changes, and competitors
- The market is a never-ending battlefield
- Entrepreneurs in the market are like generals on the battlefield

Etc. Etc. Etc.

The Double Star Market Theory once made some economic theorists to be stunned. Wang said, "**Since I wear my own shoes, I have to go my own way. To survive and develop, enterprises have only one way, that is, to take the highest leadership and remember that the market as the standard for testing all work of the enterprise. The market is the highest-level official of the enterprise! If an enterprise is not competitive in the market, all of efforts will be meaningless!**" He asserts, "**Practice has proved that the brilliance achieved currently in Double Star is closely related with the Double Star Market Theory.**"

Wang is an entrepreneur with ideas and theory. In addition to the Double Star Theory, he proposes the following theories: market theory, rules theory, new cat theory, ABW theory; contradiction theory, 3-emotion theory, 3-nature theory, 3-win theory, 3-character theory, tiger theory, big quality theory, big tech theory, big innovation theory; three-seven theory, red plus expert theory, piety and loyalty theory, and upgrade theory etc.

The way of thinking determines the way out, the theory guides practice. At every critical point in the development, Wang always analyzes the actual situation of Double Star, and proposes new guiding ideas and new theories. Therefore, Double Star can grow healthily and steadily for more than 30 years. These innovative ideas and new theories are mainly in his four monographs on management: (1) Market, Enterprise, Innovation; (2) Market, Enterprise, Brand; (3) Secrets of Double Star; (4)

Market: Root of Enterprise. His theoretical books having 2.284 million words cover the following aspects: (1) Double Star Forum; (2) Theory of Reform, Development, and Innovation with Double Star; (3) Double Star Market Politics Theory; (4) Double Star Market Management Theory; (5) Double Star Marketing Theory (6) Double Star Technology Management Theory; (7) Double Star Quality Management Theory; (8) Double Star Brand Management Theory; (9) Double Star Talent Management Theory; (10) Double Star International Market Theory; (11) Double Star Financial Management Theory; (12) Double Star Macro Management Theory; (13) Double Star Basic Management Theory; (14) Double Star Production Management Theory; (15) Double Star Management Theory of Tertiary Industry. It can be seen that these monographs are his encyclopedia of enterprise management.

Wang often says to his staffs, "**Enterprises without theory and thought are hopeless; cadres without theory and thought are hopeless; employees without theory and thought are hopeless. Without good theory and thought, the cause will have no direction; it will fail and even suffer crushing defeat**." He not only is insightful, but also is practical.

(5) Market general who is resourceful and flexible

John W. Tiz as a world-renowned corporate strategist pointed out, "**The strategist's task is not to see what the company is like currently, but to see what the company will look like in the future**."

Confucius, a great thinker, politician and educator in ancient China, said, "**Worries will soon appear if one gives no thought to a long-term plan**." Chen Danran, a famous scholar during the reign of Guangxu in the Qing Dynasty, also said, "**From ancient times to the present, those who do not have long-term considerations will inevitably have immediate worries; those who do not consider the overall interests will solve the**

immediate problems." The long-term overall problem is the strategic issue, which is the most critical issue that determines the survival of the enterprise.

The words of these experts show that to be a successful entrepreneur, you must be a strategist and strive to be forward-looking and consider the overall situation so forth.

Wang has a deep understanding on it. He often says, "**It is necessary to consider the development of the enterprise in future 10 years. Entrepreneurs must the courage to do things with the awareness of being ahead and bravely take risks. Entrepreneurs may be different from staffs and may make decisions before the agreement among all the member of the leadership team, to be able to capture the business opportunity. Indeed, the market is like the battlefield.**"

Wang has a General's Complex. While being a child. he decided to grow up to be a general in the army and serve the motherland. However, the arrangement of fate made him give up the general's dream. By chance, after being transferred from the army to the civilian work, he created the famous Double Star brand and became a well-known general in the market. The military career has made him familiar with the military law, and he can skillfully apply the strategic tactics in the military field to the commercial field, thereby repeatedly obtaining good results. Here are a few exciting strategies from him:

· To create a brand: He gave up Jiefang shoes and produced

shoes of Double Star. He proposed the resounding slogan of promoting the national spirit, creating national brands, and revitalizing national industries, and determined to create the famous brand belonged to our Chinese people. He also became the pioneer of the brand strategy, including the band being used, promoted, developed and strengthened etc.

· Expansion: He expanded the business into the tire industry.

· Diversification: Shoes and tires were taken as main businesses. At present, Double Star has been involved in the five pillar industries (shoes, tires, clothing, machinery, and so forth); and a total of eight industries such as printing, embroidery, tertiary industry.

· Internationalization: That is, Double Star is rooted in his local region, faced with China, goes out of Asia, and goes to the world.

· To go westwards: In Double Star, the production base is transferred from the bustling downtown area of Qingdao to the old revolutionary base - Yimeng Mountain area and the suburbs area of Qingdao; also transferred to the west and southwest of China.

· M & A: The M & A strategy is adopted. That is, through the transplantation of corporate culture, Double Star acquired Qingdao Huaqing Tire (like a small fish to eat a big fish) and acquired Dongfeng Tire (like a state-owned enterprise to eat the second state-owned enterprise) and etc.

· Differentiation strategy – means that the company creates distinctive features or characteristics for its products or services in the competition of target markets within the industry;

· Cooperation and competition: That is, competition and cooperation are concurrently carried out to achieve a win-win situation. This is the highest level of competition.

· Shoe-tire linkage: That is, the shoe and clothing are linked with the tire in sales, to achieve the goals of a mutual promotion, a win-win situation, and an increased sale.

· Big-scale Double Star: Under the Double Star brand, there are 10 business areas, more than 60 operating branches, and more than 5,000 chain stores across the country. Each business area has its own business network and factory with its assets registered locally and its one-stop pattern of production, supply and sales.

The book entitled Art of War written by Sun TZU, which is hailed as a military classic, also says, "**All warfare is based on deception.**" "**What is of supreme importance in war is to attack the enemy's strategy. Next best is to disrupt his alliances by diplomacy. The next best is to attack his army. And the worst policy is to attack cities**." "**In all fighting, the direct method may be used for joining battle, but indirect methods will be needed to secure victory**." "**Attack him where he is unprepared, appear where you are not expected. These military devices, leading to victory, must not be divulged beforehan**d."

In all the fighting, the commander should attach importance to the use of the strategy. Therefore, the best method is to win the enemy by strategy; next best is to win the enemy by diplomatic means; the third best is to use force to defeat the enemy; the last resort is the siege around the city of the enemy. The fighting is based on the deception. In the warfare, the enemy is held off by the face-to-face contact and is beat by the non-contact or indirect method. To carry out an attack when the enemy is unprepared. An attack is launched when the enemy has no preparation, and an action is taken when the enemy does not expect it. These are secrets of military strategists to win, which cannot be disclosed in advance.

Wang has a deep understanding on and skillfully uses the tactics of battles. Here are a few exciting battles that Wang plans and leads:

· On the battlefield of the market, Wang gains surprising victories by using the arts of war, including strategies, tactics, strong points developed, and weak points avoided etc. The ones that best reflect this feature are three major battles that he has carefully planned and personally directed during the development of the shoe market:

The first battle: He led staffs to enter the domestic market. He won the victory by using the methods of key breakthroughs and wave-style advancement

The second battle: He led staffs to enter the global market. He won the victory by using the methods of direct and fierce competitions as well as completely driving competitors away from the market.

The third battle: He led staffs to build the production base in the rural area. He won the victory by using the methods of planning and ingenious moves etc.

· The shoe industry, which was a sunset industry in developed countries, faced with the difficulty to survive in coastal open cities like Qingdao. In such a grim moment, Wang followed the principle of seeking truth from facts and developed the three-step scheme of the development strategy for Double Star, which enabled the Double Star to not only get rid of the predicament, but also develop into a world-famous enterprise group.

The first step: from Qingdao to Shandong;

The second step: from Shandong to the entire country;

The third step: from the country to the world.

In addition, Wang has many wonderful cases in battle and tactics. E.g:

· During the press conference in New York on August 28, 1992, faced with the provocative questions of journalists with ulterior motives, he was adaptable and answered them humorously. He took off his shoe on this press conference to make an advertisement and won the glory for our Chinese people.

· In the fall of 1992, at the 124th International Footwear Expo held in Germany, he used the surprising tactic: designing and carrying out the Oriental Shoe Culture Performance. This cultural performance showed to the Westerners the splendid shoe culture history of thousands of years in China. It let the Double Star brand cause a sensation throughout Europe and spread all over the world.

· When the KOSOVO War broke out in 1995, the people around the world were concerned about its outcome and impact with the investors who successively withdrew from there. However, Wang felt that this would be an appropriate time for the marketing of Double Star Shoes. He seized the market opportunity and sent sales representatives there. As a result, during this war, Double Star sold 2 million pairs of shoes.

· In 2000, the world's top ten tire brands almost monopolized the markets of the United States, Europe and Asia, but Africa, with relatively poor geographical conditions and relatively backward manufacturing, was outside their field of vision. With the use of reverse thinking, Wang ignored the mainstream market represented by the United States and Europe, instead, he spent a lot of effort on the African market for the sake of avoiding the strong competitors. He finally realized his dream in Africa. Now, in the great deserts of Africa, there are tires of Double Star which are like beautiful sunflowers everywhere.

(6) Adventurer who dares to reform and is good at innovation

David Silver, a well-known American entrepreneur and an expert on entrepreneurial activities, pointed out in his book entitled The Career Life, "**Entrepreneurs and artists have much in common. They are problem solvers. Artists try to solve many problems in life by expressing solutions on the canvas. Entrepreneurs do their best to focus on one issue, constantly expressing and re-expressing the problems that have been grasped until they are prepared to paint with a huge canvas. Both artists and entrepreneurs as individualists are exotic, sensitive, imaginative, enthusiastic, energetic, and creative etc.**"

Peter Drucker pointed out, "**Entrepreneurs must shift resources from areas with low returns or reducing returns to areas with high returns or rising returns. They must abandon the past and give up what they already exist and are already known to create the future. The entrepreneur spirit is to create a future enterprise. In this task, it is necessary to innovate.**" Another management guru, Tom Peters, warned, "**If you don't innovate, you will perish!**"

On the wall behind his official desk, there is a slogan (**Dare to Be the First in the World**) written by Guan Dongsheng member of the National Committee of CPPCC and professor of Central Institute for Nationalities. What this slogan says is the true portrayal of his personality. As the World Man of the Year, Wang often says, "**Personality is the symbol of entrepreneurs. Personality and personal worship are two concepts. Without personality, there will be no development or creation.**"

The vicissitudes and hardships of China's national industry are reflected in the first 60 years of development with Double Star. In the 30 years after the reform and opening, under the leadership of President Wang, people at Double Stars always insists on the following principles: Daring to be a pioneer in the world, crossing the river by feeling the stones, bravely innovating, constantly exploring and advancing. He leads Double Star to continuously succeed and create brilliance in the national industry during the new era of market economy. In the ups and downs, Wang successfully plays six roles:

1. Market pioneer
2. Reform adventurer
3. Brand pioneer
4. Innovative developer
5. Management founder
6. Business decision maker

Wang claimed himself to be an ordinary shoemaker. However, only with the courage and daring spirit, can a common shoemaker achieve excellent results. Wang has led people at Double Star to create several firsts in the same industry of China.

The first to realize 100% self-sales of products;

The first to achieve a horizontal integration among the enterprises;

The first to hold a national trade fair in the name of the company;

The first to change the settings of the enterprise according to market needs;

The first to participate in the World Expo in the name of the enterprise;

The first to hold a shoe culture show and performance at abroad;

The first to create a world-famous brand belonged to China;

The first shoe-making enterprise to be restructured and listed in the capital market;

The first to realize the transformation from an enterprise only producing shoes to one engaging in both tire and shoe.

Etc., etc., etc.

These firsts are the vivid manifestations of his personality. He is brave to take a lead. He is insightful. He is good at decision-making. His personality and leadership style have made Double Star to seize the opportunity, win the market, and greatly expand the development space.

Until now, people at Double Star led by Wang are still unsatisfied with recently achieved results and never stop, because the market constantly changes. Wang often says, "**We follow the market, turn around the market, and change with the market**." He insists on the following idea: "**Not innovating today means a falling behind tomorrow, and not innovating tomorrow means a failure the day after tomorrow.**" He tries every means to inspire the innovative thinking of cadres and employees, persists in calling for the innovation of all staffs and their participation in the people's war in the market.

According to the earliest definition, the **entrcpreneur** refers to the **person who undertakes all kinds of adventure activities**. So, in this sense, **the entrepreneur is an adventurer**. Wang is an entrepreneur and naturally an adventurer. However, he is not a blind adventurer, but an adventurer who is both daring and knowledgeable and who who dares to innovate and is good at innovation.

(7) Management expert who is good at learning from others and has his own management style

Wang says, "**The development of Double Star, including the development of the domestic and foreign markets, depends on our excellent management which is the most admired and is a magic weapon for us to win the market and maintain unbeaten competition**."

One of his contributions to the business circle of China is to create Chinese-style philosophy and model of management which can be summarized as: **absorbing essentials at home and aboard in both ancient and modern times, learning from others, and being unique etc**.

The ABW theory by him is an outstanding example of Chinese-style management. This management model has 18 tactics: The eighteen tactics described in this book are: (1) the culture is the soul; (2) the theory is the guide; (3) the strategy is the dragon head; (4) the mechanism is the driving force; (5) the leadership is the role model; (6) the innovation is the vigor; (7) the system is the law of heaven; (8) the quality is the life; (9) the cost is the key; (10) the detail is the art; (11) the competition is the lever; (12) the environment is the foundation; (13) The family affection is the bond; (14) the money management is the guarantee; (15) the brand management is the sublimation; (16) the assessment is the essential; (17) the market is the standard; (18) the entrepreneur is the core.

With adherence to the principles of inheriting traditional excellence, absorbing foreign achievements and creating our own distinct products, he learns from others and creates his own unique ABW theory.

The ABW theory has its unique features. The management described by it is neither management under the planned economic system nor management under the market economic system; neither traditional nor blindly westernized. It is a new management innovation that comprehensively absorbs various management advantages at home and abroad in ancient & modern times. In other words, it is a hybrid management model that absorbs various advantages from other models.

For him, A is the big shot and means that our entrepreneurs and enterprises should stand taller and look farther as well as dare to be the best in the world or compete for the first place. B consists of two parts: 1 and 3 and means a big country and a big market with a population of 1.3 billion. W is like an eagle in shape and is also the first letter of his name, so the letter W means that the entrepreneur should be like the eagle to bravely fly in the sky.

Being rooted, he absorbs cultures at home and abroad in ancient and modern times, seeks truth from facts, and actively carries out innovation activities. Moreover, he integrates the market philosophy, management philosophy, social philosophy, and life philosophy.

An outstanding creation of Wang in management is the **Nine plus Nine Management Method**. This new management method has the following rich connotations:

Three Rings: inherit the tradition, absorb foreign achievements, and innovate our distinct products. With Three Rings being complementary to each other, Double Star has its own road of innovation.

Three Wheels: Refers to ideological education, economic means and administrative measures. The three wheels are turned together to make the development of the enterprise fruitful.

Three Principles: Educating employees to be practical, carrying out active integration, being democratic & open. The three principles require employees to work hard, take care of the overall situation, and unite as one.

Mr. Wang uses Three Rings, Three Wheels and Three Principles as the warp of the management, and uses Three Separates, Three Joints and Three Developments as the weft.

Three Separates: Hierarchical management, layered contracting, and separate accounting. Three Separates clarify the relationship between cost and benefit.

Three Joints: Joint processing, joint sales, and joint stock. Three Joints can make the enterprise unit with external forces for expansion.

Three Developments: Talent development, tech & product development, market development. Three Developments can make the enterprise have more vigor.

This scientific management system is well-organized and complicated. It enables Double Star to have standards and rules in cost management, personnel management, and technological innovation etc. Further it is practical and efficient, thereby enabling Double Star to embark on the track of market-oriented management. Double Star skillfully implemented the modern management, which were not yet familiarized by a lot of other enterprises at that time.

Wang believes that **enterprises can be managed well**. His Chinese-style management model, which, not created on imagination by scholars, is created by him in management for more than 30 years and is proven to be effective in the practice. The Americans commented that "Double Star has the best-managed factory in the world." The Japanese took the initiative to visit the factory of Double Star, and the South Koreans offered a high salary to hire supervisors from Double Star. Double Star has won the recognition of the market with its excellent management, won the respect of the industry and won the admiration of foreigners.

(8) Doer who is persistent and down-to-earth

His style is to **always take the lead and be down to earth**. The motto - A Journey of A Thousand Miles Begins with A Single Step - put in his own officer, always reminds him to do things in a down-to-earth manner and be serious in attitude. He often says, "**Only when the leader cares for and respects the staffs, can they regard the enterprise as their home**." For more than 30 years, during which Double Star has developed into a group with tens of thousands of staffs from a factory with thousands of staffs, President Wang has the same style of work. He stays at the workshop and the market most of the time, while wearing his work clothes. He pays attention to the site management, contract management, and product quality etc. He pays attention to the market by his visits to the mall and the chain store, whereas enough information are collected as the basis of decision-making. For example, according to market information, he leads staffs to successfully develop several new products. As a good hands-on manager, he always sets a good example for the cadres and staffs.

Wang often says, "**I am always a soldier in the market, who works hard and is never satisfied with what have been achieved. On the other hand, the society develops and the environment changes, so we must constantly improve ourselves to keep up with the times**."

One of his pet phrases is "**We take ourselves as a backbone**." He practices what he promises. For example, in early days of entering the market, people at Double Star **set up a goal** and create a brand. In the face of difficulty, they **take themselves as a backbone** to overcome it. In the face of setbacks, they are **still optimistic** with a good attitude. When achieving results, they are **not satisfied with them**. In case of the brand being popular, they still **put pressure on themselves** to be more successful. Thus, the same management model is adopt in Double Star Group with 60,000 staffs, including 10 business areas, nearly 50 production plants, more than 60 operating branches, and more than 5,000 chain stores. Wang believes that **enterprises can be managed well**.

For another example, the street named SI DA Sen where the staffs of Double Star resided, faced with a poor security situation. Female workers after night work must be picked up by their family members, otherwise, they might be harassed by hooligans. Due to the relocation of the factory, about 7,000 people lost their job, who did not work. What should these people will do? Could they be pushed to the society and pushed to the government? Or should they find a solution by themselves? At this moment, Double Star took take the initiative to adjust the industrial structure. To arrange these personnel, Double Star entered the tertiary industry. For example, Double Star City built by Double Star, having an excellent architectural style, integrated the catering, entertainment and sauna as a whole. Since then, Double

Star has developed into other fields and become a comprehensive enterprise group which is shoe-based and diversified.

(9) Passionate speaker

Wang is a towering man from the north part of China. He loves laughing and wearing a red hat, with attractive dimples and smiley eyes. He is simple in his life and sincere in his attitude.

His speech level is first-class among entrepreneurs. He can focus your thinking and vision on him within a few minutes, because his conversation is full of wit. His speeches, which are characterized by lively stories, idioms, allusions, arguments, quotations and so forth, let audiences be excited and fascinated. Here are two examples:

1. APEC

At the beginning of the new century, Wang attended APEC meeting in Shanghai as the vice chairman of the Asia-Pacific Economic Association.

In the meeting, each speaker was given 10 minutes to speak and was asked to submit a speech manuscript before the meeting, to make subtitles when speaking. Wang was also one of the spokespersons. When he attended the meeting, he had a new idea. That is, he wanted to speak without a written manuscript.

It was the turn of Wang to speak. He strode to the stage, putting off his watch on the podium and beginning his impromptu speech. He said, in the integration of the world economy, some so-called experts and scholars and individual senior officials over-emphasized the economic activities and advocated China to be a world manufacturer but did not mention the national industry; and were afraid that keeping the traditional things would inevitably affect the internationalization of enterprises. He said that it is a wrong idea. He attached importance to **the national spirit, national brand, and national entrepreneur**. He said, "**It is necessary to invigorate the national spirit, create national brands, and cultivate the**

national entrepreneurs, to develop the national industry and revitalize the national economy." These views put forward by Wang have profound significance for current ideological work and long-term economic work.

He put forward a new view to the participants, "**not innovating today means a falling behind tomorrow, and not innovating tomorrow means a failure the day after tomorrow**." Then, with the success story and development track of Double Star, he explained this view in a concise manner. Finally, he said, "**Where is the advantage of Chinese people creating brands? China has a large market having a population of 1.3 billion. We have cost advantages, resource advantages, and cheap labor advantages. We are a tiger. We are not afraid to dance with the wolf. We are self-confident**." Finally, he waved his hand and said: **"I am a tiger** and I am fearless." The audience sounded a thunderous applause.

There were newspapers commenting that his speech level was admirable and that his ability to control time was amazing. We feel proud of him who is such a brave entrepreneur with both enthusiasm and ideas.

2. Peking University

"Wang is a master of storytelling; Wang is a wizard who creates a wealth story; Wang is the god of health for people at Double Star; Wang is the creator for the brilliance of Double Star. Do you want to discuss how to create wealth with him face-to-face? Do you want to know his stories in the process of creating national brands? Do you want to have a glimpse of him who is one of the first generation of outstanding entrepreneurs? Dear students, let us meet him tomorrow afternoon in the library. He will tell us about his stories and share his experiences with us."

"Whether it is the battlefield filled with smoke or the dazzling market, we must have a spirit and need a kind of ambition. We must raise this spirit to the cultural level and let it become a kind of faith. This faith is the national culture which is created and inherited; and is closely related with the national spirit." This is his typical opening remark for which he receives a warm applause.

"It is necessary to be with a national spirit, but there must be strategies in the commercial war. Shoes of Double Star entered the European market through the 124th International Footwear Fair held in Germany which was a grand occasion attracting 1,400 shoe-making enterprises. Double Star was the only enterprise from China to attend it. How could we attract the attention of foreign businessmen? At that time, Chinese companies were at our family. How can we attract the attention of foreign businessmen? We thought of the proposition: the more national, the more international. We decided to carry out the Chinese shoe culture performance. This performance caused a huge sensation. Foreigners thumbed up and said: CHINA! DOUBLE STAR!"

With his first-class storytelling level, he pushed the atmosphere to a climax.

Someone handed a note and asked him how to transform an obscure enterprise into a world-famous brand. He said with a smile, first, he applied the Chinese traditional culture in modern enterprise management; second, he had a united leadership team; he worked with Wang Zengsheng, deputy secretary of the party, paying attention to reform, innovation, and quality etc. He also said, the environment was good, including the relevant government policies, from which Double Star was benefited.

"Double Star has developed from an enterprise on the verge of collapse, while other shoe enterprises have fallen one after another. During the Cultural Revolution, there were more than 3,000 shoes manufacturers in China. Nowadays, we are the only state-owned shoe enterprise to survive in China, why? For me, there are numerous factors, but the important point is our culture. I know that, in your Peking University, culture plays a very important role. Good product quality is the biggest doing-good and gathering of blessings; otherwise, it is impossible to create a brand. famous brands without doing honorable deeds. Any kind of temptation can make a brand fall apart overnight."

"As a state-owned enterprise, Double Star has its magic weapon to obtain its brilliance. It is the first listed company in the footwear industry of China, and the first national brand with the first place in exports. At present, its combined export of tires and shoes is 300 million US dollars. Some students asked me: what is the key factor in the development of Double Star? In fact, I say that it is the culture."

"In the market, the culture should be created according to the actual conditions of the enterprise. The new culture that is in line with the world and the times is able to promote the continuous development of the enterprise and improve its management. Double Star is successful as a state-owned enterprise, and what is the secret of the success? A question asked already by several students. I can tell you that Double Star now has a combination of three mechanisms: the first is to set up 6,000 chain stores, all of which are self-employed; the second is that all companies in the market are joint-stock companies; the third is Double Star is state-owned. These mechanisms are are carried out at the same time and do not contradict each other. We have a good management model, more importantly, the enterprise culture plays a key role in management."

Who say that we Chinese are not good at management? Who say that we are worse than foreigners in management? I do not agree with them. The development of Double Star proves that Chinese enterprises are excellent, and it is the spiritual strength that supports their development. Double Star creates its own new culture in each historical stage. The new culture is summarized as inheriting the traditional excellence and absorbing the achievements at home and abroad. We have our own modern culture. For us, the culture is the soul, the mind, and the spirit;

the culture is the productivity, the competitiveness, the driving force in the development of the enterprise.

A boss without the awareness of brand can't cultivate the staffs with the awareness of brand. Staffs without brand awareness can't create products that match the brand. In short, only if everyone is free to use their creativity, can Chinese enterprises really have hope. China's hope lies in you as young people.

In the applause, Wang was appointed as its researcher by Peking University.

(10) Graceful diplomat

Wang is both an outstanding entrepreneur and a well-known diplomat. He is the second Man of the Year in China after Deng Xiaoping and is one of the two communists who took off their shoes in front of the public in the United State (the other is former Soviet leader Khrushchev). His amazing move to take off his shoe promoted the Double Star brand, countered the provocation of those with ulterior motives, won the respect of the Americans, and won the glory for Chinese People. Therefore, he diplomatic style is unique.

In the summer of 1992, it was extremely hot. China was suffering from the hardship. To regain MFN status, it was engaged in a tug-of-war with the United States. Every move between China and the United States affected the situation. At this time, Wang decided to go to New York to hold a press conference. Hearing the news, Liu Qizhong, the leader of the Xinhua News Agency in the United States, became worried, because he thought that the decision to hold a press conference on the name of the enterprise in the sensitive time would affect relations between China and the United States, and that no one could bear the related responsibility. So this leader told the relevant personnel that this press conference should not be held.

The news came back to Wang. He knew the seriousness of the matter, because it was no longer a commercial issue but a political issue. Wang thought that he should personally negotiated with this leader; otherwise, the plan to go to the United States would be not successful.

On the phone. He said to this leader emotionally that although he was a shoemaker, I understood interests of the country; that he moved from the military to the local unit and was an entrepreneur; that Chinese people were not afraid of Americans on the battlefield, so were they in the market; that, as a person who represented a Chinese enterprise to hold a press conference in the United State, he knew what should be said and what should not be said; that he would win the glory four Chinese people!

Hearing these words, this leader felt excited and was impressed by the generous speech and strong patriotism from Wang. He made an exception and agreed to Wang's request. As a result, the press conference was not canceled.

At 9 o'clock on the morning of August 28, 1992, this leader came to the conference venue. When seeing the foreign journalists who came in and out, this leader became worried again, because of the thought, "Wang is not a politician after all. Can he cope with this situation?" This leader very admired Wang for his courage and eloquence, but this was the first time a domestic company to hold a press conference in the United States, could Wang, who was a business leader rather than a politician without diplomatic experience, cope with it? Thought of this, Thinking of this, this leader of the news agency sweated a bit from the forehead. Suddenly, his gaze inadvertently met Wang, while the latter was calm and relaxed and nodded to him. His nervous emotions eased.

The press conference started. Wang released five news about business activities and business management of Double

Star. Then the press conference entered the most intense stage - the reporter asked questions.

Initially they asked questions about the size, the basic construction, the number of employees of Double Star and etc. With his words pouring forth like rushing water, Wang gave satisfactory replies. The face of this leader finally showed a smile. However, it didn't take long for this leader to be afraid of something. It turned out that the US Sing Tao Daily reporter Zhen Rongguang raised sensitive issues.

"I would like to ask you as Chinese shoe king, if the United States cancels China's MFN status and implements Special 301, will your business be affected? What is your attitude?" This leader of the news agency looked nervously at Wang.

Wang calmly replied, "For this issue, my government has a clear attitude. I am just a shoemaker. I don't want to talk about politics. But as a Chinese, as the head of a large state-owned enterprise, my answer is: First, the MFN status means reciprocal treatment and reciprocal interests. The United States can let China unable to get benefits, and China can also." Hearing these words, this leader felt relived.

Wang continued, "Second, if the United States implements Special 301, our corporate development will definitely be affected. But we may lose here and gain there. The United States has a population of 200 million people, China 1.2 billion, and the world more than 5 billion. It does not matter if the US market is lost, because we still have a market of 4.8 billion people worldwide. Our high-quality shoes have taken a place in Europe. American consumers are also fond of high-quality and low-priced shoes from us. Today's market is free and open, rather than dependent on which person and which government. One clause can't stop our products from entering the US market. On the other hand, the United States would have lost China's best market in the world with the greatest potential."

At this point, there was some commotion in the venue, and this leader laughed and smiled at Wang. The latter continued, "Third, the high-quality products of Double Star have won the trust of God and the recognition of the market, including the love of the American people. Even if Special 301 is implemented, we still have the means to continue to enter the US market. This is determined by market rules and economic laws rather than controlled by someone's will."

Being neither humble or pushy, Wang made rational replied with the silence among the audience. This leader of the news agency proudly raised his head and looked directly at the reporters under the stage. He said to himself that Wang was very powerful and could coped with it. Hardly has one wave subsided when another rise.

A senior reporter from the New York Times, stood up, with a cunning look, said with a sneer, "Mr. Wang, you are the celebrity in the shoe industry of China. So, I took the liberty to ask, are shoes of Double Star on your feet?"

This reporter noticed the beautiful shoes on his feet and wanted to let him become a laughing stock by asking such a question. Yes, Wang were wearing leather shoes. We have to admit that this reporter observed carefully.

On the spot, the reporters and the representatives of the Chinese side stared at the black shoes on his feet. This leader of the news agency felt that it would turn out to be a dreadful thing. If Wang wore shoes from other countries, especially Nike, there would be an adverse impact in the world.

Laughing and smiling with the light of joy in eyes, Wang said excitedly, "I am very grateful to you as a reporter for asking this question. You give me a good opportunity to promote our products. I know that taking off shoes in public is a very uncivilized act, but..."

He started to take off his shoes. The audience were surprised with their eyes wide open. Look, Wang started to take off his shoe. This leader wanted to stop him from doing so, but it was already late. It was an impolite behavior.

Wang held the shoes high in his hand, and said in English with his local accent, "CHINA DOUBLE STAR! Look at this trademark. I wear shoes from our Double Star. If I do not wear our Chinese shoes, can I be worth being called Chinese shoe king? Truly speaking, I wear our shoes all the year round, and so do all our staffs. We put our shoes on feet to travel the world."

The spotlights flashed again.

The next day, his photo with a smile and a shoe in hand was published in a prominent position in many newspapers in the United States. The press circle of the United States commented, "In our memory, there are only two communists from socialist countries who took off shoes in front of the American public. One is Khrushchev who was the United Nations headquarters in New York, took off his shoe and knocked against the table with them. The second is Wang who stood at the forefront of the state-owned enterprise reform in China, smiling and promoting his own products in the US market with their own products, so embodying a heroic spirit!"

A Chinese American was moved. She excitedly ran to the stage and held his hand and said, "Mr. Wang, you have won the glory for Chinese people and you let us see the confidence, pride and self-esteem of the Chinese. You also let us see the hope of the national industry of the motherland. Our overseas Chinese must buy and publicize products from China."

At that moment, the said leader was very excited. He witnessed a warrior from the business community of the motherland and bravely showed a strong national spirit in front of the Americans. He took Wang's hand for a long time and said, "Old Wang, I have been in New York for five years. I have participated in many press conferences. You successfully held a press conference here. You are great! Our Chinese people are proud of you!"

After returning to the office, this leader immediately sent a message back to the relevant department of China: Wang has done a wonderful job. Congratulations on his success! We should more people like him!

(11) Evergreen tree

On the wall opposite his desk, a couplet is hung, which was written by Zhao Puchu president of Chinese Buddhist Association. This couplet reads, "**Always pursuing the dream without attention paid to the fame and wealth.**" Therefore, it is the true portrayal of his soul and morality.

Whether in forums of domestic higher education institutions or in the international high-level forums, President Wang often says that he is only a shoemaker and a salcsman. Before good comments and titles given to him by the outside world, including market general, world man of the year, and so forth, he always keeps a clear head.

A must-have quality for business leaders is to never be greedy for money. he often says, "**The person in charge of the enterprise should always cultivate the virtue, often remembering the disaster due to the greed and always remembering to be self-disciplined**." In 1996, he declined the invitation (high-paying + equity) by an American company to work in it. He said, "**I follow the CPC leadership, try my best to do the work, and pay attention to the harmony in the family.**"

He commented on himself, "For more than 30 years, I am proud to have two points: one point is that I am an excellent party member and that I provide jobs for nearly 100,000 persons. The other point is that I am an entrepreneur and that I create the Double Star brand." Due to outstanding contributions, Wang has successively won the following honors: national excellent management personnel, national May 1st labor medal, national labor model, one of first national outstanding entrepreneurs, one of young and middle-aged management experts having outstanding contributions, one of top champions nationwide in poverty alleviation, one of top ten management talents nationwide, one of top ten figures in chemical field, national quality management advanced worker, one of first men of the day in national petrochemical industry, most influential entrepreneur in national apparel industry, one of top ten news figures in China, most concerned entrepreneur and so forth. In 1993, he was included in Five Thousand Personalities of the World. In 1995, he was named World Man of the Year after Deng Xiaoping. Subsequently, he won the International Outstanding Entrepreneur Contribution Award and the World Outstanding Person title. He became the only Chinese diplomatic entrepreneur selected in the large-scale documentary film Diplomatic Records of P.R.C. His personal value has reached 32.142 billion Yuan, being the highest in the community of entrepreneurs in China.

In the 1980s, a batch of outstanding entrepreneurs were selected for the first time in China and cordially met by the party and state leaders in the latter's office room. At present, among these outstanding entrepreneurs, some have risen, some have fallen, some have fled to foreign countries, some have been jailed and so forth.

However, as director of Ninth Rubber Factory in Qingdao at that time, now president of Double Star Group, he still works hard in the same unit. He is known as Market General, Long-lived President, and Evergreen Tree in the Chinese business community.

He says, "**In China, it is easy and not easy to beat down a reformer. According to my experience, there are two points that I think are very important. If you don't handle them improperly, you may beat yourself down. One point is the temptation of money, the other point is the relationship with the woman. As an entrepreneur, we should pay attention to**

these two points. If we can properly handle them, we will never be beat down."

He often admonishes cadres: "**We enter the market and let our products become world brand products. Without a good cadre team, it is impossible. A corrupt cadre team can do nothing. If our cadre team and our staffs are not corrupt, I believe that our Double Star can catch up with and exceed the leading enterprises in the world. It is not a problem**."

(12) Long-lived president

In 2008, a reporter once asked him, "You are 67 years old this year. Have you considered your life after retirement? What do you plan to do?"

He replied, "I do not know. I cannot make my decision in this regard. If I can, I hope to live to be 98 years old, work until my death. Now, I am more than 60 years in age, but healthy in body and young in mind. Of course, I say so for the sake of publicity. Maybe one day my superior asks me to retire, then I at once go home."

"State-owned enterprises have no lifelong tenure. One of objective laws in the universe is to replace the old with the new. I let nature take its course. **On the other hand, I love Double Star very much. If I am still a responsible person in the future, I will continuously work hard and make my contributions. I love Double Star and my staffs!**"

He says, "**For decades, there have been many fault-finders who put bad labels on me. I ignore them and still dare to go forward. Why? Because I believe that I am right. Why am I right? Because I seek truth from facts and I believe that the party's policy of reform and opening will never change. If we want to engage in a market economy, we must seek truth from facts. If we do not seek truth from facts, we must suffer from poverty**." One pet phrase he likes is: "**Think, create; be earnest, pragmatically, and happy**."

Entrepreneurs who have succeeded in the market for a long time are the real entrepreneurs. He says, "**Entrepreneur should be market-oriented. He is optimistic no matter the market is prosperous or poor. He can let the enterprise survive in the poor market and develop in the prosperous market. He has a strong leadership; he bravely breaks the routine and always does things that others think are impossible; he is able to keenly predict risks and has a strong determination**." Indeed, he is a real entrepreneur with outstanding achievements; he is the core and the soul of Double Star.

Today's Double Star has opened the curtain of the historic development turning point. Under the leadership of President Wang and the impetus of the people's war in the market, inspired by the national spirit, we will continue to improve the new path of market economy development, create new features of market economy development, realize the goal of the brand being built to last, and win a new victory!

III. Expert Comments

The term entrepreneur first appeared in French in the early 16th century and referred to **the person who engaged in the military expedition**. After 200 years, the French began to extend the definition of the term by referring to **the person engaging in other kinds of adventure activities**. Finally, French economist Richard Cantillon defined **entrepreneur** as **the person who bears the risk of business** in the book entitled **Business Overview** published in 1755, while the entrepreneur was interpreted as **a part of economy**. Other French economists further expanded the definition of entrepreneur, using this nickname to refer to **the person who takes the risk in construction, farm and industry**. The latter is also known as the **capitalist taking a risk**. Thus, in the early days, **entrepreneurs were related with venture capitalists**. In this sense, **an entrepreneur is an adventurer**.

After years of evolution and refinement, the term entrepreneur has become indispensable in the economic system of China and has become an important field of research in economics, sociology, management, culture and psychology. Entrepreneur has also become an important reflector of the terms innovator, blazer and arbitrager.

David Silver, a well-known American entrepreneur and an expert on entrepreneurial activities, pointed out in his book entitled The Career Life, "**Entrepreneurs and artists have much in common. They are problem solvers. Artists try to solve many problems in life by expressing solutions on the canvas. Entrepreneurs do their best to focus on one issue, constantly expressing and re-expressing the problems that have been grasped until they are prepared to paint with a huge canvas. Both artists and entrepreneurs as individualists are exotic, sensitive, imaginative, enthusiastic, energetic, and creative etc**."

George Gilde, an American electronics industry expert and economist, wrote in his book entitled The Soul of the Enterprise, "The key to economic growth is simply that creative people own banknotes. I believe that the vitality of entrepreneurs is the most critical factor in economic growth." He continued to write, "**The vital role of entrepreneurs, which is similar to the most important role of scientists, is to create a whole new market and theory. In this respect, entrepreneurs are only limited by their own imagination and persuasion. They are like a painter who faces with a piece of empty canvas, like a poet who faces with a blank piece of white paper, like a creative artist who brings something new to the world**."

Since the Industrial Revolution, entrepreneurs have been a group of geniuses who have discovered the problems and needs of humanity and sought to solve them and meet human needs. They have transformed contemporary scientific and technological achievements into products, turned them into social productive forces, and enabled the workers' strength and wisdom to be displayed through the social organization (namely, **enterprise**), thereby creating economic miracles and promoting social progress. The historical merits of this great social role have been most prominent in the United States since the advent of the third technological revolution. Therefore, in the United States, people from this perspective say that "**contemporary entrepreneurs are the new heroes of the United States and are the new generation of heroes in the United States since Lincoln and Roosevelt**."

The key role for entrepreneurs generalized and described by above-mentioned experts only applies to the entrepreneurs at the early and middle stages, that is, stages of modern history after the world industrial revolution. The common limitation of this generalization and depiction is that we only see the natural attributes of the role of entrepreneurs, that is, the role in developing social productive forces and solving problems and needs faced by human beings, while ignoring the social attributes of the role of entrepreneurs. The social attributes are that entrepreneurs must serve a certain nation and a certain class, also known as national attributes and class attributes.

Since the success of the October Socialist Revolution in the Soviet Union, the world has entered the stage of modern history. Especially after the world formed the two camps of socialism and capitalism, the social attributes of entrepreneurs, namely nation and class attributes, become more and more obvious. Correspondingly, for entrepreneurs in the modern history stage, the connotation of their role is more enriched, and the requirements for the quality and ability of entrepreneurs are more, wider, higher and stricter.

In the business and academic circles of our country, there are many definitions of entrepreneurs: for example, entrepreneurs are leaders who exert the influence on an organized group to promote the realization of their goals;

entrepreneurs are innovators who create new products and propose new ideas through the recombination of production factors; entrepreneurs are organizers and promoters to improve the efficiency of enterprises; entrepreneurs are asset owners or corporate asset managers; entrepreneurs are adventurers who can eliminate the uncertain factors; entrepreneurs are experts in business management who allocate resources to form productive capacity; entrepreneurs are arbitrageurs and value creators; entrepreneurs are those making decisions on the allocation of scarce resources; entrepreneurs are a kind of high-level, special human capital, and is a group of business management managers; and etc. The term entrepreneur has a rich connotation.

Among entrepreneurs of China, he is the first to make a comprehensive, refined, vivid generalization and description on the concept, role, quality and ability of the entrepreneur.

He says, "**The most basic thing for entrepreneurs is to regard the enterprise as their own home and to devote themselves to the enterprise. As a national entrepreneur, we must have the minds of politicians, the thinking of philosophers, the vision of theorists, the strategies of military strategists, the romantic style of the poets, the hardworking spirit of the doers, the graceful bearing of the diplomats, the passion and the talent of the agitators, the courage of the adventurers. At the same time, more importantly, we must have the following traits: first, we have our unique management theory created based on our national culture; second, we have a keen sense of national responsibility and a national spirit. Only national entrepreneurs can create our own national brands**." Indeed, he is one of best entrepreneurs in China.

April 21, 1995, Yuan Baohua, director of China Enterprise Management Association and director of China Entrepreneur Association, published the article entitled **On the Cultivation of Entrepreneurs** for the Entrepreneur Activity Day, proposing that entrepreneurs should have ten basic qualities, this is: **(1)**

Everyone is responsible for the rise and fall of the country; (2) down-to-earth while understanding the overall situation; (3) working hard plus dedication; (4) emancipation of the mind and active thinking; (5) clean and honest, reliant on the masses; (6) a strong hatred of evil practice, readily accepting good advice; (7) modest and cautious, guarding against arrogance; (8) insatiable in learning and tireless in teaching; (9) spending a great effort on the market with a practical attitude; Lose fantasies and fight the market; (10) insisting on brave innovation.

Postscript

An expert in teaching, research, training and consulting in corporate strategy and management and a founder of success science in China, I am particularly interested in stories, activities and experiences of successful entrepreneurs at home and abroad, especially in China, and pays more attention those who are very successful. Among them, the first entrepreneur that caught my attention is Wang Hai, the longest-lived entrepreneur among the first 20 outstanding entrepreneurs of China, and the president of Double Star Group.

I have been focusing and tracking on stories, activities and experiences of Wang leading Double Star for more than 20 years. During this period, I was both happy and proud of the amazing miracle achieved by Wang and sincerely admired him for his excellent qualities such as morality, spirit, courage, wisdom, ability and style! Therefore, in my teaching, research, training and consulting work, he and his Double Star Group have become a success case I often cite. My long-cherished is striving to sum up his successful experience and let it be recognized as immaterial wealth for entrepreneurs in China. It can be used to cultivate more entrepreneurs like Wang and create more brands like Double Star.

Opportunities always favor those who are prepared. In 2008, a good chance came to me. To celebrate the 30th anniversary of reform and opening and publicize the great achievements of 30 years, China Enterprise Confederation, China Entrepreneurs Association and China Enterprise News worked together to organize the compilation of books about Wang aiming at the first comprehensive study of his entrepreneurial management thought. This project was presided over China Enterprise Confederation and China Entrepreneurs Association executive vice president Feng Bing and former editor-in-chief of China Enterprise News

Zhang Laimin. A group of experts from across the country made a three-day trip to Double Star, meeting President Wang and visiting production workshops; and collected relevant books, reports and materials which were published by Double Star. Later, Books of Wang Hai (three volumes) were compiled and published by Social Science Literature Publishing House in February 2010.

Titles of books of Wang Hai (three volumes) are: (1) Market as the Root of the Enterprise - Collection of Works by Wang Hai as one of outstanding entrepreneurs in China; (2) Pioneer in the Reform - News Reports on Wang Hai; (3) Market Economy and Theoretical Innovation: Study on Thought of Wang Hai. Three volumes have a total of 1.243 million Chinese words.

In this set of books, I write two articles on his experiences below: First, thought of being an entrepreneur; second, thought of seeking truth from facts and being pragmatic as well as meeting wishes of people. The first thought is later compiled into the textbook entitled Enterprise Strategic Management (3rd edition) compiled by me and published by Peking University Press. This textbook of 3 editions has been printed 18 times totaling about 90,000 copies. It is the most widely printed and circulated textbook among similar textbooks in China. It is not only popular in China, but also welcome in corporate, educational, and publishing communities in the US. It was re-edited in English (entitled Business Strategy: New Vision) on request and published by North American Business Press in the US. Later, Sheng Xishun deputy general manager of Double Star Group, who was responsible for publishing books of Wang, told me that above-said two articles attracted attention from leaders of Double Star including Wang and were given favorable comments by them.

On the 90th anniversary of the founding of the great Communist Party of China, Double Star celebrated its 90th anniversary. At the same time, a comprehensive, systematic, in-depth and concrete summary of successful experiences of Double Star under the leadership of Wang, including management experience, not only has great practical significance, but also has innovative theoretical significance and far-reaching historical significance.

In May of this year, the said deputy general manager was entrusted by President Wang and went to Beijing to invite me to help comprehensively and systematically sum up the management experience of Double Star for more than 30 years. According to the plan, it would be published on the 90th anniversary of Double Star.

I would like to thank the leaders of Double Star Group with Wang as the core for their high trust. This arduous, urgent and glorious task to me was both a serious challenge and a fantastic opportunity to realize my long-cherished wish. I vowed to successfully complete this task through my life's accumulated wisdom, knowledge, experience and ability!

After several months of intense work including revision many times, the books are finally published. The completion of this daunting task in such a brief period of time is the result of a collective effort.

First, the brilliant achievements, successful experiences and typical cases created by the leaders with Wang as the core and all the staffs have provided the original materials.

Second, the works and reports of writers, editors and journalists who publicize the achievements and experience of Wang and Double Star also have provided many reference materials for this book series.

Third, Comrade Wang Zengsheng deputy secretary of the party branch and general manager put forward many valuable opinions on the design and compilation; Comrade Sheng Xishun deputy general manager was responsible for its publication, providing a guarantee for this work.

Fourth, Director Guo Lin, Director Chen Xuemei, Director Sun Weipeng, and Editor Wang Kailiang of the political propaganda department in Double Star wrote many rich and typical materials for the books' compilation.

Finally, Ms. Zhang Yuhui, my assistant and office director, has done a lot of work on data collection, text collation and proofreading.

I would like to express my heartfelt thanks to all the above-mentioned leaders, writers, editors, journalists, comrades and friends for their work and contributions.

I would like to mention here in particular that Yuan Baohua, over 90 years old, founder and honorary president of China Enterprise Confederation and China Entrepreneurs Association, who enjoys high prestige in the business management community of China, specially sent a congratulatory letter to all staffs of Double Star Group on its 90th anniversary. In it, he not only fully affirmed and highly praised the brilliant achievements and successful experiences of Double Star in the past 90 years, but also hoped that the national business community would research, think and learn from the new management model of Double Star. Here, I would like to express my heartfelt gratitude to him for his concern and support, and I wish him good health and longevity!

Due to limited personal level and experience plus urgency, inadequacies are inevitable. Entrepreneurs, managers, experts, and readers are cordially welcome to give valuable advice! My email address: zxy9780@139.com

Zhang Xiuyu

Appendix

Appendix 1: Bolshevik Thinker
-- Entrepreneur Wang Hai in State-owned Enterprise Reform

Zhu Jianhua, People's Daily

Karl Marx was born in a small town called Trier in West Rhineland. On an autumn day in the late 1980s, a Chinese Communist who made a special trip to Trier and solemnly entered the former residence of Karl Marx. After saluting to the statue of the world's proletarian revolutionary leader, he began a two-hour thinking.

After reviewing the great history of the worldwide workers movement, this party member from China concluded that the theory of the socialist road with Chinese characteristics proposed by Comrade Deng Xiaoping, the chief architect of China's reform and opening, has a strong vitality, because it captures the essence of Marxism and conforms to the principle of seeking truth from facts. He seriously thought about a question that is both very sharp and unavoidable: Why are there now many people who are unfamiliar with the truth of the development of human society - Marx's theory? In the ocean of market economy, and how should contemporary Bolsheviks go along the right direction?

When this visitor named Wang Hai was about to leave the three-story building, he once again looked at the long-haired bearded Marx portrait above the door in a very revered mood, and from the bottom of his heart, vowed to devote his lift to the great cause of communism.

General who dares to break through the restricted area

Wang as a well-known leader of Double Star began his great journey from the emancipation of his mind. In 1995, the world's most influential celebrity directory selection units — the American Celebrity Biography Association and the American Celebrity Institute — jointly elected Wang as World Man of Year 1995. He is the first entrepreneur of China to win this honor.

There is a long road to reform. From the planned economy to the market economy, Double Star has experienced a great change. What is the secret of the success of Double Star? The creator of this miracle, Wang, who is known as the market general, has attributed these achievements to the ideological emancipation movement in the depths of the soul for people at Double Star. The success of Double Star is first of all the political success.

Wang often says to some visitors who have explored the secrets of Double Star, "If you want to do a good job in state-owned enterprises, you must first have the courage to break through the restricted area of thought, hold high the sword of Marxism — that is, seeking seek truth from facts — to open up a new path."

Perhaps, one morning, the air is filled with mist or one night, the sea breeze blows with stars in the sky. Wang as a thinker in the rapids stands on the beach of Jiaozhou Bay and carries out the most profound and difficult theoretical exploration of the economy at the end of the century. Questions he asks: is the root cause of sluggishness in some large and medium-sized state-owned enterprises really a so-called ownership problem? The capitalist countries generally adopt the private ownership structure with clear property rights, but why they still have a large number of companies failing? What kind of theory of thought should be used to guide our reform of state-owned enterprises today?

Wang, who participated in aiding Vietnam in its resistance to the US, says, "The dazzling market is a battlefield and the entrepreneurs in the market are the generals on the battlefield."

Wang as a party member, who is bold, wise, and humorous, began his emancipation of his mind after the painful thinking.

While the prevailing thought was against the emphasis on the role of money, Wang said, "The good use of money is the biggest political work." Both gain and fame exist objectively, and the key is to how we guide. While the prevailing thought was against the emphasis on the personality, Wang believed that personality is a symbol of entrepreneurs, that personality and personal worship are two different concepts. Without personality, there is no development and no creation. While the prevailing thought was against the practice of being different, Wang said that entrepreneurs in the market should be different by innovation. Wang also said that we should be proud and self-confidential than arrogant; otherwise, we would lose our national spirit...

The rapid of Double Star stems from its courage to create and advanced ideas!

Creating brands is the biggest politics in the market economy

While holding high the patriotic flag, Wang embarked on the journey with his staffs. Brands are the inevitable outcome of the market economy. Since you recognize the market economy, you must recognize the existence and role of brands. It is based on this sober thinking that Wang loudly said at a seminar that we should plan to create our brands in the 21st century; that domestic consumers currently worn foreign clothes and drove foreign cars; that foreigners occupied our economic fields with brands, and this was a war without smoke; that we should have the obligation and responsibility to create our own brands and revitalize the national economy!

Wang often says to staffs of Double Star, "We stress the political awareness, how to carry out political work in the enterprise? I think that creating is brand is a kind of political work. Marx once said that war is a concentrated expression of politics. We are here. In the market accompanied by more complicated globalization, the creation of brands is the biggest politics! The brand is the atomic bomb and the aircraft carrier. Where there is no famous brand in the market, there will be the largest failure in politics. We talk about patriotism every day, where is it embodied? When a company can create its own brand, is it not the biggest patriotism?"

Revitalize the Chinese nation and hold high the banner of Developing Our Count through Industry in Double Star!

However, it is not easy to create a brand. The development of a brand needs a long time: Nike taking 30 years and Adidas 70 years. If we hear that Double Star creates a brand in 10 years, then image the efforts it has spent.

Wang as a general in the market holds high the sword of patriotism and leads his army to enter the international market.

In 1986, when the volleyball team won consecutive championships in the world, when the national flag with the national anthem played, Wang was proud of our heroines. But when he heard that these heroines worn Japanese brand shoes for competitions again and again, he felt the sting in the heart.

This is a shame for the footwear industry of China! Chinese people are not shorter than foreigners when standing and lying. Why can we not do it?

Wang began eating and living in the office to act as a commander for the 100-day battle. Finally, he let these heroines put on the shoes from Double Star.

Then, Wang led the staffs to cast Double Star into a world-famous brand, and receive the orders of PONR, CVO, and Brooks. After more than 60 days and nights, the three-international brand-name shoes were successfully developed in China for the first time with one million pairs each year sold back to the European and American markets. the bell of victory was rung, Wang as the commander fell ill again. The workers felt distressed, "During the creation of the brand, we worked hard, but Wang worked harder!"

After recovering, he stood beside a production line and began to dream. He declared to the staff: "Double Star has fully equipped the ability to produce all kinds of international famous brand sports shoes. Now it is time to develop our own sports shoes that are comparable to international famous brands."

"The person who dares to dream is the strongest person in life. We should think broadly and do things meticulously. This is the secret of a winner." He said with eyes sparkling with confidence.

In the middle of 1980s, a high-end sneaker named after Double Star was born. It not only has all the advantages of PONR, but also is stronger, more comfortable and more beautiful than it. In the market, it has become a famous brand...

Persistence is the key to success. There is such a set of numbers enough to make our Chinese people proud: At present, the number of shoes sold to the United States by Double Star has reached 17 million pairs per year. On average, one out of every 15 Americans has ever worn its shoes. At the University of California, 12% of college students love sports shoes from Double Star. In the fiercely competitive US market, it is extremely rare for a national industrial product of a developing country to achieve such a high market share.

Wang, a communist in the new era, finally realizes his lifelong wish. The national footwear market survey showed that Double Star brand exceeded Nike and Adidas and other foreign brands in the market influence and market share. For the first time, it defeated these two world famous brands which had a leading position in China for more than ten years...

His practice of creating a brand shows that persistence leads to the success.

The market is the standard for testing all work in the enterprise

Wang often says: we did not recognize private ownership in the past, and now we recognize it; we did not recognize the market economy in the past, and now we recognize it. The idea is changed, can the theory remain unchanged? We must create a new set of market theories to guide today's reform practices.

On September 29, 1998, Double Star Group held a seminar on the 15th anniversary of Double Star entering the market at its Qingdao headquarters. Participants reached a consensus: the Double Star market theory created by Wang is the magic weapon and action guide for Double Stars to succeed in the fierce and complicated market competition! It is the market that forces the enterprise to change and expand its business through the use of various measures (including the transfer of the production line to the rural area the like). Therefore, Double Star has become a famous modern company at home and abroad that can produce a variety of brand-name sports shoes...

Q: Your market awareness?

A: The market is the driving force for enterprise development.

A: The market is always right.

Q: What are your three principles of market economy?

Q: Your market philosophy?

A: Users are God with gold medals obtained in the market.

Q: Your market attitude?

A: The market is the highest leader of the company; the market is the standard for testing all work; and the market is the best balance for measuring the enterprise.

When many investigators send questions to him, we may pay attention to his mechanism revolution initiated. Double Stars has been in the market for more than 30 years. Wang led people of Double Star to get ride of the rigid old ideas and create a new pattern; get ride of the planned economy and create a new mechanism; and etc.

The new mechanism is to let all staffs enter the market and participate in competition. Since 1993, Double Star has let subordinate units lease factory buildings, land and other equipment from it and pay depreciation expenses etc. Through the measure, every unit has become a profit center. Double Star is like a solar system around which more than 100 units go. The staffs led by him are always vigorous!

This is a mechanism that actively operates according to market rules, a mechanism that develops according to industry rules, or a mechanism that is based on the market demand.

This is a mechanism from Double Star, which possesses the following advantages: American-style scale, Japanese-style rapidity in response, flexibility in operation of township and village enterprises, and other advantages in shareholding and lease systems etc.

The product structure changes constantly with the market; the business strategy changes constantly with the market; and the internal mechanism changes constantly with the market. Where there is a market, there is a production base and a chain store of Double Star. Nowadays, Double Star has become a powerful domestic marketing system, which takes the initiative to make a big step towards the international market.

With the brilliance achieved, people at Double Star never forget the hardships of the past. That year, Double Star Group held an important meeting to which Wang could not attend because of illness. When he wrote an open letter to all the staff, he could not help but shed tears. Does Wang as a tough man have a heartbreaking experience?

His first step into the market began after he served as the party secretary of Qingdao Ninth Rubber Factory. At that time, the factory was on the verge of bankruptcy due to the backlog of products. The workers could not receive wages. Wang said to them, "Let us unite together and work hard and depend on ourselves than saviors."

With the spirit of daring to be the first, Wang led his staffs to bring their shoes and bravely enter the market...

In the historical process of the development of Double Star and at every turning point, there was a market theory as a guide, where Wang worked hard with the staffs under the force of courage. Thus, Double Star has set a number of first in the business community of China: The first to implement the horizontal economic integration; the first to implement the east and west development strategy (in which the strategic shift is achieved, including shoe cities - Luzhong and Hanhai and the production base built in Yimeng old revolution base area so forth); the first to hold a press conference in the United States in the name of the company; the first to promote the oriental shoe culture at the international fair; the first to create a family, militarized, moral, scientific high-level management system; the first to break the practice of eating from the same big pot; the first to strengthen political work with the view of market economy; the first to enter the tertiary industry; the first to move shoe workshops and production lines out from the prime location in the urban area (which are replaced by the entertainment city, commercial building, securities company and bowling city so forth); the first to propose the philosophical view of market politics and market theory; the first to implement the brand strategy; the first to create the world famous brand belonged to our Chinese people...

As an entrepreneur, Wang dares to be the first in the world, dares to think creatively, dares to innovate, dares to take risks, and dares to compete with any opponent. It is not the spirit of the times that the party members are required to have today?

Summarizing the experience of the market with Double Start, Wang as the Bolshevik thinker says, "Only the market is the standard for testing all work in the enterprise!"

High quality of product is the biggest doing-good and gathering blessings

The theory of seeking truth from facts proposed and applied by great men Marx, Mao Zedong and Deng Xiaoping is a powerful ideological weapon to guide the reform of state-owned enterprises. Following this theory, Wang creatively proposes a new concept: the high product quality is the biggest doing-good and gathering blessings in the enterprise management.

In 1841, the first professional entrepreneur was born in the history of modern industry. The management science has since entered the historical arena. In the twentieth century, Henry Fayol, the father of modern business management, Hugo Munsterberg, the father of industrial psychology, and Max Weber, the father of the social system methodology, were born in the world. We can't help but ask, "Where is the Master of Business Management in China as the world's largest nation?"

"Inheriting traditional excellence, absorbing foreign achievements and creating our own distinct products." Wang, who grew up in the land where Confucius and Mencius were born, knows that the profound Chinese traditional culture is the most effective culture to mobilize social resources. He always thinks about the management work. He believes that Confucianism, Taoism, and Buddhism are the representatives of ancient Chinese culture and that the predecessors have left us with so many precious cultural heritages. How to inherit them? The traditional things contain excellent ideas which can be applied in modern enterprise management. To this end, Wang instills Chinese traditional excellent culture among all employees and advocates moral management to achieve a higher level of management. For example, most of the production bases of Double Star are in mountainous areas and remote areas. Some employees have low cultural level. How to accept the preaching of serving the people and quality being the life of the enterprise? Wang puts forward slogans, for example, high quality of product is the biggest doing-good and gathering blessings, and the quality is the first. These easily understood slogans unite the president's wish with the wishes of the staffs. Moreover, this quality management perspective shortens the distance between the company and the staffs.

This is an exploration from Wang as a Chinese Communist who dares to be the first in the enterprise management culture. It is a breakthrough in the traditional management theory. It is the most powerful embodiment of the Marxist principle of seeking truth from facts in economic work. It is also the best combination of the traditional excellent culture and modern enterprise management.

In 1995, Wang was invited to fly to Singapore to elucidate the idea of applying traditional culture to modern enterprise management for the first time at the World Management Forum. His lecture won a series of prolonged applause, in which he organically combined Marx's philosophical view (that is, seeking truth from facts), moral view (that is, doing-good and gathering blessings), and market view of Double Star. This is probably also an important reason why Wang was selected as World Man of the Year by an authoritative institution for celebrity selection in the United States which was consisted of scholars who had a political prejudice again China.

July 3, 1999, Wang was exclusively interviewed by Dr. Kuhn of K2 Communications in the US.

Kuhn: Do you give full play to the traditional culture when operating Double Star?

Wang: We apply the excellent culture of Chinese Confucianism, Taoism, and Buddhism to our management. This is our creation. Don't think that Buddhism is a form of superstition. Chinese traditional culture is different from feudal superstition.

Kuhn: Are there any conflicts between Taoism, Confucianism, Buddhism and communism?

Wang: I think that culture is a national thing, so we must inherit an excellent culture. This is a completely different concept from the belief of a historical stage. It is also the great creation of the entrepreneur in China to integrate the excellent culture into the faith.

Kuhn: What let you have the idea to use the traditional culture?

Wang: According to the dialectical materialism of our ancestor, Marx, according to Comrade Xiaoping's theory of seeking truth from facts, according to the actual situation of the enterprise, especially based on the actual conditions of staffs, I think that our traditional culture has promoted the humanity progress in history. Enterprises can adopt the excellent things in Chinese traditional culture to their management, letting them serve the market and promote the development of productivity. All the cultures that are usable must be used. This is the principle of seeking truth from facts.

It is precisely because of profound thoughts, excellent culture, and novel ideas that the management model of Double Star is unique in the enterprise community.

Century Declaration

"Think, create; be earnest, pragmatically, and happy." This is a century declaration of a Bolshevik thinker!

Wang dared to take off his shoes in public at a press conference in New York and announced to the world that he led the staffs into the global market. There are only two communists from socialist countries who took off shoes in front of the American public. One is Khrushchev who was the United Nations headquarters in New York, took off his shoe and knocked against the table with them. The second is Wang who stood at the forefront of the state-owned enterprise reform in China, smiling and promoting his own products in the US market with their own products, so embodying a heroic spirit.

In the hometown of Marx, Germany, at the Düsseldorf International Footwear Expo, the Oriental Shoe Culture performance of Double Star sensationalized the entire exhibition hall and shocked the editor-in-chief of the European Footwear Newspaper who had watched the performance for three consecutive days. He took the initiative to met Wang and said to him, "We used to regard Chinese as rabbits and Europeans snakes, Snakes to scare rabbits, and the latter tremble. Today, after watching your cultural performance, I feel that Chinese should be snakes and Europeans rabbits." Wang laughed, "Sir, your metaphor is not appropriate. Don't you know that the Chinese nation is a great dragon?"

Wang won the glory for our country. This is the most sacred gift from him as a firm reformer for the motherland.

In the new era, party member Wang realizes his goal with his own actions.

Wish Bolshevik thinkers more successes in the future.

(Source: People's Daily, October 19, 1999)

Appendix 2: Great Form without Shape

——Wang and National Rejuvenation

Zhu Jianhua, People's Daily · Overseas Edition

From the Opium War of 1840 to the Eight-Power Allied Forces invasion of 1900, the Western imperialist powers had brought enormous disasters to the Chinese nation. To wipe off the centuries-old national disgrace, our Chinese people had advanced wave upon wave and launched one struggle after another.

In the 1980s, Deng Xiaoping launched the reform and opening-up, which has inspired the Chinese nation to once again embark on the road of revival.

Though the world changes, the hegemonic strategy of Western powers still exists. With the opening of the gate with our country, mud and sand are carried along - the bad get mingled with the good, a dazzling phenomenon. Some people did know how to do, some worshiped everything foreign, some were minded-rigid, and some fell into a trap in the market. At that time, Wang as one of outstanding entrepreneurs, was clear-headed and looked at the world. He led a national enterprise with a history of 90 years to compete with the enterprises from the West. This also meant that the ancient Chinese nation once again begun to face with the Western powers. Wang, who called himself a shoe-maker and was called a general in the market, became the pioneer of the market, the adventurer of reform, the promoter of the brand, the expert of the manager, the innovator of the theory and mechanism, and the decision-maker of the enterprise in the wave of reform and opening. He has led Double Star to be at the leading position in mechanism, culture, model, spirit etc. He has created a successful road for state-owned enterprises to enter the market, held high a banner of bright and colorful national industry, and created a miracle in the success of national industry and national brand in the new era of market economy.

Entrepreneur Wang devotes himself into the great rejuvenation of the Chinese nation. He believes that our country will be more brilliant and more beautiful in the future...

Thoughts of A Thinker

Wang and his enterprise were once again forced to a dead end.

The price skyrocketing of raw materials in the international market, the Obama government to impose special protectionist tariffs on tire imports from China, and the sanctions of the EU etc., were a challenge to Double Star as a national enterprise of China which manufactured both shoes and tires.

On one day of March 2011, Wang suddenly appeared in Dubai known as the World Trade Capital. At the prestigious Atlantis Hotel, a dealership annual meeting of Double Star Tire had just been held. People could not help but ask a problem: at this moment, what would he do in the Middle East having a great possibility of political turmoils, riots, and terrorist attacks regardless of personal safety?

However, perhaps many people still did not know that it is not the first time for him to take a risk in sales of shoes. As early as the mid-1990s, during the KOSOVO War in the Yugoslavia, Wang was in a war-torn place where the locals felt surprised and admired him.

On a flight to Manhattan, New York, in the car to run in the European Union, in the deep reflection with the face toward the Jiaozhou Bay and so forth, a serious and unavoidable problem again and again appeared in his mind: Why is there a high price of a product made in China and affixed with a foreign brand? Why do foreigners suspect our ability to develop our our own technologies? What's more, multinational corporations not only monopolize the international raw material market, monopolize profits, but also set unreasonable standards and force us to implement them to curb the export of our products. West powers restrict the development of China using measures: that is, brand exploitation, tech barriers, anti-dumping sanctions, and transnational groups aggression.

After a hundred years of struggle, the Chinese Communists led the suffering Chinese people and overthrew the three mountains of imperialism, feudalism, and bureaucratic capitalism. To realize the great rejuvenation of the Chinese nation, we must constantly enhance the sense of crisis. There are words in our national anthem, “The Chinese nation has reached the most dangerous time." We must be aware of them!

Wang as a brave and enthusiastic entrepreneur is one of first peoples to understand this point and leads people of Double Star to launch a new round of competition in the global market.

As a thinker of the Chinese Bolsheviks, Wang had a profound understanding on this more than ten years ago: In the 21st century, with the acceleration of the so-called integration of the world economy, whether China has its own economic development strategy is particularly important. An independent economic foreign policy is related to China's economic development.

However, at that time, a small number of officials, theorists, and economists seemed to abandon the Marxist political economy theory as the Bolshevik heirloom, and proposed that China should be a world processing factory, while not mentioning the national industry any more.

While delivering a speech at annual APEC meeting held in Shanghai and speeches in higher education institutions such as Peking University and TSINGHUA University, DAVOS Forum, BOAO Forum, and Microsoft Forum, Wang clearly pointed out that all of contradictions in the world can be resolved except ethnic contradictions. During the development of the economy, the political work cannot be ignored. In today's world, no one can give up national interests and national interests. This is an indisputable fact. We must not continuously exchange market for tech, resources for foreign currency, preferential policies for political achievements, cheap labor for investment, and land for GDP. Indeed, with his thoughts and insights, Wang won the glory for our motherland.

Wang proposes his three principles of developing the industry: to revitalize our national industry, it is necessary to inspire national spirit, create national brands, and cultivate a team of national entrepreneurs. No matter in what era we are in, the national spirit is the driving force for inspiring the people's struggle, and the cornerstone and guarantee for the rise of a country and a nation. In the globalization of the world economy, whoever dominates the economy will dominate the world, and the symbol of strong economic strength is the national brand, so creating a national brand is urgent! National brands play a key role in the national economy: reflecting the national spirit & dignity, representing the national image, safeguarding national interests, and being the symbol of national strength. To realize the goal of created-in-China, we must vigorously cultivate a team of national entrepreneurs. With his thinking, vision, and enthusiasm, he has created a strategy of independent economic development with Chinese characteristics.

Over 30 years of reform and opening, Double Star has been successfully brilliant, which is credited to Wang who also is a thinker.

There is no ready road to reform and opening. Deng Xiaoping said, "We should cross the river by feeling the stones." Without a new theory to guide, reforms cannot move forward. In the past, we did not recognize the private ownership, nor did we recognize the market; there were no brands...

The thinker Wang dares to be the first. In the exploration and practice, he has answered many problems in the forbidden zone. He is the first to put forward values of market economy and point out the direction of advancement; the first to propose that the good use of money is the best ideological and political work, which is a theoretical breakthrough; the first to put forward that the market is the standard for testing all work of the enterprise and takes the lead in entering the market; the first to say that creating a brand is the biggest politics of enterprises and hold high the banner of the national brand; the first to say that the high quality of product is the biggest doing-good and gathering blessings. He applies the excellent traditional culture of Buddhism, Taoism and Confucianism in modern enterprise management, and creates the management philosophy belonged to our Chinese people.

His theories include: market theory, rules theory, new cat theory, ABW theory, contradictory theory, three-nature theory, three-win theory, three-quality theory, tiger theory, big quality theory, big tech theory, big innovation theory, 3-7 theory, red and competent theory, loyalty and filial theory, and upgrade theory...

Wang as a thinker completes ice-breaking journeys again and again, and Wang as a doer leads a national enterprise to go from one victory to another. He has a great thought which is his driving force to work hard in the national rejuvenation.

Road of Brand

The correct strategy is the guarantee for commanders to take the initiative and obtain the final victory. Today, the success of Double Star is credited to Wang who is the first to understand the words of Deng Xiaoping chief designer of the reform and opening ("We must have our own competitive products, we must create our own national brands) and formulate the brand strategy in an insightful manner. As a party member, Wang actively takes part in national rejuvenation through the creation of the brand.

In the 1980s, many people did not hear of the concept of the brand, while Wang put forward his views: creating the brand is the biggest politics in the market economy; creating the brand is the best patriotism; the brand is the atomic bomb of market economy. He also published an article in the People's Daily to call for creating the brand for Chinese people. Therefore, Wang is the first entrepreneur to understand the importance for the brand.

Afterwards, known as the general of the market, Wang wore the shoes of Double Star to go global for the brand journey. In 1992, the first overseas press conference was held in New York, USA, whereas he took off his shoe to make an advertisement; in the shoe culture performance at the German World Expo, the Double Star brand sensationalized the global shoe industry.

Involvement in sports is another important step for Wang to carry out the brand strategy. He established China's first professional badminton team club and formed a professional basketball club in Double Star. Famous athletes wore his shoes to obtain the victory, including Lang Ping, Zhang Rongfang, Zheng Haixia, Cai Zhenhua, Li Yongbo and etc. From the 1980s, Double Star has participated in the following events: sponsoring the first national soccer tournament for women; holding the first ceremony of China Football Golden Shoes Award; supporting the female runner team led by Ma Junren in Eighth National Games to win the championship; acquiring the naming right twice in Sudirman Cup World Badminton Tournament; supporting the Chinese mountaineering team to climb the peak; sponsoring the National Street Dance Competition (for consecutive four years), and sponsoring the Clipper Yacht Race. Head coach Yuan Weimin led the women's volleyball team members (who won five consecutive championships) and Ma Junren led his runners to Double Star for visits to Double Star. Special shoes were made for basketball giant Mu Tiezhu. With the development of sports industry, Double Star brand has become more popular.

Double Star amazes the public in its creation of the brand. In early 1980s, Double Star went from imitation to innovation and produced the first pair of high-end cold-bonded sneakers, and the first pair of CVO heat-vulcanized shoes with the leather upper, thereby being at the leading position in the global footwear industry. In the 1990s, it achieved the strategic development goal of generations of products co-existing in research, development, production and storage, and set up the only national-level technology research and development center in the footwear industry; its products had new features: lightweight, being suitable for a special field, comfortable and sanitary, healthy, environmentally friendly and casual etc. Double Star is the first to consider the occupational characteristics to introduce the following shoes: air-conditioning shoes, ventilation shoes, journalist shoes, nurse shoes, driver shoes, teacher shoes, and so on; and consider the needs of different groups of people to induce the shoes for the elderly, mothers, fathers. Double Star introduced the especially functional shoes: insulated shoes, safety shoes, waterproof shoes, etc. Double Star also designed and developed the spaceflight shoes for Shenzhou 6, Shenzhou 7, and Shenzhou 8. Therefore, it contributed to the national rejuvenation.

People at Double Stars have always adhered to his development strategy: that is, to seize the opportunity and take the initiative in the market that is a battlefield filled with smoke. With its advantage of unique and advanced technology, Double Star closely follows the consumption trends of being beautiful, personalized, fashionable and casual, spends more efforts on development of luminous, fragrant and non-odor shoes, and meet the specific requirements of consumers at all levels with new materials, new processes and new tech, including ultra-large size, ultra-small size, and special shape among others. Double Star has successfully designed and developed more than 400 kinds of scented shoes (included in 60 categories) which are popular in the global high-end market.

From shoes to tires, Double Star's creative practice is fantastic. In the past, Double Star was a private tire enterprise that was on the verge of bankruptcy. Now, it has acquired Huaqing Tire (as a state-owned tire enterprise that was controlled by a Malaysian enterprise for 10 years but still failed) and Dongfeng Tire. These M & A stories are very wonderful, including a story of the small fish eating big and a story of the fast fish eating slow etc. Double Star Tire has become a famous brand at home and abroad, with its independent innovation and its products going into the high-end market. Specialized and serialized products are ultra-wide flat tires, tubeless radial tires, military tires, colorful tires, two-color trademark tires, environmentally friendly tires.

June 17, 2011, at Double Star Product Promotion Conference in Jinan, a taxi driver used a hammer to press a long steel nail into a tire. This tire with the nail pulled out was submerged in water. There was no leakage of gas! The audience gave a round of applause.

The road of Double Star brand continues to expand. In the new century, foreign equipment successively entered the domestic market. In particular, domestic products were rarely seen in the high-end equipment market. Wang, with a strong sense of responsibility, deeply worried about this and made a strategic decision: To speed up technological upgrading, create the core technology, realize the leap from made-in to created-in, and build Double Star into the largest machinery manufacturing group in China.

Since then, Double Star Machinery has won victories in independent R & D: the world's first four-mode vulcanizing machine, China's first vacuum process modeling line with independent property rights, China's first stainless steel belt shot-blasting cleaner, China's largest resin sand mixer, and other cleaning equipment for Shenzhou 6, Shenzhou 7, and Chang E No. 2 and the like. Double Star Machinery has created more than 30 firsts in the industry and developed more than 90 new products, including nearly 70 products at the domestic leading level, more than 30 products filling the domestic gap, and more than 50 core technologies obtaining national patents. Double Star

Machinery has involved in more than 20 industries in China, including aerospace, military, shipbuilding, automobile manufacturing, train locomotives, heavy-duty machine tools, engineering machinery, and so forth, thereby making contributions to the revitalization of national industries including defense industry. In the international bidding, Double Star Machinery defeated the foreign competitors such as Germany and Japan, wining the glory for our country and nation.

From 1995, Double Star won the first "China Famous Brand", Double Star Professional Sports Shoes, Double Star Travel Shoes, Double Star Leather Shoes and Double Star Tires have successively won the title of "China Famous Brand", which is the only one in China's rubber industry with four Chinese famous brand products. Enterprise, double star brand value up to 50 billion yuan!

In all stages of creating the brand, Double Star relies on the national spirit, decision-making, strict management and never-stop innovation. Double Star is the first to cast a brand belonged to Chinese people, of which Chinese people feel proud. Thus, Double Star has realized the brand dream of national industry in China.

Through the creation of the national brand, Wang invigorates the national spirit, unites the staffs, go global and makes products popular in the international market. Is not this the biggest success achieved by Wang?

Successful Management

The success of Double Star is first the success in the mechanism and management.

Wang's contribution to the domestic industry is the development the management theory with Chinese characteristics. When the MBA model from the West that did not meet actual conditions of China was very popular in China, Wang introduce the ABM theory with Chinese characteristics, which was derived from his Nine Plus Nine Management Method.

Wang's interpretation of ABW theory is as follows: A refers to the first or the leader. We should be a leader at home and abroad. B consists of two parts: 1 and 3 means a big country and a big market with a population of 1.3 billion. Entrepreneurs must be diligent and down-to-earth. W is like an eagle spreading wings. It means that the entrepreneur leads his team to meet the challenge and is never satisfied with what he has achieved.

The ABW theory is an enterprise development theory with Chinese characteristics, which absorbs the essences from Chinese and western cultures in ancient and modern times and integrates principles in market and management the like. It shows that Chinese people are clever and practical.

What is his new model of Double Star in the market management that is in line with actual conditions of China and its enterprises?

Through the strict management, Double Star gets rid of the problems (namely, the working site being dirty, chaotic and lowly efficient) left in the planned economy. The post, position, and staff number are fixed, which is the breakthrough. The management is strict, meticulous and highly standard. Double Star the first to use the digital tracking card, which enables the enterprise basic management to enter dynamic management from static management. The difficult problem of the rubber industry is solved. With on-site management as a breakthrough, Double Star achieves a standard, military and family style effect.

The meticulous management solves the problem (that is, only paying attention to production and not considering the cost) left in the planned economy. Cost management is characterized by capital blocks, cost of each order known, cost of current day known and so forth. On the basis of capital blocks, the factory currency is creatively applied. Family-type consumption management is also carried out. Every link of management is paid attention. In Double Star, everyone is responsible, and everything is paid attention. This is a new model in management of manufacturing and processing.

The use of money in management challenges old ideas and thoughts. For the product, the quality responsibility system is adopted. In case of a problem in quality, relevant leaders and staffs will be held accountable. Salaries are known on the current day and are publicized on the wall, including the rewards and punishments. Staffs who make the outstanding contributions are granted rewards, e.g., color TV sets, houses, and cars among others. Every year, Double Stars selects quality models, innovative experts, stars in job competition, best managers and salesperson in chain stores. The use of money in management leads to the best combination of material and spirituality in the market economy. With the enterprising spirit, people at Double Star uphold high the banner of uprightness and create a new politic and economic model in management.

Integrity management has let Double Star get rid of the old model in the planned economy. The new model of integrity management is created, whereas moral ideas are combined with quality of product. With the principle of the quality being first, Double Star is the first to use the integrity as a moral standard to evaluate the quality awareness of staffs. For Wang, the product is equal to the moral character and the quality is equal to the conscience. His creation is to link the enterprise management to people's morality and conscience. People at Double Star uses the moral character and conscience to guarantee the product quality. Everyone in Double Star keeps integrity and honesty; everyone is an inspector; and every post is responsible for the quality.

With the people-oriented principle, Double Star respects staffs and gets rid of its old image as a impersonal organization in the past. Its slogan says: relentless discipline and compassionate leadership. Decision-making, management, and supervision are democratic. In case of birthdays, staffs can enjoy a day off and a birthday cake from Double Star. Staffs are encouraged to make a rationalization proposal. Double Star sets up its telephone supermarket, electronic reading room, and kindergarten the like. This is a comfortable living environment eliminates. While carrying out cultural activities and talent competitions, Double Star selects outstanding staffs to its education center for further study and creates a good atmosphere in which everyone learns, grows and loves the enterprise. This is a harmonious environment it creates.

Double Star replaces the old model with the new contracting model. For Wang, an important creation is to let staffs buy out equipment production lines and to implement contracted operations in the reform of state-owned enterprises. It enhances the awareness of staffs in quality, capital, cost, and consumption reduction, and stimulate their enthusiasm. Workers, who hated machines in the past, now regard them as partners and actively maintain them with production efficiency increased by more than 30% on average. The harmony is achieved between man and machine and between individual and collective, letting Marx's century-old dream become true.

The reform led by Wang in the enterprise enables staffs to become enthusiastic in work with their attitude changing from passive to active. Currently, people at Double Star are highly spirited and strive for being more capable.

The American rates Double Star as the best-managed factory in the world. The Japanese makes a visit to Double Star Factory. The Korean offers a high salary to find the director from Double Star. With its excellent management, Double Star wins the respect of peers and the admiration of foreigners.

This is the best combination of ABW theory and enterprise production and management. This is a concrete manifestation of the unique 3-in-1 management method (namely culture, management and system mechanism). This is the new creation, new breakthrough and new leap of Chinese enterprise management mode!

The practice of Double Star proves once again that management is the foundation of success in uniting staffs and obtaining the survival and development of enterprises.

In Double Star, the all-steel load-bearing radial tire can run 300,000 kilometers without damage; the maximum error of vacuum modeling line of more than 180 meters is less than 0.15 mm; the shoe production line is fully without full-time inspectors. Do these miracles not show a success of his new theories, methods & philosophies?

From an enterprise, we can see the revival of a nation. The revival of Double Star led by Wang in corporate culture and corporate management is a result of management innovation fully manifesting the national spirit and the enterprising spirit the like. This, which becomes a conscious act from non-conscious in Double Star, is a road to the management of socialist enterprises with Chinese characteristics that leads the direction of enterprises and contributes to social development.

Boundless Road

Like ships that must have wise helmsmen n a long voyage, an outstanding company must have an outstanding entrepreneur.

As the first generation of outstanding entrepreneurs in China, Wang is the creator of the Double Star brand, the core and soul of the Double Star development, the spiritual leader of the Double Star employees, and the outstanding representative of the national entrepreneurs.

With the braveness of being a pioneer and the courage of crossing the river with stones, Wang has found the road for revitalization of national enterprises.

Wang is an entrepreneur representing an era. He has experienced the entire process of reform and opening in the position of factory director and manager. With great courage and wisdom, Wang bravely devotes himself to the ice-breaking activities in revitalizing state-owned enterprises in the new era. He is the first to implement the staff appointment system, carry out low-cost expansion and develop western parts of China, select the talented people - no matter whether his is a cadre or worker, enter the tertiary industry, invigorate tangible assets via invincible assets. He is also the first to let the shoe enterprise into the stock market, possess the rights for import and export, let the shoe enterprise sponsor sports events, use traditional excellent culture in enterprise management, absorb the self-employed into the sales network, hold the national order fair in the name of the enterprise, cooperate with the media, and let the shoe enterprise go global...He emancipates the mind and breaks old systems including the Three Irons so forth and achieves a great success. He creates a new model in Double Star as a state-owned enterprise revitalizing under the market economy. Thus, he is a pioneer of the reform and opening-up.

More than 30 years ago, in case of many people being still unfamiliar with and even not recognizing the market, Wang took risks and bravely led staffs to enter it, despite of being threatened, cursed, blamed, and even possibly dismissed by the higher authorities. He set up self-operated sales channels, organized press conferences in the name of the enterprise, and carries out reforms in the enterprise, including the property rights system reform and those in forbidden zones etc. While being not afraid of bureaucratic forces, he makes active explorations and develops the market theory of Double Star as a labor-intensive enterprise that conforms to the laws of the market and creates a lot of firsts: entering the market, looking for customers and funds, looking for partners, carrying out the job transfer, going global and so forth. For him, the enterprise should follow and turn around the market as well as change with it. Thus, while exploring the path for the socialist market economy, he is the pioneer of the market.

Wang has led the reform of Double Star for more than 30 years. He always believes that under the background of most of state-owned shoe-making enterprises falling into bankruptcy, the reason why Double Star still can successfully brilliant is that it relies on the national spirit and the conviction of wining the glory for the country and that it relies on the successful exploration in the creation of the national brand and relies on the ambition of revitalizing the national industry. He is the first to propose the creation of the brand, and the first to promote, develop, and use the brand. He finds the way to create a brand, realizes the brand strategy through the national brand. Thus, he is the pioneer of the brand.

With a high sense of national responsibility, in the process from planned economy to market economy, Wang courageously seeks for the truth and develops the management philosophy and theory that is characteristic of Chinese national culture under the conditions of market economy. He launches Chinese-style management and creates the unique Chinese-style corporate culture in which the Buddhist culture is used in modern enterprise management, thereby making Double Star to be a leading Chinese enterprise in the world, creating a new management model including new theories and new systems for China's socialist market economy. Thus he is the founder of management in the modern Chinese enterprise.

The development process of Double Star for more than 30 years is the process of continuous theoretical innovation, product innovation, technological innovation and management innovation. The successful history of Double Star for more than 30 years is a history of continuous innovation, which is a process of continuous independent innovation and development. It also is a history of people's war that has the following characteristics: self-transformation and self-improvement; theoretical innovation, all-staff innovation, team innovation and the like; recent changes in the aspects from theoretical innovation to innovative consciousness, innovative objects, and innovative contents. As a result, the new phenomenon of Double Star appears. Wang has found the innovative way of continuous advancement and development and has become a promoter of innovation.

In the rising price of raw materials and the increasingly fierce market competition, Double Star is still developing rapidly. The reason is that Wang is insightful. More than 20 years ago, he carried out low-cost expansion and brand operation. In 1990s, he was the first to propose the new idea of development in west and east. He has found a new development idea for Double Star. In the era of high-tech parks being successively built even in villages and counties, Wang unexpectedly chose the tires (which are the traditional industry) as a new growth point for the development of Double Star...Wang dares to enter the market, dares to be pragmatic, dares to persist, dares to take risks, dares to practice, and dares to make decisions. Wang believes that it is entrepreneurs who decide the destiny of the enterprise no matter how the ownership is important. Thus, he is a successful decision maker of Double Star in the market.

As a thinker, politician, strategist, philosopher, diplomat, and speaker, Wang fulfills the duties of national entrepreneurs. The courage of entrepreneurs is embodied in the decision-making. He is a symbolic figure in the reform and opening; a banner in the transformation of traditional manufacturing industry; and an example in the development of national industry.

Double Star has no unique condition for the old and established name, no advantage for state-owned monopoly industry, no favorable policies for joint ventures, no flexible environment for township enterprises. However, Wang has enabled it as an old state-owned enterprise in a labor-intensive and low-profit industry to be in an invincible position. Is this not a success of Wang as a reformer?

Now Double Star has obtained a good result: total assets increasing from less than 10 million yuan in the early 1980s to 6.7 billion yuan. In the past 20 years, the accumulated profits and taxes were more than 3 billion Yuan, sales revenue increasing from about 30 million Yuan to 12 billion Yuan, and foreign exchange earned from exports increasing from 1 million US dollars to 300 million US dollars. Double Star has developed into a large-scale group company with 60,000 employees involving in 23 industries such as shoe, tire, clothing, machinery, packaging and printing, and tertiary production etc.; that is, it goes from the sunset industry to the sunrise industry. Is this a success of Wang as a Bolshevik thinker?

In his simply decorated and clean office, we can see that on the desk he has been using for 30 years, there are various kinds of shoe molds collected from all over the world showing that he loves the shoc-making job and reminding the visitors always that the owner of this room is a shoemaker. The walls are decorated with the calligraphic works which read below: Dare to be the first in the world; The road is under the foot; Always pursuing the dream without attention paid to the fame and wealth. Therefore, above works are the true portrayal of his character and life attitude. On the other hand, as a pioneer of the reform and opening for 30 years, Wang casts two votes for himself: one is that he is an excellent party member in the era of market economy; the other is that he is a market entrepreneur.

He says, "I do not want to be a governmental official, instead, I want to go into the market. I am forever with the party. National responsibility is very important." These words from him as an adventurer, a practitioner, and a survivor reveal the secret of the success obtained by him as a long-lived entrepreneur in China.

"We Communists can set the world by the ears with what we do." Yes, they can come out of nowhere. As a proverb goes, it never rains but it pours.

With the unremitting pursuit for 90 years, a 30-year surprising leap is obtained. The success of Double Star is from the leadership of Wang as a party member who obeys the laws of the market economy and scientific development.

There will be a better future for the development of the market economy in China, and the Chinese nation will be able to rejuvenate itself - our great Chinese dream that is shining! *(Source: People's Daily · Overseas Edition, September 5, 2011)*

Index

A

B

C

D

E

F

G

H

I

J

K

L

M

N

O

P

Y

Z

About the Author

Professor Zhang Xiuyu, a famous consultant in management, is an enterprise strategy expert, management expert, founder of China Success science, special researcher of Peking University, former dean of business administration department at Beijing Institute of Economic Management, and founder of Beijing Successful Key Consulting Co., Ltd. where he acts as chairman of the board of directors and general manager. He serves as a guest professor at many famous universities, such as Peking University, Tsinghua University, Rennin University of China, China Europe International Business School (CEIBS). He is postgraduate supervisor at the Central Party School, member of Beijing SME Expert Advisory Committee. He is also co-editor-in-chief of Contemporary China Series published in the United States by North American Business Press.

Professor Zhang Xiuyu engages in the teaching, scientific research, training and consulting work in areas of enterprise strategy management, operation management and success science for a long time. He has published 14 works, e.g., Enterprise Strategy Management, Strategy Management, Management Science Principle, Total Competition Management, Welcome Challenge-How the Enterprise Practices the Internal Power, How to Succeed, China Human Resources Development and Research, Human Resources Management, Labor Quota Formulation and Management, Labor Remuneration Science and etc. He has undertaken more than 10 provincial or ministerial level research subjects and has published about 100 theses.

Among them, Enterprise Strategic Management as a textbook published by Peking University Press has been produced 20 times in three editions of 100,000 copies; so far, it has the highest number of printings and the largest circulation in China among the same kind of textbooks; requested by North American Business Press, he has re-edited it as Business Strategy: New Vision (English) published in the United States. Professor Zhang won honorary titles of The Republic's Meritorious Person and Pioneer of Motherland. In October 2012, he was selected to be included in the new edition of World Who's Who (Chinese version) collected in British Museum and won the honorary title of World Celebrity.

Made in United States
Orlando, FL
04 November 2026

90206781R00302